Riding the Populist Wave

In spite of the fact that Conservative, Christian democratic and Liberal parties continue to play a crucial role in the democratic politics and governance of every Western European country, they are rarely paid the attention they deserve. This cutting-edge comparative collection, combining qualitative case studies with large-N quantitative analysis, reveals a mainstream right squeezed by the need to adapt to both 'the silent revolution' that has seen the spread of postmaterialist, liberal and cosmopolitan values and the backlash against those values – the 'silent counter-revolution' that has brought with it the rise of a myriad far-right parties offering populist and nativist answers to many of the continent's thorniest political problems. What explains why some mainstream right parties seem to be coping with that challenge better than others? And does the temptation to ride the populist wave rather than resist it ultimately pose a danger to liberal democracy?

TIM BALE is an expert on European politics and political parties. He won the UK Political Studies Association's W.J.M. Mackenzie prize for his book, *The Conservative Party: from Thatcher to Cameron* (2010) and is a frequent contributor to broadcast, print and social media in both Britain and beyond.

CRISTÓBAL ROVIRA KALTWASSER is an expert on populism, who has held visiting appointments at Nuffield College, Sciences Po, the Social Science Research Centre Berlin (WZB) and Uppsala University. He is the co-author of the book, *Populism: A Very Short Introduction* (with Cas Mudde, 2017) which has been translated into more than ten languages.

Riding the Populist Wave

Europe's Mainstream Right in Crisis

Edited by

TIM BALE
Queen Mary University of London
CRISTÓBAL ROVIRA KALTWASSER
Universidad Diego Portales, Santiago

CAMBRIDGE
UNIVERSITY PRESS

CAMBRIDGE
UNIVERSITY PRESS

University Printing House, Cambridge CB2 8BS, United Kingdom

One Liberty Plaza, 20th Floor, New York, NY 10006, USA

477 Williamstown Road, Port Melbourne, VIC 3207, Australia

314–321, 3rd Floor, Plot 3, Splendor Forum, Jasola District Centre,
New Delhi – 110025, India

79 Anson Road, #06–04/06, Singapore 079906

Cambridge University Press is part of the University of Cambridge.

It furthers the University's mission by disseminating knowledge in the pursuit of
education, learning and research at the highest international levels of excellence.

www.cambridge.org
Information on this title: www.cambridge.org/9781316518762
DOI: 10.1017/9781009006866

© Tim Bale and Cristóbal Rovira Kaltwasser 2021

First published 2021

A catalogue record for this publication is available from the British Library.

Library of Congress Cataloging-in-Publication Data
Names: Bale, Tim, 1965– author. | Rovira Kaltwasser, Cristóbal author.
Title: Riding the populist wave : Europe's mainstream right in crisis / edited by
Timothy Paul Bale, Cristóbal Rovira Kaltwasser.
Description: Cambridge, United Kingdom ; New York, NY : Cambridge University
Press, 2021. | Includes bibliographical references and index.
Identifiers: LCCN 2021024885 (print) | LCCN 2021024886 (ebook) | ISBN
9781316518762 (hardback) | ISBN 9781009009058 (paperback) | ISBN
9781009006866 (ebook)
Subjects: LCSH: Populism – Europe. | Political parties – Europe. | Right and left
(Political science) – Europe. | Europe – Politics and government. | BISAC:
POLITICAL SCIENCE / American Government / General | POLITICAL SCIENCE /
American Government / General
Classification: LCC JN40 .B34 2021 (print) | LCC JN40 (ebook) | DDC 320.56/
62094–dc23
LC record available at https://lccn.loc.gov/2021024885
LC ebook record available at https://lccn.loc.gov/2021024886

ISBN 978-1-316-51876-2 Hardback
ISBN 978-1-009-00905-8 Paperback

Contents

Contributors

Tarik Abou-Chadi, Assistant Professor, Department of Political Science, University of Zurich

Sonia Alonso Sáenz de Oger, Associate Professor, Georgetown University in Qatar (GUQ)

Tim Bale, Professor, Queen Mary University of London

Pietro Castelli Gattinara, Assistant Professor, Centre for Research on Extremism (C-REX), University of Oslo

Jocelyn Evans, Professor, School of Politics and International Studies, University of Leeds

Bonnie N. Field, Professor, Global Studies Department, Bentley University

Caterina Froio, Assistant Professor, Centre for European Studies and Comparative Politics (CEE), Sciences Po

Eelco Harteveld, Assistant Professor, Department of Political Science, University of Amsterdam

Richard Hayton, Associate Professor of Politics, School of Politics and International Studies, University of Leeds

Reinhard Heinisch, Professor, Department of Political Science, University of Salzburg and Associate at the European Studies Center at the University of Pittsburgh (ESC)

Gilles Ivaldi, Researcher in Politics, CEVIPOF, CNRS/Sciences-Po Paris

Werner Krause, Postdoctoral Researcher and Lecturer, Department of Social Sciences, Humboldt-Universität zu Berlin

Anders Ravik Jupskås, Deputy Director, Center for Research on Extremism (C-REX), Department of Political Science, University of Oslo

Cristóbal Rovira Kaltwasser, Professor, School of Political Science, Universidad Diego Portales and Associate Researcher at the Centre for Social Cohesion and Conflict Studies (COES)

Stijn van Kessel, Senior Lecturer in European Politics, School of Politics and International Relations, Queen Mary University of London

Annika Werner, Senior Lecturer, School of Politics and International Relations, Australian National University

Sarah E. Wiliarty, Associate Professor of Government, Wesleyan University

Figures and Tables

Tables

Preface

The origins of this project can be traced back to 2011 when the editors of this volume were working together at the University of Sussex. During this time Cristóbal was working on a book on the right in Latin America, while Tim was doing research on the Conservative Party in the United Kingdom. Soon after Tim started a new job at Queen Mary University of London and Cristóbal started a new job at Universidad Diego Portales in Santiago de Chile. Nevertheless, we continued to stay in contact – and continued to remain baffled about the absence of comparative studies on the mainstream right in Western Europe. This bafflement led Tim to travel to Santiago de Chile in March 2018 and we started not only to write a framework for analysis on this topic, but also to think about who else might be interested in writing on the state of the mainstream right in the different countries of Western Europe. Thanks to the support of the Thyssen Foundation, we were able to organize a two-day meeting at Queen Mary University of London in March 2019, in which we discussed a first draft of several of the chapters of this edited volume. We want to thank Susan Scarrow and Thomas Poguntke, who provided invaluable feedback to all authors during this workshop.

After this, we provided detailed comments to each of the authors and we decided to commission two additional chapters covering the demand and supply sides of the mainstream right in Western Europe. We are extremely grateful to all the colleagues who have participated in this project, and to Ariel Becerra, Camila Díaz and Cristóbal Sandoval who have been very helpful in the preparation of the final version of this manuscript. At the same time, we would like to thank John Haslam from Cambridge University Press, who supported this project from the very beginning, and the two anonymous reviewers, who provided detailed comments and suggestions not only for each chapter but also to the book project seen as a whole. Moreover, we discussed the subject of this book with different friends and colleagues, who gave us invaluable comments and ideas. In this regard, we are particularly grateful to Sarah de Lange, Carlos Meléndez, Cas Mudde, Jan-Werner Müller, Kenneth Roberts, Paul Taggart, Lisa Zanotti and Andrej Zaslove.

Last but not least, Cristóbal Rovira Kaltwasser would like to acknowledge support from the Chilean National Fund for Scientific and Technological Development (FONDECYT project 1180020), the Centre for Social Conflict and Cohesion Studies COES (ANID/FONDAP/15130009) and the Observatory of Socioeconomic Transformations (ANID/PCI/Max Planck Institute for the Study of Societies/MPG190012).

Tim Bale and Cristóbal Rovira Kaltwasser
Eastbourne and Santiago de Chile

1 | The Mainstream Right in Western Europe: Caught between the Silent Revolution and Silent Counter-Revolution

TIM BALE AND CRISTÓBAL ROVIRA KALTWASSER

1. Introduction

Academic and media portrayals of the political situation in Western Europe point without fail to the dire situation in which the continent's centre-left finds itself. Social democratic parties almost everywhere – even those that previously dominated their country's political scene – are struggling to hold on to their old voters and finding it hard to attract new ones. As a result, they are far less likely than they used to be to win office, particularly at the national level. By way of illustration, the once powerful Labour Party in the Netherlands (PvdA) performed appallingly at the country's 2017 general election, getting just under 6 per cent of the vote. The situation in France is not much better. In the 2017 presidential elections the candidate of the French Socialist Party (PS) obtained 6 per cent of the vote, and the party's financial situation was so critical that it sold its headquarters on the chic Rue de Solférino in Paris. And to add one more example to the list, Germany's Social Democratic Party (SPD) won just 20 per cent of the vote at the 2017 general election, representing its worst electoral result in the post-war period thus far.

However, the political debate in Western Europe is not marked only by discussions of the decline of social democracy. The other topic receiving increasing public attention is the rise of populist radical right parties, particularly after the refugee crisis that garnered so many headlines in 2015 and 2016. Indeed, hardly a day goes by without the media across Europe making at least some mention of the actions and ideas of the leaders of these parties. Most countries have at least one reasonably well-established populist radical right party that normally wins between 5 per cent and 15 per cent of the vote (Mudde 2013). Moreover, these parties are not necessarily treated as pariahs. In fact, they have been in office in Austria, Finland, Italy, the Netherlands, Norway and Switzerland, and have provided regular and reliable parliamentary support to minority governments in Denmark – and all this in spite of the fact that they have not, as many expected them to, become somehow more moderate over time (see Akkerman 2015a; Akkerman, de Lange and Rooduijn 2016; Wagner and Meyer 2017; Twist 2019).

One might have assumed that the corollary of both the increasing political relevance of the populist radical right and the electoral decline of social democracy would be the success of the mainstream right – in other words, the conservative, Christian democratic and (market) liberal parties that have sold themselves as strong supporters of capitalist economies and, certainly in the first two cases, of 'traditional' values. Yet in reality many of those parties are also in trouble electorally, even if the rate at which they run into trouble can vary considerably (see, e.g., Bale and Krouwel 2013). True, partly because that trouble has not generally been quite as serious as that faced by their centre-left counterparts and partly because they often have more coalition options, they seem – for the moment anyway – to be better able to hang on to office. But that should not blind us to the problems they face. As Jan-Werner Müller (2018) has recently suggested, mainstream right parties have become so pragmatic over the years that it is often unclear what, other than their desire to cling to power, animates them in the first place. Moreover, the electoral results of mainstream right parties are very uneven across Western Europe, and some of the once electorally strongest cases are facing tougher times today. To demonstrate this, we have collected data on the electoral results of all mainstream right parties in Western Europe in national elections from 1980 until 2019.[1] The following graph (Figure 1.1) presents the average per decade in percentages for each of the three party families of the mainstream right that we discuss below (Christian democrats, conservatives and liberals), as well as for the populist radical right. Looking at this graph, the picture is very clear: while the populist

---

[1] At the end of the chapter we provide information about all the parties included in the analysis and their classification in the different party families. We include only those parties that have obtained at least 4 per cent of the vote in national elections.

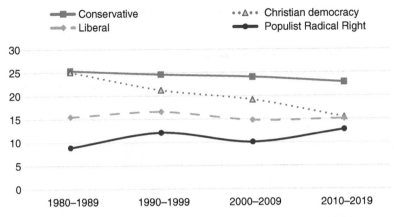

Figure 1.1 Electoral results in national elections of right-wing parties in Western Europe (average per decade in percentage)

radical right party family has been able to establish itself and expand its electoral appeal, the conservative and Christian democratic party families have experienced declining support. This leaves the liberals as the only mainstream right party family which seems to have maintained a degree of stability over time.

Although the focus of our book is on the mainstream right, it is also important to note the electoral situation of left-wing parties in Western Europe, the better to understand the situation in which mainstream right parties find themselves today. Accordingly, we present data on the electoral results of left-wing parties in Western Europe in national elections from 1980 until 2019.[2] Figure 1.2 gives the average per decade in percentages for each of the three main party families of the left that are normally identified in the academic literature on Western Europe: social democratic, green/ecologist and radical left parties. At least three issues stand out. First, the decline of the social democratic party family is a relatively recent phenomenon, albeit one that becomes acute in the last decade (2010–2019) and is probably related to disillusion with the so-called Third Way politics pursued by social democratic leaders such as Tony Blair in the United Kingdom and Gerhard

---

[2] At the end of the chapter we provide information about all the parties included in the analysis and their classification in the different party families. Again, we include only those parties that have obtained at least 4 per cent of the vote in national elections.

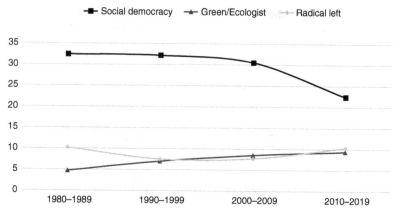

Figure 1.2 Electoral results in national elections of left-wing parties in Western Europe (average per decade in percentage)

Schröder in Germany. Second, the green/ecologist party family has almost doubled its electoral strength, but on average gathers a lower proportion of the vote than the populist radical right. Third, by comparing Figures 1.1 and 1.2 it becomes clear that both social democratic and Christian democratic parties are losing electoral ground in dramatic fashion. The decay of the former may be more abrupt, but both party families have suffered significant electoral losses since the 1980s.

One of the main ideas behind this book is that scholars have in recent years devoted so much attention to the decline of social democracy and the rise of the populist radical right that they have paid less attention than they should have done to the mainstream right – a range of parties which continue to play a part (in some places the major part) in the representative governments of contemporary Western Europe. Of course, there are single-case studies of the evolution of specific mainstream right parties such as the Conservatives in the United Kingdom (e.g., Bale 2010) or the Christian Democratic Party in Germany (e.g., Wiliarty 2010; Green and Turner 2014). However, there is a relative and noticeable lack of *comparative* research on the mainstream right in Western Europe.[3] Indeed, to the best of our knowledge, the last

---

[3] Partial exceptions of this absence of comparative research on the mainstream right in Western Europe are Jensen (2014) on the right and the welfare state, and the special issue on the centre-right and immigration edited by Bale (2008), as well as some studies on the evolution of Christian democratic parties (e.g., Frey 2009; Kalyvas and van Kersbergen 2010; Wagner 2014; Invernizzi-Accetti 2020).

comparative collection on this subject was published in the late 1990s (Wilson 1998).

There are two main reasons why scholars may have (at least relatively speaking) ignored this topic. First, if it is the case that most political scientists feel more of an affinity with the centre-left and progressive causes, then it was always likely that they would devote more attention to the analysis of the parties with which they tend to identify (such as the social democrats) and the parties that they strongly reject (like the populist radical right) than to the situation of the mainstream right (conservative and Christian democratic parties). Second, as Figures 1.1 and 1.2 show, the decay in support experienced by Christian democrats and conservatives has been much more gradual than the one experienced by social democrats, while the liberal party family, by maintaining its position, seems even less newsworthy. As a result, mainstream right parties are often – in our view mistakenly – seen as both dependably dull and dependably stable. In fact, as we aim to show in this book, mainstream right parties are undergoing significant and, in our opinion, fascinating transformations, not least as they confront an ever more serious challenge from the populist radical right.

This relative lack of attention should be a cause for concern given how big a role the mainstream right has played and continues to play in governments throughout the continent. As such, its role in preserving the liberal order in a continent struggling with the changes brought about by the gradual erosion (and subsequent demand for re-imposition) of national borders is a vital one. Moreover, as Daniel Ziblatt (2017) has shown, the birth and endurance of democracy in Western Europe is directly related to the extent to which right-wing political parties were able to recast themselves and deal with the emergence of their more radical counterparts. Given that mainstream right parties '… represent wealthy establishments that can squelch the democratic aspirations of the poor and politically weak, it is especially vital that such parties accept their democratic responsibility' (Grzymala-Busse 2019: 41). One only has to look at the other side of the Atlantic, where Donald Trump's rise to the presidency, and the apparently unquestioning support given to him in Congress by his co-partisans, casts doubt on whether the Republican Party can be considered a mainstream right party anymore – something that has consequences for the current state and future of democracy in the United States (Liebermann et al. 2019; Roberts 2019a).

The central aim of this book, however, is to bring the mainstream right back into our analysis of contemporary Western European politics. In order to undertake this task properly it is also crucial, we will argue, to take into account the interaction between the mainstream right and the populist radical right – an interaction that, it should be noted, is sometimes more reciprocal, even symbiotic, than many imagine (Bale 2018). That said, our main focus is firmly on the former rather than the latter. This is partly in order to redress the imbalance in coverage already referred to, but partly, too, because analysing how mainstream right parties in different countries in Western Europe have been changing over time and adapting (or struggling to adapt) to the current context might contribute not just to us getting a clearer picture of the continent's politics but also to the efforts made by those parties to think things through. If the mainstream right continues, as some allege it has begun to, to hollow out ideologically and become little more than a pragmatic problem-solver, the agenda will be set by other political forces, meaning – presuming it survives electorally at all – that it will end up importing their ideas and policies rather than bringing to bear its own.

The rest of this introductory chapter is divided into three parts. We begin by trying to bring some conceptual clarity and offering working definitions of both the mainstream right and the far right in Western Europe. After this, we argue that mainstream right parties in Western Europe experience a tension between, on the one hand, adapting to segments of the electorate that express the liberal and progressive values of the so-called 'silent revolution' (Inglehart 1977, 1990) and, on the other hand, representing voters who sympathize with the arguably authoritarian and nativist ideas associated with the so-called 'silent counter-revolution' (Ignazi 1992, 2003) pursued by the populist radical right. As we will argue in this section, this tension presents mainstream right parties with four policy and political challenges in particular – namely, European integration, immigration, moral issues and welfare. Finally, we conclude by presenting a short summary of each of the contributions included in the book.

2. Concepts: The Mainstream Right and the Far Right

Contested concepts are hardly uncommon in the social sciences. Scholars often disagree about the best way to define key notions that we employ to make sense of the political world. The distinction between 'left' and 'right' is itself an example. Although most scholars agree that the German Christian Democratic Party (CDU) is a mainstream right party and that the Spanish Socialist Workers' Party (PSOE) is a mainstream left party, they often debate the criteria one should employ in order to make this distinction (e.g., Jahn 2011, 2014; Franzmann 2015). Similar discussions arise when classifying (populist) radical right parties and (populist) radical left parties, such as the Alternative for Germany (AfD) and We Can (*Podemos*) in Spain, respectively. Given this, it is incumbent upon us to offer some conceptual clarification.

We cannot pretend to have the final word on this complex and much-debated issue, but we nevertheless hope to present clear and concise definitions that can be used to undertake comparative research (Sartori 1970). Minimal concepts are characterized by the identification of a reduced set of attributes that need to be used to define said concept: they are based, if you like, on finding 'the lowest common denominator'. For instance, Sartori (1976) argues that a political party should be thought of as 'any political group identified by an official label that presents at elections, and is capable of placing through elections (free or non-free), candidates for public office'. Of course, one could argue that this definition is in some ways *too* minimal since it does not say anything about the organizational features of political parties. This is why Sartori claims that minimal definitions should be seen as a starting point in distinguishing phenomena (e.g., political parties from, let us say, social movements or interest groups), after which it is often necessary to go one step down the 'ladder of abstraction' in order to include additional criteria to identify subtypes of the phenomenon under analysis. For example, Panebianco's (1988) book on political parties deliberately distinguishes subtypes of political parties depending on their degree of institutionalization and links with other organizations.

When it comes to distinguishing between 'left' and 'right', it is common knowledge that the origins of this distinction can be traced back to the French Revolution (Laponce 1981), after which this spatial notion of politics rapidly took root all over Europe because of its direct connection with the struggle between the defence of the *ancien régime* and the push for democratization (Ziblatt 2017). Seen in this light, one can argue that those on the right 'are primarily invested in the

importance of hierarchical relationships or some more or less naturalized conception of inequality. They do not simply emphasize the particular and the potential importance of its preservation; they attribute
differential value to a particular set of human beings, and they emphasize that certain social arrangements distributing power unequally are
unalterable' (Müller 2006: 363). However, this does not mean that the
right always and necessarily defends the status quo by all means,
because it usually recognizes that staying in power requires adaptation.

   This notwithstanding, the left–right divide is perhaps best thought of
'as a permanent cleavage about equality, which is sufficiently open to
be redefined with time and allow shifting alliances' (Noël and Thérien
2008: 16) – an argument that recalls the work of Norberto Bobbio
(1996), whose succinct definition of the left–right divide we use as the
yardstick for our own work. According to Bobbio, 'left' and 'right'
refer to opposing political ideologies that are structured around the
idea of equality. Whereas the right conceives most inequalities as
natural and as difficult (and probably unwise) to eradicate, the left
considers most inequalities as socially constructed and therefore amen-
able to progressive governmental action. Thus, our minimal definition
of the right is a political ideology characterized by the belief that the
main inequalities within society are natural and largely outside the
purview of the state. One way of operationalizing this ideology is to
observe the extent to which political actors and parties promote state
involvement in the economy in order to counter inequality.
Nevertheless, as we will argue in more detail later on, it is also possible
to examine whether political forces posit the existence of natural
inequalities (the right) as opposed to socially constructed inequalities
(the left) when it comes to sociocultural issues such as gender, national
identity and morality.

   Following Sartori's (1970) dictum, this minimal definition is useful
for distinguishing between 'left' and 'right'; but to differentiate subtypes one has to look at additional criteria. In fact, the literature on the
right in Western Europe normally recognizes two important subtypes:
on the one hand, the mainstream right, and on the other hand, the far
right. At the same time, it is possible to distinguish specific party
families within each of these two subtypes. While the Christian democrats, the conservatives and the liberals are normally seen as examples
of the mainstream right, the populist radical right and the extreme right
are usually depicted as examples of the far right. In the following

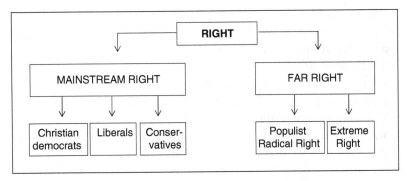

Figure 1.3 Typology of right-wing parties in Western Europe

paragraphs we provide working definitions of each of these party families and outline their main characteristics.

As per Figure 1.3, the right – understood as a political ideology characterized by the belief that the main inequalities within society are natural and largely outside the purview of the state – can be divided into two subtypes: the mainstream right and the far right. Although this is a common distinction in the political science literature, it has not received much conceptual attention. One of the few exceptions is the recent study by Akkerman, de Lange and Rooduijn (2016: 6–7), who aptly note two complementary meanings of the term 'mainstream'. First of all, it alludes to parties that tend to adopt centrist and moderate programmatic positions. This means that when they defend a left or a right ideology, they normally do not advocate extreme solutions. Second, the term also refers to parties that are not only long-established, but also – and more importantly – loyal to the political system. This means that when they defend a left or a right ideology, they normally support existing norms and values as well as refrain from calling for an overthrow of the political system.

By contrast, far right (or left) parties are characterized by the opposite. These are parties that take radical positions and show little commitment to the formal and informal rules of the game that are intrinsic to (liberal) democratic regimes (Mudde 2007: 49). To paraphrase Linz (1978), far right parties behave as semi-loyal or disloyal political actors, while mainstream right parties behave as loyal political actors. In summary, our distinction between the mainstream right and the extreme right relies on two features that are commonly employed in the academic literature: spatial attributes (moderate versus hard-core positions) and attitudes towards the (liberal) democratic system (acceptance versus rejection) (e.g., Ignazi 1992, 2003; Mudde 2007, 2013; Rydgren 2007).

Of course, nothing is immutable in the long term, and there is considerable debate in the academic literature about the extent to which mainstream right parties and far right parties move and morph over time. Recent work on the populist radical right shows that, in spite of some adaptation and modification of its programmatic profile (Rovny 2013; Eger and Valdez 2015), it continues to be located at the far end of the political spectrum and shows limited commitment to *liberal* democracy (Akkerman, de Lange and Rooduijn 2016). At the same time, there is research on the transformation of mainstream right parties in response to the populist radical right: depending on the countries included, parties studied, methods employed and time frame considered in the analysis, some scholars find that mainstream right parties have been radicalizing (e.g., van Spanje 2010; Han 2015; Wagner and Meyer 2017; Abou-Chadi and Krause 2020), others do not detect huge changes (e.g., Alonso and da Fonseca 2012; Rooduijn, de Lange and van der Brug 2012; Mudde 2013; Akkerman 2015b), and some claim that there is significant variance across cases (e.g., Bale 2003; Odmalm and Bale 2015; Schumacher and van Kersbergen 2016). Moreover, we need to be careful not to fall into the trap of assuming that each and every shift in that respect is down to established parties reacting to new challen*gers* rather than new challen*ges*. After all, it is possible to argue that '[r]ather than the populist radical right, it has been the mainstream right-wing that has pushed West European politics to the right, in part in response to media and popular responses to relatively recent developments (such as multi-ethnic societies, the Maastricht Treaty and 9/11)' (Mudde 2013: 13). All these are clearly open questions and ones which our contributors will analyse in detail, along, of course, with the possibility that the challenged and the challengers, notwithstanding their electoral rivalry, may be able, in the wake of elections, to cooperate in order to form a tacit or explicit right-wing bloc in the legislature that will help keep more liberal, progressive and left-wing rivals out of office (Bale 2003).

2.1 Mainstream Right

Western Europe is characterized by the existence of different party families, which have specific ideological profiles and are therefore relatively homogeneous (Mair and Mudde 1998). As stated above, the mainstream right alludes to a family of parties with two main attributes. On the one hand, it believes that the main inequalities within society are natural and largely outside the purview of the state, whether those inequalities are framed in sociocultural or socioeconomic terms. On the other hand, it not only adopts fairly moderate programmatic positions but also supports existing norms and values that are intrinsic to the liberal democratic regime – support which distinguishes it from the far right. However, the mainstream right is not a monolithic bloc, but rather a set of parties that have important differences despite their mainstream and right-wing character. In fact, the mainstream right should be thought of as 'a coalition of heterogeneous political currents with distinct, and at times clashing, ideological visions and social bases of support' (Gidron and Ziblatt, 2019: 23). In fact, three party families within the mainstream right can be distinguished in contemporary Western Europe: Christian democrats, conservatives and liberals. We analyse each of these in turn.

In spite of the relatively limited attention paid to the mainstream right in Western Europe, there are a number of key comparative studies on Christian democratic parties in the region, which offer important insights into their evolution and right-wing character. For instance, Kalyvas (1996) postulates that this party family emerged at the beginning of the twentieth century not as a result of the will of the Catholic Church but rather as the decision of political entrepreneurs, who opted to endorse moderate religious views by forming confessional parties that put forward a distinctive Catholic political identity separated from the official position of the Church. Van Kersbergen's classic study (1995) claims that Christian democracy is characterized not only by the promotion of integration, class compromise, accommodation and pluralism, but also by the development of a particular welfare regime that, amongst other things, privileges families over individuals and is based on the principle of subsidiarity. Last, but not least, Christian democracy has been a pivotal actor in the process of Europeanization (van Hecke 2004). Transnational networks of Christian democrats played a key role in the formation of the European Community, which was seen as a solution to war, a mechanism to tame national sovereignty and a vehicle for fighting Communism (Kaiser 2007).

The historical relevance of Christian democracy for the consolidation of democracy in post-war Western Europe cannot be emphasized enough. By offering a moderate religious identity and embracing liberal democracy, Christian democratic parties were able to develop a catchall profile that became electorally very successful in various countries of the region (Kalyvas and van Kersbergen 2010: 188–9; see also Buchanan and Conway 1996). As Jan-Werner Müller (2011: 130) has indicated, '[i]n the core countries of continental Western Europe – Germany, Italy, the Benelux countries and France – it was actually Christian democracy which proved central to constructing the post-war domestic order, and the welfare and modern administrative state in particular. Its leaders were willing to innovate politically, while its intellectuals could present innovation in the guise of largely traditional languages.' Seen in this light, Christian democratic parties were some of the most important actors in shaping the post-war settlement in Western Europe. Whether they can continue to exert such a huge influence, however, is highly doubtful. Whether down to spectacular collapse, as in Italy, or gradual attrition, as in the Netherlands, Christian democratic parties, operating in an increasingly secular environment and finding it harder and harder to hold on to working-class voters, have been haemorrhaging votes and losing office (see Bale and Krouwel 2013). Even the apparent exceptions to the rule – the CDU/CSU in Germany and the ÖVP in Austria – are not what they once were: both have had to rely on grand coalitions to maintain their grip on government, the only alternative (one recently taken in Austria but harder to imagine happening in Germany) being to form an administration with radical right populists (although in Austria the latter have now been dumped – somewhat counter-intuitively perhaps – in favour of the Greens). True, the European Peoples Party (EPP) group remains one of the strongest in the European Parliament but only because it contains parties from Western Europe that are clearly conservative rather than Christian democratic (such as the Spanish *Partido Popular*) and parties from Eastern Europe that cannot really be classified as such (see Bale and Szczerbiak 2008; Grzymala-Busse 2013).

The second party family that belongs to the mainstream right is the conservatives. Unlike Christian democracy, which is usually identified with a common historical worldview, there is no single conservative tradition in Western European politics. The origins of conservative parties can be traced back to the industrialization process in the nineteenth century, since during this period of time pro-regime groups – the elites that concentrated power, wealth and privilege – decided to form political parties to defend their ideas and interests. As the very name indicates, conservatives wanted to keep the existing economic and political order. However, they realized over the years that it was necessary to adapt by acceding to demands for democracy and then appealing to workers as well as owners, often by appeals to the nation rather than class. According to Ziblatt (2017), two strategies were implemented by conservative forces to adjust to the democratic era. While the first involved manipulation to contain the uncertainty of electoral results (e.g., electoral fraud and clientelism), the second entailed the construction of political parties with well-funded organizations capable of mobilizing voters across the board. When conservative forces adopted this second strategy, they were usually able to develop strong conservative parties.

Although it is true that the roots of conservative parties are related to preserving the status quo, one should not overlook the fact that these parties adapted to modern democracy over time and therefore were able to promote transformative policies. Probably the archetypal case in this regard is the development of the neoliberal revolution seeking to downsize both the state and the welfare regime (Harvey 2005; Pierson and Hacker 2010; Jensen 2014). In fact, conservative parties today are generally characterized by the promotion of free-market economics and therefore have a clear right-wing ideology in socioeconomic terms. Another important difference between conservative and Christian democratic parties lies in their relationship with nationalism. As indicated above, the latter have been key in supporting the European project, while the former are much more reluctant to cede national sovereignty to supranational institutions (Gidron and Ziblatt 2019).

The paradigmatic example is, of course, the British Conservative Party. It had always been much less inclined than its main rival for office, the social democratic Labour Party, to spend money on the welfare state, to countenance high and redistributive levels of taxation, to regulate business and to tolerate trade union power. But it had more or less acquiesced in all of them for electoral reasons for three decades after the Second World War. Then, after a prolonged period of economic crisis, along came Margaret Thatcher. The party's first ever female leader proved to her colleagues that cutting public services, lowering direct taxes, getting rid of red tape and taking on the unions could be popular with voters – as long, that is, as the economy appeared to be delivering (at least to those in work) and the programme was accompanied by restrictions on immigration and an assertive foreign policy built around military force (deployed in the Falklands and invested in against the Soviet Union) and increasing criticism of 'Europe'. Few continental conservative parties adopted the full Thatcherite package – particularly when it came to the EU. But many went with parts of it: the Swedish Moderates (M), for instance, swung sharply to the neoliberal right for a while before returning to the centre in search of office; Sarkozy attempted to do the same in France, in his case adding a harder line on immigration for good measure.

Finally, the third party family that forms part of the mainstream right is the liberals. There is much conceptual debate about the very notion of 'liberalism' and its use in the political world is 'polysemous' (Freeden 2015). Conceived as a political ideology, there are three main attributes that are normally associated with liberalism: first, the protection of individual rights, particularly from governmental interference and oppression; second, the promotion of the free market as an efficient and beneficial mechanism for the exchange of goods between individuals; third, the recognition of diverse individual beliefs and group lifestyles. Of these three attributes, only the first and the second are clearly related to the right-wing worldview: on the one hand, the defence of individual rights often implies suspicion towards state involvement and this sometimes translates into the protection of private property (Freeden and Stears 2014: 332); on the other hand, the promotion of free markets is akin to the assertion of the existence of a natural economic order with which the state should not interfere (O'Sullivan 2014: 303). The third, pluralistic strain in liberalism sits less comfortably with right-wing politics, meaning that liberal parties can be more difficult to classify on the left–right axis than conservative and Christian democratic political parties (Kirchner 1988: 3–4; Close and van Haute 2019).

When considering the origins of liberal parties in the nineteenth century, there is little doubt that they were opposed to the *ancien régime*. After all, they represented the interests of the rising bourgeoisie that sought personal liberties, freedom for economic enterprise, constitutional reform and secularization of the state (Smith 1988: 17).

However, the introduction of universal adult suffrage implied a major transformation in European politics that challenged the relevance of liberal political parties. By widening the electorate to impoverished social sectors, communism and socialism became more powerful at the expense of liberal ideas. In addition, the post-war period was marked by the consolidation of *liberal* democracy across Western Europe, making many of the demands of liberal political parties relatively superfluous. At least since the end of the 1990s, many liberal parties across Western Europe have adopted clear stances in favour of the free market, and, in consequence, they can be classified as belonging to the mainstream right. Nevertheless, given that liberal parties tend to stress individual rights and freedoms, they often adopt more moderate positions (and sometimes even left-wing views) on sociocultural issues – one reason why in some of our country case studies they are not considered to be part of the mainstream right that is our focus.

Liberal parties' access to power may, generally speaking, have paled in comparison with their conservative and Christian democratic counterparts, but they should not be dismissed too lightly in this respect. For instance, the Liberal Democrats in the United Kingdom entered into a minimum winning coalition with the Conservatives in 2010, although it has to be said that the move shocked many of their voters, who were used to thinking of them as a social-liberal, rather than a market-liberal party, hence the collapse of their vote at the following election in 2015. That the Lib Dems hung on to a handful of seats, however, meant they were ostensibly in a better position than their German sister party, the FDP. Long used to using its pivotal position between Christian and social democrats to play kingmaker, the FDP's even more thorough-going move towards market liberalism and away from social liberalism – along with its coalition with the CDU/CSU and the departure of some of its more culturally liberal voters to the Greens – saw it wiped out of parliament altogether in 2013. Indeed, had the new right-wing party in Germany, AfD, stuck to its initial stress on liberal economics and not moved towards a strongly anti-immigration position, the FDP's very survival may have been in doubt. As it is, it made a comeback four years later and may one day play kingmaker again. Indeed, across the Rhine, its Dutch counterpart – or rather one of its Dutch counterparts, the other being the traditionally more left-leaning liberal party, Democrats 66 (D66) – is now more king than kingmaker, however. Partly because, unlike its British and German sister parties, the VVD has chosen to fuse market liberalism with a tough stand on migration and multiculturalism, it has recently become the Netherlands' biggest party, taking the premiership in 2010 for the first time since the end of the First World War.

2.2 Far Right

Much of the academic and public debate in contemporary Western European politics relates to the electoral growth of diverse varieties of far-right forces. These are different types of political parties, which share one important commonality: when defending right-wing ideas, they not only adopt hard-core positions but also oppose existing norms and values that are intrinsic to (liberal) democracy. Their attack against the (liberal) democratic regime is sometimes fairly explicit (e.g., proclamation of the use of violence against opponents), but often can be rather more subtle (e.g., weak commitment to certain rules of the game such as basic civil and political rights). In other words, not all far right parties show the same level of disloyalty to (liberal) democracy. In fact, although debates about terminology and concepts are widespread, many, if not most, scholars make a distinction between two subtypes of far-right parties: the extreme right and the populist radical right. While the former is openly undemocratic, the latter is nominally democratic (Mudde 2007: 49).

Extreme right ideas and parties are nothing new in Western Europe. Fascism is the paradigmatic example. Following Roger Eatwell's (2003, 2014, 2017) work, the latter can be defined as a political ideology with three partly overlapping core themes. First, the construction of the 'new man' – masculine, martial and devoid of bourgeois individualism. Second, the forging of a holistic nation with deep cultural and racial roots. Third, the quest for an authoritarian state that reconciles classes by transcending capitalism and socialism. As this conceptualization reveals, the right-wing nature of fascism is not necessarily related to the degree of state involvement in the economy, but rather to the assertion of natural inequalities in sociocultural terms (e.g., inferior and superior races). In effect, extreme right ideas and parties tend to portray the existence of a natural community with clear internal hierarchies and external enemies who are usually distinguished on the basis of ethnic and racial criteria. Moreover, the extreme right is at odds with democratic values and therefore openly defends authoritarianism.

Besides the classic historical instances of fascism, extreme right parties with roots in fascism could be found in post-war Europe in several countries. Amongst the most well-known examples are the British BNP, the Dutch CP89, the Italian MSI, the German NPD and the Spanish FN (Ignazi 1992, 2003). Most of these parties are on the fringes or even essentially defunct today, and, as a consequence, Golden Dawn in Greece represented something of an exception in Western Europe since it was one of the few extreme right parties that for a while at least was still somehow competitive in the electoral arena (Ellinas 2013; Vasilopoulou and Halikiopoulou 2015). For most of these parties, however, their frontal attack on democracy and their links with fascism mean they are normally treated as pariahs by other political parties and are usually portrayed negatively in the media (for a recent overview, see Charalambous 2015).

In contrast to the extreme right, the populist radical right nominally supports the democratic system, which presumably makes it more palatable to the wider public. This party family emerged in Western Europe in the 1980s and its origins are directly linked to the *Nouvelle Droite* in France, a group of intellectuals who, inspired by the work of Gramsci on the left, tried to counter its cultural hegemony by arguing for ethno-pluralism – the idea that, rather than one being inherently superior to another, each ethnicity has its own value and that they are different, incompatible and incommensurable (Betz and Johnson 2004; Rydgren 2013). This notwithstanding, ethno-pluralism should be thought of as a right-wing doctrine because it argues in favour of the existence of natural inequalities between different cultures and within society in a particular country. This means that the populist radical right is right-wing primarily because of its sociocultural positions and not so much because of its socioeconomic positions (Rydgren 2007; Mudde 2013).

Although different concepts are applied in the academic literature to this right-wing party family, Cas Mudde's is probably the most widely cited (Mudde 2007). According to him, the populist radical right has three defining attributes. The first attribute is nativism, which 'holds that states should be inhabited exclusively by members of the native group ("the nation") and that non-native elements (persons and ideas) are fundamentally threatening to the homogeneous nation-state'

(Mudde 2007: 22). The second attribute is authoritarianism, which is not defined as a regime type but rather as the belief in a strictly ordered society, in which authority should be respected and deviant behaviour should be severely punished (i.e., law and order). Finally, the third attribute is populism, which alludes to a specific set of ideas that not only claims that society is based on the moral distinction between 'the pure people' and 'the corrupt elite', but also argue that politics should be about respecting popular sovereignty (Mudde 2004; Mudde and Rovira Kaltwasser 2013, 2017).

Nativism is certainly the key ideological feature of the populist radical right. It can be thought of as a combination of nationalism and xenophobia that is directly related to the doctrine of ethno-pluralism discussed above. However, populism is particularly influential when it comes to understanding the type of political regime supported by such parties. By advancing a populist critique against 'the establishment', they insist that they are in favour of democracy but are at odds with the *liberal* democratic regime. According to them, the problem is that Western European democracy has granted too much power to institutions which are neither elected nor controlled by 'the people' (Rovira Kaltwasser 2014). In short, populist radical right parties are semi-loyal opponents of *liberal* democracy: while they defend the principles of majority rule and popular sovereignty, they implicitly and/or explicitly reject liberal values.

There is a vast academic literature on the populist radical right in Western Europe, including excellent case studies and comparative studies. This is not the place to summarize this literature (on this, see amongst others, Bale 2013; Mudde 2013, 2014; Rydgren 2018). Suffice to say here that populist radical right parties are well-established in most West European countries and they have been able to enter government in a few places, most recently in Austria (FPÖ) and in Italy (*Lega*). And, even where they have not, they exert considerable influence in public discourse, particularly on immigration: witness the Danish People's Party (DF) in Denmark, the National Front (now the National Rally) in France, UKIP in Great Britain and, more recently, the Sweden Democrats (SD), whose roots in the Nazi underground prompt interesting questions about the potential extreme right parties might possess to transform themselves (more or less convincingly depending on one's point of view) into supposedly more benign populist radical right parties (Ivarsflaten, Blinder and Bjånesøy 2020). In addition, scholars agree that the rise of the populist radical right has engendered a profound change in the ways in which the political system is structured throughout Western Europe. That change challenges mainstream parties in general and mainstream right parties in particular.

3. The Silent Revolution versus the Silent Counter-revolution

This book seeks to better understand the current political situation and fate of the mainstream right in Western Europe: just how daunting is the challenge it faces? To answer this question, one has to acknowledge an important transformation that has shaken the party system of the continent: the unfreezing of the existing cleavages and the emergence of new lines of conflict. Not long ago, any introduction to comparative politics in Western Europe started by citing Lipset and Rokkan (1967) to the effect that Western Europe was still characterized by a limited number of traditional cleavages that structure the political game – cleavages which were the result of the Industrial Revolution and the National Revolution, which generated socioeconomic and sociocultural divisions which became entrenched and gave birth to the political parties that still dominated politics a century or more afterwards (Boix 2007). By representing different sides of these social divides, parties were able to politicize issues relevant to specific constituencies, who then became loyal supporters – not least because political parties invested time and resources in socializing voters, who then developed strong partisan identifications that lasted over generations (Caramani 2008: 326).

Nevertheless, '[t]he empirical observation of relative party system stability in Europe over some period of time, however, did not compel Lipset and Rokkan to deny that such systems may get caught up in a profound process of systemic dealignment and realignment' (Kitschelt 2007: 542). In other words, if European societies experience new revolutions that effectively thaw existing cleavages and the previously 'frozen' party systems to which they give rise, we should expect new lines of conflict and therefore a process of 'creative destruction': old parties can decay, new parties might emerge, and novel patterns of coalition formation may well become possible. This is indeed the situation we see in Western Europe today. Two revolutions have shaken Western European societies, which have made possible the emergence of two new party families: while the silent revolution fostered the appearance of the Greens, the silent counter-revolution helped to give rise to the populist radical right.

The concept of the silent revolution was introduced by Ronald Inglehart (1971, 1977), who some time ago argued that the economic prosperity experienced by Western European countries during the post-war period was generating a gradual process of value change. Sustained economic growth permitted the emergence of a robust middle class that began to worry less about material needs and started to place more emphasis on post-material concerns. This was not an abrupt transformation, but rather a slow-motion development that was championed first by younger generations who cared about issues such as fair trade, international peace, respect for the environment and women's rights. By the 1980s, this generation was able to trigger a shift in the political agenda of most Western European societies, putting pressure on the existing political parties to adapt to this new scenario – one marked by the growing relevance of post-material values and thus the declining strength of traditional class voting. The clearest expression of this transformation was the emergence of Green parties which advanced a left-wing agenda on cultural issues that was supported by affluent citizens rather than by the working class (Inglehart and Rabier 1986). Even in those Western European countries where the Greens were unable to consolidate electoral support, processes of electoral dealignment and realignment have taken place, with left-wing parties increasingly attracting highly skilled middle-class voters favouring post-materialist values (Kitschelt 1994; Kriesi 1998). Seen in this light, the silent revolution forced the left to rethink its policy proposals so as to incorporate the progressive cultural demands raised by new generations.

However, the Western European right has also been affected by post-industrialization and the gradual process of value change that has taken place. Increasing support for progressive values by the middle class implied a major challenge to the mainstream right, because the left threatened to expand its base of support beyond the traditional working class. At the same time, as mentioned above, the populist radical right adopted the framework developed by the *Nouvelle Droite* to advance a novel conservative identity focused on a full-frontal attack against multiculturalism and immigration. To paraphrase Piero Ignazi (1992: 6), it can be said that the Greens and the populist radical right are, respectively, the wanted and the unwanted children of the expansion of post-material values across Western Europe: while the Greens come out of the silent revolution, populist radical right parties derive from a reaction to it – a silent counter-revolution. This means that both party families are essentially a post-material phenomenon based primarily (albeit not exclusively) on sociocultural rather than on socioeconomic issues (Mudde and Rovira Kaltwasser 2012: 167). Not by chance, several scholars argue that Western Europe is experiencing the formation of a new political cleavage that is primarily centred on sociocultural issues and is producing a transformation of the party system in most countries of the region (see, among others, Kriesi et al. 2008; Bornschier 2010; Rydgren 2013).

Interestingly, the early work of Inglehart devoted little to almost no attention to the issue of immigration and multiculturalism. He rather emphasized that post-materialism is mainly to do with values around environmental protection, gender equality, secularism, as well as attitudes towards European integration as an example of support for cosmopolitan stances. Piero Ignazi (1992) was probably the first scholar who explicitly argued not only that the silent revolution involved attitudes towards immigration, but also that this process of value change paved the way for the emergence of a silent counter-revolution later on in reaction to post-materialism. It is only in his most recent work that Inglehart develops a cultural backlash theory linked to the original silent revolution thesis (Norris and Inglehart 2019), although several scholars adopted the silent revolution thesis much earlier to argue that the populist radical right should be seen as a new party family that politicizes a set of sociocultural ideas at odds with the post-materialist agenda (Mudde 2007, 2010; Rydgren 2007, 2013).

In summary, post-industrialization should be thought of as a sociological transformation – akin to the National and Industrial Revolutions analysed by Lipset and Rokkan – that, by fostering the gradual formation of a new political cleavage, has paved the way for the transformation of the Western European party system from a unidimensional to a multidimensional conflict space (Ignazi 2003; Mudde 2007; Kriesi et al. 2008; Bornschier 2010). The most obvious sign of this new political dynamic triggered by the silent revolution and silent counter-revolution is not only increasing polarization but also growing fragmentation. Battles around sociocultural issues are becoming increasingly intense across the region. In addition, more parties have entered the electoral arena as each of them embraces constituencies with different positions in an increasingly multidimensional conflict space.

What are the implications of this political scenario for the mainstream right in Western Europe? To answer this question it is crucial to recall that mainstream right parties experience a tension between, on the one hand, the need to continue to appeal to well-heeled (and often highly educated) voters, many of whom express the liberal and progressive values associated with the silent revolution and, on the other hand, the need to appeal to voters who sympathize with the authoritarian and nativist ideas associated with the silent counter-revolution pursued by the populist radical right. In more concrete terms, this translates into four key policy challenges that we briefly spell out below – European integration, immigration, moral issues and welfare – that are explored by the case studies included in this book. Certainly, these are not the only challenges that the mainstream right needs to confront in Western Europe today, but they are particularly pressing because they involve a difficult trade-off between the office-seeking, policy-seeking and vote-seeking dimensions of political parties identified by Strøm and Müller (1999). While the office-seeking dimension alludes to the aim of maximizing control over political office benefits, the policy-seeking dimension refers to the goal of maximizing impact on public policy and, finally, the vote-seeking dimension indicates the interest of parties in maximizing electoral support. The various contributions to this edited volume point out how the mainstream right attempts to manage the trade-offs between these different dimensions and they also try to assess if these four key policy challenges are of equal magnitude or rather if some of them are proving, for the mainstream right at least, more daunting than others.

3.1 European Integration

A transnational entity like the European Economic Community (then the European Community and finally the European Union) was always going to prove more problematic for one of the three component parts of the mainstream right than the other two. Christian democrats were heavily invested, indeed instrumental, in the project from the very start, seeing it as a means by which to put a lid on, and perhaps even bring an end to, the virulent nationalism and ultimately anti-religious extremism that had torn the continent apart between 1939 and 1945. Internationalism, free trade and a rules-based order had long been part of the credo of many liberal parties. For conservatives, however, things were rather more complicated – especially outside France, whose conservative leaders, unlike their counterparts in other countries, could at least dream (initially at least) of running the show in their country's own interests. On the one hand, the possibility that it might encourage economic growth and at the same time help to form a bulwark against Soviet Communism was an attractive one – as was the opposition to European integration (seen by many socialists as a capitalist 'rich man's club') on the part of their left-wing opponents. On the other hand, not all of them had entirely abandoned the idea that economic protectionism was sometimes necessary, while the defence of national sovereignty, as well as electoral appeals to patriotism bordering on jingoism, were very much still part of their DNA. Conflict over European integration has also become more acute in the wake of the Great Recession, as the EU has sought to impose fiscal rectitude on member states, particularly those in the Eurozone, thereby sharpening the distributive conflict among them and arguably increasing the democratic deficit in the EU (Sánchez-Cuenca 2017).

As integration and enlargement proceeded apace, bringing with them greater power for the European Court of Justice and increased freedom of movement from a wider range of countries, things became complicated for all concerned (Hooghe and Marks 2018). Those voters who held the kind of liberal, progressive, even cosmopolitan, values associated with the silent revolution welcomed the pluralism and the opportunities offered by the freedoms of the single market and EU citizenship. However, those whose values were more in tune with the silent counter-revolution saw downsides instead – change they had never been consulted on and were uncomfortable with; interference from people they had either never voted for or felt no connection with; scarce resources that supposedly could and should have been used at home given to 'undeserving' foreigners. Conservative parties – with the UK's Tories in the vanguard – started to wonder, especially once the Cold War was over, as growth slowed, and as they came under pressure from populist radical right insurgents, whether the bargain they had reluctantly made was really worthwhile any more. As Marks and Wilson have argued (2001: 454–8), conservative parties support European integration as part of their effort to generate capital-friendly environments, but increasingly oppose European-level market regulation and the weakening of national sovereignty. Even Christian democrats, still very much the heart of the European project, began to worry: the single currency, and the rules required to make it work, were causing arguments between nations rather than always knitting them closer together; and their support at home was shrinking still further as voter antipathy towards migration and spending on poorer member states mounted. Liberal parties were equally worried, particularly because of the democratic deficit in the EU and its growing bureaucratization.

3.2 Immigration

The silent revolution implies that Western societies (or at least substantial sections of them) have become more open-minded about multiculturalism than they were in the first few decades following the post-war settlement – something that might have led mainstream parties both on the left and the right to adapt by accepting more liberal progressive positions on the immigration that inevitably results in more ethnic variation. That said, one could perhaps argue that the previously more marginalized groups have been able to improve their societal integration, the greater the possibility of the backlash (Ignazi 1992; Bustikova 2014). Not by chance, the rise of the silent counter-revolution and of the populist radical right has arguably produced 'contagion effects' on the issue, affecting mainstream parties and the party system as a whole (e.g., Rydgren 2005; van Spanje 2010; Alonso and da Fonseca 2012). In any case, anti-immigration attitudes remain relatively widespread across certain segments of the electorate in Western Europe, providing fertile breeding ground for those parties wishing to exploit it (Mudde 2010). This anti-immigrant sentiment is particularly problematic the mainstream right parties – not just because, generally speaking, they approve of a degree of business-friendly labour market flexibility but because, ideologically, they are all about defending right-wing ideas yet adopting moderate policy positions and adhering to liberal democratic values. So while they can advance an 'accommodative strategy' towards more nativist, radical rivals (Meguid 2008; see also Bale 2008), there are limits to this approach. As well as posing a threat to the immediate economic interests of some businesses, the adoption of harsh positions on immigration can hurt the image and reputation of mainstream right parties among voters who, generally speaking, approve of markets but not authoritarianism, and might therefore withdraw their support. Moreover, since the populist radical right has in many countries effectively seized 'issue ownership' of migration and multiculturalism, a focus on them risks driving up their electoral salience, thereby doing the members of that party family a huge favour (Mudde 2007: 241–2).

But if immigration represents a challenge to the mainstream right, it may well affect its component different party families in dissimilar ways. In the case of the Christian democrats, it is worth indicating that the adoption of harsh anti-immigrant positions is at odds with Christian values. In the words of Cardinal Reinhard Marx, chairman of the German Bishops' Conference, '[a] party that has chosen the C in the name has an obligation, in the spirit of Christian social teaching, especially in its attitude toward the poor and the weak'.[4] Various studies have found that Christian voters are not freely 'available' to the populist radical right (e.g., Arzheimer and Carter 2009; Immerzeel, Jaspers and Lubbers 2013; Montgomery and Winter 2015). For conservatives, however, moral arguments against restricting immigration are likely to play less of a role. Instead, opening the economy to immigrants can be seen as something positive for the free market and therefore business actors supporting conservative parties are normally in favour of having relatively open borders. Finally, liberal parties should in theory find themselves at odds with anti-immigration policies, since they are in favour of both the free market and the very idea of tolerating different cultures, although, as we will argue below, by presenting Islam as a religion at odds with pluralistic values, radical right parties may disrupt that logic.

3.3 Moral Issues

There is little doubt that since the beginning of the 1980s, Western European societies have become more liberal on issues such as abortion, divorce, gay rights and gender equality (Inglehart and Welzel 2005, 2010). Younger generations have played a crucial role in this process of cultural change, which has forced mainstream right parties to rethink their programmatic positions and the policies they pursue in government – not always an easy task (Engeli, Green-Pedersen and Larsen 2012). Take, for instance, the case of David Cameron, who as

---

[4] Interview with Reinhard Marx, published in the weekly newspaper *Die Zeit*, 18 July 2018.

the UK's Conservative Prime Minister introduced same-sex marriage in England and Wales in 2013 in spite of the fact that over half of his MPs failed to support the legislation when it passed through Parliament. By contrast, Chancellor Angela Merkel from the German Christian Democratic Party voted against same-sex marriage in the Bundestag in 2017, but because polls were showing strong support for the Bill and her party was divided on the topic, she did not try to impose party discipline, meaning that it eventually passed into law with the support of seventy-five members of her CDU–CSU bloc.

Despite the fact that Western European societies have become more liberal, there are sections of the electorate – particularly, but not exclusively, poorly educated men in favour of traditional family values (e.g., Mudde 2007; Arzheimer 2009; van der Brug and van Spanje 2009; Rydgren 2013) – who disapprove of this development and are willing to back the populist radical right. As Tjitske Akkerman (2015b) has shown, populist radical right parties tend to adopt more traditionally conservative positions than their mainstream right competitors. This notwithstanding, she also reveals an important change over time: in the last few years, some populist radical right parties have been shifting their stances by presenting themselves as defenders of gender equality and sometimes even gay rights, stating that these are part and parcel of Christian and/or Western values that are under attack by Islam (see also Spierings and Zaslove 2015; Moffitt 2017).

This new rhetoric is particularly challenging for liberal parties, since they are in favour of cosmopolitan values and therefore against conservative principles defended by certain immigrant communities. It also poses problems for Christian democratic parties, since some of their values are bound to be at odds with other religious doctrines that are said to put the 'Judeo-Christian' normative underpinnings of Western European societies at risk (Brubaker 2017). Conservative parties, however, face less of an issue since they can more easily redefine traditional values by advocating a restrictive definition of the 'nation' yet simultaneously defending relatively open-minded positions on sociocultural issues such as gay rights and gender equality.

3.4 Welfare

The right has always been able to live with what it sees as naturally occurring inequalities, and this translates into support for less state intervention in the economy and a more residual welfare state. This approach, however, is not identical to the one advanced by the populist radical right. Anti-immigration may constitute its main pitch to the electorate, but it tends to adopt blurred positions on economic issues (Rovny 2013) and various scholars have shown that it embraces welfare chauvinism – support for a comprehensive safety net but one whose protection does not extend to 'foreigners' (e.g., Rydgren 2013; Eger and Valdez 2015; Schumacher and van Kersbergen 2016). This is not a trivial aspect. Given that the populist radical right is supported mainly by poorly educated (male) voters, it is prone to portray itself as the defender of working-class interests and therefore traditional social insurance schemes (Arzheimer 2013). This means that labour market 'insiders' (often male blue-collar employees with secure jobs) are one important constituency that previously voted for the traditional left and now increasingly supports the populist radical right (Häusermann, Picot and Geering 2013: 228–9).

According to this interpretation, mainstream right and populist radical right forces have conflicting economic positions, thus hindering the possibility of their forming a governing alliance between them. There is indeed some truth to this argument, but the real-world interaction between the two reveals that under certain circumstances they can work together and build a powerful right-wing bloc (Bale 2003). If mainstream right and populist radical right parties increasingly converge on tougher positions on certain sociocultural policies (e.g., immigration), the former might be keen on forming a government with the latter as long as it can impose its own socioeconomic policies (Mudde 2013: 16). This approach represents something of a win–win situation, since each member of the coalition obtains something relevant for its own constituencies (de Lange 2012) and enables the formation of a cross-class alliance between middle-/upper-class voters sympathetic to a right-wing socioeconomic agenda and lower-class voters favourable to a right-wing sociocultural agenda.

Recent studies have shown a more complex picture, however (e.g., Afonso 2015; Röth, Afonso and Spies 2018). It appears that the populist radical right has learned from its governmental experience that it is wise to preserve redistributive economic policies (e.g., social spending and welfare generosity) while permitting the pursuit of deregulatory economic policies (e.g., privatization of state-owned companies and liberalization of financial markets): the former are in tune with the ideas and interests of the working class, while the latter help the populist radical right to diminish the power of labour unions sympathetic to social democratic competitors and to please the mainstream right party with whom it is willing to work. At first glance, at least, this approach offers a potential 'winning formula' that will allow mainstream and populist radical right parties to come together in stable governing coalitions.

4. Outline of the Book

The main aim of this book is to offer a comprehensive picture of the mainstream right in Western Europe, which is experiencing growing challenges because of the tension between the silent revolution and silent counter-revolution. To better understand quite how daunting is the challenge faced by its constituent parties, this edited volume combines individual case studies with contributions that take a broader comparative perspective. The book begins with two large-N case studies that look at the demand side and the supply side, respectively. After this introduction, Eelco Harteveld (Chapter 2) provides a picture of the voter base of the mainstream right in Western Europe since the 2000s. Amongst other things, his contribution reveals that, although the strategic environment of mainstream right parties has undergone profound changes, mainstream right electorates evince a remarkable continuity. Despite the electoral decline of social democratic parties (and class voting more generally), the mainstream right has, for the most part, found it difficult to expand its base of electoral support in poorer sections of society. In fact, occupation – with its ensuing associated interests and outlook (as well as income) – is still overall the strongest sociodemographic predictor of mainstream right voting: managers, small business owners and the self-employed are clearly over-represented among the mainstream right in Western Europe as a whole.

To complement this demand-side approach, Tarik Abou-Chadi and Werner Krause (Chapter 3) take into account the supply side by examining party manifesto data in order to reveal the extent to which mainstream right parties have shifted their policy positions since the

1980s. Their analysis shows that, in general terms, the mainstream right has seen a strong shift towards more anti-immigrant positions, while on questions of traditional morality it has become rather more progressive and therefore seems to have adapted to the silent revolution. This trend is almost identical for all mainstream right party families when it comes to becoming tougher on immigration, but this is not the case when it comes to moderating the position on traditional morality. Christian democratic parties reveal a less pronounced shift towards more progressive stances on moral issues (e.g., gender equality, minority rights or same-sex marriages) than conservative and liberal parties. And, as the authors convincingly argue, this transformation of mainstream right is not without risks. By adopting harsher positions on immigration, mainstream right parties risk alienating their core constituency, which is strongly pro-business and usually prefers investment in human capital as well as global economic integration and trade. Given that many of these voters also have relatively pro-immigration attitudes, this transformation opens up the possibility for new centrist and progressive challengers that may 'steal' votes from the mainstream right.

After these two large-N case studies, the edited volume presents eight individual case studies focused on the mainstream right in different Western European countries, which encompass often very different levels of electoral success. Subsequently, we briefly explain the main findings of each of these contributions by following the alphabetical order of the countries included. The Austrian case study (Chapter 4) is written by Reinhard Heinisch and Annika Werner, who analyse the evolution of the Austrian Christian democratic party (ÖVP) in the last three decades. This case study is particularly interesting because Austria was one of the first West European countries that experimented with the formation of a government coalition between the mainstream right and the populist radical right (2000–2007) and that repeated this type of government coalition (2017–2019). Under which conditions does the mainstream right opt to build a government with the populist radical right? The Austrian contribution answers this question by advancing a two-pronged argument. On the one hand, when the ÖVP was polling behind the FPÖ, the former experienced strong incentives to shift from dismissive to accommodative strategies towards the latter. On the other hand, decisions to accept the FPÖ as a coalition partner depend on changes in the balance of power among the ÖVP's most important intra-party groups. At the same time, the contribution demonstrates that, although the ÖVP has been affected by massive voter dealignment since the 1980s, its ongoing programmatic transformation is an answer to the silent counter-revolution and the resulting surge of nativism by means of emulation of, and cooperation with, the populist radical right.

Chapter 5 deals with the situation in France. In it Jocelyn Evans and Gilles Ivaldi argue that after the mid-1980s the French mainstream right was able to build a relatively stable alliance between conservative and progressive factions – one which had the capacity to establish a 'liberal consensus' in favour, on balance, of the silent revolution rather than the silent counter-revolution. However, Emmanuel Macron's victory in the 2017 French elections marks a critical point for the mainstream right in the country. The latter is no longer able to maintain an equilibrium between conservative and progressive factions. While the former seem to be moving towards the populist radical right, the latter appear to be willing to support Macron's centrist project. Under these circumstances, there seems to be little space for the existence of an electorally strong conservative party, and, in consequence, the right-wing bloc will probably become increasingly divided between two competing projects that attract voters with very different sociological profiles.

In contrast to Austria and France, Germany is characterized by the very late appearance of an electorally strong populist radical right party. Nevertheless, Sarah Wiliarty shows in Chapter 6 that the challenges that the German Christian Democratic Party (CDU) is experiencing today have actually been long in the making and are closely related to the tension between the silent revolution and the silent counter-revolution. The party took time to adapt to the former but suffered less than it might have due to the fragmentation on the left occasioned by the rise of the Green Party. Meanwhile challenges posed by the silent counter-revolution – primarily around immigration and integration – proved less problematic owing not just to the continuing illegitimacy of the far right stemming from Germany's history, but also to the CDU/CSU's determination, nevertheless, to be seen to be doing something about the issues it raised. Merkel's decision to welcome so many refugees in 2015, however, seems to have changed everything, allowing the AfD – initially founded as a conservative, Eurosceptic party – to exploit the issue and take off electorally. Whether its rise will be limited by the fact that it proved more reluctant than some other populist radical right parties to embrace a more centrist, pro-welfare (and on some issues less morally conservative) stance, as well as by its Euroscepticism, remains to be seen. But as Wiliarty points out, the AfD's presence is potentially extremely problematic: if it continues to be treated as a pariah at the federal level, then this could force the CDU/CSU into either staying in or forming coalitions that serve only to reinforce the insurgents' claim that politics has been 'stitched up' by 'the establishment' in order to exclude the voice of 'the people'. Inevitably, that would reduce the Christian Democrats' room for manoeuvre and their ability to make policy choices that, in their view anyway, would help them close down the space available for the AfD.

The next contribution (Chapter 7) deals with the Italian case study. Pietro Castelli Gattinara and Caterina Froio persuasively argue that Silvio Berlusconi's personalist political parties worked for almost two decades as a sort of 'functional equivalent' of the mainstream right in Italy. To better understand this, one needs to recall that the country experienced a collapse of the party system in 1994 that led to the disappearance of the once mighty Italian Christian Democratic Party. As the authors show, Berlusconi played a pivotal role by constructing personalist electoral vehicles that were able to access power by establishing alliances with the populist radical right. Nevertheless, the different Berlusconi governments were not strongly driven by the silent counter-revolution and the non-mainstream right parties were always the junior partners in the coalition. This situation changed dramatically after the Great Recession, which paved the way for the emergence of a new populist party (the Five Star Movement) and the electoral growth of the populist radical right (the Northern League). Nowadays Berlusconi's influence is all but gone and the League is clearly the main actor in the right-wing bloc, implying that the silent counter-revolution is gaining preponderance in contemporary Italy and this has important consequences for the liberal democratic regime in the country.

In Chapter 8, Stijn van Kessel offers an interesting analysis of the transformation of the mainstream right in the Netherlands since the 2000s. In effect, his contribution reveals that the interplay between the silent revolution and the silent counter-revolution triggered major changes in the Dutch party system; a system that is increasingly fragmented today. The agenda of the silent counter-revolution has been

advanced by different populist radical right parties that play an important role not only because of their electoral results, but also due to their
capacity to influence public discourse and debate. In turn, the balance
of power within the mainstream right has changed: while the Christian
Democratic Party (CDA) has been losing votes over time, the Liberal
Party (VVD) has been able to become electorally stronger. Part of this
change has to do with the fact that the VVD has taken more restrictive
immigration stances while at the same time presenting itself as a
defender of individual freedoms and progressive values. As van Kessel
shows, the strategy of the VVD consists in the defence of an idiosyncratic understanding of liberalism, which can be very illiberal towards
immigrants and therefore is quite compatible with building a governmental alliance with the populist radical right.

One of the most neglected case studies of the West European mainstream right is the Partido Popular (PP) in Spain. To fill this research
gap, Sonia Alonso and Bonnie Field provide a compelling study
(Chapter 9) that reveals three particularities of the evolution of the
mainstream right there. First, the silent revolution has been quite
evident in Spain, a country that after the transition to democracy in
the late 1970s experienced major societal transformations, particularly
in terms of the expansion of post-material values and the gradual
formation of a progressive political culture. Second, the PP was able
to adapt to this new scenario with great success as it became the
hegemonic electoral force in the right-wing bloc and was able to govern
the country under Aznar (1996–2004) and Rajoy (2011–2018). Third,
this success has seemingly come to an end in the last few years. Today
the PP is ideologically sandwiched between two right-wing party challengers, the more centrist Citizens and the far right *Vox*. This political
fragmentation is due to a favourable opportunity structure for the rise
of new parties after 2010 – one related to the Great Recession, political
corruption and the push for independence in Catalonia. In summary,
the Spanish mainstream right now confronts similar dilemmas to those
of most of its West European counterparts.

Chapter 10 deals with the situation of the mainstream right in
Sweden, a country that in many ways has been deeply affected by the
silent revolution. In effect, as Anders Ravik Jupskås argues, since the
mid-1980s, established parties in Sweden have rarely emphasized traditional morality in their manifestos and 'green issues' have become
increasingly salient. At the same time, the welfare state is deeply

engrained in Swedish political culture and therefore mainstream right parties cannot afford to be seen as anti-welfare parties. Not by chance, the most relevant player within the Swedish mainstream right (the Moderates) moved towards the kind of centrist economic pragmatism that allowed it to govern the country between 2006 and 2014. This comfortable situation for the mainstream right came to an end, however, when a populist radical right party – the Sweden Democrats (SD) – entered parliament in 2010. After this, the agenda of the silent counter-revolution started to gain greater traction in the country – a development that has proved challenging for the mainstream right, which, on the one hand, has been reluctant to build a coalition with the populist radical right and, on the other hand, is increasingly adopting nativist positions with the aim of stealing voters that support it.

The last case study included in this edited volume is the contribution by Richard Hayton on the transformation of the Conservative Party in the United Kingdom (Chapter 11). The Tories (as they are often called in the UK) are the most successful political party in British electoral history and probably one of the most successful mainstream right parties in Western Europe; but Hayton convincingly demonstrates that the tension between the silent revolution and the silent counter-revolution has presented them with quite a challenge. Faced with the electorally successful 'New Labour' project of Tony Blair, the Conservative Party under self-styled 'liberal conservative' David Cameron (2005–2016) started to adapt to the silent revolution in order to attract progressive voters. Nevertheless, the outcome of the 2016 Brexit referendum dramatically changed the agenda pursued by the party, which became badly divided between liberal and reactionary factions, only to see the latter triumph so completely that some fear it is teetering on the cusp of becoming a populist radical right party itself.

Last, but not least, the edited volume finishes with a conclusion (Chapter 12) that not only summarizes the main findings of the book but also proposes three new avenues of research. First, we reflect on the long-term consequences of what some mainstream right parties see as their 'winning formula', namely, to adapt to the silent counter-revolution on issues such as immigration with the aim of closing down the space available for the populist radical right. The second aspect worth exploring is the extent to which the modification of the programmatic profile of the mainstream right should lead us to rethink and/or be more cautious about the concepts that we use to define and understand this group of parties. Third, we suggest that future studies look into how 'negative partisanship' could impact on support for both the mainstream and the far right.

Annex

Parties Included in Figure 1.1

Christian Democratic Parties

Austria: Austrian People's Party (ÖVP); Belgium: Christian Democrats and Flemish (CVP/CD&V), Humanistic Democratic Centre; Finland: Christian Democrats (KD); Germany: Christian Democratic Union (CDU), Christian Social Union (CSU); Italy: *Unione/Centro, Democrazia Cristiana*; Luxembourg: Christian Social People's Party (CSV); Netherlands: Christian Democratic Appeal (CDA); Norway: Christian Democratic Party (KrF); Sweden: Christian Democrats (KD); Switzerland: Christian Democratic People's Party (CVP).

Conservative Parties

Belgium: New Flemish Alliance; Denmark: Conservatives (KF); Finland: National Coalition Party (KOK); France: Rally for the Republic (RPR), Union for a Popular Movement (UMP); Greece: New Democracy (ND); Iceland: Independence Party (Sj); Italy: *Forza Italia*; Luxembourg: Alternative Democratic Reform Party (ADR); Norway: Conservative (H); Portugal: *Centro Democratico y Social/Partido Popular, Partido Social Democrata* (PPD/PSD); Spain: *Partido Popular* (PP); Sweden: Moderate Party (MSP); Switzerland: Conservative Democratic Party (BDP); United Kingdom: Conservative Party.

Liberal Parties

Austria: The New Austria (NEOS), Liberal Forum (LIF); Belgium: Reformist Movement (MR), Flemish Liberals and Democrats (PVV/VLD), Liberal Reformist Party (PRL); Denmark: Liberal Party (V), New-Liberal Alliance (NLA), *Radikal Venstre* (RV); Finland: Centre Party (KESK), Swedish People's Party of Finland; France: Union for French Democracy (UDF), *En Marche!*; Germany: Free Democratic Party (FDP); Greece: The River (TP); Iceland: Progressive Party (F), Bright Future (Bf), Revival (V), Liberal Party (Ff); Italy: *Italia dei Valori*, Republican Party (PRI), *Scelta Civica*; Luxembourg:

Democratic Party (DP); Netherlands: People's Party for Freedom and Democracy (VVD), Democrats 66 (D66); Norway: Liberal Party of Norway (V); Spain: *Ciudadanos*; Sweden: People's Party (FP); Switzerland: Radical Democratic Party (FDP-PRD); United Kingdom: Liberal Democrats.

Populist Radical Right Parties
Austria: Freedom Party of Austria (FPÖ), Alliance for the Future of Austria (BZÖ); Belgium: Flemish Block, People's Union (VU); Denmark: Danish People's Party (DF), The New Right (NB); Finland: Finnish Party/True Finns; France: National Front (FN); Germany: Alternative for Germany (AfD); Greece: Independent Greeks (ANEL), Popular Orthodox Rally (LAOS); Italy: *Fratelli d'Italia*, Northern League (LN); Netherlands: Party for Freedom (PVV), Pim Fortuyn List; Norway: Progress Party (FrP); Spain: *Vox*; Sweden: Sweden Democrats; Switzerland: Swiss People's Party; United Kingdom: United Kingdom Independence Party (UKIP).

Given the peculiarities of the Irish political system, which make it hard to slot both Fine Gael and Fianna Fáil convincingly into party families, we do not include Irish parties in this graph. The collected data comes from the database ParlGov[5] and we classified the parties in the different party families according to our own knowledge, secondary literature and the feedback from some scholars.

Parties Included in Figure 1.2

Social Democracy
Austria: Social Democratic Party of Austria (SPÖ); Belgium: Socialist Party (Francophone) (PS), Socialist Party – Different (SPa); Denmark: Social Democrats (SD); Finland: Social Democratic Party of Finland (SSDP); France: Socialist Party (PS); Germany: Social Democratic Party of Germany (SPD); Greece: Democratic Left (DIMAR), Democratic Social Movement (DIKKI), Panhellenic Socialist Movement (PASOK); Iceland: Social Democratic Party (A), Alliance of Social Democrats (BJ), Social Democratic Alliance (SAM), People's Movement (TH–FF); Italy: Democratic Party (PD), Italian Democratic Socialist Party (PSDI), Italian Socialist Party (PSI), Centre Left (*Centro-sinistra*, CeS), Democrats of the

---

[5] See at: www.parlgov.org.

Left (DS); Luxembourg: Socialist Party (SP); Netherlands: Labour Party (PvdA); Norway: Norwegian Labour Party (DNA); Portugal: Socialist Party (PS); Spain: Spanish Socialist Workers Party (PSOE); Sweden: Social Democrats (SAP); Switzerland: Independents Alliance (LDU–ADI), Social Democratic Party of Switzerland (SP–PS); United Kingdom: Labour Party (LAB), Scottish National Party (SNP).

Green/Ecologist

Austria: The Greens–The Green Alternative (*Grüne*), JETZT–Pilz List (PILZ); Belgium: *Agalev–Groen* (AGL–GR), Confederated Ecologists for the Organisation of Original Struggles (ECOLO); Denmark: The Alternative (A); Finland: Green League (VIHR); France: Europe Ecology–The Greens (*Europe Écologie–Les Verts*); Germany: Greens (B90/Gru); Iceland: Women's Alliance (KL), Left-Green Movement (GRAEN); Luxembourg: The Greens (GRENG), Green and Liberal Alliance (GLA/GLEI); Netherlands: GreenLeft (GL); Sweden: Greens (MP); Switzerland: Greens (GRUE), Green Liberal Party (GLP–PVL).

Radical Left

Belgium: Workers' Party of Belgium (PA–PTB); Denmark: Red–Green Alliance (EN–O), Socialist People's Party (SF); Finland: Democratic Union | Left Alliance (DL | VAS), Democratic Alternative (DEVA); France: Unbowed France (FI), French Communist Party (PCF); Germany: PDS–Die Linke/The Left (PDS | LI); Greece: Communist Party of Greece (KKE), Coalition of the Radical Left (SYRIZA), Coalition of the Left (SYN); Iceland: People's Alliance (AB), People's Party (FlF); Italy: Communist Party (PCI), Communist Refoundation Party (PRC); Luxembourg: The Left (DL), Communist Party of Luxembourg (KPL); Netherlands: Socialist Party (SP); Norway: Socialist Left Party (SV); Portugal: United People Alliance (APU), Bloc of the Left (BE), Unified Democratic Coalition (CDU); Spain: Communist Party | United Left (PCE | IU), *Podemos* (P); Sweden: Left Party (*Vänsterpartiet*) (VP).

Given the peculiarities of the Irish political system, which make it hard to slot both Fine Gael and Fianna Fáil convincingly into party families, we do not include Irish parties in this graph. It is worth indicating that we included only those parties that have obtained at least 4 per cent of the vote in national elections. The collected data comes from the database ParlGov[6] and we classified the parties in the different party families according to our own knowledge, secondary literature and the feedback from some scholars.

[6] See at: www.parlgov.org.

2 | The Demand Side: Profiling the Electorate of the Mainstream Right in Western Europe since the 2000s

EELCO HARTEVELD

1. Introduction

This chapter aims to provide a picture of the voter base of the mainstream right in Western Europe. It asks three related questions. First, how has the mainstream right electorate developed in the last two decades in terms of its sociodemographic characteristics and attitudes? Second, how does this profile and development differ across the mainstream right subfamilies and between West European countries? And, third, which factors distinguish the mainstream right voter from the supporters of its most recent electoral competitor, the populist radical right?

Much more attention has been given to the profile of the populist radical right electorate and, in its wake, the populist radical left electorate (see Rooduijn 2018) – and more recently the electorate of the mainstream left (see Abou-Chadi and Wagner 2019) – than to those who vote for the mainstream right, although they occasionally have a cameo role in such studies (see, e.g., Zhirkov 2014; Pardos-Prado 2015; Steenvoorden and Harteveld 2016). Still, we do know some things about them. Across the board, mainstream right voters tend to self-identify as right-wing (liberals least so, conservatives most), have conservative views on economic and cultural issues, and often belong to the higher socioeconomic strata in society (see Gidron and Ziblatt 2019). However, these straightforward patterns might well have been shaken up by changes in the structural conditions and political competition faced by the mainstream right discussed in the introductory chapter. Has the profile of mainstream right voters in the last two decades shifted accordingly?

I answer these questions using the European Social Survey between 2002 and 2016. Over this period, I map the mainstream right voter in seventeen countries in terms of their educational level, income, occupation, age and gender, as well as their views on immigration, European integration, moral issues (concretely, LGBT rights) and redistribution. Where relevant, I zoom in on the three subfamilies of liberals, Christian democrats and conservatives, and I explore whether the trends are uniform across countries. While they reveal some changes, the analyses in this chapter highlight above all else a surprising level of stability (and in some respects convergence) in the general profile of the mainstream right voter. In short, while the strategic environment of mainstream right parties has undergone profound changes, the mainstream right electorates evince a remarkable continuity.

2. Theoretical Background

While the aims of this chapter are descriptive in nature, it is informed by the theoretical expectations discussed in the introduction to this volume. Dealignment and realignment in post-industrial societies, as well as the counterforces of the 'silent revolution' and the 'silent counter-revolution', could be re-shaping the mainstream right electorate in important (but diverging) ways. Below I briefly discuss which patterns could be expected.

2.1 Sociodemographic Profile

Famously, as the attachment of working-class voters to the mainstream left weakens, this opens up electoral potential for other parties, including the populist radical right but also the mainstream right (Kitschelt 1994). For this group, the appeal of the mainstream right likely lies in its cultural, rather than economic, positions. An important dividing line in this respect is education, which increasingly structures values and political preferences. As mentioned in the opening chapter, the conflicting demands of different educational groups have the potential to split mainstream right parties down the middle (as they allegedly do with the mainstream left).

The (increasingly salient) culturally conservative positions of the mainstream right are especially likely to resonate with less-educated voters. Conversely, as the salience of cultural issues increases (de Vries, Hakhverdian and Lancee 2013), the better-educated might leave the mainstream right for a culturally progressive alternative. As a result, the mainstream right's relative success among less- and reasonably well-educated voters might have increased. On the other hand, while less- and reasonably well-educated voters with culturally right-wing affiliations constitute a potential market for the mainstream right, they are also likely to be captured by successful populist radical right challengers (see Spies 2013). The sociodemographic make-up of the mainstream right therefore likely depends on the presence, and size, of such right-wing challengers. To make things even more complicated, not all parties have positioned themselves equally clearly in a culturally conservative direction. Conservative parties seem to have taken the lead in this respect (Abou-Chadi and Krause, Chapter 3, this volume). By contrast, some liberal parties have redefined themselves at the progressive end, possibly swapping the primarily well-off for the primarily university-educated (and culturally progressive) electorate.

Apart from education, 'classic' class considerations (for instance, income) still structure the vote, too. A useful lens to understand class is therefore to look at occupational groups, which embody multiple aspects which are relevant to somebody's class position (Oesch 2006a; see also Abou-Chadi and Krause, Chapter 3, this volume). For instance, both sociocultural professionals (who tend to vote mainstream left) and higher managers (who tend to vote right) are better-educated, but they differ in terms of their interest and outlook (Kitschelt and Rehm 2014). An overarching question is whether, in the face of all these tensions, the mainstream right has managed to hold its previous class alliance together.

Generational differences are relevant, too. I expect younger voters to be less likely to show partisan attachment to mainstream right parties, and more inclined to support ideologically specialized 'boutique' parties rather than parties of the (formerly) 'catch-all' type. Furthermore, generational shifts in values make younger voters less likely to support parties that are conservative on 'globalization issues' such as immigration and the EU (Rekker 2018). More generally, trends among younger cohorts can tell us something about what the future might hold for the mainstream right.

2.2 Attitudinal Profile

Through mechanisms of representation and cueing, the attitudes of mainstream right *voters* can be expected to be (more or less) congruent with broader issue positions of the mainstream right *parties*. This means many mainstream right voters are economically conservative (i.e., market-liberal). In recent years, as many mainstream right parties have moved in a nationalist and Eurosceptic direction, a similar shift is likely to have occurred (as a cause and/or consequence) in the attitudes of their electorate. At the same time, views on these issues are probably less restrictive and Eurosceptic among voters of liberal and Christian democratic parties, compared with the electorate of conservative parties.

As Chapter 3 by Abou-Chadi and Krause (this volume) shows, mainstream right stances on moral issues have become more progressive across the board. Among voters I also expect a shift in this direction. All in all, given the shifts in salience of the public and political debate, I expect that the mainstream right vote is increasingly structured by attitudes towards immigration and the EU, and less by the welfare or moral issues on which their electorates are probably more divided.

2.3 Populist Radical Right Competition

It is often assumed that much of the electoral 'traffic' towards the populist radical right (PRR) comes from the mainstream or radical left. This is because much of the discussion around the PRR has focused on working-class voters (which are supposedly dominant in the PRR electorate), and also because of the co-occurrence in many cases of the PRR rise and the social democratic decline. However, in most countries electoral competition between the mainstream or radical left and the PRR right is in fact less substantial than is the case between the mainstream and radical right (van der Brug et al. 2012). In this respect the PRR is best located in the right-wing 'choice set' (van der Meer et al. 2012).

What the mainstream right and the PRR voter have in common is a right-wing stance on the 'globalization issues' of immigration and EU integration. In this respect, the PRR voter can be characterized as a more extreme version of the mainstream right voter. When it comes, however, to economic and moral issues (neither of which are central to PRR ideology), PRR voters often have mixed or blurred views (Rovny 2013; Spierings, Lubbers and Zaslove 2017). This likely sets them apart from mainstream right voters.

In terms of sociodemographics, some differences can be expected. While the 'proletarianization' (Betz 1994) of the PRR electorate should not be overestimated, PPR parties do draw relatively large numbers of voters with lower incomes and levels of education (Harteveld 2016). This profile obviously differs from the more affluent picture of the mainstream right voter, even if this affluence is easily overstated.

3. Data and Method

3.1 Data

The analysis in this chapter is based on the European Social Survey (ESS). The ESS consists of biennial high-quality surveys among population-representative samples across Europe.[1] Importantly, the ESS offers highly consistent, repeated, cross-sectional measures of electoral support, sociodemographics and attitudes across seventeen West European countries: Austria, Belgium, Denmark, Finland, France, Germany, Greece, Ireland, Iceland, Italy, the Netherlands, Norway, Portugal, Spain, Sweden, Switzerland and the United Kingdom.[2] This allows us to track the mainstream right electorate between 2002 and 2016 using identical indicators. This is crucial in order to establish trends.[3]

The independent variables are education, income, occupation, age, gender, as well as attitudes on immigration, European integration, moral issues (LGBT) and redistribution. I describe the details of their operationalization in the respective sections on social-demographic characteristics and attitudes. The classification of parties as either

[1] See at: www.europeansocialsurvey.org.
[2] Italy only took part in two waves. To avoid relying on a very limited number of data points, I did not include it in the longitudinal analysis.
[3] On the downside, the ESS waves do not coincide with national elections. The dependent variable is the self-reported vote *at the last national election*, which might be several years (sometimes more than one wave) ago. I nevertheless opt for this data source for the following reasons. First, there is strong evidence that, in surveys, voters 'mis-remember' their past vote choice in the direction of their current electoral preference (van Elsas, Miltenburg and van der Meer 2016). Second, even if the reported vote refers to an election that lies – say – two years in the past, major sociodemographic characteristics will not have changed much since. To the extent that attitudes have changed, this will lead to an underestimation of the correlation between vote choice and attitudes. This makes any correlations I do find in this chapter conservative.

liberal, Christian democratic or conservative follows the classification presented in the introductory chapter to this volume.

3.2 Design

The data used in this chapter provides variation across time (2002–2016), countries and subfamilies (liberal, Christian democrat and conservative). Most attention is devoted to trends that emerge across Europe as a whole, given that other chapters will discuss individual countries in much more depth. Where relevant, I split the sample by subfamily. In several cases, multiple parties belonging to different subfamilies are present in a country (think, for instance, of the FDP and CDU/CSU in Germany). However, in most instances there are too few observations to make reliable inferences about each of these at one particular election. I therefore analyse the individual subfamilies only in an aggregated manner across Europe as a whole.

While at first sight it seems straightforward to map trends in the sociodemographic and attitudinal characteristics of an electorate, there are two competing approaches. The first is to look at (trends and variation in) the *relative size* of a group – say, the better-educated – among the mainstream right electorate. This might show, for instance, that a certain mainstream right party's electorate is increasingly composed of university-educated voters, whereas numbers of less-educated voters are dwindling. This, of course, has important implications for a party. However, these shares are also strongly dependent on the size of the respective group within society at large and would not tell us whether this particular mainstream right party is indeed relatively (let alone increasingly or dominantly) popular among this group – say, again, the university-educated. For that reason I add the distribution of these groups among the remainder of the electorate.[4]

A second approach is to look at *relative propensities* (or, relatedly, marginal effects): does being better-educated influence the probability of voting for party X? This number can be compared with the same

---

[4] Party electorates are always coalitions of groups, and it is hard to qualify when a group counts as 'over-represented enough' to be considered an important 'base' of a party. The most relevant comparison is therefore between variables, i.e., comparing the relative roles of education and income. Significance tests provide no solution either given that even slight over-representations will appear as significant in a dataset of this size.

propensity among the less-educated, and in this way tell us which group is over-represented. It also allows to control for other co-variates. However, the downside of this approach is that it does not say much about how sizeable a particular group is within the electorate as a whole. Even if voters with only primary education were to be strongly over-represented, this would still remain a very small part of a party's voter base. For that reason, I include both analyses. Given space constraints, I show the analysis most pertinent to the question at hand (usually the relative size of groups). All analyses use design weights.[5]

4. Sociodemographic Background of the Mainstream Right Electorate

In this section I show the socioeconomic profile of the voters of the various mainstream right subfamilies, as well as of the remainder of the electorate, between 2002 and 2016. I use the following indicators. First, education, measured in three categories (lower secondary or less, upper secondary and tertiary). Second, occupational group based on Oesch's classification (self-employed professionals and large employers, small business owners, technical (semi-)professionals, production workers, [associate] managers, clerks, sociocultural [semi-] professionals and service workers). Third, age in five categories (under 20, 20–34, 35–49, 50–64 and 65 plus). Fourth, income (measured in five quintiles based on the original ten categories used in ESS; available only from 2008 onwards[6]). Fifth, gender (male or female).

4.1 Trends over Time

The following series of figures shows the distribution of the variables among the liberal, Christian democratic and conservative electorates. For a comparison, it also presents the distribution for the rest of the electorate (i.e., respondents voting for all other parties).[7] Starting with

---

[5] These weights correct for the different probabilities of respondents to be included in the national samples (due to sampling procedures). Replications using post-stratification weights show highly similar results.

[6] In 2002, 2004 and 2006 income was measured using twelve categories in ESS, which is difficult to compare.

[7] This means the category 'Rest of the electorate' does not include non-voters. At any rate, non-voting is highly under-reported in survey research.

education, Figure 2.1 shows that, with ongoing expansion of tertiary education, mainstream right parties as well as other parties increasingly rely on this group. Liberal parties attract relatively large numbers of voters with a tertiary education, whereas conservative parties perform slightly better among voters with only a lower secondary education. That said, the educational profile of the mainstream right electorate does not deviate enormously from that of other parties.

Moving on to occupational groups (Figure 2.2), there is little evidence that the mainstream right class coalition has collapsed. Self-employed professionals are strongly over-represented, even though they constitute a relatively small group in absolute terms. (Associate) managers remain over-represented, as do small business owners. Production workers or sociocultural professionals feature less. All of this is rather stable and does not differ very much across the subfamilies.

The measurement of income changed in 2008 (moving from ten to twelve categories), which makes it difficult to compare trends before that year (Figure 2.3). Nevertheless, we can conclude that there is a clear over-representation of higher income groups (the fifth quintile), especially in the liberal and conservative camps. In line with expectations, this over-representation seems to fade somewhat as middle-income groups grow (slightly) in electoral importance among the mainstream right. There is little evidence of growing support among those on the lowest incomes. Despite the decline of social democratic parties (and class voting more generally), the mainstream right as a whole has not been able to expand its base of electoral support in poorer sections of society.

In terms of generations (Figure 2.4), the following pattern emerges. Christian democratic and conservative parties are somewhat over-represented among older voters (over sixty-five) and do not capture voters below thirty-five as well as liberals or other parties. While these differences are not very substantial, it could be worrying (from the mainstream right's point of view) that they are growing: Christian democratic and conservative electorates are more skewed towards older voters than was the case in the early years of the century.

Finally, looking at gender likewise reveals more stability than change (Figure 2.5). Christian democratic parties remain slightly (but not substantially) more popular among women; male voters are over-represented in the electorates of liberal and conservative parties – but, again, only slightly so.

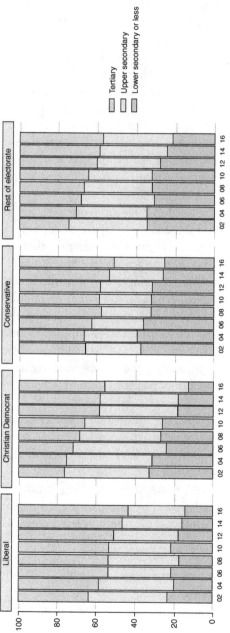

Figure 2.1 Educational level of mainstream right and other voters, by subfamily

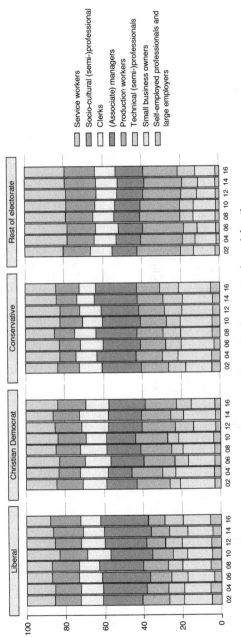

Figure 2.2 Occupational groups of mainstream right and other voters, by subfamily

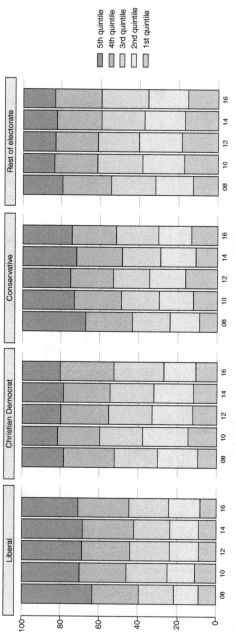

Figure 2.3 Income groups of mainstream right and other voters, by subfamily

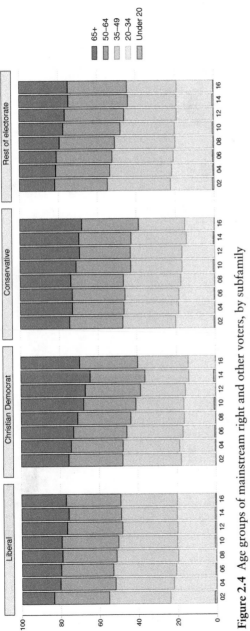

Figure 2.4 Age groups of mainstream right and other voters, by subfamily

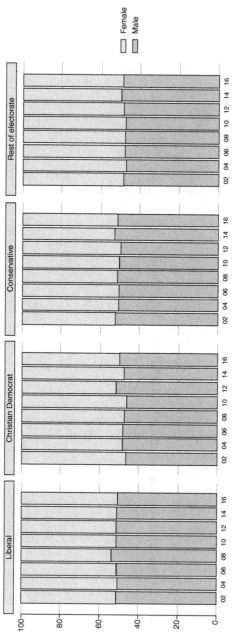

Figure 2.5 Gender composition of mainstream right and other voters, by subfamily

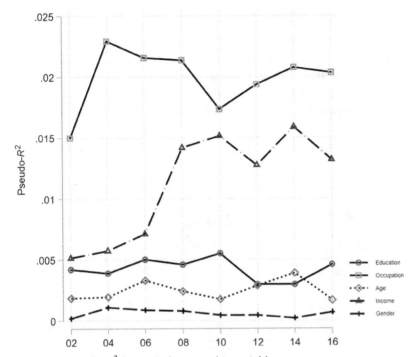

Figure 2.6 Pseudo-R^2 for sociodemographic variables

Finally, Figure 2.6 provides the explained variance – measured as pseudo-R^2 – for each of the variables across time and for all mainstream right parties combined. It confirms the trend visible in previous figures – namely, that the mainstream right has actually remained remarkably stable in terms of the sociodemographic profile of its electorate. The clearest over-representation occurs when it comes to occupations (the 'petit bourgeoisie' and managerial class) and income, followed by education and age. At the same time, these differences should not be blown out of proportion. After all, even accounting for the fact that this model lumps very different contexts together, the explained variance is remarkably low. In that respect the mainstream right remains, in terms of class, a relatively 'big tent'. The next section continues to collapse the three subfamilies and instead focuses on differences between countries.

4.2 Trends by Country

The main differences between countries relate not so much to *which* groups are over-represented, but rather to *the extent to which they are over-represented*. This section therefore summarizes trends in individual countries by comparing which variable has most explanatory power. Figure 2.7 below does so by showing the trends in pseudo-R^2

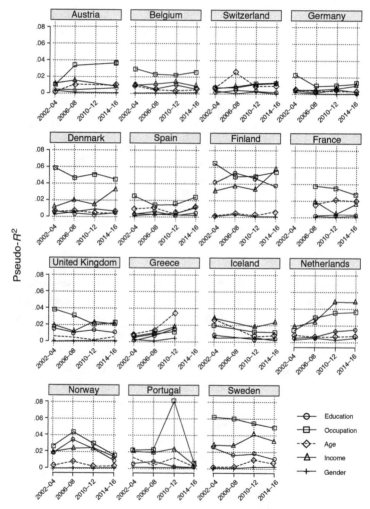

Figure 2.7 Explanatory power (pseudo-R^2) of sociodemographic variables, by country

of each variable in each country over time. To reduce sensitivity to individual surveys and improve readability, the eight ESS waves were collapsed into four two-wave pairs.[8]

It shows, first of all, that there is variation in which variable predicts the mainstream right vote best. Usually, occupation and income are the best predictors. This is most true in the Nordic countries, often presented as societies in which class voting has remained important. However, in Norway this seems to be in decline (after a peak in 2008). The same is true for the United Kingdom, which has experienced a decline in the explanatory power of all sociodemographic indicators over the period. Education plays a role everywhere, sometimes more prominently so, but it is very rarely the most important predictor. The result, in most countries, is a mix of factors, all of them providing limited explanatory power. In some cases, such as France, Greece and Ireland, age is on the rise as a structural characteristic of the vote – perhaps reflecting alignment along generational lines in the wake of the Great Recession.

There are no clear trends shared across the continent. Across the board, occupation and income seem to become slightly less important, but they increase in explanatory power in some cases. Neither is there strong evidence that the role of education is becoming more important. All in all, the most striking pattern is that mainstream right support in Western Europe is generally still structured above all by income and occupation.

5. Attitudinal Background of the Mainstream Right Electorate

This section maps the attitudes present among the mainstream right electorate. We again start by sketching the development across Europe as a whole, before turning to the trends in individual countries. We follow the four issues identified in the introductory chapter, using one item for each: European integration ('European integration should go further or has gone too far'); immigration ('Immigrants make [country] a better or worse place'); moral issues ('Gays and lesbians should be free to live as

---

[8] I opt to show the bivariate explained variance, rather than marginal effects in a multivariate analysis (which will be provided in section 6). To be sure, indicators such as income and education correlate and will share explained variance. However, given that the goal is to uncover the extent of over-representation of *groups*, the nominal correlation is more informative than the marginal effect.

they wish'); and welfare ('The government should reduce differences in income levels'). The latter item does not exclusively pertain to the welfare state, but no closer operationalization was available in the ESS.

The first two of the items have a ten-point answer scale ranging between the two ends implied in the question (e.g., 'A worse place to live' to 'A better place to live'). The items about LGBT rights and welfare have five answer options ranging from 'Agree strongly' to 'Disagree strongly'. All variables were recoded so that higher values correspond with the generally right-wing, conservative or nationalist option. In the interest of visualization, in Figure 2.8 the attitude scales of various lengths have been further subsumed into three categories that make substantive sense and are of roughly equal size (as far as possible).

5.1 Trends in Europe

We start with the distribution of attitudes, subsumed in three categories for readability purposes, across Western Europe as a whole.[9] Figure 2.9 shows that the one item that clearly sets mainstream right voters apart is income redistribution, which is far less popular among any of the subfamilies' voters than among the rest of the electorate. This difference with all other voters is sizeable: the mean scores on this item differ by almost half a standard deviation.

Looking at the other issues, it becomes clear that mainstream right voters are (and have often been) pretty average when it comes to their views of the EU and immigration, although, as might be expected given conservative parties' greater tendency towards nationalism, conservatives are more Eurosceptic than liberals and Christian democrats – indeed, increasingly so. In terms of moral issues, all mainstream right subfamilies were more conservative than average at the start of the century, but they have become steadily more progressive since, and – with the exception of the Christian democrats – they have caught up with the general distribution since. This convergence reflects broader shifts in public perceptions of LGBT issues; most respondents in Western Europe now strongly agree with this particular statement, although a more strongly worded question on an issue that reflects some of the current debates on moral issues might, of course, show

---

[9] An analysis of the full range of answer options, or mean scores, paints a very similar picture.

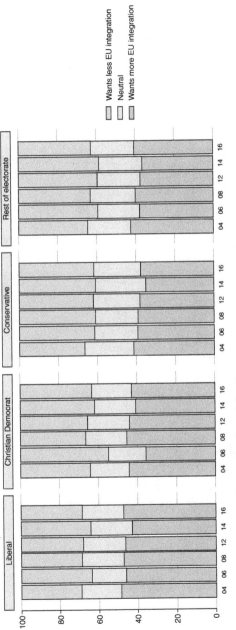

Figure 2.8 Distribution of attitudes, by subfamily

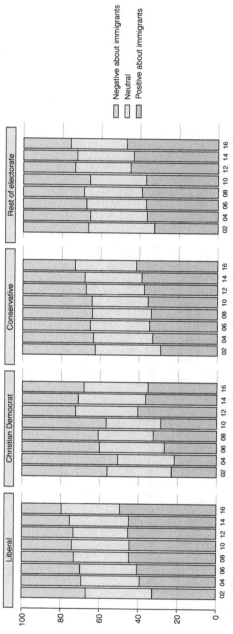

Figure 2.8 *cont.*

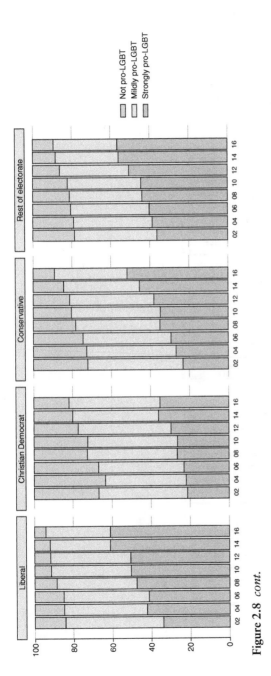

Figure 2.8 *cont.*

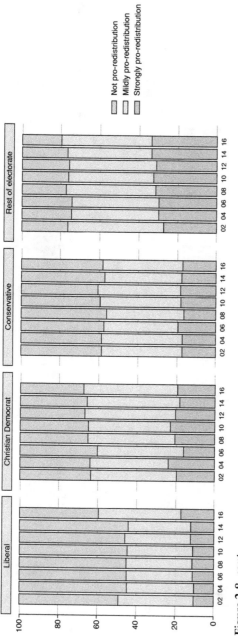

Figure 2.8 *cont.*

rather less convergence. Still, the convergence between the mainstream right and the rest of society clearly fits the finding by Abou-Chadi and Krause (Chapter 3, this volume).

Even if the distribution of attitudes remains fairly constant, there could still be changes in their relative salience. We therefore first look at how well these attitudes predict mainstream right support over time. Figure 2.9 shows the marginal effects of each attitude (controlling for sociodemographics) on support for a liberal, Christian democrat or conservative party.[10] Positive values mean that higher scores on a variable (i.e., a more right-wing or conservative stance) *increase* the probability of voting for that party. Negative values mean that such a stance *decreases* this probability. An overlap with zero score means there is no significant effect on support for the party.

It immediately becomes clear that support for both liberal and (especially) conservative parties is (still) best predicted by views on economic issues. Immigration, interestingly enough, only predicts support for conservative parties. Support by Christian democratic voters is primarily predicted by their views on moral issues, as might be expected, but it does so to a decreasing extent.

Liberal voting is predicted by a pro-EU stance, but, interestingly, so is conservative voting (if decreasingly so). Interestingly, in spite of the European tradition of the Christian democrats, support for that sub-family is not predicted by EU attitudes either way.

5.2 Differences between Countries

Of course, these general patterns might very well hide potential differences between countries. If we look at the marginal effects by country (Figure 2.10), differences do indeed emerge. Antipathy to redistribution appears especially central to the mainstream right voter in Northern Europe (Denmark, Finland, Iceland, Netherlands, Norway and Sweden, and to some extent the United Kingdom and France). Apart from that, the variation within and across countries in the salience of the various issues is striking; there are very few general trends. Neither are there clear correlations with the rise of the PRR. All this

---

[10] Including 95 per cent confidence intervals. These figures do not include 'Other' parties than the mainstream right, because support for all of the other options will not be predicted in the same direction.

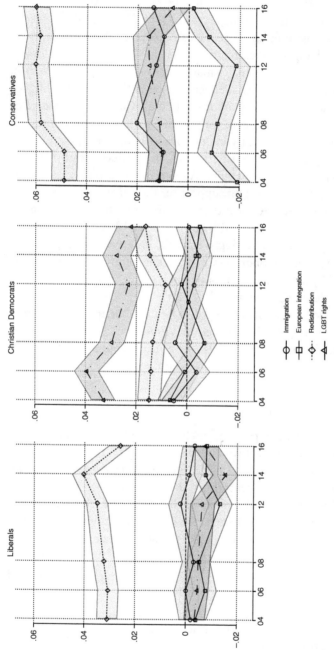

Figure 2.9 Marginal effects of attitudes, by subfamily

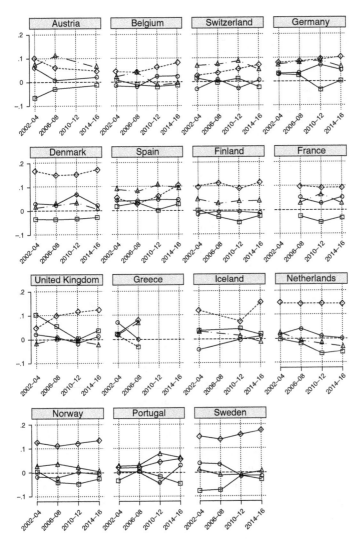

Figure 2.10 Marginal effects of attitudes, by country

reminds us how contingent the strength of attitudinal predictors are to the specifics of the party system, country and election.

6. Competition with the Populist Radical Right

In this section we zoom in on the factors that set the mainstream right apart from the PRR. To do so, we look at the marginal effects of both

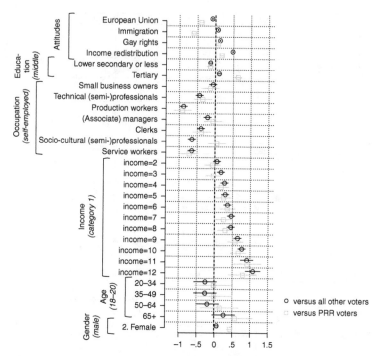

Figure 2.11 Marginal effects of sociodemographic and attitudinal variables on mainstream right support vs. (1) all other voters and (2) PRR voters
Note: reference categories of ordinal/nominal variables between brackets.

sociodemographic and attitudinal variables. The coefficient plot of Figure 2.11 shows two models. First, a model predicting mainstream right support compared with the rest of the electorate. This model provides a summary of the previous two sections. Second, a model predicting mainstream right support compared with the PRR only. The models combine data from all years. The models have two random intercepts, one for elections and one for countries. Because the attitudes were standardized, effect sizes can be compared across attitudes. Similarly, the effects of dummies can be compared, too.

In Figure 2.11, the black dots represent a model in which mainstream right voting is predicted relative to all other available parties. For the attitudinal variables, this model basically replicates section 5 above: among the attitudes examined, the most important is income redistribution, followed at some distance by gay rights, pro- (rather than anti-) European stances, and finally immigration.

The grey squares represent a model in which mainstream right voting is compared relative to the respective PRR party. Here, the substantial negative effect of immigration stands out: compared with the PRR voters, mainstream right voters are much less restrictive on immigration. The same is true regarding European integration. In other words, the PRR voter is above all characterized by their 'demarcationalist' (Kriesi et al. 2008) views on 'globalization issues'. While this is well-established as the defining feature of the PRR voter in general, this analysis confirms that it also sets them apart from their counterparts on the right.

In terms of sociodemographics, the black dots again replicate the findings from section 4. Mainstream right voting is only slightly related to educational level: compared with those with middling education (the reference category), the under-representation of the less-educated as well as the over-representation of the better-educated is small. Occupation and income are stronger predictors. Compared with the reference group of the self-employed, all occupational groups except small business owners are less likely to be mainstream right voters. (Associate) managers, however, are still very likely to be so. The groups least likely to vote for the mainstream right are sociocultural professionals or service and production workers. The effect of income is neatly linear: the higher the income group, the more likely the people in it are to vote mainstream right. Finally, neither age nor gender predicts mainstream right voting very well.

Moving to the comparison with the PRR, the following picture emerges. Compared with PRR voters, mainstream right voters are much more likely to be well-educated, slightly richer and more often female rather than male. In other words, the PRR captures the lower-educated and slightly (but not overwhelmingly) less affluent voter. While this fits the profile of the PRR voter as a 'loser of globalization', it is important not to overstate it. To be sure, the mainstream right voter is almost twice as likely to have completed tertiary education. However, voters who have been through higher education nevertheless constitute a sizeable proportion of the PRR electorate, too (albeit 22 per cent against 39 per cent). The under-representation of women in the PRR electorate has been noted often, and in the case of the mainstream right likely reflects the stigmatized image of the PRR, or stronger ties among (older) women with organized religion and associated parties (Harteveld et al. 2015).

7. Conclusion

This chapter has sketched the sociodemographic and attitudinal base of the mainstream right electorate between 2002 and 2016 based on data from the European Social Survey. One of the guiding expectations was that the mainstream right electorate's structuring in terms of 'classic' class indicators such as income would have been weakened, and that the 'globalization' issues of immigration and EU integration would have become the main predictors of mainstream right voting. Neither of these expectations is fully borne out.

I found that the mainstream right has a relatively stable base in sociodemographic terms. A person's income bracket is (still) a stronger predictor than their educational level. Occupation – with its associated interests and outlook (as well as income) – is overall the strongest sociodemographic predictor of mainstream right voting: managers, small business owners and the self-employed are clearly over-represented among the mainstream right in Europe as a whole. These occupational groups vary in terms of their formal education. Indeed, the data shows that, in terms of its educational level, the mainstream right electorate is often quite representative of the population at large. While individual countries and elections show variation in the relative weight of the various sociodemographic predictors, there are few shared trends.

The issue position that predicts mainstream right support is, above all, economic conservatism. The dominant, as well as stable, effect of economic issues is somewhat surprising, given all the scholarly emphasis on the rise of cultural issues. It does, however, dovetail with the relative importance of occupation and income over education, as established above.

To a weaker (but growing) and more variable extent, mainstream right support is also predicted by restrictive views on immigration, although this is mostly restricted to parties of the conservative party family. In line with expectations, moral issues are less predictive than a decade ago, and morally conservative stances by now define only the Christian democratic voter. In fact, the importance of moral issues rather than economic issues sets the Christian democratic voter apart from the others, and probably constitutes the most important difference between the subfamilies. However, the waning importance of moral issues even among Christian democrats means that the Christian democratic and conservative electorates are converging. There is also some evidence that liberal parties are disconnecting from the rest of the mainstream right on cultural issues: their electorates are increasingly characterized by neutral or progressive stances on immigration, moral issues and the EU, although conservative stances on economic issues are still the most dominant feature among this group of voters. However, the liberal party family (at least as classified by MARPOR) is quite a mixed bag that covers a lot of variation between national parties.

Finally, a comparison of mainstream right voters with PRR voters confirms that the latter are often less educated. However, class differences should not be overestimated: differences in affluence and occupation are less stark. Above all, the PRR voter is much more restrictive on immigration and the EU than the average mainstream right voter. If PRR parties manage to expand their electoral base by capturing the most restrictive mainstream right voters, this gap will only grow.

All in all, the relative stability of the mainstream right electorate in terms of composition and even (to a lesser extent) vote share, is in contrast to the fate of the mainstream left. While the class coalition on the left – for example, tertiary-educated sociocultural professionals and the less-educated working class – is allegedly under constant pressure due to wedge issues like immigration, the mainstream right coalition has proven quite durable. Gidron (2020) notes that 'there are many ways to be right', finding that it is often enough to be right-wing on either economic or cultural issues to identify with the right. This asymmetry might partly explain the relative stability of the mainstream right electoral coalition. It also creates strategic space for alliances with the PRR, suggesting a division of labour of sorts (Bale 2003). Such a right-wing bloc can capture complementary constituencies (the somewhat lower and higher strata of society) since each of the party families involved emphasizes a different issue dimension (cultural and economic, respectively) while blurring on the other. As such, it alleviates some of the trade-offs the mainstream right faces between office-seeking, policy-seeking and vote-seeking objectives.

Of course, such a strategy depends on the continued cohesion of the mainstream right's class and issue coalition – one which can disintegrate in the face of strong cross-cutting pressures. Nevertheless, despite the fragmentation of Western European party systems, the mainstream right's electoral coalition has so far shown a remarkable resilience.

3 The Supply Side: Mainstream Right Party Policy Positions in a Changing Political Space in Western Europe

TARIK ABOU-CHADI AND WERNER KRAUSE

1. Introduction

European party systems have undergone tremendous change in the past thirty years. Most notably, we have witnessed a decline in mainstream party vote shares and an increase in support for challenger parties such as green or radical right parties. Research has extensively studied the determinants and consequences of challenger and niche party success (Meguid 2008; Hobolt and Tilley 2016), as well as the dilemmas of mainstream left parties in a changing political space (Kitschelt 1994; Abou-Chadi and Wagner 2019). However, parties of the mainstream right have received far less attention. While some mainstream right parties, such as the German CDU/CSU, still dominate their national party systems, others, such as the Dutch CDA or the Italian *Forza Italia*, have experienced significant electoral decline. In order to understand the electoral fortunes of parties of the mainstream right, it is necessary to investigate the development of their policy positions over the last decades. We follow a large literature that has described the transformation of a multidimensional political space (Kitschelt 1994; Kriesi et al. 2008; Beramendi et al. 2015), and in this chapter demonstrate how mainstream right party positions have evolved.

We set out to do two things. First, we describe the evolution of mainstream right party policy positions since the 1980s. In contrast to many studies, ours does not limit itself to one or two super dimensions, such as the left–right scale, but tracks the developments on more specific issue dimensions. While recognizing that analysing party strategies within larger dimensions comes with many advantages, we are especially interested in those issues that have shaped the transformation of European politics in the last decades. Whether or not these issues fall into previously existing dimensions or instead form a new one has frequently been a subject for debate (see, e.g., van der Brug and van Spanje 2009). Moreover, how these issues become integrated within the dimensionality of the political space is a function of party competition itself. We study mainstream right party developments on four issue dimensions: immigration; European integration; investment versus consumption; and traditional morality. We argue that general trends in the development of mainstream right party positions can be regarded as the result of structural transformations that have made different electoral groups available to the mainstream right. In particular, the working class, which used to be the core support group of the mainstream left, has become a target of mainstream right strategies. As Harteveld points out in this volume, these strategies are not necessarily successful.

Second, we investigate mainstream right party positions not only as a response to broad socioeconomic transformations, but also as a reaction to the competitive space in which they manoeuvre. In particular, we analyse how mainstream right party positions can be explained as a response to the success of radical right party challengers. We argue that, when facing a populist radical right challenger, mainstream right parties feel incentivized to strategically accommodate the positions of the radical right in order to try to win back voters (for similar arguments, see Meguid 2008; van Spanje 2010; Han 2015; Abou-Chadi 2016; Wagner and Meyer 2017; Abou-Chadi and Krause 2020).

We thus investigate how the policy positions of mainstream right parties have developed as a response to the broad structural changes of the silent revolution (Inglehart 1977), as well as the changes in the competitive context resulting from the silent counter-revolution (Ignazi 1992).

While we find no specific time trend on the left–right dimension, we can see that mainstream right parties have clearly become more authoritarian–nationalist on second dimension issues. Looking at more specific issue dimensions, we can see that, on economic issues, mainstream right parties turned towards more consumption-oriented policies after the 1990s. The shift towards more authoritarian–nationalist positions is largely driven by immigration issues, while for questions of traditional morality these parties have become rather less conservative. We do not find a trend for their positions on questions of European integration. In addition, we can show that mainstream right parties largely react to the success of far right challengers by shifting their position towards a more anti-immigration stance but shift much less on other issues.

2. Mainstream Right Parties in a Changing Political Space

In order to understand the positions of political parties, we need to take into account the socioeconomic transformations that shape the demand side of the political space as well as more short-term shifts in incentive structures based on party competition. There is by now broad agreement that party positions in post-industrial societies should be understood in an at least two-dimensional space (Kitschelt 1994; Hooghe, Marks and Wilson 2002; Kriesi et al. 2008). The first dimension – often referred to as the left–right dimension – subsumes questions of economic redistribution and ranges from a pole that emphasizes state intervention to one that favours the free allocation of resources based on free market competition principles. In contrast to the first dimension, the content and relevance of the second dimension have been subject to much more debate. According to Kitschelt's (1994) seminal work on the question, the second dimension represents preferences for the basic principles of organizing societies ranging from authoritarian to libertarian values. Others describe this dimension as green–alternative–libertarian versus traditional–authoritarian–nationalist (Hooghe, Marks and Wilson 2002) or focus on global integration versus national demarcation (Kriesi et al. 2008). How the issues of immigration and European integration fit this cultural dimension has been especially subject to debate (van der Brug and van Spanje 2009; Kitschelt 2012).

Here, we argue that in order to properly explain the movements of mainstream right parties, we need to focus on more specific issue dimensions than just these two super dimensions. We derive four issue dimensions that structure conflict in post-industrial societies and provide different incentive structures for mainstream right party positions. These different incentives, in turn, are based on varying group preferences on these dimensions. We generally follow Kitschelt (1994) and Oesch (2006b) and argue that socioeconomic class groups that go beyond a simple distinction of material means are crucial in order to explain party appeals in post-industrial societies (see also Abou-Chadi and Wagner 2019). In line with the theoretical framework of this edited volume, we regard mainstream right party strategies as the response to the challenges of two developments: the silent revolution and the silent counter-revolution. Inglehart (1977) famously described the silent revolution as a development in which citizens in societies that have reached a certain level of affluence turn to post-material issues such as gender rights or environmentalism. On these issues, increasing levels of education in particular lead societies to have more progressive values over time. For mainstream right parties, this means that the preferences of the electorate are increasingly moving away from their traditional positions. In contrast, the mobilization of anti-immigrant sentiment that resulted from the silent counter-revolution (Ignazi 1992) has led to the emergence of what is so far the most successful challenger for the mainstream right: the radical right. Within this framework of structural pressure and more short-term competitive incentives, we investigate mainstream right positions in four policy areas: investment versus consumption; traditional morality; immigration; and European integration.

As Beramendi et al. (2015) argue, distributional conflicts in post-industrial societies are no longer shaped only by demands for more or less redistribution but revolve around questions of investment versus consumption. Investment-oriented policies aim at improving social conditions such as poverty or social inclusion through investment in individual skill development instead of direct transfers (Gingrich and Ansell 2015). While consumption policies such as unemployment insurance or public pensions are targeted at maintaining standards of living and generally decommodifying citizens, social investment policies such as public education or childcare aim at human capital development and more successful participation in the labour market (Hemerijck 2013). In an age that is characterized by global financial integration, changing labour market structures (e.g., through automation and digitalization) and family relations, as well as seemingly permanent austerity when it comes to social spending, questions of investment versus consumption have gained increasing importance. In terms of electoral groups, investment spending generally appeals more to educated voters and professionals with general skills, while workers with specific skills who are labour market insiders should favour consumption (Rueda 2007; Fossati and Häusermann 2014; Garritzmann, Busemeyer and Neimanns 2018).

In order to describe mainstream right reactions to the silent revolution and counter-revolution appropriately, we argue that it is necessary to distinguish strategies on immigration, traditional morality and European integration. Morality issues such as gender equality, abortion or LGBT rights have been politicized as a consequence of the social movements of the late 1960s and 1970s in what has become known as

the silent revolution (Inglehart 1977; Kitschelt 1994). The politicization of immigration, in contrast, largely started in the 1980s and 1990s
and is strongly linked to the silent counter-revolution that can be
regarded as a backlash against the value changes associated with the
progressive movements of the 1960s and 1970s (Ignazi 1992). The
politicization of European integration can be described as a move
from permissive consensus to constraining dissensus (Hooghe and
Marks 2009). While European integration for a long time was an
elite-driven project and described as a 'sleeping giant' issue (van der
Eijk and Franklin 2004), the success of Eurosceptic parties has led to a
politicization of European integration in the domestic arena in some
countries (de Vries 2007). For the electorate, we usually find that liberal
cultural positions in favour of LGBT rights or less restrictive immigration positions are more popular among highly educated voters and
sociocultural professionals (Kitschelt and Rehm 2014). Since
European integration issues relate to cultural and economic issues,
preferences are usually not as clear-cut as they are on other second
dimension issues (de Vries 2018a).

Confronted with the politicization of these new issue dimensions,
mainstream right parties need to decide how to strategically position
themselves. We see three long-term developments that should affect the
positions of mainstream right parties on these issues. The de-alignment
of the working class that started in the 1980s provides mainstream
right parties with a strong electoral opportunity. While a large share of
workers used to be strongly attached to social democratic parties, this
type of attachment is much less pronounced in post-industrial societies
and the knowledge economy (Gingrich and Häusermann 2015;
Gingrich 2017). This provides an opportunity for mainstream right
parties to appeal to working-class voters and thereby expand their
electorate. Since voters with less education tend to have more authoritarian and nationalist preferences, we should expect parties of the
mainstream right to use these positions to appeal to this segment of
the electorate. However, culturally conservative positions might not be
enough to appeal to working-class voters if mainstream right parties
are still seen as strongly anti-welfare and anti-consumption. Hence, we
should generally expect to see mainstream right parties move towards
more culturally conservative and pro-consumption positions.

However, parties' incentives are not identical for all second dimension issues. Positions on traditional morality were long based on

conservative and Christian democratic parties' strong relationships with churches and a religious electorate. Secularization and post-modern value change have made conservative positions on morality issues such as abortion or gender equality less electorally attractive. Especially for Christian democratic parties, politicization of these issues comes at a high electoral risk (Engeli, Green-Pedersen and Larsen 2012). The most striking example of this is LGBT rights, where a fundamental value change has taken place in Western European countries over the last thirty years (Abou-Chadi and Finnigan 2019). Now, many conservative and even Christian democratic parties support same-sex marriage.

In contrast, immigration issues provide mainstream right parties with a much clearer electoral opportunity. While many traditional morality issues have seen a liberalization of attitudes, this is not the case for immigration. Large shares of the European electorate remain highly sceptical about immigration (Sides and Citrin 2007). In addition, immigration can serve as a potential wedge issue (van de Wardt, de Vries and Hobolt 2014) against social democratic parties as it pitches the preferences of the working-class electorate (which is often critical of immigration) against the preferences of more educated sociocultural professionals.

European integration issues generally have high electoral potential as the electorate holds less positive positions on European integration than do parties and political elites (Hobolt and de Vries 2016). However, politicizing anti-EU sentiment should be problematic for parties of the mainstream right. First, since many core supporters of the mainstream right strongly support European integration, particularly for economic reasons, a politicization of the EU at the domestic level carries the risk of splitting mainstream right parties' own support base (van de Wardt, de Vries and Hobolt 2014). In addition, mainstream right parties are often part of government coalitions. Being involved in European policy-making as part of the government, they are much less able to deliver on Eurosceptic rhetoric (Green-Pedersen 2012). Hence, politicizing these issues comes at the risk of being seen as hypocritical and flip-flopping.

In sum, we expect parties of the mainstream right to have moderated their economic positions and moved towards more support for consumption-oriented policies. This should be especially the case after the global financial and economic crisis. We also expect parties of the mainstream right to have moved towards more conservative positions on the cultural dimension. This shift, however, should be largely driven by immigration issues and should be less visible on issues relating to traditional morality. For European integration we do not expect to observe a move towards more anti-EU positions.

In addition to mainstream right parties' reactions to these general sociostructural trends there is one crucial factor that will affect the competitive space and provoke a reaction from mainstream right parties, namely, the success of far right parties. Far right parties constitute an important competitor for mainstream right parties and will be especially likely to attract working-class voters. We expect that far right success thus accelerates the dynamics described above and, if facing a successful far right challenger, mainstream right parties will move towards more consumption-oriented and culturally conservative positions. This should be especially visible when it comes to immigration (see also Abou-Chadi 2016; Abou-Chadi and Krause 2020).

3. Development of Mainstream Right Party Positions

As a first step, we inspect the positional movements of mainstream right parties from an aggregate view by focusing on the two super dimensions that dominate political competition in Western Europe. We then explore the positional development of the mainstream right for a set of issue dimensions. In addition, we present marginal effects plots showing the results of OLS regressions. These allow us to assess the extent to which the observed trends are driven by the success of far right parties.[1]

Our sample includes issue positions of fifty-eight mainstream right parties for 177 national elections in eighteen West European countries for the period from 1980 to 2018. To estimate parties' policy positions on several issue dimensions, we make use of data provided by the MARPOR group (Volkens et al. 2018). The MARPOR dataset provides information on parties' policy stances based on hand-coding of election programmes. Each quasi-sentence of a manifesto is assigned to one of fifty-six pre-defined policy categories. Based on the resulting scores, we can calculate parties' positions on a wide set of policy areas and issue dimensions. For example, to estimate parties' policy positions on immigration we employ items referring to positive and negative views towards multiculturalism, nationalism, minority rights, and

---

[1] See Appendix B for more detailed information on our estimation strategy.

Table 3.1 *Mainstream right parties in Western Europe, 1980–2018*

Country	Liberals	Christian democrats	Conservatives
Austria	Liberal Forum (LF) The New Austria/NEOS	Austrian People's Party (ÖVP)	
Belgium	Open Flemish Democrats (openVLD; also PVV and VLD) MR (also PRL, PRL-FDF and PRL-FDF-MCC)	Christian Democratic and Flemish (CD&V also CVP) Humanist Democratic Centre (cdH also PSC)	New Flemish Alliance (N-VA)
Denmark	Liberals (V) Danish Social-Liberal Party (RV)		Conservative People's Party (KF)
Finland	Centre Party (KESK) Swedish People's Party (RKP/SFP)	Christian Democrats (KD)	National Coalition (KK)
France	Republic Onwards! (*En marche!*) Union for French Democracy (UDF; also MoDem)		Gaullists Rally for the Republic (RPR) The Republicans (also UMP)
Germany	Free Democratic Party (FDP)	Christian Democratic Union/Christian Social Union (CDU/CSU)	
Greece	The River (TP)		New Democracy (ND)
Iceland	Progressive Party (F) Liberal Party (FF) Bright Future (Bf) Liberal Reform Party (V)		Independence Party (Sj)
Italy	Italian Republican Party (PRI) Civic Choice (SC) List di Pietro – Italy of Values (IdV)	Christian Democracy (DC; also PPI) Pact for Italy (PI) Union of the Centre (UdC)	*Forza Italia* (FI; also House of of Freedom and People of Freedom)
Luxembourg	Democratic Party (DP/PD)	Christian Social People's Party (CSV/PCS)	Alternative Democratic Reform Party (ADR)
Netherlands	Democrats'66 (D'66) People's Party for Freedom and Democracy (VVD)	Christian Democratic Appeal (CDA)	
Norway	Liberal Party (V)	Christian People's Party (KrF)	Conservative Party (H)
Portugal			Social Democratic Party (PSD; also PàF) Social Democratic Centre- Popular Party (CDS-PP)
Spain	Citizens (C)		People's Party (PP; also AP)
Sweden	Liberals (L)	Christian Democrats (KD)	Moderate Coalition Party (MSP)
Switzerland	Radical Democratic Party (FDP/PLR; also FDP/PRD)	Christian Democratic People's Party of Switzerland (CVP/PDC)	Conservative Democratic Party of Switzerland (BDP/PBD)
United Kingdom	Liberal Democrats		Conservative Party

law and order.[2] It is exactly this flexibility that allows us to map developments on a variety of issue dimensions that make the manifesto data set the ideal source for our task at hand.

To get a fine-grained picture of mainstream right parties' positional adjustments, we present analyses for the three main party families of the mainstream right: liberals, Christian democrats and conservatives (see Table 3.1). Importantly, we include countries with and without successful far right parties in order to identify trends that are indeed dependent on the success of challengers from the far right. Far right parties were identified following the categorization put forward by Mudde (2007). All in all, our analysis includes eighteen West European countries. The findings of our empirical analysis remain essentially the same even if we restrict our sample to the member states of the European Union.

4. Competition on the Two Super Dimensions

Figure 3.1 depicts the development of mainstream right parties' positions on the economic left–right dimension for our three party families of interest. The plot shows mean issue positions for each mainstream right party family (dots) along with smoothed trend lines. These lines suggest some movement of conservative, liberal and Christian democratic parties. However, the size of the shifts is modest and overall we can observe only a slight trend towards more leftist positions at this aggregate level.

In contrast to this, all mainstream right party families have made considerable shifts towards more authoritarian stances on cultural issues (Figure 3.2). While conservative parties have only moderately shifted towards more authoritarian positions, liberal and Christian democratic parties have undertaken a sharp authoritarian turn during the 1990s. It is therefore unsurprising that in some Western European countries liberal parties, such as the Dutch VVD or Danish Liberals, now constitute the main party of the right.

As we have argued earlier, focusing on the two super dimensions might hide important variation in mainstream right parties' positions

---

[2] See Lowe et al. (2011) for more information on our estimation strategy. Appendix A provides detailed information on the policy items that were used to calculate the scores.

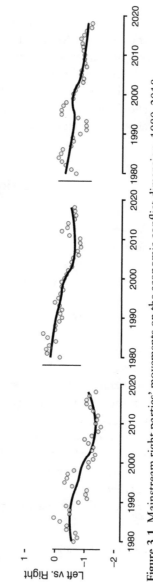

Figure 3.1 Mainstream right parties' movements on the economic conflict dimension, 1980–2018

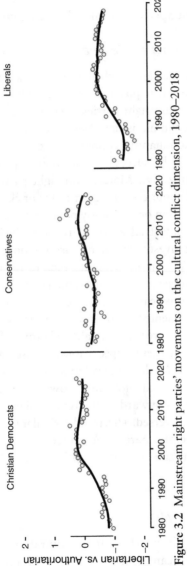

Figure 3.2 Mainstream right parties' movements on the cultural conflict dimension, 1980–2018

on more specific issue dimensions. For that purpose, we now leave the bird's-eye view and look at four specific issue dimensions that have been prominent throughout the last decades in Western Europe: consumption versus investment; traditional morality; immigration; and European integration.

5. Competition on Specific Conflict Dimensions

5.1 Consumption versus Investment

First, we turn to the question of whether mainstream right parties have strategically modified their position on distributive issues. Figure 3.1 suggests that mainstream right parties have only moderately adjusted their position on economic issues. Nevertheless, recent research has found that it is predominantly economically leftist parties that tend to respond to radical right success by promoting pro-welfare stances (Krause and Giebler 2019). Mainstream right parties, however, are less inclined to talk about economics in terms of classic 'leftist' issues such as welfare extension or unemployment benefits. Rather, distributional issues in post-industrial societies are increasingly framed in relation to questions of investment versus consumption. For that reason, we expect to capture a more accurate picture of mainstream right parties' positional movements on this dimension. As we have argued, we would expect mainstream right parties to have tended to promote more consumption-oriented stances throughout recent decades in order to appeal to the increasingly unaligned group of skilled workers.

Figure 3.3 confirms these expectations. Conservative and liberal party families show a curvilinear development on this issue dimension. While there was a general movement towards investment-oriented politics from the 1980s onwards, this trend peaked at the turn of the millennium and then reversed. This trend is similar but less pronounced for Christian democratic parties. All three mainstream right party families now promote similarly consumption-oriented policy positions as in the 1980s.

5.2 Traditional Morality

Next, we take a more detailed look at the cultural conflict dimension on which all three mainstream right party families (as per Figure 3.2) have

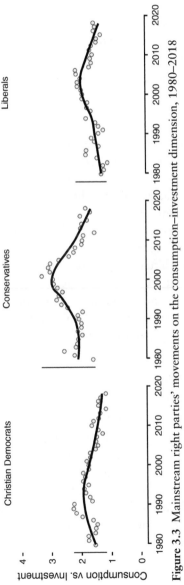

Figure 3.3 Mainstream right parties' movements on the consumption–investment dimension, 1980–2018

exhibited a tendency to promote more authoritarian stances. With regard to issues related to traditional morality, we expect that mainstream parties are confronted with clear incentives to moderate their stances. As a result of fundamental value shifts within West European societies since the 1970s, traditionalist conservative stances on issues such as gender equality, minority rights or same-sex marriage constitute less promising electoral strategies. In line with this expectation, Figure 3.4 shows a negative trend for all three party families that began at the turn of the millennium. These results stand in contrast to the development identified for the cultural super dimension.

5.3 Immigration

Looking at issues relating to immigration (Figure 3.5) explains why mainstream right parties look to have shifted towards more authoritarian positions on cultural issues in spite of progressive trends with regard to issues of traditional morality. Overall, we see a uniform movement towards anti-immigrant positions that is also substantial in size: while the average mainstream right party promoted more moderate values with regard to immigration at the beginning of the 1980s, this value has shifted by approximately 1.5 points towards the anti-immigrant pole of the scale. Although the positions of Christian democrats and liberals underwent little change during the first decade of the twenty-first century, the anti-immigrant trend that began in the 1980s restarted for these party families in the last ten years.

5.4 European Integration

The issue of European integration relates equally to the economic and cultural issue dimension of political competition within Western Europe (Hooghe, Marks and Wilson 2002). On the one hand, the European Union constitutes a community designed to deal with common questions concerning national economies, such as trade or infrastructure projects. On the other hand, the EU sees itself increasingly confronted with collective cultural questions, such as the distribution of immigrants among its member countries in times of an increasing influx of foreign populations. Mainstream right parties, bounded by pro-European attitudes among their support base and governmental

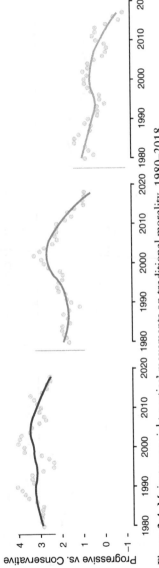

Figure 3.4 Mainstream right parties' movements on traditional morality, 1980–2018

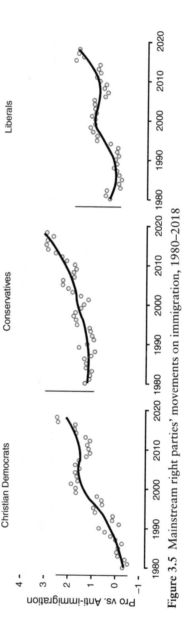

Figure 3.5 Mainstream right parties' movements on immigration, 1980–2018

responsibilities, have little room to manoeuvre on this issue dimension. As a consequence, we do not expect to find a clear time trend.

Overall, we see this expectation confirmed in Figure 3.6. However, Christian democrats have tended to take more critical stances towards European integration since the beginning of the European debt crisis in 2008.

6. Mainstream Right Party Positions and the Impact of the Far Right

After investigating the positional development of mainstream right parties over time, we now turn to a more systematic test of whether the identified trends are associated with the rise of the radical right in Western Europe. As outlined above, far right parties represent a growing challenge for entire party systems. In this context, mainstream right parties are most strongly affected by this development since they are – in terms of positional proximity and issue ownership – the far right's closest competitors. The credo that there should be no democratically legitimized party to the right of these parties – uttered by the former chancellor candidate of the German CDU/CSU, Franz-Josef Strauss – was key to ensuring the electoral strength of many mainstream right parties in the past. With the rise of far right challengers, electoral support for the mainstream right has diminished, and conservatives, Christian democrats and liberals alike are being forced to deal with political parties who are unmistakably addressing parts of their (formerly uncontested) core constituencies.

Figure 3.7 shows the results of models in which we regressed mainstream right parties' positions on the vote share of far right parties. The effect sizes shown indicate to what extent the mainstream right has adjusted its position on specific issues in correspondence with the electoral support for the far right. Moreover, the confidence bands depicted tell us whether the estimated effects are statistically significant, that is, different from a null effect.

Considering, first, mainstream parties' re-positioning on consumption- and investment-oriented policies, we see that the overall effect is negative, suggesting that the centre-right tends to promote more consumption-oriented policies in response to radical right success. This finding is in line with our expectations that mainstream right parties seek to attract increasingly unaligned working-class voters, who favour

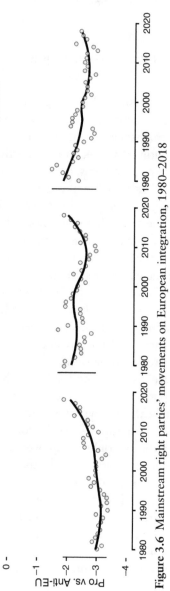

Figure 3.6 Mainstream right parties' movements on European integration, 1980–2018

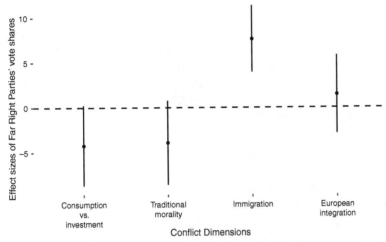

Figure 3.7 Coefficient plot: the impact of populist radical right success on mainstream right parties' policy positions on different conflict dimensions
Note: Dots represent point estimates of OLS regressions with party fixed effects, standard errors clustered by election and party, a lagged dependent variable, and additional covariates (government status, vote share). Error bars show 95% confidence intervals.

less market-liberal policies. That said, the corresponding confidence bars indicate that this effect is only borderline significant (90 per cent level), so we should be cautious about the robustness of this result.

The finding is clearer with regard to issues relating to traditional morality. Here, the error bar includes the zero line and we can conclude that this effect is not different from a null effect. Although the point estimate is negative, mainstream right parties thus do not alter their positions in this policy domain in response to radical right success. As outlined above, value change in Western Europe now results in increased public support for more progressive policies with regard to women and minority rights. Promoting strong conservative policy positions might thus alienate significant parts of the support base of the mainstream right. As a result, mainstream right parties refrain from adopting far right parties' positions in this issue domain – positions that predominantly oppose policies relating to improved gender equality or minority rights.

Third, the regression confirms previous findings concerning the effect of radical right party success on mainstream parties' positions towards immigration (van Spanje 2010; Abou-Chadi and Krause 2020): the stronger the radical right is in electoral terms, the more restrictive are the positions of mainstream right parties on immigration. Although anti-immigrant shifts constitute a 'double-edged sword' for the mainstream right as they run into the danger of making the views of the far right socially acceptable (Thränhardt 1995; van Kersbergen and Krouwel 2008), they tend to tighten policy proposals in order to remedy electoral losses to the radical right and win back vote switchers. The rationale behind this movement is straightforward (Meguid 2008): by promoting more culturally protectionist issue positions, the mainstream right not only aims to crowd out far right challengers by moving into their issue space; mainstream right parties also aspire to regain or preserve their status as issue owners of this core concern for the radical right. As a result – the argument goes – voters will consider mainstream right parties as a more authentic and, due to their chances of government involvement, a more efficient vote choice.

Lastly, we have already explained that European integration constitutes an issue domain with little room to manoeuvre for the mainstream right. As a consequence, we do not find a strong relationship between increasing vote shares of the radical right and mainstream right parties' positions on European integration. While the point estimate is positive – indicating shifts towards more Eurosceptic stances – it fails to reach standard levels of statistical significance.

7. Conclusion

In this chapter, we have documented the policy shifts of mainstream right parties over the last four decades. We have argued that structural shifts in voter demands lead to changing incentives for mainstream right parties in post-industrial societies. On economic issues, we do not find a general trend for the left–right super dimension, but we can document a shift towards more consumption-oriented policies in the past twenty years. On second dimension issues we have seen a strong shift towards more anti-immigrant positions, while on questions of traditional morality mainstream right parties have become rather more progressive. We find that shifts on the immigration dimension in particular happen in response to radical right success.

In this chapter, we have focused on parties' positional strategies. The literature on party competition, however, emphasizes the increasing importance of issue competition, that is, parties competing over attention for issues instead of taking different positions (Green-Pedersen 2007). Future research should investigate how parties of the mainstream right strategically engage with some issues but avoid others. Similarly, a question remains as to whether these strategic shifts of mainstream right parties then translate into policy.

All in all, our findings suggest that mainstream right parties have shifted their policy positions in order to expand their electorate towards less-educated and working-class voters, who generally prefer more consumption-oriented economic policies and more restrictive immigration regimes. These attempts do not come without risks of course. They also entail important trade-offs in terms of parties' policy-, office- and vote-seeking strategies. By taking on a more right-wing-populist profile, mainstream right parties risk alienating their core constituency that has strong pro-business orientations and usually prefers investment in human capital as well as global economic integration and trade. From an economic perspective, many of these voters also have pro-immigration attitudes. This constellation opens up the possibility for new centrist and progressive challengers that may take away votes from the mainstream right. In this regard, liberal parties might be best equipped to expand their electorate through anti-immigrant positions, while at the same time not losing out to more centrist parties as a result of, for example, an association with traditional morality issues. The Dutch VVD and the Danish Liberals exemplify successful applications of this strategy.

Appendix A

The MARPOR dataset provides information on parties' salience scores for fifty-six policy categories. We follow Lowe et al. (2011) and calculate logit-transformed scales in order to estimate parties' policy positions on different issue dimensions. The MARPOR coding scheme does not provide specific categories for all issue dimensions that are of interest in our study. For that reason, deciding which items should be used to estimate parties' policy positions is crucial. In this regard, we rely on measures that have been tested and applied in previous studies.

The following list reports the items used to estimate parties' policy stances on our six conflict dimensions of interest.

Economic Left–Right Dimension (Benoit and Laver 2007):

Right: Free Market Economy (per 401), Incentives: Positive (per 402), Protectionism: Negative (per 407), Economic Orthodoxy (per 414), Welfare State Limitation (per 505)

Left: Market Regulation (per 403), Economic Planning (per 404), Protectionism: Positive (per 406), Controlled Economy (per 412), Nationalization (per 413), Welfare State Expansion (per 504), Education Expansion (per 506), Labour groups: Positive (per 701)

Cultural Issue Dimension (Wagner and Meyer 2017):

Authoritarian: Political Authority (per 305), National Way of Life: Positive (per 601), Traditional Morality: Positive (per 603), Law and Order: Positive (per 605), Civic Mindedness: Positive (per 606), Multiculturalism: Negative (per 608)

Libertarian: Freedom and Human Rights (per 201), Democracy (per 202), Anti-Growth Economy: Positive (per 416), Environmental Protection (per 501), Culture: Positive (per 502), National Way of Life: Negative (per 602), Traditional Morality: Negative (per 604), Multiculturalism: Positive (per 607), Underprivileged Minority Groups (per 705), Non-economic Demographic Groups (per 706)

Consumption vs. Investment (Abou-Chadi and Wagner 2019):

Investment: Incentives: Positive (per 402), Protectionism: Negative (per 407), Technology and Infrastructure: Positive (per 411), Education Expansion (per 506)

Consumption: Protectionism: Positive (per 406), Keynesian Demand Management (per 409), Controlled Economy (per 412), Labour Groups: Positive (per 701)

Traditional Morality:

Conservative: Traditional Morality: Positive (per 603)
Progressive: Traditional Morality: Negative (per 604)

Immigration (Alonso and da Fonseca 2012):

Anti-Immigrant: Multiculturalism: Negative (per 608), National
                 Way of Life: Positive (per 601), Law and Order:
                 Positive (per 605)
Pro-Immigrant: Multiculturalism: Positive (per 607),
                 Underprivileged Minority Groups (per 705)

European integration (Bischof 2017):

Eurosceptic: Protectionism: Positive (per 406), European
               Community/Union: Negative (per 110)
Pro-European: Protectionism: Negative (per 407), European
               Community/Union: Positive (per 108),
               Internationalism: Positive (per 107)

Appendix B

In order to investigate the impact of radical right party success on mainstream right parties' policy position, we ran a number of OLS regressions. Our dependent variables are the policy positions of conservative, Christian democratic and liberal parties since 1980, and our main explanatory variable is the vote share of the strongest radical right party in a general election. We include two co-variates (mainstream right parties' vote share and government status) as well as party fixed effects in the regression equations in order to diminish the risk of finding spurious correlations. Moreover, we add a lagged dependent variable to deal with potential serial correlation that might result from the quasi-panel structure of the data. Lastly, the standard errors are clustered by party and election because the error terms might be correlated across parties or time. The following table lists the corresponding results.

Table 3.2 The impact of radical right success on policy positions of the mainstream right – regression results

	Investment vs. Consumption	Traditional Morality	Immigration	European Integration
Radical right vote share	−4.242 (2.282)	−3.927 (2.389)	7.634** (1.888)	1.450 (2.214)
MRP government status	.006 (.213)	−.262 (.251)	−.118 (.204)	−.084 (.249)
MRP vote share	−1.147 (1.476)	−.012 (2.176)	1.463 (1.859)	−.746 (2.273)
LDV	.148* (.066)	.044 (.076)	.170** (.075)	.152 (.089)
Constant	2.579** (.202)	.410 (.484)	1.000** (.254)	−3.329** (.379)
N	318	318	318	318
R-squared	.280	.603	.441	.459

*p<.05; **p<.01

4 | Austria: Tracing the Christian Democrats' Adaptation to the Silent Counter-Revolution

REINHARD HEINISCH AND ANNIKA WERNER

1. Introduction[1]

Austria serves as clear example of a political system in which the silent revolution and (not so) silent counter-revolution have shaped politics from the 1980s on. As a result, both major parties of the centre left and the centre-right, the Social Democratic Party (SPÖ) and the Christian democratic Austrian People's Party (ÖVP), underwent a prolonged period of decline and electoral de-alignment. However, it is the Christian democrats on which our analysis is focused for they displayed much greater strategic shifts in their responses, especially to the growing challenge posed by the populist radical right Freedom Party (FPÖ). In the ten national elections following the transformation of the FPÖ into a populist radical right party in 1986, the ÖVP could have achieved governing majorities in partnership exclusively with the Freedom Party on seven occasions. Yet they formed such coalitions on only three – in 2000, 2002 and 2017. Instead, in all other instances or, put differently, in twenty-four out of those thirty-two years, the People's Party chose to govern as the junior partner in so-called grand coalitions with the Social Democrats. This decision by the ÖVP is puzzling because non-leftist parties have had continuous majorities in Austria since the 1990s.

Although the Christian democrats generally portray themselves as a centrist and especially pro-European party, they have shown periodic openness towards the populist radical right FPÖ – both at the national and at the sub-state level. How, then, do we explain, on the one hand, the general reluctance to form centre-right governing majorities under ÖVP

[1] Research for this chapter has received funding from the European Union's Horizon 2020 research and innovation programme for the project 'PaCE' under the grant agreement No. 822337.

91

leadership and, on the other hand, alliances with a party whose radical agenda seemed to run counter to core positions held by the ÖVP?

To answer these questions, this chapter traces the development of the ÖVP from 1990 to 2019 at the electoral, supply and demand, as well as coalition-formation levels. Using election results, polling and manifesto data we show how the Austrian Christian democrats have oscillated between the rejection of, and adaptation to, the FPÖ's radical right positions.[2]

We argue in the next section that the switch from dismissive to accommodative strategies (Meguid 2008) occurred only when the Christian democrats were polling behind the Freedom Party and decided to change strategy. This was the case in 1995 and 2017 when the party, in its distress, turned to new leaders who were seen as capable of bringing about strategic change. In both situations, the ÖVP was not in danger of losing public office since government formation without Christian democrats was implausible; but there was a growing perception that the ÖVP would be marginalized electorally and lose its status as a major party. In 1995, the chief concern was declining economic policy influence in a coalition dominated by Social democrats, whereas in 2017 the ÖVP feared further electoral losses to the FPÖ following the refugee crisis in 2015. In response, the Christian Democrats emphasized policy-seeking in the first instance and vote-seeking in the latter (Müller and Strøm 1999), both of which resulted in the alignment of their positions with those of the FPÖ. In each case, electoral peril allowed a shift in the internal party dynamics, where the ÖVP has traditionally been split between a more centrist and social wing preferring to collaborate with the SPÖ and a more culturally conservative and economically neoliberal wing that favours an alliance with the FPÖ. Most of the time since 1990, the more centrist wing dominated the development and alliances of the ÖVP. In times of electoral trouble, however, the party followed a leader willing to open up to the FPÖ.

The third section, which focuses on the party programmes of the three dominant Austrian parties, shows that in the early 2000s this opening of the ÖVP was accommodated by the FPÖ by adopting many of the ÖVP's policy positions and appearing less radical. In 2017, on the other hand, we found less of a moderating effect but a sharp move to the right by the ÖVP. In the fourth section, we then use election survey data to show the effects of

---

[2] For the manifesto data we rely on Volkens et al. (2018).

these changes on the composition of the ÖVP's electorate. It becomes clear that the ÖVP has a wide-ranging electoral potential but pays for accommodating those voters that are friendlier towards the FPÖ by losing voters willing to consider the SPÖ and vice versa. While this situation constitutes a permanent decision-making dilemma for the ÖVP, it is also a fundamental strength and explanation for its stability since it allows the party to move in accordance with the general political developments of the day. The case of the Austrian Christian democrats is thus one of both the negative impact of silent revolutions, but also one of a relatively successful coping strategy: the ÖVP, after all, has been continuously in government since 1986 and has emerged as the dominant party in government in four out of seven national elections since 1999.

2. The Two Silent Revolutions and Their Impacts on the ÖVP's Internal Cleavages

Before delving into specific developments since 1990, some background is necessary to understand how the sociocultural shifts of the silent revolution (Inglehart 1977) in the 1970s and 1980s affected the ÖVP. The Austrian Christian democrats were initially thought to be the natural beneficiaries of the SPÖ's declining political dominance in the 1980s. Having been out of government since 1970, the ÖVP remained untarnished by a series of government corruption scandals. Moreover, the rise of radical right parties elsewhere in Europe and the influx of neoliberal ideas were meant to boost the fortunes of the ÖVP in the electoral market place. Furthermore, throughout the 1970s, the percentage of white-collar workers, a core constituency of the Christian democrats, rose steadily, reaching 42 per cent in 1980. However, the social trends under way in Austria at the time went hand in hand with a pervasive change in lifestyle and cultural values (Inglehart's 'silent revolution'), which at the same time undermined traditional Christian democratic and conservative milieux and, as such, a key pillar of the ÖVP's base.

The crucial year when the cumulative trends of the silent revolution and counter-revolution first manifested themselves in major ways in Austrian national politics was 1986. This was when the Greens first entered parliament and the Freedom Party surged from its traditional level of support of around 5 per cent to nearly 10 per cent, indicating that it was breaking out of its accustomed electoral niche of old-style nationalists (cf. Figure 4.1). Over the next decade, the ÖVP dropped from 41.2 per cent to barely

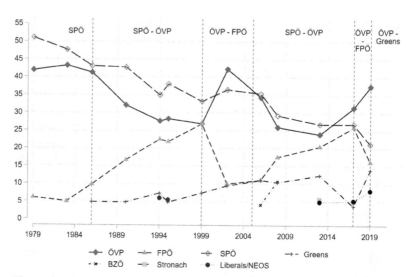

Figure 4.1 Austrian national election results and government participation
Notes: Vote shares in % in national elections; pre-populist FPÖ in 1979 and 1983; BZÖ is formed by moderate FPÖ MPs in 2005 who continue the collation with the ÖVP, serving out the parliamentary term until 2006.

28 per cent in 1995. The Christian democrats felt increasingly under pressure from both liberal and traditionalist political trends, which exacerbated internal political fault lines.

Historically, the Christian democratic ÖVP has been rooted in the petit bourgeois and bourgeois urban milieu, as well as in the rural and farming population. Its chief unifying characteristic has been political Catholicism, especially the Christian social understanding of the mutual responsibility between individual and the community. Organizationally, the People's Party has remained with a comparatively weak centre and powerful component organizations and regional branches. Its five so-called 'leagues', based on professional and demographic characteristics (Employees League, Business League, Farmers League, Women's League and Young Conservatives League), are independent under the law and can potentially act autonomously from the party leadership. The ÖVP is also shaped by powerful regional party branches and their leaders, reflecting the party's electoral and organizational strength across the country. Thus, national party leaders always strive for leverage vis-à-vis these different internal factions. It is this struggle for influence over the party's direction that characterizes the ÖVP's political stance and responses to challenger parties.

Electorally, the ÖVP has been the dominant party on the right despite a fierce challenge by the FPÖ, as Figure 4.1 demonstrates. Between 1990 and 2017, the ÖVP averaged about a 30 per cent vote share in national elections and was continuously in government. Figure 4.1 shows that the ÖVP formed a government with the Social Democrats whenever it was the second largest party in an election, while it coalesced with the FPÖ when it won outright or when circumstances allowed it to act from a position of strength. At the same time, the Christian democrats changed party leaders in quick succession. For example, four of the eight leadership changes in the ÖVP since 1989 have occurred within the past decade compared with only two changes of leader in the SPÖ and one in the FPÖ.

The following analysis will show how the Christian democrats responded to the growing political challenges in terms of the supply of policy programmes and personnel and discuss the electoral consequences. It will highlight the ÖVP's decision to first pursue a policy-seeking strategy and then, the second time, a vote-seeking strategy.

3. The Supply Side: The ÖVP's Reaction to the Two 'Silent' Revolutions

In this section we ask whether the ÖVP responded to the challenges of the silent revolution and counter-revolution by adopting more centrist/moderate or instead more extreme/radical programmatic positions. Initially, the response to the silent revolution was the more crucial one after the party, headed in the early 1980s by the conservative Alois Mock, lost the 1986 elections. The People's Party then embraced two moderate and ostensibly liberal party leaders, Josef Riegler (1986–1991) and Erhard Busek (1991–1995). In a nod to the silent revolution, Riegler's electoral programme was labelled 'eco-social market economy', seeking to reconcile environmental and social policy goals. His successor, Busek, a vocal critic of party conservatives, maintained the ÖVP's centrist sociocultural orientation, but also began pushing the party into a more liberal economic direction (Heinisch 2002: 64–77). Being the junior partner in a grand coalition with the Social Democrats from 1987 onward, however, significantly constrained the ÖVP's modernization agenda. Thus, although the ÖVP found itself in public office, its business faction saw the market-liberal policy agenda blocked and was increasingly eager to change the status quo. Meanwhile, the FPÖ recast itself from a primarily 'anti-statist populist party' focused on an overbearing corporatist state and partitocatic clientelism (McGann and Kitschelt 2005: 151; cf. Müller 2002: 157–8) to a predominantly ethnocratic and nativist formation. As the ÖVP experienced massive losses in the elections in 1990 and 1994 (Figure 4.1) largely to the Freedom Party, ÖVP conservatives together with the party's business faction represented by Wolfgang Schüssel pushed out Busek in 1995 (Heinisch 2002: 169–83). When Schüssel took over the party, he ended the grand coalition, moved the party to the right, and called for new elections in the same year.

At the time, the ÖVP had its programmatic profile challenged by both the SPÖ and the FPÖ. Figures 4.2 and 4.3, which show the economic and the social left–right positions of all three parties over time, illustrate this pattern in a general way. On the one hand, the EU accession process had the effect of pushing the Social Democrats closer to the ÖVP on issues such as European integration, economic modernization, welfare state reform and budgetary retrenchment (Müller, Plasser and Ulram 2004: 163–4), making it more difficult for the ÖVP to stake out a distinct profile. This made it even more necessary for the party to implement a policy agenda that was distinct from both the SPÖ and the FPÖ and centred on reforming the state bureaucracy, liberalizing economic governance and further reducing public spending.

On the other hand, EU membership, coupled with the influx of migrant workers and refugees from the Balkans, presented Social Democrats and Christian democrats with a series of political choices that were unpopular with voters (Müller 2002: 162–4), and perceived by many in the ÖVP as unloved compromises with the resented SPÖ coalition partner (Heinisch 2002: 64–77). The Freedom Party offered the only credible alternative for voters concerned about the austerity measures in preparation for Austria's integration into the Single Market, mass immigration and rising crime (Müller 2002: 164–70). Criticizing globalization and economic modernization, the FPÖ in the mid-1990s moved to the left of the ÖVP on welfare questions and to the right on sociocultural issues (Czernin 2000: 81). Thus, the ÖVP was not just caught between the positions of the SPÖ and FPÖ, but had to face the fact that these two parties were converging towards its middle position.

Under the leadership of Schüssel, the ÖVP then moved further to the right but eventually reversed course after another disappointing election result in 1995. In that campaign, social policy issues and concerns about neoliberal economic reforms dominated, handing an unexpected election victory to the Social Democrats. In response, the ÖVP paired its goal of further economic liberalization with reviving conservative ideas about family politics and maternity pay (Heinisch 2002: 202–10), all of which was opposed by the SPÖ. At the time, the FPÖ began developing a more policy-oriented focus (Luther 2010: 81–2), and laying the ideological and political groundwork for an alliance with the Christian democrats. The Freedom Party aligned itself increasingly with the conservative social policy positions and deregulatory economic agenda advocated by the ÖVP. After 1998, it became clear that from a policy-seeking perspective, an alliance with the FPÖ was preferable. That the ÖVP was to end up in such a dominant position in government while the FPÖ would eventually collapse in public office was unforeseeable at the time, given that the ÖVP came in only third in the 1999 elections (cf. Figure 4.1). Subsequently, both the ÖVP and FPÖ formed a coalition and implemented very speedily a substantial economic and social policy agenda unprecedented in Austria at the time in its economic liberalism and social conservatism.

If we take a closer look at the positions of the ÖVP, FPÖ and SPÖ in Figures 4.2 and 4.3, we see the effect that the change in the ÖVP leadership had on their positions. In general, Figure 4.2 shows that the SPÖ – as we would expect of a social democratic party – was taking a stable position on the left (lower) side of the scale. More importantly, Figure 4.2 shows that after 1995, with the ÖVP leadership going to Schüssel, both the ÖVP and the FPÖ moved to the left in terms of economic positions and continued to do so until 2008, when all three parties converged. Thus, the ÖVP's response from the mid-1990s on became more cautious when advocating further deregulation and privatization. Subsequently, the ÖVP and FPÖ formed a government from 2000 to 2005 and aligned quite closely in terms of socioeconomic positions. However, the FPÖ was paying a high price in the polls (Figure 4.1) both for becoming more of a mainstream party (Heinisch 2003; Akkerman, de Lange and Rooduijn 2016) and for its support for specific welfare retrenchment measures designed to weaken organized labour. Thus, even though the FPÖ moved away from its previously fairly neoliberal positions, it was still nearly always located to the socioeconomic right of the other parties. This led to its large blue-collar electorate feeling 'betrayed' (Afonso 2015) and resulted in massive losses for the FPÖ. On the other hand, the ÖVP, thanks to its somewhat different electorate, benefited from the same policy positions in 2002 and suffered a setback only later in 2005. The ÖVP reacted to this setback by backing away from its socioeconomic position after 2008 when the leadership changed from Molterer to Pröll. This trend continued under his successor Mitterlehner. However, as Figure 4.2 shows, it was the leadership passing to Sebastian Kurz in 2017 that was decisive in taking the ÖVP back to a market-liberal profile and thus a position it had last held under Schüssel.

The apparent gap between the ÖVP's market-liberal and the FPÖ's more 'leftist' position may conceal the fact that the two parties are in reality much closer than they appear since both engage in welfare chauvinism – promoting the idea that state support should go to

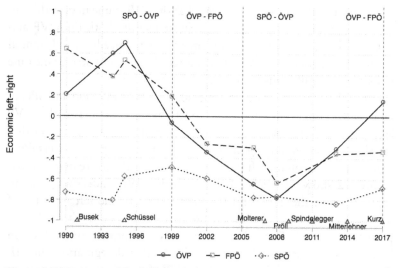

Figure 4.2 Economic right–left score of main Austrian parties, MARPOR data[3]
Note: Own calculation based on manifesto categories and left–right categorization by Franzmann (2009).

---

[3] Markings for the respective names of ÖVP leaders. The Y-axis shows the extent to which the economic positions veered to the right (less government intervention in the economy, positive values) or the left (more government intervention, negative values); position = (right–left)/(right+left).

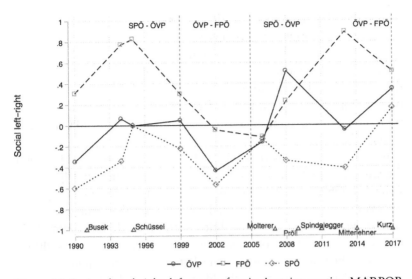

Figure 4.3 Sociocultural right–left score of main Austrian parties, MARPOR data[4]

Note: Own calculation based on manifesto categories and left–right categorization by Franzmann (2009).

Austrians in genuine need rather than to so-called scroungers and supposedly undeserving foreigners. This is evidenced by a package of welfare retrenchment measures which the ÖVP–FPÖ coalition government introduced in parliament in 2018. It intended to cut social spending primarily to those who are not Austrian citizens but also to those viewed as not fully contributing to the social and economic system. Thus, neoliberal and anti-immigration agency support one another.

On the sociocultural issue dimension, the FPÖ stayed to the right of the ÖVP, which remained more closely aligned with the SPÖ until 1995, as shown in Figure 4.3. Despite this, Christian democrats and Social Democrats were also moving to the right relative to their position in 1990, seemingly pulled in that direction by the FPÖ. Figure 4.3 indicates also the relative moderation of the Freedom Party even in the sociocultural dimension in 1999 because it was pursuing an office-seeking strategy. This moderation made it possible even for groups in the ÖVP with a centrist social policy orientation to

---

[4] The Y-axis shows the extent to which parties veered to the right (positive values) or to the left (negative values) when we combine issues such as tradition, religion, nationalism and immigration; position = (right–left)/(right+left).

accept the FPÖ as a new coalition partner under Schüssel's leadership. Thus, government participation pulled the FPÖ towards the middle between 1999 and 2005 but led to severe electoral losses (Heinisch 2003; Heinisch and Hauser 2015). Delving deeper into the sociocultural dimensions, we see that on issues such as the roles of tradition and religion, law and order, nationalism and immigration, the FPÖ is nonetheless furthest to the right and the SPÖ furthest to the left.

By 2005, the three parties, FPÖ, SPÖ and ÖVP, converged around the Christian democrats' position. This changed dramatically in that same year when the FPÖ split. Its more moderate, office-seeking wing broke away, forming a new party, the Alliance for the Future of Austria (BZÖ), which continued the coalition with the ÖVP. The rump of the FPÖ left government, moving sharply to the right in the sociocultural domain while staying towards the left on economic policy. These positions were designed to rebuild the FPÖ's radical electoral base after years of mainstreaming.

By the mid-2010s, the ÖVP found itself once more as the junior partner in a coalition with the Social Democrats and again in great electoral distress. The 2013 elections had resulted in another defeat under yet another party leader. Moreover, from 2014 to 2017 the FPÖ was leading in opinion polls whereas the Christian democrats were mostly in a distant third place. The reverberations of the refugee crisis of 2015 threatened to result in further defections by conservative voters to the Freedom Party. As in 1995, the Christian democrats again saw themselves in danger of political marginalization. In addition, the SPÖ had managed to install a new leader and chancellor, Christian Kern, in 2016, who gave his party a boost in the opinion polls. In response, the Christian democrats turned again to new leadership by bringing in Sebastian Kurz, who had been a vocal critic of Austria's handling of the refugee crisis. He quickly embarked on a vote-seeking strategy by distancing himself from the 'old guard' of the party, abandoning electorally unpopular positions such as the ÖVP's staunch pro-European stance, and adopting right-wing positions on immigration and Islam that were previously deemed to be unacceptable for a mainstream party in public office. The shift to the right found its expression less in coherent policy proposals but, rather, mainly in campaign rhetoric and a right-wing discourse reminiscent of the FPÖ's.

How can we explain this rapid turn of events? At this point, it is important to recall that the ÖVP is a heterogeneous party, divided in multiple ways and often pulling in different directions. In the context of the ÖVP's decline in the polls, the traditional heterogeneity gave way to a division between two larger camps. The first, consisting of liberal Christian-social groups, centrists and the ÖVP labour wing, prefers national-level coalitions with the Social Democrats to collaborating with the Freedom Party and favours alliances with the Greens and Liberals at the regional level if and where they are possible. The other group, consisting of market-liberals, social and rural conservatives, and the youth wing, generally support cooperation with the FPÖ more than with the SPÖ. They see the Social Democrats as the ÖVP's principal ideological antagonist. While it can appear that the ÖVP changes its policy positions and alliance preferences rapidly, it rather reflects one internal group prevailing over another. Under party leader Mitterlehner (2014–2017), as was the case under Riegler and Busek, the ÖVP seemingly eschewed cooperating with the FPÖ while express-ing its commitment to the coalition with the SPÖ. As soon as Mitterlehner was replaced by Kurz in 2017 (as had happened with Schüssel in the 1990s), these preferences changed. The willingness to switch from the SPÖ to the FPÖ, already manifest in the ÖVP under Mitterlehner, was evident in the frequent attempts made by party insiders to undermine his leadership and the partnership with the SPÖ. The shift, however, occurred only with the change in leadership. Under Kurz the differences within the ÖVP became so explicit that he rebranded that part of the ÖVP loyal to his political direction as the 'New People's Party' and gave it a new party logo and colour (tur-quoise). Prior to these changes, the ÖVP's centrism was perceived as a lack of political profile and the centrist faction stood accused by the FPÖ of enabling leftist policy solutions.

It is also clear that the shift within the ÖVP from the moderates to the hardliners was a consequence of the refugee crisis. That this affected Austria in profound ways can be seen in Figure 4.3 by the fact that all three parties converge on the right (upper) area of the dimension, in a space previously mainly occupied by the FPÖ. Thus, while Figure 4.2 shows the ÖVP to be the main proponent of right-wing economic policies vis-à-vis both the SPÖ and FPÖ positioned to the left, the picture in Figure 4.3 is very different. In terms of social and societal values and policies, the ÖVP clearly reacted to the radical right profile of the FPÖ by repositioning in the 2017 elections following greater demand for right-wing positions in the population.

These patterns on the social left–right scores are reflected in the strategy of the ÖVP towards the FPÖ. The Christian democrats (and also Social Democrats) initially reacted to the Freedom Party's surge after 1986 by seeking to isolate the latter politically, applying what Meguid (2008) called a 'dismissive strategy'. The SPÖ enacted a policy of ostracization by enacting a strict *cordon sanitaire* in its party statutes. The ÖVP used the concept of the 'constitutional arch' implying that the FPÖ was not fit to govern (*regierungsfähig*) as long as its leadership continued its 'cultural revolution', opposed Austria's consensus democracy and social partnership, rejected European integration, and distanced itself only half-heartedly from Nazism (Luther 2010: 81–2). Nonetheless, whereas in the SPÖ's case this was a matter of principle requiring a decision by the party congress, for the ÖVP it was a matter of political evaluation on the part of the leadership and their standing within the party. In both cases, the governing parties sought to marginalize the FPÖ by portraying the latter as politically irresponsible. This strategy of excluding the FPÖ from political dialogue was intended to signal to the electorate that votes for the Freedom Party were essentially wasted. This was more difficult for the ÖVP because the FPÖ's traditionalist discourse appealed to the Christian democratic voter base.

In the second half of the 1990s, the dismissive strategy adopted by the major parties towards the FPÖ was tacitly but increasingly abandoned. The shift to an accommodative strategy was most pronounced in the areas of immigration and, to a lesser extent, law and order (Meguid 2008). Figure 4.4, thus, turns to the multiculturalism positions of the ÖVP, FPÖ and SPÖ, as well as to the salience of this issue attributed by the FPÖ and the ÖVP.[5] The figure shows that this is an issue that was salient mainly for the FPÖ, whereas its salience oscillated for the Christian democrats at generally lower levels. In terms of its position, the ÖVP was very positive towards multiculturalism in the early 1990s, but then converged with the FPÖ in the late 1990s and early 2000s. In this context, Hafez and Heinisch (2018) have shown that the Freedom Party's anti-Islamic rhetoric was gradually taken up by ÖVP politicians in the 2000s and reflected as well in an ever more

---

[5] We use multiculturalism as a proxy for immigration and openness to cultural diversity as the Manifesto data does not provide a direct measure.

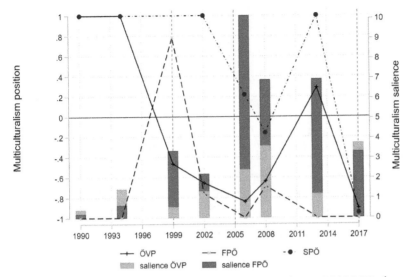

Figure 4.4 Multiculturalism in Austrian parties' manifestos, MARPOR data
Note: Own calculation based on manifesto categories 607 (pro-multiculturalism) and 608 (anti-multiculturalism), salience = (per 607 + per 608), position = (per 607 – per 608)/(salience). Salience bars overlap, higher bar in the background.

restrictive immigration and asylum policy (Bauböck and Perchinig 2006: 732–4). These negative stances towards multiculturalism persisted until 2013, when the ÖVP, under a more liberal leadership, again temporarily took a more positive stance on this topic. However, with the party leadership changing to Kurz, the ÖVP once more converged with the FPÖ in 2017.

Finally, the party's position on European integration is of particular importance because the aforementioned temporary *cordon sanitaire* against the FPÖ by the ÖVP was partially driven by this question. The ÖVP made the acceptance of the European integration process a central condition for any cooperation in 1999. Figure 4.5 shows that until 2017, the ÖVP had a very stable pro-European position. Thus, when the two right-wing parties first formed a coalition between 2000 and 2005, it was the FPÖ that moved from a Eurosceptic to a pro-EU stance. After this government collapsed in 2005, the FPÖ returned to rejecting European integration. In 2017, precisely the opposite happened: whereas in 2000 it was the FPÖ that changed to make the first

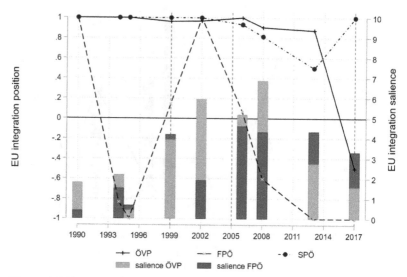

Figure 4.5 European integration in Austrian parties' manifestos, MARPOR data

Note: Own calculation based on manifesto categories 108 (pro-EU) and 110 (anti-EU), salience = (per 108 + per 110), position = (per 108 − per 110)/ (salience). Higher salience bar in the background.

coalition possible, now it was the ÖVP that moved to a much more Eurosceptic position. Although the ÖVP–FPÖ coalition agreement affirmed a fundamental commitment to the EU and European integration (Regierungsprogramm 2017: 33), it added several qualifiers, reform demands and caveats, which was clearly a departure for the Christian democrats.

Summing up, the changes undertaken by the ÖVP after 1990 were clearly reactions to the counter-revolution. This is underlined also by the breakaway of a group of party liberals who subsequently merged with an existing liberal formation (Liberal Forum) to form a new party (New Austria/Neos) in 2012, which entered parliament in 2013 (cf. Figure 4.1). Had the ÖVP tried to accommodate a more liberal agenda, these party liberals would likely not have seen the need to leave.

Facing the prospect of political marginalization as the junior partner in government, the ÖVP undertook important strategic changes that prepared the way for a coalition with the FPÖ. In the first such instance, the Christian democrats changed their strategy to policy-seeking so as to re-establish a distinct profile and cater to the interests of important client groups notably in the business sector. This ended up aligning ÖVP and FPÖ positions when the latter adopted conservative positions on welfare and liberal positions on economic governance. Two decades later, the ÖVP reacted with a vote-seeking strategy by aligning its sociocultural discourse more with that of the FPÖ and thus moving to the right. In both cases, the changes in the ÖVP leadership were preceded by the shifts of power between the two dominant groups within the party and driven largely by feared electoral defeats. The party thus strongly reacted to its voters' signals, shifting between moderate and more extreme versions of its positions.

The ÖVP changed its strategy again following the collapse of the coalition with the Freedom Party in 2019 due to the notorious Ibiza-video affair, which implicated FPÖ leader Strache and the head of its parliamentary faction Johann Gudenus in a public corruption scandal. Although Kurz seemed by all accounts initially unwilling to end the coalition with the FPÖ, key groups in the ÖVP, notably several regional leaders, nudged him to change course. The frequent implication of the FPÖ in embarrassing episodes and public controversies represented a permanent threat to the stability of the government and thus to the ÖVP's own dominant position in public office. As a result, following the 2019 elections, Kurz preferred a coalition with the ideologically more distant Greens to renewing cooperation with the FPÖ in the interest of office-seeking. As in 2002 and 2005, the Freedom Party proved to be an unstable and unreliable partner in government, in response to which a minimum-winning coalition with the Greens was the safer political bet for the ÖVP.

4. The Demand Side: The ÖVP's Shifting Electorate

In this section, we examine whether the sociological profile of ÖVP voters has changed over time. We proceed from the assumption that this may have been the case every time the party radically changed its programmatic orientation, especially in 1999, 2008 and 2017. In order to investigate these patterns, we collated the Austrian election study surveys from 1990 to 2017.[6] We first identified the typical ÖVP voter in the period from 1990 to 2017.[7] Table 4.1 shows that ÖVP voters were predominantly male (until 2008), either employed or retired and are either (white-collar) employees or (blue-collar) workers.[8] With the exception of gender, this profile of a 'typical' ÖVP voter is generally stable.

When it comes to the first ÖVP shift in 1999, the social group composition does indeed show subtle changes in comparison with the earlier elections. Although the gender composition does not change, the category 'occupation' does: while the percentage of white-collar employees in the sample increased, its corresponding share among ÖVP voters declined. This dovetails with an increase in the proportion of blue-collar workers. The same applies to education, where the voters with only vocational training increase relative to other educational categories and relative to the corresponding proportion in the sample. The effect seems especially pronounced after 1995 when Schüssel took the leadership of the ÖVP culminating in the 1999 election that led to the coalition with the FPÖ. The effect is also in evidence in 2008 when Schüssel's hand-picked successor Wilhelm Molterer ran a conservative campaign centred on law and order, and finally in 2017 when Kurz moved the party to the right. Indeed, while less-educated (primary and vocational only) voters made up 73.5 per cent of ÖVP voters in 2006, this share increased by nearly ten percentage points to 82.2 per cent in 2008 (without seeing major shifts in the sample composition that might have caused this change).

Furthermore, our data reveal that the ÖVP's electorate is generally evenly distributed among age groups. However, we find some shifts in these patterns when the ÖVP opened up to the FPÖ the first time. Both

---

[6] We were kindly provided with the raw data for the elections between 1990 and 2006 by Fritz Plasser and Gilg Seeber, available at: https://www.sora.at.

[7] For the 2008, 2013 and 2017 elections, we relied on post-election survey data from the Austrian National Election Study.

[8] Changes in survey questions make it impossible to investigate changes in ÖVP voters' ideological positions or reasons for vote choice. Systematically available information includes respondents' voting behaviour, key demographic information and, for the 1990s, 2002 and 2017, their recalled vote in the previous election. As the sample weights are not consistently available, we rely on unweighted respondents. To account for this, we benchmark the distribution of the social groups among ÖVP voters against the sample distribution of these groups.

Table 4.1 *Demographic characteristics of ÖVP voters*

Election year	Education				Occupation				Gender
	Primary	Vocational	Secondary	Tertiary	Worker	Employee	Civil servant	Self-employed	Male
1990	21.3	50.6	20.7	7.3	29.5	40.6	11.7	14.5	61.3
	(36.1)	(42.8)	(23.5)	(7.6)	(29.8)	(38.6)	(14.8)	(10.9)	(50.3)
1994	16.9	54.6	23.2	5.4	–	–	–	–	64.2
	(18.9)	(43.8)	(28.1)	(9.2)					(51.4)
1995	19.2	55.6	19.5	5.6	32.5	38.1	10.8	14.4	61.8
	(20.0)	(43.6)	(26.9)	(9.5)	(24.9)	(39.5)	(15.4)	(12.9)	(50.2)
1999	15.8	55.0	24.2	5.0	37.6	33.3	10.8	15.1	62.0
	(15.8)	(44.2)	(29.5)	(10.5)	(24.0)	(42.4)	(14.8)	(12.7)	(51.2)
2002	21.4	54.9	20.1	3.6	34.8	45.2	6.5	12.9	58.0
	(21.4)	(44.4)	(24.9)	(9.3)	(23.4)	(48.4)	(10.7)	(13.0)	(46.5)
2006	19.1	54.4	17.0	9.5	20.5	61.5	3.9	9.0	55.8
	(16.4)	(42.2)	(23.6)	(17.8)	(12.3)	(54.7)	(12.8)	(14.8)	(45.0)
2008	18.3	63.9	13.9	4.1	30.5	53.3	3.8	10.5	47.5
	(23.0)	(49.0)	(16.3)	(11.7)	(24.9)	(46.9)	(10.6)	(12.0)	(45.5)

Table 4.1 (*cont.*)

Election year	Education				Occupation				Gender
	Primary	Vocational	Secondary	Tertiary	Worker	Employee	Civil servant	Self-employed	Male
2013	3.5	51.0	34.1	11.4	20.0	55.3	14.3	10.5	48.5
	(4.2)	(38.0)	(36.6)	(21.2)	(12.5)	(60.5)	(13.4)	(12.3)	(48.4)
2017	11.2	67.1	12.8	8.9	23.2	53.0	13.5	9.4	53.6
	(10.8)	(52.7)	(21.5)	(15.1)	(17.5)	(58.9)	(11.9)	(11.1)	(49.1)

Note: Sample percentages in parentheses (e.g., in 2017, 49.1% of the sample reported to have voted for the ÖVP were male while 53.6% of those respondents reporting to be male); highlight when share of group in ÖVP voters at least five percentage points higher than in sample. Sum total not 100 due to rounding. Occupation data not available for 1994.

in 1999 and in 2002, the share of those aged between eighteen and thirty-nine rises to over 50 per cent of the ÖVP voters, before then dropping again to around 40 per cent during the 2000s and early 2010s. We may conclude that the ÖVP increased its share of young (at least during the first coalition with the FPÖ), less educated and blue-collar voters, which suggests a subtle but noticeable change of the ÖVP electorate towards a profile that we associate more with a radical right party in that they are male, young, blue-collar and relatively less educated.

In sum, we do find shifts among the voter profile of ÖVP voters that coincide with the large programmatic moves of the party, especially with regard to the education and the occupational status of these respondents. Of course, we cannot establish a causal relationship on the basis of these data. However, the ÖVP attracts largely a more radical right type of electorate when it breaks its coalition with the SPÖ, attacks the left and projects strong leadership. We see these developments in 1995 (when the ÖVP under Schüssel broke the coalition), 1999 (when Schüssel vowed to go into opposition), 2002 (collaboration with the FPÖ), 2008 (ÖVP breaks coalition) and in 2017, when Kurz took over and opened the ÖVP up to the FPÖ again.

When we look at the changes among ÖVP voters, another important angle is the party's capacity to hold on to its own voters as well as to win voters from other parties. In 1986, the Christian democrats found themselves confronted for the first time with new competitors on the radical right as well as on the liberal and environmental end of the spectrum. Whereas the Greens managed to attract only 2 per cent of former ÖVP voters, the populist radical right FPÖ induced 7 per cent of former ÖVP voters to switch (Hofinger, Jenny and Ogris 2000). Thus, the Christian democrats encountered for the first time a problem that would plague them for the following decades: their declining capacity to retain voters.

Figure 4.6 gives us more insight into the movements of the ÖVP voters by showing the parties for which the ÖVP voters recalled having voted in the previous election. Because of data limitations, we can only present the results for the 1990s, 2002 and 2017. While Figure 4.6 shows that the Christian democrats did indeed have problems retaining its voters in the 1990s, we also see a trend of increasing success in this regard later on. While in 1990 and 1994, less than 50 per cent of ÖVP voters reported having voted for the Christian democrats in the previous election, this number reached 80 per cent by 2002 and in 2017. Focusing on 1999 and 2017 as our years of interest, we see that in 1999 the ÖVP gained

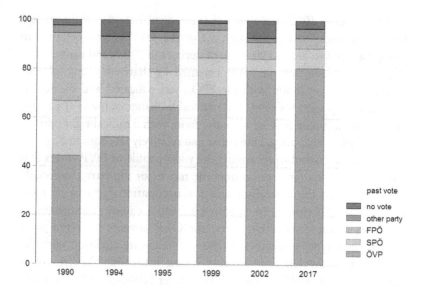

Figure 4.6 Who did ÖVP voters elect in the previous election?
Note: Data not available for 2006, 2008 and 2013 elections.

a considerable number of voters from both the SPÖ and FPÖ. The results in 2017, on the other hand, show that most ÖVP voters had already voted Christian democrat in 2013 and that those who had voted for other parties previously came in equal measure from the latter as well as from the camp of non-voters.

5. Conclusion

How has the Austrian mainstream right party reacted to the silent revolution and silent counter-revolution? Initially, the effects of the silent revolution on the ÖVP seem to be less pronounced. While the ÖVP did lose voters during the 1980s, it remained a stable and strong party attracting more than 40 per cent of the national vote. This situation changed with the counter-revolution, which in Austria was far from silent and began as far back as 1986 when the Austrian Freedom Party adopted a strong radical right profile.

The FPÖ's development was possible because, from the 1980s onward, modernization and European integration resulted in signifi-cant de-alignment processes between Austria's major parties and their traditional voter base. With growing voter defections from the major parties, the newly reconstituted populist radical right Freedom Party was able to tap into this process, appealing to former mainstream voters by promising radical change. Initially, the FPÖ's agenda was political corruption, before shifting more to immigration, globalization and Euroscepticism. In general, the FPÖ showed a pattern of policy-driven behaviour, which was strongly encouraged by their voters. While the FPÖ did not eschew the opportunity of seeking office, it generally paid for the moderation of its platform on election day. Thus, there is a close connection between a policy-driven party strategy and a strongly ideological voter base.

Of the two government parties, the smaller and weaker ÖVP was more vulnerable to the challenge by the counter-revolution. Although the party was politically unlikely to lose its lock on public office, electoral decline jeopardized its major party status and ability to shape the government agenda. On at least two occasions, in 1995 and 2017, important factions within the ÖVP perceived this development as being so severe a threat that they pushed for a leader who was likely to change the status quo. In the first instance, the ÖVP under Schüssel adopted a clearly defined social and economic policy agenda which was largely copied by an office-seeking FPÖ. In the second case, Kurz embarked upon a political discourse during the election campaign in 2017 that parroted the far right rhetoric of the FPÖ (cf. van Spanje and van der Brug 2007). In both cases, we see an alignment of positions between the ÖVP and FPÖ that resulted in a coalition between the two parties.

Mainstream parties like the ÖVP engage in strategic positioning, combining office-seeking with policy-seeking or vote-seeking strategies. However, they are also beholden to internal factions and important party groups. The ÖVP is internally heterogeneous, split both along regional and interest group lines. Thus, the ÖVP has had working coalitions with both the FPÖ and Greens at the regional level. In the latter case, this was often to avoid cooperation with the FPÖ or the Social Democrats. In so doing, the Christian democrats react to, and accommodate, both the silent revolution and the counter-revolution. However, since the latter is electorally more significant, accommodating the radical right was the much more important issue for the ÖVP.

It would, however, be an exaggeration to assume the ÖVP was pushed in this direction or that it was demand-led. In fact, we cannot say empirically whether or not people ended up flocking to the ÖVP only after the party had selected leaders who represented a change from the status quo and projected strength. More importantly, both of the leaders who proved decisive in the ÖVP's two rightward moves (Schüssel and Kurz) favoured the opportunity to achieve liberal market reforms, welfare retrenchment and tax cuts popular with Austrian business. Therefore, we should not look at the relationship with the radical right only in terms of a sociocultural convergence, but have to recognize, too, the opportunities for the ÖVP presented by such cooperation, not least in socioeconomic policy terms. We cannot therefore simply dismiss the right-wing agenda as merely 'parroting the pariah' (e.g., van Spanje and van der Brug 2007) because the Christian democrats were able to implement substantive policy changes during coalitions with the FPÖ.

The dynamics of electoral success, changing party leaders and shifting party positions together provide the ÖVP with a broad platform that reaches beyond traditional but shrinking Christian democrat milieux into voter groups that are otherwise serviced by the social democratic SPÖ and the radical right FPÖ. Indeed, our voter analysis has shown that these strategic changes worked insofar as ÖVP voters took on a profile more akin to typical radical right voters (i.e., young, male and relatively less educated). In hindsight, this strategy has so far proven successful for the ÖVP only when executed resolutely. This success faded when the ÖVP started to move back to its traditional voter hunting grounds in the centre-right of the political spectrum. When reacting to the twin pressures of the silent and counter-revolution, the ÖVP accepted the exodus of one of its liberal factions to become a new party competitor but could not tolerate the persistent challenge from the radical right. It saw itself in great peril as a result of the FPÖ's dominant position on right-wing sociocultural issues and also welcomed the opportunities for market liberal reforms – reforms to which the radical right was a willing accomplice.

5 | France: Party System Change and the Demise of the Post-Gaullist Right

JOCELYN EVANS AND GILLES IVALDI

1. Introduction

The French mainstream right finds itself at its weakest point in the history of the Fifth Republic. As the political bloc dominating the first twenty years of the Gaullist regime, the governing right – principally *Les Républicains* (LR), the latest manifestation of the former Gaullist movement – find themselves fragmented and electorally diminished. After holding the presidency from 1995 to 2012, the incumbent, Nicolas Sarkozy, was defeated by the Socialist François Hollande. Five years later, despite strong public discontent with Hollande, LR's frontrunner, François Fillon, was unable to make the run-off ballot with 20 per cent of the vote, falling third behind centrist candidate Emmanuel Macron (24 per cent) and Marine Le Pen of the populist radical right *Front national* (FN, now *Rassemblement national*, RN) at 21 per cent. In the legislative elections that followed, the right lost 68 of its 199 seats, while Macron's new centrist formation, *La République en Marche!* (LREM), together with their centrist allies, won an overall majority of 61 per cent of parliamentary seats.

Whilst there were idiosyncratic reasons for the right's failure both in 2012 and 2017 – the 2008 financial crisis during Sarkozy's presidency, Fillon's financial scandal in 2017 – the party system dynamics and electoral realignment evident over the past twenty years led to a situation where the electoral collapse of the mainstream right has certainly become possible if not necessarily inevitable. The role of LR in legitimizing, then losing control of what may be termed the cultural values of the silent counter-revolution (Ignazi 1992) – reactionary law and order, morality, and ethnocentric values, as well as neoliberal economic reaction to the post-materialism of the silent revolution (Inglehart 1977) – has pushed the party into a position that lacks credibility in challenging the status quo, and lacks currency in representing it.

In 2017, the simultaneous challenge of centrist and radical candidates proffering political renewal forged the perfect storm for LR. Moreover, the systemic marginalization of LR and the narrowing of its electoral space has allowed Macron's LREM to broaden its own political space into areas traditionally well inside the mainstream right bloc. In the European elections of May 2019, support for LR fell to an all-time low of 8.5 per cent of the vote, casting doubt on the viability of the post-Gaullist right in the new party system that has emerged from the 2017 elections.

This struggle to identify an electorally viable political offer resulted from a gradual shift in values and social structure over the last half-century. This chapter asks how mainstream right parties in France have tried to adapt over time to the policy and political challenges caused by sociodemographic and value changes that have taken place in Western countries since the 1970s as part of the silent revolution and the conservative backlash against it. We look at how these parties have attempted to reposition themselves within a transforming political space produced by processes of internationalization such as European integration, immigration and economic globalization.

We argue that, whilst the core values of the post-materialist revolution such as environmentalism, feminism and egalitarianism were essentially absorbed by the left in France, notably through a Green party (*Les Verts*, now EELV) within the leftist electoral bloc, and whilst the counter-revolutionary backlash has doubtless fuelled support for the FN, the pull of the populist radical right has primarily taken mainstream parties further to the right on the cultural dimension – most particularly immigration issues – and, more recently, European integration, balancing vote-seeking and policy-seeking motivations. As our analysis suggests, however, successive periods of electoral outbidding of the FN on such issues by the mainstream right since the mid-1980s have gone against a more general trend towards cultural liberalization and greater support for the EU amongst many moderate right-wing voters. This opened a political space for Emmanuel Macron's LREM as a credible centrist liberal and pro-European alternative.

This chapter is organized as follows. First, we present the key actors of the right, and the institutional context in which they operate. We then look at the path dependency of the reshaping of the party system which occurred in 2017. We focus on historical changes in competitive patterns and voter demand along issue dimensions as well as the institutional continuities in political opportunity structure. We argue that these developments have not been monotonic, however, and we look at four main periods since the early 1980s which are characterized by significant variation in voter demand, party supply and strategy. Finally, we examine possible implications of those developments for the future of the mainstream right in a party system currently dominated by Macron's liberal centre and Le Pen's populist radical right.

2. The French Right in Context: Heterogeneity under Majoritarian Constraints

2.1 The Two Streams of the Mainstream Right: Conservative Gaullists and Liberal Centrists

The mainstream right has, since 1959, constituted a coherent political bloc, only twice losing the presidency and holding government for thirty-eight of the Republic's fifty-eight-year existence. Historically, the mainstream right in France has been divided into two main components, namely, the conservative Gaullists and non-Gaullist liberal centrists (Knapp and Wright 2006).

From the mid-1970s to the early 2000s, the main Gaullist party was the *Rassemblement pour la République* (RPR). The first viable centrist alternative to traditional Gaullist dominance was Valéry Giscard d'Estaing's *Républicains Indépendants* (RI) in the early 1970s, which later provided the organizational basis for the *Union pour la Démocratie Française* (UDF) federation, formed in 1978. During the 2000s and early 2010s, the conservative right continued into the *Union pour un mouvement populaire* (UMP), which changed its name to *Les Républicains* (LR) in 2015 following a series of political scandals. From the early 2000s onward, the liberal wing of the French right was embodied in the new UDF led by centrist leader François Bayrou, which later transformed itself into the *Mouvement démocrate* (MoDem), setting out a new direction further away from the right. By 2017, Emmanuel Macron's newly formed LREM took over this 'independent' political centre, winning moderate voters from both left and right (Evans and Ivaldi 2018).

While these two streams of the right relate to distinct ideological traditions, they have also been marked by internal ideological diversity. Additionally, personal rivalries and presidential ambitions have been important factors in party strategies on the right, and these interact with the Fifth Republic's institutional constraints. We will consider the broader institutional incentives in the next section. But to summarize here briefly the impact of presidential ambition as well as of variations in affiliation at the subnational level: the non-Gaullist, centrist pole in particular has traditionally been more fragmented, accommodating a wider array of small parties including liberals and Christian democrats, and has been organizationally unstable over time. This diversity of actors with different positions and strategies makes it difficult to draw a clear line of demarcation between the subcomponents – Gaullist and non-Gaullist – of the French right. Nonetheless, five areas of divergence can be identified.

First, since the early 1970s, the centrists have generally been more economically liberal than the Gaullists. In contrast, the typical Gaullist political economy has traditionally been defined by its support for state intervention and a planned economy (*'dirigisme'*), reflecting its appeal to voters across the left–right divide and the strong working-class component in the Gaullist movement (Demker 1997: 411).

Second, culturally, the Gaullists represent the conservative pole of the French mainstream right, while centrists have traditionally supported more progressive and culturally liberal policies – for example, the Veil reforms to contraception and abortion laws during Giscard's presidency – despite their accommodating Christian democrats with conservative views.

Third, the Gaullist and non-Gaullist strands of the right have diverged in their support for European integration over time. The defence of national independence and national sovereignty has always been at the heart of the Gaullist ideology, resulting in scepticism, if not outright hostility, towards the EU, as well as international alliances such as NATO. In contrast, centrist liberals have traditionally been more supportive of federalism and a more integrated EU.

Fourth, centrist liberals have historically been more open to institutional reform and modernization, whereas Gaullists would strongly defend a strong leadership and the institutions of the Fifth Republic as the legacy of de Gaulle.

Fifth, and finally, Gaullist and centrist parties also differ in terms of party organization. The successive iterations of the Gaullist party – from the UNR in the 1960s to the UMP during the 2000s and 2010s – generally follow a model of mass party with large membership (by French standards) as opposed to the constellation of small cadre parties that form the centrist pole, with low membership and strong local notables.

As can be seen from Figure 5.1, which shows electoral results of right-wing parties in France, in the 'modern' period of the Fifth Republic, that is, when the system finally alternated in 1981 to a left executive, the story has ostensibly been one of relative consolidation of the conservative right, at the expense of the liberal centre-right, particularly post-2002, and the implantation of the third stream, the populist radical right. In 2017, however, these three political blocs achieved similar levels of presidential support, attesting to the reshaping of the party subsystem on the right of French politics.

2.2 Enter the Populist Radical Right FN

The FN was formed in 1972 from a collection of far right groupuscules, monarchists, Vichy nostalgics and remnants of the anti-Gaullist OAS. While it originated in the far right milieu, by the mid-1980s the FN had pioneered a new 'populist radical right' agenda combining nativism, authoritarianism and populism (Ivaldi 2018a). The FN under Jean-Marie Le Pen challenged the right flank of the Gaullists, first as an economically neoliberal, national sovereignist party, drawing on the shopkeepers, small entrepreneurs and petit bourgeois traders who supported the Poujadists of the 1950s and setting itself in opposition to the variants of *dirigisme* offered by both left and the conservative right. As we will discuss later, support from the blue-collar class, which would underpin much of the electoral analysis of the FN from the 1990s onwards, was notable by its absence in the mid-1980s – just 9 per cent, the lowest of any intra-occupational class proportion, in 1984 (Ysmal 1984: 9). To a large extent, Bell's observation from the 1970s, that the FN's ideological profile was largely indistinct from the conservative right's (Bell 1976: 103), remained valid long into the 1980s and 1990s. Only with the welfare chauvinist shift leftwards by the FN from the late 1990s did bloc differentiation begin to emerge (Ivaldi 2015).

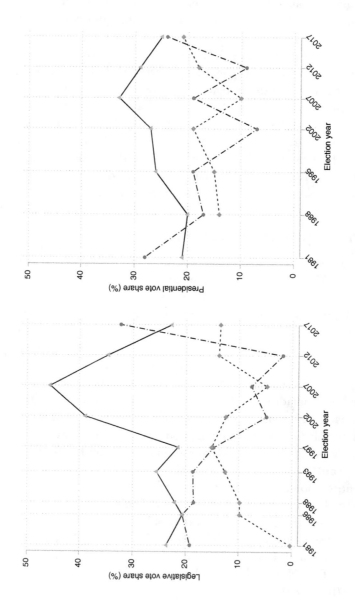

Figure 5.1 Electoral results in legislative and presidential elections of right-wing parties in France since 1981

What differentiated the FN from the conservative right was its anti-establishment populism, anti-system position partly forced upon, partly embraced by, the former, and a niche strategy primarily emphasizing cultural issues such as immigration and law and order. The FN's reactionary roots and greater willingness to play upon growing anti-immigrant sentiment made it an attractive alternative for working-class and lower-middle-class voters who had been ignored by a post-materialist left and subsequently disappointed by a socially conservative right. This silent counter-revolution position remained the preserve of the FN, given the moderate right and centre's erection of the *cordon sanitaire* following a failed ideological and electoral flirtation with the populist radical right in the late 1980s.

That the ideological affinity between moderate and radical right, which extended to voters as well as parties well into the 1990s (Andersen and Evans 2003), did not result in bloc consolidation owed much to the institutional and competitive context. To understand the impact of value change on the right's support, we must take into account the rules of the game under which it competes.

2.3 Institutional Context

France's two-ballot majoritarian electoral formula plays a significant role in shaping the behaviour of parties and voters (Elgie 2006). Paradoxically, whilst incentivizing fragmentation through its presidential race, it also provides strong incentives for parties to cluster within the two dominant party subsystems, in order to achieve electoral competitiveness. This limits structural opportunities for independent centrist and radical forces. The main threat to the mainstream right, namely, the FN's 'nuisance potential' in legislative three-way run-offs (*triangulaires*), never realized its potential, despite costing the right well over thirty seats to the left in 1997. This was partly due to the reaffirmed right-wing cooperation through the UMP from 2002 onwards, but it owed far more to the realignment of the electoral calendar as part of the five-year presidential term (*quinquennat*) reforms two years previously. Since 2010, the primacy of the presidential race has turned the Assembly elections into essentially the third and fourth rounds of the presidential election (Dupoirier and Sauger 2010), with a steep fall-off in support for presidential losers and smaller parties.

Furthermore, the majoritarian electoral system manufactures highly disproportional parliamentary majorities which are primarily detrimental to peripheral parties, favouring more established parties with strong local bases, such as a well-implanted conservative right with networks of its own and other right-wing (*divers droite*) candidates – either regional conservative groups or independent local politicians (Knapp and Wright 2006: 216). On average, since 1981, the winning parties of the left and right have received over 61 per cent of all parliamentary seats in French legislative elections. Finally, voter apathy and record high abstention rates in legislative elections result in a rise in effective thresholds for second-round entry in a fragmented and highly competitive race, which creates a favourable context for larger parties. Reflecting such institutional mechanisms, there have been on average three effective parliamentary parties in France since 1981, compared with an average 5.5 effective competitors in legislative elections over the same period.

Because of this strong bipolarizing effect of majoritarian rule, the centre was assumed not to be a threat, and certainly not a viable location for a presidential challenger. As we shall see in the next section, this was illustrated by centrist candidate François Bayrou's albeit creditable third place in the 2007 presidential election. Ideologically, a viable centre space existed on the right, between a conservative right-wing UMP candidate and the entrenched Socialist agenda of Ségolène Royal. Perversely, however, the lower level of fragmentation and the weakness of the radical vote across both sides of the spectrum helped to maximize support for the two dominant parties of the left and right, contributing significantly to Bayrou being unable to disrupt the more traditional pattern of left–right competition (Evans and Ivaldi 2018). That said, the 2007 presidential race first illustrated the growing tension between this institutional logic and the silent revolution shift of traditionally more centre-right electorates, especially in larger conurbations with service and graduate-level employment, moving to more liberal positions hitherto more associated with the left. So, while 2007 and 2012's traditional left–right run-off seemed to confirm the resilience of the bipolarity of France's electoral politics (Grunberg and Haegel 2007; Grunberg 2008), increased political fragmentation and the rise of radical alternatives would, by 2017, see support for traditional parties of the mainstream diminish, ultimately making room for Macron.

With these institutional parameters in mind, we turn now to unpicking the two (counter-)revolutionary logics across four main periods, focusing on three key elements – the competitive array in play; party supply in terms of issue positions; and voter demand, particularly in terms of attitudinal profile.[1] We look at how these elements have changed across different periods and for each period we analyse the reconfiguration of the party subsystem of the right.

3. The Four Periods of the French Right since 1981

The start of each period may be defined by a critical juncture affecting one or more of the above elements. The main features of the four periods of right-wing politics in France since the early 1980s are summarized in Table 5.1. We look at each period in turn in the sections below.

3.1 The Mitterrand Years, 1981–1991

During the Mitterrand incumbency, the mainstream right was split between two blocs of relatively equal size, namely, the conservative Gaullists of the RPR and centrist Liberals of the UDF. The victory of the left and first alternation in power in 1981 had produced strong incentives for party cooperation, eventually seeing the formerly separatist liberal UDF effectively ceding leadership to Chirac's conservative Gaullists following Giscard's failure to secure a second presidential term. During this first period, both the RPR and UDF opted for formal cooperation in all legislative elections, while presenting individual candidates in the 1981 and 1988 presidential races. In terms of party supply, two critical junctures were decisive. First, as reflected in the manifesto data, the rise to power of the Socialists and Communists in 1981 resulted in a market-liberal policy backlash by the mainstream right, with the Gaullists in particular moving away from Colbertist state intervention and *dirigisme* to unambiguously endorse free market economics, small government and deregulation. In so doing they moved closer to their traditionally more liberal centrist counterparts (Figure 5.2).

---

[1] Here, we must rely upon a small number of items that are comparable across national election surveys in France over the period covered in this chapter.

Table 5.1 *Four main phases of the mainstream right in France since 1981*

	Mitterrand years (1981–1991)	Chirac era and the 'social fracture' (1992–2002)	Sarkozy period and 'the France that gets up early' (2003–2012)	Fillon and the social-conservative moment of the right (2013–)
Critical juncture	Victory of the left (1981) FN electoral break-through (1984)	Maastricht referendum (1992)	Le Pen–Chirac run-off (2002) ECT referendum (2005) Financial crisis (2008)	Victory of the left (2012) EU migration crisis (2015) Copé, Wauquiez
Leadership	Chirac	Chirac	Sarkozy	
Economic policies	Liberal free market 'moment'	Moderation of free market neoliberalism	Productivism, workfare and the 'hardworking' people Post-2008 crisis economic orthodoxy and austerity	Economic orthodoxy and market liberal policies
Cultural policies	Co-optation of FN cultural issues (immigration, law and order) Cultural conservatism continued from pre-vious period	Stability of right-wing cultural agenda and policies	Persistence of right-wing cultural agenda Co-optation of FN ethnocultural agenda (Grenoble speech, 2010)	LR shift towards social conservatism and reactionary right Cultural liberalism of Centre

Europe		Gaullist support for Maastricht	UMP support to ECT and Lisbon Treaty	Soft-Euroscepticism
Voter demographics	Gaullist move towards pro-EU positions	Beginning of decline of bourgeois centre (post-Balladur 1995, Bayrou 2002)	Sarkozy/UMP – mobilization of *couches populaires* (2007)	Loss of *couches populaires* and farmers to Le Pen
	Partisan Gaullism	Alignment of farmers' vote destabilizes	Ageing, Catholic right-wing electorate	Consolidation of (petit) bourgeois, ageing, Catholic + entrepreneurs by UMP
	Class/religious basis to RPR/UDF support – private sector, managers, petit bourgeoisie plus farming community; Catholic		Educated, young centre (2007)	Educated, urban young centrists to Bayrou
Voter attitudes	Shift to neoliberal economic positions from authoritarian-social/moral positions	Middling economic positions	Attitudinal split between centre and right – social/moral liberalization of former, stability of Gaullists	LR moral conservatism but 'liberalized' on security
		Social and moral liberalization among moderate right-wing voters	Return to economic neoliberalism predating financial crisis	Centre liberalism – social and economic
		Anti-immigrant stability		

Table 5.1 (*cont.*)

	Mitterrand years (1981–1991)	Chirac era and the 'social fracture' (1992–2002)	Sarkozy period and 'the France that gets up early' (2003–2012)	Fillon and the social-conservative moment of the right (2013–)
Mainstream competition	Tactical cooperation in legislative elections Gaullist leadership UDF back to party subsystem of the right	Formal cooperation within UPF Electoral decline of UDF (2002) Fragmentation of the mainstream right Splinter right-wing Eurosceptic sovereignist parties (MPF, RPF)	UMP merger of Gaullist and Liberals UDF emancipation from the right. Splinter Eurosceptic sovereignist party (DLF)	Bayrou's endorsement of Socialist candidate (2012) UDI move away from LR since 2017 Bayrou's endorsement of Macron (2017) Accommodation of Sens Commun by LR
Party organization	RPR/UDF organizational differentiation since the mid-1970s	UPF umbrella organization Separation of DL Liberals from the UDF (1998)	UMP organizational merger Independent UDF	Split of UDI from UMP (2012) Split of *Constructifs* from LR Diaspora of moderate right-wing leaders (e.g., Juppé and Pécresse)

Populist radical right	Accommodation Tactical cooperation with the FN at local level	Republican front and *cordon sanitaire* Chirac's moral condemnation of the FN in 1990	*Cordon sanitaire* Localized and episodic Republican Front	*Cordon sanitaire* Neither/nor strategy vis-à-vis FN and left Change in FN leadership and 'de-demonization'
Average support in national elections (P & L)	Conservatives (Gaullists) = 19.5 Liberals (centrists) = 20.6 Populist radical right (FN) = 8.6	Conservatives (Gaullists) = 22.1 Liberals (centrists) = 11.2 Populist radical right (FN) = 14.9	Conservatives (Gaullists) = 32.9 Liberals (centrists) = 9.3 Populist radical right (FN) = 11.7	Conservatives (Gaullists) = 19.4 Liberals (centrists) = 28.2 (Macron) Populist radical right (FN) = 17.4
Average turnout in national elections	P = 81.3 L = 71.4	P = 75.0 L = 67.1	P = 81.6 L = 58.8	P = 77.8 L = 48.7
Average ENP (P & L) Election years	4.8 1981P, 1981P, 1986L, 1988P, 1988L	6.8 1993L, 1995P, 1997L, 2002P, 2002L	4.8 2007P, 2007L, 2012P, 2012L	6.1 2017P, 2017L

Note: ENP = effective number of parties; P = presidential; L = legislative elections

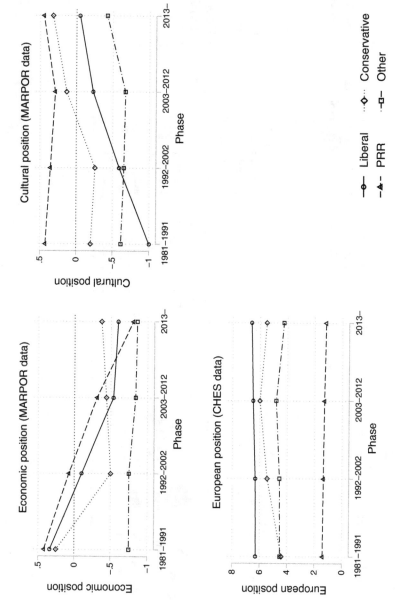

Figure 5.2 Policy positions of French parties

Among their voters, the traditional strong class and religious basis to RPR/UDF mainstream right support still obtained, with private sector employees, managers, the petite bourgeoisie plus the farming community showing high levels of support for parties of the right. Within the last two of these social groups, shopkeepers and freehold farmers declined in numbers, marginalizing them electorally and thereby placing them firmly in the silent counter-revolutionary pool of voters. Such a typically right-wing sociodemographic profile dovetailed with voters' economic attitudes during the period, with both RPR conservative and UDF liberal supporters being firmly located to the right on the economic dimension, showing strong neoliberal preferences in reaction to the failed interventionism of the PS-led left-wing coalition in power between 1981 and 1986.

A second critical event was the electoral breakthrough of the FN in 1984. During its period of identity formation, the FN managed to establish a distinctive appeal, primarily galvanizing voters on immigration and law and order, in due course politicizing opposition to European integration and competing directly against the mainstream right on a free market capitalist agenda strongly influenced by the international wave of Reaganomics. In its entry phase in the mid-1980s, the FN drew most of its electoral support from the right in national elections. It posed only a moderate electoral threat to both the RPR and UDF, most visible in regions such as Mediterranean France where traditionally anti-Gaullist, and previously anti-system (Bartolini 1984) centrist voters constituted a significant electoral pool for the FN.

In response, the mainstream right incorporated a number of the FN's positions on immigration and law-enforcement (Schain 2006) – a crucial legitimizing step in terms of the silent counter-revolution, polarizing the mainstream right towards the populist radical right challenger. Meanwhile, cooperation with the populist radical right occurred in a small number of cases, mainly in the south – mostly as a response to the shock caused by the victory of the left in 1981, and because the ideological borders between the mainstream right and radical right were historically more 'porous' there. By the early 1990s, however, conservatives and liberals under Chirac's leadership put an end to attempts to incorporate the FN, reflecting the moral condemnation of the party's far right legacy (Ivaldi 2018a).

Furthermore, beyond such tactical co-optation of radical right themes, Chirac's conservative Gaullists also upheld their traditionally more social conservative agenda, which continued to set them apart from some (though certainly not all) UDF centrists,[2] as well as from the Socialist left which timidly began to adopt silent revolution-oriented, culturally liberal policies such as the abolition of the death penalty, granting more rights to immigrants and liberalizing the media. Demand-side data for the 1981–1991 period suggest that authoritarian social and moral positions were already predominant amongst RPR voters (more so than amongst UDF centrists) and, even more prominently, supporters of the left. In contrast, both the centrist and Gaullist electorates showed more convergence on immigration. Possibly, this reflected the impact of this issue's politicization by the FN on both conservative and liberal sectors of the mainstream right after 1984, and independently from traditional moral values associated for instance with age and religiosity (Figure 5.3).

Finally, while not a prominent issue for voters at the time, Europe began to gain salience during this pre-Maastricht Treaty period. Increasing cooperation between centrists and Gaullists saw the latter progressively move towards more pro-EU positions, in sharp contrast to the old Gaullist agenda of national sovereignty and independence pushed by leading Gaullist figures such as Pierre Juillet and Marie-France Garaud – an agenda endorsed by Chirac himself in his notorious Appel de Cochin (Call of Cochin) (Schonfeld 1986: 21) in 1978, in which Giscard and the UDF were simply labelled the *parti de l'étranger* ('party of the foreigner'). As the expert survey data for France suggest, however, the RPR remained much more sceptical of European integration during the 1980s when compared with both the UDF and the PS.

3.2 The Chirac Era and the 'Social Fracture', 1992–2002

The Chirac era of the mainstream right, from 1992 to 2002, showed substantial changes from the previous period. Party system fragmentation and polarization rose significantly, epitomized by the 2002 presidential election's record high number of candidates and a substantial rise in support for radical parties at both ends of the spectrum. Meanwhile, electoral turnout began to decline in both national and

---

[2] Unfortunately, the MARPOR dataset does not include data for the UDF between 1981 and 1988. The available data for 1993 suggest, however, that the UDF was more culturally liberal than the RPR, which is corroborated by the data for their predecessor parties during the 1970s.

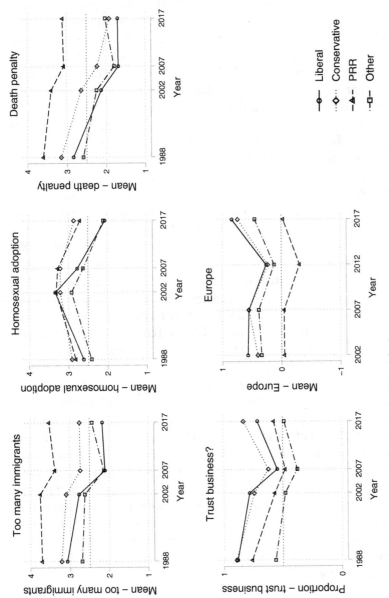

Figure 5.3 Mass attitudinal positions of French electorate

subnational elections, reflecting growing popular discontent with the political establishment.

The period saw a significant change in the balance of power within the right as Chirac's conservative Gaullists firmly established their leadership over an electorally declining UDF. Similarly, the FN enjoyed a significant rise in support, predominantly from working-class voters traditionally affiliated with the left (Evans 2000), as well as from disenfranchised voters outside the classic left–right divide (Mayer 2002). As revealed by both Balladur and Bayrou's failed attempts to challenge Gaullist dominance in the 1995 and 2002 presidential elections, electoral support for the bourgeois liberal centre declined, while rural voters increasingly turned to the populist radical right in protest against EU agricultural policies as agricultural protectionism began to falter (Ivaldi and Gombin 2015).

Important organizational changes occurred within the UDF as both Alain Madelin's neoliberal *Démocratie Libérale* (DL) and social conservative Catholics rallying behind Christine Boutin left the federation. Both DL and Boutin's small party, the *Forum des républicains sociaux* (FRS), ran independently against UDF leader, François Bayrou, in the 2002 presidential election, eventually joining the conservatives of the new UMP under Gaullist tutelage. The 2002 presidential election showed a record high level of fragmentation within the right, with no fewer than five candidates, mostly accounted for by the schism in the UDF of its historical components. While the UDF had continued electoral cooperation with the Gaullists under the *Union pour la France* (UPF) during the 1990s, by the end of the period, Bayrou turned the centrists' strategy into one of greater independence from the right, positioning the UDF as a new 'neither left nor right' actor at the centre of the political spectrum.

As illustrated by the manifesto data, in the context of the economic recession of the early 1990s, all parties of the right – including the FN – shifted positions and converged towards the economic centre. In 1995, Chirac secured his first presidential term by campaigning on the 'social fracture' (*fracture sociale*) advocating social justice and solidarity, clearly breaking with the laissez-faire economic policies of the mid-1980s. Amongst RPR and UDF voters, the failed neoliberal experiment by the right during its years in power between 1986 and 1988 led to the consolidation of middling economic positions.

Culturally, the manifesto data suggest that the push of silent counter-revolution values was most evident in the rightward shift by DL liberals, who were increasingly at odds with the somewhat more progressive agenda advocated by UDF moderates who had rallied behind Bayrou; meanwhile, the Gaullists maintained their previous social conservative agenda, as did the FN at the authoritarian end of the GAL/TAN dimension (Hooghe, Marks and Wilson 2002).[3] Particularly notable was the emergence in the 1992 regional elections of the Green party pushing a strong silent revolution agenda. As the Greens became rapidly incorporated into the subsystem of the left, entering a formal *gauche plurielle* alliance with the Socialists and the Communists between 1997 and 2002, polarization over cultural issues continued throughout the 1990s.

The implementation of a silent revolution policy agenda by the left in power fuelled a silent counter-revolution reaction by liberals and conservatives on the right of the party system, at a time when, as voter surveys suggest, support for socially conservative values was beginning to decline amongst voters of the RPR and UDF. Those voters were displaying more support for homosexual adoption and less support for the death penalty, for instance, thus widening the gap between right-wing party elites and voters, most visibly amongst supporters of a 'split' UDF. Meanwhile, attitudes towards immigration remained stable within the electoral base of the mainstream right, thus providing a pool of particularly conservative voters in the RPR susceptible to the FN's ethnocultural appeal. In response, the mainstream right under Chirac's leadership adopted a *cordon sanitaire* against the FN, refusing tactical alliances both nationally and locally, while endorsing the *Front Républicain* (Republican Front) – the unwritten rule that mainstream parties automatically support each other in a run-off election where the FN is still running.

Finally, the 1992 Maastricht referendum represented a critical juncture that significantly increased the salience of European integration issues for both parties and voters. As conservatives in the RPR in particular continued their move towards more pro-integration positions, Maastricht provoked a split resulting in the formation of a new Eurosceptic party by Gaullist Charles Pasqua, the *Rassemblement pour*

---

[3] The Green–Alternative–Libertarian and Traditional–Authoritarian–Nationalist scale is a composite attitudinal scale used to map sociocultural attitude and policy positions, normally orthogonally to the traditional economic left–right.

la France (RPF). In the UDF, a schism occurred with the break by Philippe de Villiers and the creation of the *Mouvement pour la France* (MPF). While ambivalent about the EU during the 1980s, the FN took a clear Eurosceptic turn in the mid-1990s, voicing its opposition to Maastricht and the deepening of European integration, thus contributing to the growing polarization of party competition over Europe (Ivaldi 2018b).

3.3 The Sarkozy Period and 'the France that Gets Up Early', 2003–2012

Despite Jacques Chirac still being president until 2007, for the right the final four years were a period of power-building for Nicolas Sarkozy ahead of his electoral campaign for the Elysée, officially taking over the party in 2004. The formation of the UMP after Chirac's victory in 2002 was designed as much to set up a party machine for the next election as it was to secure a parliamentary majority for the incumbent. That the FN candidate had progressed into the 2002 presidential run-off had been a major political shock, producing strong incentives for all mainstream actors to build more competitive unified blocs.

Under the leadership of François Bayrou, the UDF (which would become MoDem in December 2007) was organizationally and ideologically separate from the UMP. Having left the EPP in 2004 and co-founded ALDE in the European Parliament, Bayrou's formation increasingly opposed the UMP in the National Assembly, culminating in supporting a vote of no-confidence in the de Villepin government, together with the Socialists and Communists, and refusing to endorse Sarkozy's second-round candidature in the 2007 presidential election. Ideologically, the party pushed for a social liberal economic agenda, while maintaining the centrist tradition of strong Europeanism.

Whilst now remembered as culturally conservative and authoritarian on the GAL/TAN scale, the conservatism in Sarkozy's initial presidential programme was more pronounced in economic terms, proposing reductions in welfare and social protection. As the manifesto data illustrate, the UMP under Sarkozy moved towards materialist, growth-oriented policies focusing on productivity, while reviving the right-wing mythology of the 'hardworking people' – as reflected in Sarkozy's appeal to 'France that gets up early' (*la France qui se lève tôt*) – and adopting a soft anti-establishment rhetoric against 'liberal elites'. However, the 2008 financial crisis and growing public deficit shifted the neoliberal economic agenda back to a hybrid centrist position, eventually forcing the right in power to implement unpopular austerity policies. It was only subsequent to the infamous Grenoble speech in December 2010, in response to riots caused by police shooting an armed robber, that a more authoritarian, ethnocentric profile emerged.

Finally, Europe returned to the forefront of the political agenda following the rejection by the French of the EU's proposed constitution in the 2005 referendum and subsequent adoption of the Lisbon Treaty. However, despite increasing polarization over Europe and a split from the sovereignist right of Nicolas Dupont-Aignan and *Debout la France* (DLF), the expert survey data suggest that the conservative UMP did not significantly deviate from the pro-EU positions of the Chirac years.

From an electoral demand perspective, this polarization of positions followed the silent counter-revolution trajectory of legitimizing the FN's position which had remained strongly towards the authoritarian end of the GAL/TAN dimension. During the last days of Jean-Marie Le Pen's leadership of the party, the FN had begun to lose support and its split in the late 1990s had weakened its grassroots potential. And the persistence of the *cordon sanitaire* alongside the hostile institutional environment faced by an isolated extremist party, exemplified in the 2002 presidential run-off, had not helped. Additionally, Sarkozy's agenda of workfare helped the moderate right to reclaim petit-bourgeois, middle- and working-class voters who had previously defected to the populist radical right, thus temporarily rebuilding the traditional cross-class electoral alliance of Gaullism. The basis of Bayrou's 2007 centrist liberal challenge (in contrast to its more socially conservative, religiously active strain which was still in evidence in 2002) lay in mobilizing an electorate that in many ways appeared prototypically new left – younger, educated, well-off, secular and socially liberal – but which fell equidistant between the left and right candidates on matters of economic liberalism and welfare (Sauger 2007: 451).

The early 2010s saw a drop in support for the mainstream right, an electoral revitalization of the FN under Marine Le Pen, and the PS building a more competitive bloc to the left. By the end of the Sarkozy period, the right's (albeit relatively moderate) electoral decline was rooted as much in the failure of its neoliberal economic agenda as in any silent revolution-driven leftist agenda – an agenda that had lost traction as a result of the *gauche plurielle*'s own tribulations in 2002. Rather, silent counter-revolution issues of cultural and moral conservatism which had become salient in the late 1980s and 1990s as a result of a pushback against the more centrist and immobilist policies from cohabitation experienced a 'second wave'. By the early 2010s, on issues of law and order, immigration and broader identity issues, the FN was credibly placed to exploit the failure of governments of both the left and right to address flash-points of social unrest, as well as broader economic sclerosis after the 2008 crisis.

Perhaps the most revealing element in a growing divide that was pushing the mainstream right towards the populist radical right, and away from a liberal centre, was the increasing fragility of the so-called *front républicain*. In 2011, the UMP formally adopted a '*ni-ni*' approach for the local elections, supporting neither the PS nor the FN in the second round, thereby strengthening the FN by default. This indirect weakening of the *cordon sanitaire* was as much a product of an ideological shift towards the FN as a purely competitive strategy against the PS (Perrineau 2014: 85). Nonetheless, as a competitive strategy, it contributed to the legitimization of a supposedly 'banalized' FN, which, in the most recent period of the post-Gaullist shift to the right, would encourage much greater osmosis between moderate and radical right actors.

3.4 Fillon and the Social-Conservative Moment of the Right, 2013–

Perhaps the most significant reorientation of the right bloc has occurred in the last decade, with the destabilization of LR (successor to the UMP since 2015), and the displacement of the right pole towards the political centre. Bayrou's presidential campaigns had evidenced the competitive viability of the centre under conditions of weakness among the two main blocs. But the establishment of Macron's LREM with an absolute majority in the National Assembly, in part through poaching a liberal wing of LR increasingly at odds with the conservative right of the party (Evans and Ivaldi 2017), has established a new market liberal centre pole – one predicated upon some of the cultural values associated with the silent revolution, tempered by a realist economic positioning and more restrictive policies in the areas of immigration and law and order.

Bayrou's own role as centrist precursor saw a growing entrenchment of a divide between conservatives in LR and MoDem liberals. Bayrou's endorsement of Socialist François Hollande rather than Sarkozy in the 2012 presidential second round signalled a critical juncture, ending MoDem's role as a potential right-wing ally. Only the federation of the UDI, extending a hand to both MoDem and the UMP, offered a short-lived bridge between the former cooperating blocs. By 2012, however, the UDI had emancipated itself further from the UMP, forming an independent group in the National Assembly, pursuing a dual strategy of cooperation with both the MoDem and LR. The party reluctantly supported Fillon's candidacy in the 2017 presidential election, having previously endorsed Alain Juppé in the 2016 primary. In June 2017, the UDI's centrists were joined by *Les Constructifs* – LR moderates such as Thierry Solère and Franck Riester – who had failed to resist the radicalization of LR. Conversely, in October, liberals who had gathered in Hervé Morin's *Centristes* left the UDI to maintain the alliance with Laurent Wauquiez's LR, effectively splitting the party in two.

The recent period shows a re-orientation of the mainstream right on both the economic and cultural dimensions of competition. Despite the rapid curtailing of Sarkozy's new right programme after the financial crisis, Hollande's commitment to supply-side measures rather than austerity provided LR with the opportunity to revive market policies as an economic orthodoxy. As the manifesto data suggest, François Fillon was placed the furthest right in economic terms in the 2017 presidential race, as were LR voters according to survey data. Yet events during the Hollande presidency pushed the right towards harder stances on non-economic social and moral issues. Particularly important in this respect were the following: the 2015 Paris and 2016 Nice terrorist attacks, with the ensuing state of emergency; the 2015 refugee crisis; and, internally, the social movement mobilizations by *Manif pour Tous* and *Sens Commun* against same-sex marriage, which were supported by hard right conservatives in LR, as well as former UDF centrists such as Christine Boutin, and intensified the social conservative position of the right against the cultural liberalism of the Taubira Laws.

Cultural issues represented a significant divide in the 2016 right-wing presidential primary, exposing a growing gap between the victorious hard conservative core of LR supporters rallied behind

Fillon and the more liberal preferences of the general right-wing electorate. Centrist Alain Juppé could have enhanced LR's electoral competitiveness against Macron. Instead, as shown by the manifesto data,
LR continued its rightward shift on the cultural dimension, if anything
extending the hard right strategy initiated by Sarkozy in the early
2010s. Moreover, expert survey data show that this has been accompanied by a substantial move towards more Eurosceptic positions since
2014, further shrinking the electoral basis for the right and tipping the
balance of pro-EU voters further towards the political centre, allowing
Macron to further encroach on right-wing territory.

Whilst it may be tempting to see this as a unified reaction in line
with the silent counter-revolution hypothesis, we must be careful to
acknowledge dynamics that do not line up with this theory. First, as
Figure 5.2 shows, all parties were already moving towards more
culturally conservative positions at the beginning of the Hollande
presidency. Second, from the demand side, the liberalization affecting all electorates in the late twentieth century is not reversed – even
the FN sees its voters stabilize on an albeit still conservative position. The largest change in the demand side is seen in the widening
of the gap between centrist liberals, on the one hand, and LR's
conservatives and populist radical right voters, on the other, not
least in terms of their position on moral issues such as same-sex
adoption.

But, for LR, this growing schism with the liberal centre represents
a further diminution of its social and political relevance. Whilst the loss
of the more liberal LR notables to the centre has homogenized the
conservative core of the party, in line with its membership's values,
such a hardening of its reactionary post-silent-counter-revolution positioning threatens to impose longer-term electoral penalties, as seen in
the 2019 European elections. Swathes of LR voters have decamped
either to LREM, or to the RN, which continues to attract lower
middle- and working-class voters of the *couches populaires* (working-
and lower middle-class voters). Figures 5.4 and 5.5 separate out the
conservative electorate by age and religious practice. Contrasting the
youngest (18–24) and oldest (over 65) subpopulations of the conservative electorate over time, its younger supporters have always been more
culturally liberal; but the gap in 2017 has widened – even among those
younger voters who supported Fillon in spite of the financial scandals
whirling around him.

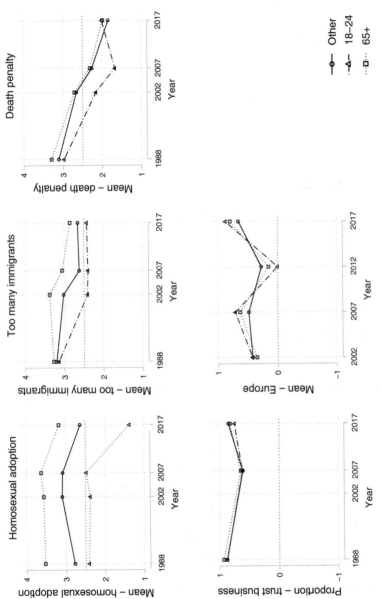

Figure 5.4 Age differentiation on mass attitudes of the conservative electorate

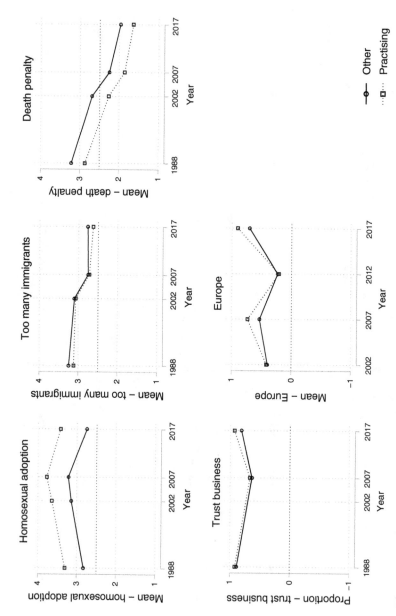

Figure 5.5 Religious practice differentiation on mass attitudes of the conservative electorate

There is greater consonance between younger voters and the centre on modern cultural tolerance – an issue which, on the conservative right, LR would claim as its own. A similar situation pertains to religiosity and conservative support. Those who practise regularly – almost exclusively Catholics – are much less tolerant and more culturally conservative. Clearly, this disparity has existed for some time – from 1988 at least. However, this disparity is one where the centrist offer of Macron and LREM, rather than the silent counter-revolution alternative of the FN, is more fully in line with non-Catholic support. In short, the silent counter-revolution logic towards which LR has recently moved indulges older, traditionalist supporters, rather than targeting a broader electoral pool in the way that LREM has.

4. Conclusion

Since the mid-1980s, the core values of the post-materialist revolution have been essentially absorbed by the left in France, through a relatively stable political bloc including the Socialists and the Greens. Meanwhile, the counter-revolution backlash together with processes of internationalization such as European integration and economic globalization have fuelled support for the populist radical right, in particular amongst working- and lower middle-class voters.

Electorally, pressure from the populist radical right has taken Gaullist conservatives further to the right on the cultural dimension of competition. Over time, this shift has been most discernible in the area of immigration and, more recently, European integration, primarily reflecting vote-seeking motivations and the attempt to win back voters defecting to the FN. In contrast, policy-seeking orientations have dominated the socioeconomic agenda of the right, depending on the electoral incentives produced by shifts in public opinion, as exemplified by Chirac's social fracture agenda in the mid-1990s or Sarkozy's productivist policies in the mid-2000s. Similarly, policy-seeking goals were well in evidence in the reactionary turn by Fillon in the 2017 elections, aligning his presidential bid with the preferences of core conservative voters.

Electoral outbidding of the FN on cultural issues by the mainstream right has opened a political space at the centre of French politics, which is now occupied by Emmanuel Macron's centrist liberal and pro-European LREM. The adoption by the conservative right in France of silent counter-revolution values has located it closer than ever to a progressively 'de-demonizing' RN, and threatens to reduce the once-dominant party to a reactionary minor party on the flank of the upstart LREM. The positioning of LREM, particularly as a new movement devoid of ideological baggage, remains fluid and will largely be determined by its tactics in the next presidential race in 2022. But it certainly has the potential to displace the Gaullist movement as France's most obvious party of government.

Macron's success in 2017 confirmed the viability of social liberal, centrist electoral support, at least under certain political conditions – namely, sufficient fragmentation of presidential candidate supply; ideological polarization of the governing parties; and, connected to this, the strength of radical challengers. Without both the post-materialist value change among previously bourgeois, centre-right voters, many of whom are now closer to centre-left liberals on the social dimension, and the subsequent counter-revolutionary backlash pulling older cohorts of voters to a reactionary social conservative position, the traditional left–right balance in the bipolar system might well have continued. Whether Macron continues to occupy a more traditional rightist space, as current policy proposals suggest, or once again attempts to build a bridge to more leftist silent revolution-based values will potentially influence whether the mainstream right can once more find competitive space in French politics.

6 | Germany: How the Christian Democrats Manage to Adapt to the Silent Counter-Revolution

SARAH E. WILIARTY

1. Introduction

The German Christian Democrats are one of the most successful parties of the mainstream right in post-war Europe. Consisting of two 'sister parties' – the Christian Democratic Union (CDU) and the Christian Social Union (CSU)[1] – the Christian Democrats have held the Chancellor's office for nearly fifty years, compared with less than twenty years for the Social Democrats (SPD), their primary opponents on the mainstream left. The framework proposed in this volume, that the mainstream right is under threat from the silent revolution and the silent counter-revolution, can help to explain this long-term trend of Christian Democratic success in Germany. The CDU/CSU gradually shifted its position to adapt to the sociocultural changes that occurred as part of the silent revolution. Instead of paying a price at the ballot box for this move, the CDU benefited from increasing fragmentation on the left caused by the silent revolution. The German silent counter-revolution, on the other hand, has been exceptionally weak historically and therefore caused few problems for the Christian Democrats. The recent rise of the Alternative for Germany (AfD) marks the arrival of a genuine political presence associated with the silent counter-revolution, and the CDU/CSU has yet to figure out how to manage this change, even if its initially sure-footed handling of the coronavirus crisis appeared to have helped it regain support in the short term.

The CDU has never been a policy-seeking party, preferring pragmatism to ideology (Pridham 1977). The Christian Democrats have not faced serious trade-offs between office-seeking and vote-seeking, partly because their ideological flexibility has meant they are willing to form

---

[1] The CSU is active only in the federal state of Bavaria, while the CDU is active in the rest of Germany.

coalitions with both the FDP and the SPD (and even the Greens, at least on the state level). The CDU/CSU generally attempts to maximize votes and then form whatever mathematically possible coalition is most attractive (Harmel and Janda 1994). The party's pragmatism and its focus on office- and vote-seeking have contributed to its lasting success.

The CDU's core constituencies have remained fairly constant throughout the existence of the Federal Republic. The Christian Democrats consistently receive more support from older voters (especially over the age of sixty), and this portion of the electorate is growing as the population ages (Green 2013). In terms of regional divisions, voters in the southern and southwestern states of Bavaria, Baden-Württemberg and Rhineland-Palatinate are regional strongholds for the Christian Democrats. Since unification, the CDU has polled close to the same or better in the former East Germany than the former West Germany in all elections except 2005, doing especially well in Saxony, Saxony-Anhalt and Thuringia. For comparison, the SPD has only done better in the former East than the former West in one election (2002), and the Social Democrats often fare significantly worse in the former East. The FDP and the Greens also do better in the former West with the Left Party and the AfD unsurprisingly faring better in the former East.[2]

The Christian Democrats have also been able to hold on to female voters at much greater rates than Christian Democratic parties in most other Western European democracies. Even with fairly dramatic changes in female employment patterns, with more women working and a much lower fertility rate, women have continued to support the CDU. Continued support from female voters may be because of the party's successful outreach to female constituents, because of Angela Merkel's leadership or because the CDU has modernized more than comparable Christian democratic parties (Wiliarty 2010, 2013).

From the beginning, the CDU has attempted to create and maintain cross-class appeal, both through support for the welfare state and by integrating Catholic labour through its internal organization, the *Christlich-Demokratische Arbeitnehmerschaft* (Christian Democratic Workers' Association; CDA) (Bösch 2002). Over time the CDU lost support among working-class voters despite these efforts. Particularly after the 1970s, the party's voters tilted more towards the middle and

---

[2] See at: www.bundeswahlleiter.de/bundestagswahlen/2017.html.

upper classes. The CDU did do better at keeping the electoral support of the working class than Christian democrats in most other West European countries, however (Krouwel and Bale 2013).

The CDU has always done well with Catholic voters, especially those who attend church on a regular basis (Debus and Müller 2013; Krouwel and Bale 2013). Part of the founding mission of the CDU was to bridge the confessional divide by reaching out to both Protestants and Catholics. Leaders of the early CDU wanted to ensure that their new party was not perceived as a reincarnated Centre Party so they established an internal party organization for Protestants, the *Evangelischer Arbeitskreis* (Evangelical Working Group; EAK), and over-represented Protestants on the party's internal decision-making bodies (Bösch 2002). This move was successful at least among religious Protestants, and the CDU gains votes among frequent church attenders of both confessions. Despite ongoing internal party debates about whether the 'C' in the CDU has lost all relevance, the German Christian Democrats have hung on to more religious voters even with increased secularization.

In summary, both the CDU and the CSU have received disproportionate support at the polls from older voters, from voters in certain regions (especially the south, the southwest and parts of the former East Germany), from women, from the middle and upper classes, and from more religious voters. Despite some shifts over time, these voting groups have remained remarkably loyal to the Christian Democrats. This consistency holds both for groups where we might expect continued support (older voters, particular regions, the middle and upper classes, the religious) and among voting groups where we might have expected more pronounced decline than has actually occurred (women, the working class, the former East more generally). The continued relative success of the German Christian Democrats is partly due to this ability of the sister parties to hang on to their core constituencies at higher rates than Christian democrats elsewhere and partly due to the SPD's struggles with the loss of its core supporters (Debus and Müller 2013).

The (West) German silent revolution has been especially strong. Although it eventually pulled the Christian Democrats *to* the left as the party followed public opinion, the primary contribution of the silent revolution has been to cause fragmentation *on* the left. The emergence of the Green Party in the 1980s created a challenging situation for the SPD. German unification further contributed to left-party fragmentation when the former East German Communist Party evolved into, first, the Party of Democratic Socialism and then the Left Party. Increased competition on the left of the political spectrum has weakened the SPD. The divided and often ineffectual Social Democrats have effectively given the Christian Democrats breathing room, allowing them to dominate politics through much of the post-war era.

The silent counter-revolution, on the other hand, has been weak in Germany. The Christian Democrats did not, historically, face much of a threat from the right side of the political spectrum. Between the Christian Democrats and the Free Democrats, the mainstream parties had the moderate political right covered. On multiple occasions, radical right movements attempted to launch a political party, but until recently these efforts have failed, leaving only extremist (and therefore for most voters effectively beyond-the-pale) options on the Christian Democrats' right flank. The AfD, which holds seats in the Bundestag and as of this writing, every state-level parliament, represents an entirely different level of threat. Certainly, before the coronavirus crisis struck in 2020, the Christian Democrats had not figured out an effective response to the new party. The next national election, scheduled for 2021, will therefore be critical.

This chapter begins by characterizing the particular ways in which the silent revolution and silent counter-revolution manifested themselves in Germany. The next section discusses the evolution of the German party system. The chapter then examines post-unification developments in greater depth, including how the Christian Democrats have managed the four issue areas that are the focus of our framework: the welfare system, moral issues, European integration and immigration. Because of the long delay in the emergence of the populist radical right in Germany, for the most part the CDU/CSU developed its policies in the absence of a radical right challenge. Under Angela Merkel, the CDU moved towards the centre of the political spectrum, which likely contributed to the emergence of the Alternative for Germany (AfD). Particularly during the Merkel era, immigration has been by far the most challenging issue for the Christian Democrats.

2. The Silent Revolution and Silent Counter-Revolution in Germany

Overall, Germany has seen a stronger-than-average silent revolution (the rise of post-materialist values and movements) and a smaller and certainly later rise of the silent counter-revolution. This combination –

more revolution on the left, less revolution on the right – has meant greater space for political manoeuvring for the German Christian Democrats. This section gives a brief overview of the trajectories of the two revolutions.

The silent revolution has its roots in the 1960s, a time of serious upheaval in German politics (Inglehart 1977). The Christian Democrats and a small liberal party, the Free Democrats (FDP), had formed the governing coalition since 1961, but this coalition broke down in the face of economic difficulties. The FDP left the coalition in 1966 over disagreements about the budget and the Christian Democrats formed a new coalition with the Social Democrats. The first so-called Grand Coalition remained in office until the next scheduled election in 1969. From 1966 to 1969, the Grand Coalition controlled around 90 per cent of the seats in the Bundestag, leaving only the small Free Democratic Party as the voice of the parliamentary opposition.

Opposition to the government became focused in groups outside the Bundestag, known as the *Ausserparliamentarische Opposition* (Extraparliamentary Opposition, APO). The APO encompassed a range of social movements in the 1960s, including the student movement. Students demanded democratization of the universities and society more broadly. The APO and the student movement – which overlapped significantly – also objected to the Emergency Acts (passed in 1968), which gave exceptional powers to the government in times of strife. Two incidents of violence marked the heyday of the APO: Benno Ohnesorg, a student protestor, was killed by a police officer at a demonstration in 1967 and in 1968, Rudi Dutschke, a student leader, survived an assassination attempt. However, the APO declined in prominence after the Grand Coalition was replaced by an SPD–FDP coalition government in 1969 (Richter 1998).

Although the APO itself declined, the movement had laid the groundwork for other social movements of the 1970s, such as the anti-nuclear movement, the ecological movement, the feminist movement and the peace movement. Germany also experienced some serious far-left terrorist activity in the 1970s. In response to the terrorist activity, the new social–liberal (SPD–FDP) coalition passed measures that limited civil liberties. The governing coalition also made overtures to East Germany that helped to ease relations between the two states. These moves, plus swift justice against convicted terrorists, helped to bring the terrorist aspect of the 'silent' revolution to an end by the late 1970s.

The social movement portion of the silent revolution, on the other hand, coalesced into the Green Party, which won seats in the Bundestag for the first time in 1983. The Greens developed into a serious political party turning into both a potential challenger and potential coalition partner for the Social Democrats (Markovits and Gorski 1993; Poguntke 1994). In the early years, the party was viewed by many as a flash in the pan, but the Greens have maintained their presence in German politics and, according to some pundits, are now poised possibly to become the major party of the left. The German silent revolution, then, left a lasting legacy on the German party system with the establishment of a new party of the left.

The silent counter-revolution was not nearly as successful as the silent revolution. West Germany experienced its first recession in the mid-1960s, contributing to the breakdown of the CDU/CSU/FDP coalition. Economic hard times also facilitated the rise of a far right party, the German National Party (NPD). The NPD won seats in a series of state-level parliaments, but failed to clear the 5 per cent hurdle for the Bundestag in both the 1965 and 1969 elections. By the late 1960s, the NDP lost political relevance in the wake of a series of internal conflicts and the end of the Grand Coalition. The silent counter-revolution and the radical right remained a non-factor in German politics until the 1980s (Ignazi 2003).

In the early 1980s, a new far right party, the Republicans (REPs), emerged in Bavaria, as a splinter group from the CSU. The REPs were dissatisfied with what they viewed as a Christian Democratic move to the centre of the political spectrum. The CDU/CSU had continued the policies of the Social Democrats to normalize relations with East Germany and they began adopting more progressive positions on social issues. The Republicans did well in elections to the European parliament and in state-level elections in Bavaria and Berlin in 1989 and again in Baden-Württemberg in 1992. However, like the NDP, they also struggled with internal divisions, largely over the question of how far to the right the party should locate itself. By the mid-1990s, the REPs were no longer a significant political party (Mudde 2000).

A variety of factors in the German political system worked against the success of a radical right party. German political institutions limited the success of the REPs. The party was unable to get over the 5 per cent hurdle to enter the Bundestag and thereby build on its success at the Land level. The Federal Constitutional Court put the party under observation for potential extremist tendencies. Germans had turned out in droves to protest the entrance of the REPs into the Berlin state parliament in 1987. The German press also ostracized the party (Art 2007). The Christian Democrats (and other parties as well) worked to limit the political potential of the REPs (Art 2007: 339). Between their own ineptitude and the response of German political parties, the German public, and German political institutions, the REPs were unable to gain a foothold in politics.

Even in the face of a significant increase in immigration in the 1990s, the REPs failed to gain ground. The REPs' success in the Land-level election in Baden-Württemberg in 1992 largely occurred because of voter concern about immigration. Even in the 1990s, immigration was an exceptionally challenging issue for the Christian Democrats. In response to electoral support for the REPs (and an increase in anti-immigrant violence), the CDU/CSU and SPD cooperated to pass compromise legislation on asylum that made existing immigration policy more restrictive. Although much criticized at the time, mainstream party co-optation of the REPs policy positions was quite effective. Furthermore, the 5 per cent hurdle and oversight from the Federal Constitutional Court also limited the ability of the REPs to gain traction at the national level. By the late 1990s, the radical right was no longer a factor in German politics. Van Spanje and de Graaf (2018) have labelled this strategy of ostracizing a radical right party while co-opting its policy positions 'parroting the pariah'. The silent counter-revolution, then, remained largely irrelevant in Germany until the rise of the Alternative for Germany just before the 2013 national election.

The German case illustrates how developments of the silent revolution and the silent counter-revolution can facilitate mainstream right-wing party success. The powerful silent revolution contributed to increasing fragmentation on the left side of the party system. This fragmentation meant that the Social Democrats lost votes and sometimes struggled to form coalitions large enough to govern. On the other hand, the weak silent counter-revolution meant that the Christian Democrats escaped serious competition on the right until recently (the small FDP never represented significant competition). The lack of threat on the right meant the CDU/CSU (especially the CDU) could move to the centre of the political spectrum without paying a penalty at the polls. Christian Democratic success in Germany is not wholly a story of Social Democratic struggle.

3. The Evolution of the Party System in Germany

This section outlines the transformation of the German party system over the course of the post-war period. As Figure 6.1 shows, we can break these developments into three eras: (1) 1950–1983: the two-and-a-half party system; (2) 1983–1990: the two-bloc system; and (3) 1990–today: increasing fragmentation post-unification. Each of these eras presents its own dynamic in terms of competition and coalition formation. Figure 6.1 shows the dominance of the Christian Democrats, the continued weakness on the far right, and the increasing fragmentation on the left.

3.1 1950–1983: The Two-and-a-Half Party System

The CDU/CSU formed following the Second World War as a response to a vacuum on the right of the political spectrum. Early Christian Democratic leaders blamed the lack of a sufficiently strong, legitimate party of the right for contributing to the rise of the NSDAP during the Weimar era and they wanted to form a strong party on the right with a clear commitment to democracy. The clearest precursor to the Christian Democrats – the Centre Party – primarily appealed to Catholics and therefore was unable to unite all conservative Germans. Bridging the confessional divide between Catholics and Protestants was therefore one of the most crucial early projects – and successes – of early German Christian democracy (Pridham 1977). A range of parties contested the first elections in the new Federal Republic of Germany, but the party system quickly consolidated to the Christian Democrats, the Social Democrats and the Free Democrats as the three parties of note.

As the lingering division between the CDU and CSU makes clear, early Christian democracy was also fraught with regional divides. The various regional Christian democratic movements had united slowly over the course of the late 1940s with the eventual exclusion of eastern Christian Democrats as the East–West division solidified. The Bavarian party, the Christian Social Union, also remained independent, but cooperated closely at the national level with its 'sister party', the Christian Democratic Union.

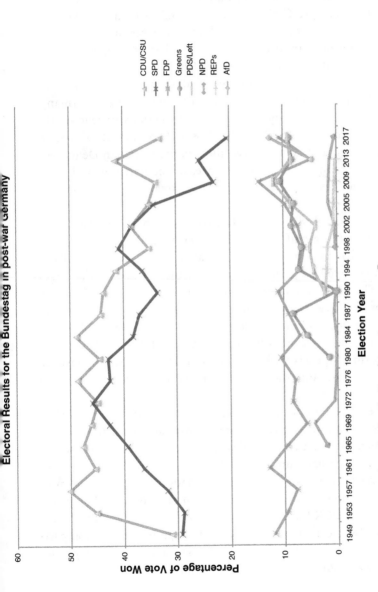

Figure 6.1 Electoral results for the Bundestag in post-war Germany

Source: Der Bundeswahlleiter: Wahlberechtigte, Wähler, Zweitstimmen und Sitzverteilung bei den Bundestagswahlen seit 1949. Statistisches Bundesamt.

The newly formed mainstream right party appealed to market-oriented business groups, conservative religious voters, and even groups such as the League of Expellees and Deprived Rights, a German refugee group with nationalist tendencies. The Christian Democrats also appealed to Catholic labour unions, which were more progressive. The CDU/CSU had internal tendencies focused on free market ideology, Catholic socialism and German nationalism. A system of internal corporatism facilitated representation of various internal groups on party decision-making bodies and helped to maintain some internal cohesion (Wiliarty 2010).

Once the division of Germany solidified, the Christian Democrats quickly dominated politics at the national level in West Germany. The CDU/CSU have enjoyed three lengthy periods of leading the governing coalition, 1949–1969, 1982–1998 and 2005–today. Long periods in government have allowed the Christian Democrats to put their stamp on many policy areas. The party proved to be pragmatic and flexible, able to adjust to an array of challenges in the post-war period.

From 1950 to 1982, (West) Germany can be characterized as having a two-and-a-half party system (Siaroff 2003). In addition to the CDU/CSU and the SPD, the smaller Free Democratic Party (FPD) often acted as junior coalition partner to one of the larger parties. The FDP is a liberal party; the party is a steadfast supporter of the free market and also tends to support the liberal position on sociocultural issues such as divorce and abortion. This liberal ideological profile has meant that the FDP has been able to form coalitions with the Christian Democrats (emphasizing economic issues) and the Social Democrats (emphasizing social issues).

In some West European countries, a liberal party has emerged as a challenger to a Christian democratic mainstream right party, but not in Germany. Given the traditional weakness of liberalism in Germany, the FDP has, perhaps unsurprisingly, remained fairly small, never winning more than 14.6 per cent at a national election and most commonly winning only 5–10 per cent of the votes. Although the FDP and the CDU/CSU to some extent compete for the same voters, they have also mostly remained each other's preferred coalition partner. Certainly, the small size of the FDP has meant that the party never emerged as a serious threat to the Christian Democrats.

3.2 1983–1990: The Two-Bloc System

In the early 1980s, the Green Party emerged in (West) Germany as a political manifestation of the silent revolution. The arrival of the Greens marked a transition in the German party system from a two-and-a-half party system to a two-bloc system. The most frequent coalition arrangements after the early 1980s were CDU/CSU–FDP and SPD–Greens. Voters tended to shift more commonly within their chosen bloc rather than change to the other bloc entirely. Even in the post-unification era, as other coalition arrangements became more common, conventional wisdom tended to expect the formation of one of these coalitions, which were both regarded as 'normal'.

3.3 1990–Today: Increasing Fragmentation in the Post-Unification Era

The left side of the political spectrum underwent additional fragmentation in the 1990s in the post-unification era with the arrival of the PDS (the former Communist Party). In the early 2000s, the PDS merged with a splinter group from the SPD to become *Die Linke*. Unlike the PDS, which focused almost exclusively on issues pertaining to the former East Germany, the Left Party contests elections in all regions of Germany. The Left Party is the party furthest left in the German party system with a platform based on democratic socialism.

The only serious parties on the right remained the CDU/CSU and the FDP – until, that is, the recent arrival of the AfD. The AfD first emerged in 2013 as an anti-euro party, but it subsequently evolved into an anti-immigration party. The AfD first entered the Bundestag in 2017, but the mainstream parties have thus far refused to work with the newcomer at the federal level.

Post-unification, the party systems in the former West and East Germany continue to look somewhat different. In the former West, the Greens and the FDP remain important players. Despite some regional variation, the remnants of the two-bloc system can still be discerned, given the greater relative strength of the Greens and the FDP and the relative weakness of the Left Party and now the AfD. Both the Left Party and the AfD have made greater inroads in the East (though in the 2017 election, the Left fared less well overall). In some regions of the East, a three-party system (CDU–SPD–AfD) is starting to take shape. These trends are still very much in flux, with significant variations each electoral cycle.

In summary, there is little doubt that the German party system has experienced something of a transformation. From the 1950s until the beginning of the 1980s, Germany had a clear two-and-a-half party system. This arrangement changed because of the silent revolution that manifested itself in the arrival and consolidation of the Greens, so that the party system moved towards a two-bloc dynamic: on the left side, the Greens and the Social Democrats; and on the right side, the CDU/CSU and the Liberals. However, the fragmentation of the political system continued because of the rise of a populist left party (*die Linke*) in the 2000s and more recently of the populist radical right party (AfD). Today Germany should be categorized as a political system characterized by six political parties and the decline of catch-all parties. As we will see in the next section, this has important consequences for the internal dynamics of the Christian Democratic Party and its capacity to build stable governmental coalitions.

4. Post-Unification Development of the CDU

The initial post-unification period represented significant adjustments for the German political system, but was largely a blessing for the Christian Democrats. In 1989, just months before the Berlin Wall came down, Chancellor Helmut Kohl (CDU) had been threatened with an internal party coup as a group of CDU elites made an attempt to dislodge him from the leadership. The attempt failed, but it illustrates the extent of dissatisfaction Kohl faced within the party. By 1989, the CDU-led government was starting to feel stale to voters as well. Kohl had been chair of the party since 1973, and many party activists thought it was time for a leadership change (Bösch 2002).

Unification extended both Kohl's term as party chair and the CDU's tenure in government. Whatever criticism Kohl faced later, his astute handling of the unification process as it unfolded won widespread support both for the CDU and for Kohl's role as Chancellor. The Free Democrats also benefited from a unification bounce at the polls, which further solidified support for the CDU/CSU–FPD coalition.

Parties on the left of the political spectrum found the immediate post-unification era more challenging. Both the Social Democrats and the Greens were wary of the costs unification might bring. Even if those concerns were justified, they were not helpful at the ballot box in 1990 in the midst of unification euphoria. The West German parties of the left were also more cautious about rejecting East German Communism than the Christian Democrats or Free Democrats. Later in the 1990s, Eastern Germans often felt (and to some extent still feel) like second-class citizens, but the ambivalence with which both the SPD and the Greens approached unification damaged their credibility with Eastern voters for quite some time. No political party got through this process unscathed. Many West German parties 'exported' some leadership from the West to the East – for which they were often accused of carpet-bagging. Figuring out how to organize and campaign in both parts of Germany was (and to some extent remains) a complex challenge. But for the first two post-unification elections, it was a greater challenge for parties on the left – in part, because they faced a direct competitor. Many observers expected the former East German Communist party (at the time the PDS) to fade from the scene. Instead, over the course of the 1990s, the PDS became increasingly anchored in the eastern Länder (Patton 2011).

By 1998, however, exhaustion with Kohl's chancellorship finally came home to roost and the Christian Democrats spent the years 1998–2005 in opposition – a time marked by significant internal wrangling, as Merkel worked to gain authority within the party. Edmund Stoiber, chair of the CSU, ran as the Christian Democratic Chancellor candidate in 2002, but when he lost, Merkel was able to cement her leadership. By the 2005 Bundestag elections there was no question as to who the Christian Democratic Chancellor candidate would be. Indeed, we might label the years 2005 until 2021 as the 'Merkel Era'. She governed in a Grand Coalition with the SPD from 2005 to 2009 and then with the FDP from 2009 to 2013, returning to the Grand Coalition in 2013 and again after the 2017 election. Merkel successfully modernized the Christian Democrats. She moved her party towards greater liberalism on issues such as immigration and family policy (e.g., on policies such as expanding access to daycare and re-conceptualizing parental leave), while sticking with the party's core tenets of a strong commitment to the social market economy and European integration.

Merkel's time as Chancellor was not, of course, been without its ups and downs. Though she was at times heralded as the 'Leader of the Free

World',[3] she struggled to find an appropriate response to the European sovereign debt crisis. She spent enormous political capital when she welcomed approximately 1 million migrants to Germany during the 2015–2016 refugee crisis. The one-two punch of these crises contributed to the rise of the Alternative for Germany. The AfD barely missed getting into the Bundestag in the 2013 election. In 2017, it won 12.6 per cent of the vote, with the CDU/CSU winning only 33 per cent, its worst result since 1949. Merkel ceded the party chair position in late 2018 and said she would not run again for Chancellor in 2021.

The relationship between the Christian Democrats and the AfD continues to develop. A serious crisis occurred in state-level elections in Thuringia. The former coalition of the Left Party, the SPD and the Greens failed to win enough votes in the October 2019 election to continue in government. In February 2020, the Thuringian Landtag unexpectedly voted in Thomas Kemmerich (FDP) as Minister President on the third round of voting. Kemmerich was elected with the support of the FDP, the CDU and the AfD. This election broke a long-standing taboo in German politics that no mainstream democratic party should form a governing coalition with the support of the AfD. The AfD had run its own candidate for the Minister President position and the CDU had abstained from voting in previous rounds so the support of these parties for Kemmerich was viewed as unexpected.

Both the FDP and the CDU were widely criticized for their support of Kemmerich, but the repercussions were more severe for the CDU. The national chair of the FDP, Christian Lindner, asked for and received a vote of confidence from his party and continued in office. CDU chairwoman Annegret Kramp-Karrenbauer, on the other hand, announced that she would resign her position as party chair and that she would not run, as Merkel's designated successor, for Chancellor in 2021 as planned. Mike Mohring, chairman of the Thuringia CDU, also resigned. Chancellor Merkel, however, received praise for her quick and severe condemnation of Kemmerich's election. The CDU was scheduled to select a new party leader at a party congress in April 2021, which was postponed due to the Covid-19 pandemic. The CDU elected Armin Laschet as party chair in January 2021. The state-level crisis in Thuringia revealed that the CDU was still divided on the question of how to manage the AfD, though Merkel's hard-line rejection of any

---

[3] See at: www.politico.com/interactives/2017/politico50/angela-merkel.

cooperation with the party certainly received more public support than did any suggestion of Christian Democrats working with the AfD.

Since the emergence of the Covid-19 pandemic, the fortunes of both the CDU and the AfD have shifted. Germans were largely supportive of Chancellor Merkel's management of the crisis.[4] The AfD protested some of the lockdown measures, but the party's support began to drop. The AfD's main issue, the refugee crisis, moved to the backburner and in late spring 2020, combined support for the CDU/CSU approached 40 per cent while support for the AfD had fallen below 10 per cent (Forschungsgruppe Wahlen n.d.). Some even suggested that the AfD might collapse altogether, sharing the fate of earlier manifestations of the radical right which suffered from an inability to negotiate just how radical a radical right party can be in Germany.[5]

5. Development of Christian Democratic Issue Positions Post-Unification

This section examines the programmatic offering of the Christian Democrats from unification until today, using Manifesto Project data as well as qualitative analysis of how the Christian Democrats' policy offering has evolved over time. The German party system has become more crowded since unification. This analysis therefore focuses on the two parties that have historically been the largest, the CDU/CSU and the SPD, as well as the FDP as a potential challenger to the CDU/CSU on the right. It includes the AfD to illustrate how, as the range of competition among established parties narrowed and shifted left, a gap opened on the far right, which the AfD has been eager to fill. The AfD has drawn support especially from previous non-voters and from voters who were particularly convinced that the Christian Democrats had moved left (Martin 2018). This dynamic is observable in general, but also on the four issue areas which we identify as particularly likely to create vulnerabilities for mainstream right parties: welfare policy, issues of morality, European integration and especially immigration.

Examining first a general left–right development of the parties, we see that both main parties drifted to the right in the decade or so after

---

[4] See at: www.nytimes.com/2020/05/18/world/europe/coronavirus-germany-far-right.html.
[5] See at: www.zeit.de/politik/deutschland/2020–05/rechtsextremismus-afd-npd-republikaner-parallelen-gemeinsamkeiten-andreas-kalbitz.

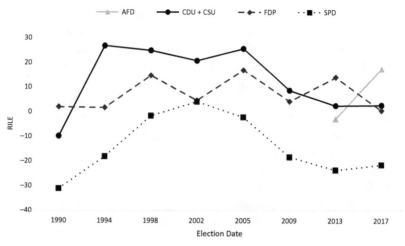

Figure 6.2 Right–left score (RILE) of German parties, MARPOR data

unification (Figure 6.2). As discussed above, the 1990s were an era in German politics when focusing on the free market economy and Western democracy was a politically advantageous way for parties to distinguish themselves from Communism and the former East Germany. After 2005, however, both major parties moved back to the centre, possibly to correct for the over-compensation of the 1990s, as well as accounting for a general leftward shift of public opinion. The FDP nearly always stayed between the two main parties, occupying an already fairly crowded space rather than creating a potential threat by moving to the right of the Christian Democrats. The general leftward shift created an opening on the right for the AfD to occupy. The similarity of the overall trajectories of the two major parties masks some variation on particular issues, however.

5.1 Welfare/economy

On welfare and economic issues, we can see from the Manifesto Project data that the two major parties actually diverged in their policy offerings in the mid-1990s (Figure 6.3). This divergence reflects the differing responses not just to unification, but more generally to the neoliberal economic climate of the 1990s, which the Christian Democrats embraced and the Social Democrats rejected. Unsurprisingly, the liberal FDP's position tracked quite closely to the CDU/CSU on these

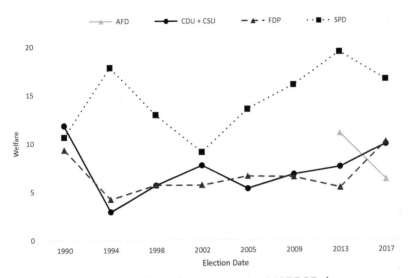

Figure 6.3 Position on welfare of German parties, MARPOR data

issues, which meant the Free Democrats did not constitute serious competition for the Christian Democrats. However, competition between Social Democrats and Christian Democrats on economic issues was pronounced.

In the early 2000s, the parties converged as the Christian Democrats returned to a more moderate position and the Social Democrats, under Gerhard Schröder, moved to the right and adopted Agenda 2010. This set of reforms marked a significant reorganization of the German labour market, including cuts in pension and unemployment benefits and the creation of new forms of part-time and short-term employment. The reforms were highly unpopular within the SPD. A splinter group accused the SPD of abandoning the working class and this group eventually merged with the PDS to form the Left Party. Schröder ultimately resigned as party chair, though he remained Chancellor until his loss to Merkel in 2005. The SPD took most of the heat for the unpopular reforms (Schwander and Manow 2017).

At the 2003 Leipzig CDU party congress, Merkel put forth an economic agenda that leaned heavily on market-oriented ideas. It initially appeared that Merkel would take the CDU in a more liberal direction, possibly abandoning some of the party's more traditional Christian Democratic support of the welfare state. Early enthusiasm quickly faded, however. Within a year, internal CDU compromises had already watered down the most neoliberal components of Leipzig, such as increasing individual health insurance contributions and raising the retirement age. The CDU did less well than expected in the 2005 election and was forced into a Grand Coalition with the Social Democrats. Both of these outcomes led the party to reassess its position on welfare and economic issues. The CDU's Basic Programme, adopted at its party congress in Hanover in 2007, was a move back towards more traditional Christian Democratic policy orientation (Clemens 2013). Even after the 2009 election, when the CDU/CSU went into coalition with the Free Democrats, the party did not implement serious welfare reform and it began advocating for the idea of a minimum wage. Thus, despite Leipzig, the CDU/CSU mostly kept with more traditional Christian Democratic support for the welfare state under Merkel's leadership. The trend of Christian Democratic support for welfare policies continued during the second Merkel Grand Coalition (2013–2017). The CDU/CSU/SPD government introduced a minimum wage and expanded pension benefits and benefits for nursing care (Voigt 2018). Both major parties backed these reforms and party competition on economic issues continued to be minimal (Engler, Bauer-Blaschkowski and Zohlnhöfer 2019).

The populist radical right often draws support from working-class voters. We might therefore expect these parties to support welfare state policies, thus distinguishing themselves from more market-oriented mainstream right parties. In Germany, this tendency is reversed. Despite their foray into the neoliberal ideology of Leipzig, for the most part the Christian Democrats under Merkel continued their support of the welfare state, regardless of whether they were in coalition with the Social Democrats or the Free Democrats. Furthermore, the German Free Democrats are in no way a radical free market party advocating major slashing of the welfare state, a position which would be unpopular with public opinion. Neither right-wing party was as far left on welfare issues as the Social Democrats – the SPD, for example, has pushed harder for a minimum wage and has advocated greater subsidies for low-income earners in healthcare reform. But the German Christian Democrats (and the Free Democrats, for that matter) are in no way hard-core opponents of the welfare state, as market-oriented parties of the right are in some other countries.

The rising AfD, on the other hand, entered politics with a commitment to liberal economic policy and it maintains what some have called radical liberal policy stances (Kim 2018). The AfD began life as a party opposed to German backing of bailouts to other member states during the Eurozone crisis. Under the early leadership of Bernd Lucke, the party opposed a minimum wage on the grounds that it would reduce German competitiveness. The AfD has subsequently reversed that stance, but without strong reasoning. At times the party has favoured eliminating some unemployment benefits entirely (Kim 2018). Even though the AfD draws support from working-class voters, it has been the German party most opposed to the welfare state. This position is not well supported by German public opinion. The AfD has therefore positioned itself on this issue in a space where there is not a lot of competition from other parties, but presumably that is largely because there are not many voters to be had with these positions either (Kim 2018). As a Christian democratic, rather than a conservative, party, then, the CDU has maintained its commitment to the welfare state and the European Union. The Free Democrats might perhaps have been more likely to put forth a neoliberal or anti-tax platform similar to the AfD's, but these positions are simply not popular with German voters.

5.2 Moral Issues

On moral and ethical issues we can clearly observe the Christian Democratic move to the left and the subsequent narrowing of competition between the two main parties. In the mid-1990s, the CDU (and especially the CSU) was still dominated by older Catholic men and their stances on moral and ethical issues were increasingly out of step with those of the German public, which had been swept along in the silent revolution. As the Christian Democrats modified their position over time, moving to the left, it meant no established party remained to represent the concerns of more traditionally minded voters. The Free Democrats' position on moral and ethical issues is (and for decades has been) quite close to that of the Social Democrats (Figure 6.4).

Abortion flared up as a contentious issue in the wake of unification because it had been legal in the former East Germany, but illegal in West Germany. The mid-1990s saw fairly intense partisan fighting on abortion, but once compromise legislation was passed, the salience of the issue dropped away.[6] On other issues, however, such as support for working

---

[6] The abortion issue flared up again after the 2017 election when a doctor was charged with advertising abortion services on her website, which was potentially illegal (advertising abortion services had been against the law). Compromise legislation worked out in spring 2019 allowed for doctors to advertise and also

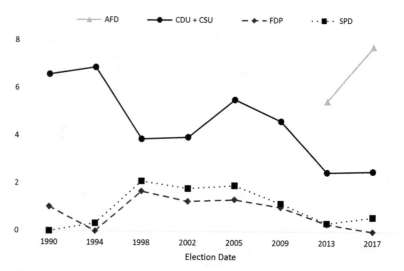

Figure 6.4 Position on traditional morality of German parties, MARPOR data

mothers and LGBTQI rights, the CDU/CSU had fallen behind the majority of public opinion. But during the Merkel era, the CDU underwent significant modernization in this respect. During Merkel's first and second terms as Chancellor, the government implemented what has been called a 'paradigm shift' on family policy moving away from the old Christian Democratic vision which supported mothers staying home with young children. The new family policies, implemented under the first Merkel government, built directly on ideas formulated (but not passed) by the Red–Green coalition of 1998–2005. The new policies increase monthly payments for parental leave, but reduce the duration of the leave in an effort to encourage women to maintain a closer connection to the workforce through their childbearing years. Subsequent policies also increased daycare offerings for younger children. Overall, the policy change represents a notable shift for the Christian Democrats to the centre in favour of gender equality and support for working mothers. The CDU also adopted the motto '*Familie ist, wo Kinder wohnen*' – 'If children live there, it's a family' – which signifies Christian Democratic support for both single-

facilitated a government-run national register. Doctors are still prevented from listing specifics on their website, use of the national register remains limited and access to abortion is still poor. Despite a rise in activism on both sides, no change was made in the actual legality of abortion – just in which procedures could be advertised and how.

parent households and gay and lesbian families. On this issue, the values of the silent revolution have gradually permeated German society and the Christian Democrats moved to catch up with societal change in the early 2000s. Furthermore, though the CDU did not advocate legalization of gay marriage as an official party stance, legislation allowing gay marriage was passed as a vote of conscience under the Grand Coalition, just prior to the 2017 election. Although official Christian Democratic doctrine opposed gay marriage, seventy-five Christian Democratic members of the Bundestag voted to support the measure (Davidson-Schmich 2018).

On issues of morality, then, the Christian Democrats shifted their positions to the left side of the political spectrum. The two major parties are much closer to each other on this issue than they used to be. The AfD has positioned itself as the party responsive to voters who maintain more traditional views on moral issues. The party does not advocate making abortion illegal, but its party programme calls for counselling directed towards preventing the procedure and it claims the overwhelming majority of abortions in Germany are performed for 'so-called "social reasons"'. The AfD supports traditional gender roles in its calls for financial support for stay-at-home mothers and its demand to eliminate gender studies at universities. The AfD also opposes gay marriage. In short, the AfD offers notably more traditional positions on cultural issues than any other party in Germany.

5.3 European Integration

The last two issue areas raised in the framework, European integration and immigration, are the ones in which the populist radical right challenge has been most severe in the German context (Figure 6.5). For much of the post-war era, the mainstream right has supported European integration. Christian democratic parties in general, and the German Christian Democrats in particular, have been loyal supporters of the EU in all its incarnations. Unlike, for example, the British Conservative Party, which has seen serious internal tension on the issue of European integration, the German Christian Democrats have remained united in their support of the EU. The Free Democrats and the Social Democrats have likewise been long-standing staunch supporters of European integration.

The near total lack of competition among mainstream parties on European integration left them vulnerable to attacks from the populist

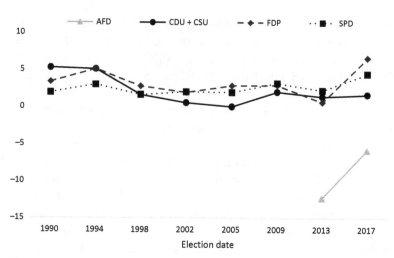

Figure 6.5 Position on the European Union of German parties, MARPOR data

radical right, particularly in the wake of the European sovereign debt crisis. Many citizens questioned German financial support for the euro and objected to the series of bailouts to Greece and other EU countries. The Alternative for Germany began life as a party opposed to the European Union in general and to the euro bailout specifically before evolving into a more typical populist radical right party (Schmitt-Beck 2017). The AfD questioned why money from hard-working Germans who balanced their budget should be spent to rescue 'lazy' Greeks who had spent well beyond their means. The AfD was willing to state publicly what many Germans were thinking privately. Emerging as a party only a few months ahead of the 2013 election, the AfD won 4.7 per cent, nearly clearing the 5 per cent hurdle necessary to gain representation in the Bundestag. Lack of major party competition on European integration and the European sovereign debt crisis provided an opening for the new party.

5.4 Immigration

The most obvious challenge for the mainstream right across Europe has been immigration and Germany is no exception. The Comparative Manifesto Project does not have data on immigration prior to 2017 for Germany. If we instead examine the parties' positive statements on multiculturalism, we see that on that topic, partisan competition on

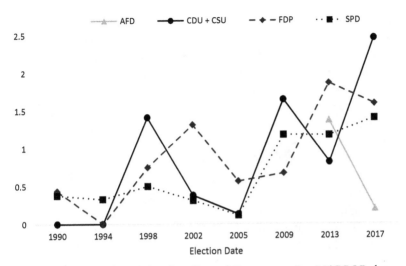

Figure 6.6 Position on multiculturalism of German parties, MARPOR data

this issue was limited. Christian Democratic, Social Democratic and Free Democratic positions on multiculturalism have been strikingly similar and trending strongly positive since unification. Here, too, the AfD has jumped into a gap in the competition space left open as the other parties moved left (Figure 6.6).

Looking more particularly at immigration policy, it is important to establish some context. In the early years of the Federal Republic, West Germany accepted ethnic Germans from formerly German territories across Eastern Europe and also recruited labour migration from Turkey, Italy and elsewhere to provide the workforce for West Germany's economic miracle. Germany's constitution, the Basic Law, established asylum provisions that were, at least on paper, quite generous. In 1973, West Germany stopped recruiting labour migrants, but many of the so-called 'guestworkers' continued to reside in Germany and subsequently brought their families to join them. Thus, West Germany received a large and diverse population of immigrants in the early decades after the war. Legally, however, Germany lacked a pathway to naturalized citizenship and had no significant regulations governing potential labour migration.

As discussed above in the section on the silent counter-revolution, Germany saw an increase in both immigration and radical right activity (both violent street attacks and voting for the far-right REPs party) in the late 1980s and early 1990s. This far-right activity died off after the mainstream parties ostracized the REPs and passed legislation restricting the right to asylum. In the mid-1990s, the Christian Democrats maintained their traditional stance on immigration, reiterated by many politicians at the time, that Germany is '*kein Einwanderungsland*' – Germany is not a country of immigration. Both actual policy and the position of the Christian Democrats were on the verge of change, however.

The transition began under the SPD–Green government led by Social Democratic Chancellor Gerhard Schröder (1998–2005). Pushed by the Green Party, the Schröder government began shifting the focus from excluding immigrants to developing a track for naturalized citizenship and facilitating integration of foreigners who already resided in Germany. The SPD–Green coalition also passed the first policies since the 1973 immigration stop to allow labour migration. Germany has subsequently implemented a series of policies to regulate immigration, citizenship and integration. The first significant changes came into effect with the 2005 Immigration Law. This act allowed highly skilled workers the chance to remain in Germany on a permanent basis and expanded somewhat the terms under which refugees might be granted asylum. It also opened a track to naturalized citizenship and implemented a range of policies intended to boost integration, including mandatory German-language classes. Changes have been wide-ranging, but the general direction has clearly been towards opening the country to more forms of immigration and integration, while also trying to direct which streams of migrants arrive and acknowledge human rights concerns.

Rather than roll back these provisions, Merkel's governments have continued this general track of policy-making. Additional legislation has included further refinement of German citizenship law, a general trend towards allowing greater labour migration, with a continued emphasis on attracting higher-skilled workers (though also with provisions for low-skilled workers). Other changes included more policies aiming to integrate refugees but also some additional restrictions on asylum. In general, the government has been enormously more active in the field of immigration and integration with the overall trajectory of bringing Germany more into line with its European neighbours. Partisan tension on the issue of immigration, which had been very high in the 1990s, eased significantly in the first decade of the twenty-first century and fewer Christian Democratic politicians seemed to be insisting that 'Germany is not a country of immigration' (Wüst 2016). True, when Merkel famously told a meeting of the CDU youth group that 'multiculturalism has failed', her remarks were often interpreted by the foreign press to mean that the CDU was maintaining its anti-immigration stance. But, as can be seen by tracing the evolution of policy, what Merkel was attempting to signal was an increased focus on *integration* of immigrants. This shift did involve measures that were sometimes seen as draconian, such as required language instruction. But the government also passed policies such as shortening the wait time from five years to three months for some asylum seekers to have access to the labour market (Laubenthal 2019). The goal was shifting from living 'side-by-side' as implied by multiculturalism to integrating immigrants into German society.

Immigration, however, became a major issue again in Germany in 2015 when the refugee crisis that had been brewing for many years erupted across the European continent (Engler, Bauer-Blaschkowski and Zohlnhöfer 2019). As refugees gathered first in Hungary and then in Austria, Merkel decided to allow them to enter Germany to relieve both the humanitarian crisis in the Middle East and the dramatically escalating tension at the borders. Germany allowed hundreds of thousands of undocumented refugees to enter the country. Over the course of the autumn of 2015, the problems with admitting the refugee population became clear. Local governments were tasked with finding accommodation and caring for the newcomers, without clarity at first about where funding was coming from to cover increased expenses. The initial outpouring of support from the German population became more limited as time wore on. Particularly after a series of attacks on German women on New Year's Eve 2015–2016 were said to have been perpetrated by men of North African descent (possibly refugees), sympathy for the refugee population shrank dramatically.

Tension between the CDU and the CSU over immigration was a significant problem as immigrants were arriving in 2015; and this issue continued throughout the 2017 electoral campaign. Immigration and the refugee crisis were serious factors in the contest. The only established party seriously questioning Merkel's decision to admit the refugees was the CSU. Voters' rejection of the mainstream parties' management of these issues contributed to a dramatic jump in support for the AfD, which, having advocated restricting immigration as the centrepiece of its campaign (Dostal 2017), won 12.6 per cent of the vote and was able to take ninety-four seats in the Bundestag. The AfD played no part, however, in the complex coalition negotiations which followed. After a record-breaking 171 days, the failure to broker a so-called Jamaica Coalition (CDU/CSU, FPD and Greens), and the refusal of President Frank-Walter Steinmeier to hold new elections (lest they produce an even better result for the AfD), the Social Democrats (many of whom preferred to rebuild in opposition) eventually yielded and re-entered the Grand Coalition with the CDU/CSU.

Of the four issue areas under consideration, then, policies on welfare and European integration proved not to be terribly problematic for the CDU/CSU. The Christian Democrats have largely stayed the course on economic policies and they have benefited from the difficult welfare reforms implemented by the SPD. Although the CDU/CSU's commitment to European integration may have left an opening for the rise of the AfD, the other German parties also remained committed to the EU and it is difficult to imagine the Christian Democrats wavering in that respect – particularly after what to many observers was a surprising willingness (especially in the wake of a potentially awkward decision on EU financing by Germany's Constitutional Court) on the part of the government to contemplate large-scale European assistance to those member states whose economies were worst hit by the Covid-19 pandemic. Issues of traditional morality, especially policies on abortion and gay marriage, have sometimes caused tension between the CDU and the CSU. The Christian Democrats' move to the centre may also have provoked conservative voters to consider the AfD. That said, immigration has certainly been the most difficult issue for the CDU/CSU. The sister parties disagreed so strenuously on the issue that the dissolution of their partnership was briefly under discussion, and the difficulties helped to open the door to the rise of the AfD.

6. Conclusion

For most of the post-war period, Germany has had a strong silent revolution and a weak silent counter-revolution. Those trends shaped the party system, contributing to fragmentation on the left and Christian Democratic dominance on the right. The CDU/CSU benefited from the strength of the silent revolution – which disrupted politics on the left – and the weakness of the counter-revolution – which left plenty of room on the political right. German political institutions, civic culture and the actions of the Christian Democrats themselves worked to maintain this situation even through the unification period. The CDU in particular has benefited from two longer periods in opposition at the national level which served as times of internal party renewal. But after nearly seventy years of success, the German Christian Democrats, at least before Europe was struck by the Covid-19 pandemic, looked as if they might finally be 'catching up' with the rest of Western Europe, where their counterparts have long since lost any dominance they once enjoyed (Bale and Krouwel 2013).

Since the beginning of the Merkel era, the situation has been changing. Under Merkel, the CDU has shifted left, following the voters influenced by the silent revolution. The CDU's shift towards the political centre, though, created a vacuum on the right and greater distance between the CDU and the CSU. These changes, in combination with the rising salience of the immigration issue, created the opportunity for the rise of a populist radical right party. Thus, Germany's party system has now begun to fragment on the political right, as well as the political left.

A problematic party system now exists in Germany. The increased fragmentation on the left has meant that the SPD is unable to unite the left of the spectrum to form a coalition at the national level. The Social Democrats are in near free-fall electorally, potentially leaving the Christian Democrats perpetually in government. The Grand Coalition is losing steam as a governing arrangement, but no other coalition seemed both mathematically possible and politically palatable. Both major mainstream parties would likely benefit from time in the opposition spent on internal renewal. However, the perceived necessity of the Grand Coalition meant neither major party seemed able to devote serious time to rebuilding.

In some countries, notably Austria, the mainstream right has 'solved' the problem of a rising populist right-wing party by entering into coalition with the political newcomer. This outcome is unlikely in the German case. German history continues to shape German politics today. Both internationally and domestically, the rise of an extreme party in Germany is viewed differently from how it would be in other countries. The threat of the AfD in German politics is not that the party will somehow come to power as a junior coalition partner and end up steering policy-making. It is that the existence of the AfD may make coalition-building so difficult that it will push the other parties into uncomfortable coalitions or that lengthy time periods for government formation will become the new norm.

One possible shift in the German party system is that the Green Party might replace the SPD as the major party on the left. Results for the Greens were trending upward before the pandemic struck. The party continues to hold the Minister President position in Baden-Württemberg, the Greens did well in the 2019 European Parliament elections, and one Forsa poll even had them ahead of the Christian Democrats in Germany in June of that year. Christian Democratic–Green coalitions have been tried at the state-level in Hamburg, Hesse and Baden-Württemberg. Germany has not yet had a Christian Democratic–Green coalition at the national level, but the Christian Democrats were open to a coalition with the Green Party and the FDP in 2017. The current Christian Democratic–Green government in Austria might facilitate a similar coalition in Germany. Such an arrangement might pull the Christian Democrats further in the direction of the silent revolution. A normalization of Christian Democratic–Green governing coalitions would be unlikely to solve coalition formation issues in the long term, however. It might provide the Social Democrats with the chance at renewal in opposition, but it would also provide even more space for the AfD on the right.

Other European countries have seen the rise of a stronger liberal party, but the German FDP has not experienced any such renaissance. The Free Democrats missed the 5 per cent hurdle at the national level in 2013 and the party appeared poised to vanish. Instead, it was able to re-enter the Bundestag in 2017. However, the FDP has almost no presence in the eastern part of Germany and it is steadily losing votes to the Greens in the western part. If the FDP were to disappear entirely, that might push the Christian Democrats more towards a coalition with the AfD, perhaps starting at the state-level. Even under those circumstances, however, a Christian Democratic–AfD coalition would be breaking enormous taboos about cooperation with the radical right. It also remains the case that East–West divisions remain in Germany and that they are especially visible in the party system. The AfD is present throughout Germany, but notably stronger in the former East. The FDP and the Greens both struggle to make headway in the East, though recently the Greens have been doing much better.

If the current situation of a highly fragmented party system continues, the AfD will likely continue to benefit, unless the party implodes from internal strife due to leadership and policy conflicts or else some of its supporters return 'home' to the CDU/CSU in the wake of the Merkel government's initially impressive handling of Covid-19. The 2021 elections will prove to be critical in assessing the longer-term future of both the mainstream right and the populist radical right in Germany.

7 | Italy: The Mainstream Right and its Allies, 1994–2018

PIETRO CASTELLI GATTINARA AND CATERINA
FROIO

1. Introduction

Italy provides a perfect context to study the relationship between
different right-wing parties in democratic politics. There are few (if
any) other places in Western Europe that have seen such a symbiosis
between the mainstream right, on the one hand, and its centrist and
radical right counterparts, on the other (though see Bale 2018). Since
the collapse of the Italian party system in 1992 and up until the 2013
parliamentary elections, Italian politics comprised a multi-party system
aggregated around two broad left- and right-wing poles (Bartolini,
Chiaramonte and D'Alimonte 2004). Throughout most of these
years, Silvio Berlusconi's personalistic parties have played an essential
role in re-building Italy's fragmented centre-right, having constantly
been the dominant force of coalitions involving minor partners both on
the right and in the centre. With their support, Berlusconi led centre-
right coalitions to three general election victories (1994, 2001 and
2008), serving as either prime minister or as leader of the opposition
from his first political experience in 1994 until his replacement in the
midst of the 2011 financial crisis. The following years, however, radically changed the balance of power between the more moderate and
radical components of the political right in Italy. The transformation
culminated in the 2018 elections, when Matteo Salvini's *Lega* (formerly *Lega Nord*) obtained more votes than Berlusconi's *Forza Italia*,
which in turn got its lowest score at the ballot box in over two decades.

These developments seem to suggest that the Italian mainstream
right succumbed to the tension between the challenges posed by the
silent revolution, and those embedded in the silent counter-revolution,
notably migration. While at the turn of the twentieth century
Berlusconi's parties embraced this issue to cement a lasting partnership
with radical right allies, this strategy ultimately proved too problematic

for the more moderate components of Italy's centre-right. In the long run, the mainstream right could not cope with the need to appeal simultaneously to voters expressing liberal and progressive values associated with post-material value change, and to electorates sympathizing with authoritarian nativist ideals of the populist radical right (Bale and Rovira Kaltwasser, Chapters 1 and 12, this volume). The Italian context, however, offers further insight into the complex relationship between mainstream and radical right politics. The party system collapse in 1992–1994, and the implosion of Italy's main centre-right party *Democrazia Cristiana* (Christian Democrats; DC), ultimately blurred the distinction between the 'liberal', 'conservative' and 'populist' components of the political right. In this scenario, the personalistic parties of Silvio Berlusconi, who dominated the scene following the 1992 juncture, effectively represented the functional equivalent of the mainstream right in Italy. Despite the populist tendency of their leader, the cadres of *Forza Italia* displayed a moderate ideological profile, similar to other liberal–conservative parties in Europe (Raniolo 2006), and their policy platforms mirrored those of 'the mainstream European centre-right' (Verbeek and Zaslove 2015; see also Ruzza and Fella 2011).

This chapter examines how the centre-right of the Italian political spectrum has evolved over the last twenty-five years, that is, from the general elections that marked the beginning of the 'Second Republic' in 1994 until the contest held in March 2018. We seek to assess how the Italian right coped with the key policy challenges thrown up by the emergence of new lines of conflict in Western Europe, notably European integration, immigration, moral issues and welfare. Looking at the patterns of competition and cooperation among the components of the Italian centre-right, the next section offers an overview of the fragmentation and re-composition of parties within this area since the 1990s, and classifies the mainstream, centrist and radical right components covered in this study. We then present the chapter's analytical strategy based on the identification of three main phases of recent centre-right politics in Italy: breakthrough (1994–2001); government (2001–2011); and decay (2011–2018). After a discussion of demand- and supply-side factors across these three phases, we conclude by presenting the implications of our findings for future research on the interaction between mainstream and radical components of the political right in Europe.

2. Party System Change and the Centre-Right in Italy

To understand mainstream right politics in Italy, we must first deal with the fragmentation of this party family (which calls into question the classification of its various components), and with the issue of its continuity (which calls for the drawing of an analytical distinction between the different phases of recent Italian politics). To address these issues, we go back to the developments of the early 1990s. As noted earlier, in fact, the Italian party system did not collapse due to the advent of new political cleavages but in the wake of corruption scandals that would radically transform the nature of its parties and of party competition over the following decades (Morlino and Tarchi 1996).

Between 1992 and 1994 the disintegration of the DC created a large opening and a considerable fragmentation on the centre-right of the Italian political spectrum. Until then, Italy had configured an imperfect two-party system dominated by the DC and the Communists (Galli 1966), with the former occupying a centrist position and being continuously in government as the largest party since 1947 (Sartori 1982). The collapse of the DC thus created a political void, which would be filled by the creation of new centre-right forces (Fella and Ruzza 2013). The early 1990s saw the emergence or breakthrough of, among others: Berlusconi's personalistic party *Forza Italia* (Go Italy; FI) (McDonnell 2013); Gianfranco Fini's post-Fascist *Alleanza Nazionale* (National Alliance; AN) (Ignazi 2003); Umberto Bossi's regionalist populist *Lega Nord* (Northern League; LN) (McDonnell 2006); as well as multiple separate, small Christian democratic parties (Paolucci 2008). While often allied in broad centre-right coalitions, the names, nature and composition of these parties changed quite regularly over the following twenty-five years. The diaspora of the Christian democrats produced the *Centro Cristiano Democratico* (Christian Democratic Centre; CCD) and the *Cristiani Democratici Uniti* (United Christian Democrats; CDU). The two joined forces in 2002 in the *Unione di Centro* (Union of the Centre; UDC), but experienced multiple splinters and changes over the following decade. Furthermore, Berlusconi's federative attempts over the centre-right resulted in a merger between FI, AN and other smaller parties in 2009 to form the *Popolo Della Libertà* (People of Freedom; PDL). Over the following years, various components splintered out of the new party, reconfiguring some of the formations that existed before the PDL. Some members left the party in

2011 following former AN secretary Gianfranco Fini. Other AN nostalgics splintered a year later to form *Fratelli d'Italia* (Brothers of Italy; FdI), whereas most of the Christian democrat component quit the party in 2013, with the result that PDL returned to its old denomination of FI.

If the 1992 implosion of the Italian party system was not triggered by the emergence of new political cleavages, the ensuing fragmentation of the Italian right was, at least to a certain extent, a response to the tensions linked to the silent revolution and silent counter-revolution outlined in the introduction to this volume. In this respect, we can identify four main political actors: a Christian democratic component; Berlusconi's personalistic parties FI and PDL; the more right-wing National Alliance and its successor Brothers of Italy; and the (Northern) League. In the light of the comparative ambitions of this volume, we consider that the personalistic parties of Silvio Berlusconi (FI, then PDL, then again FI) represent the functional equivalent of mainstream right parties in Italian politics. Previous research suggests that the concept of 'right-wing populism' is not easily applicable in Italy, since Silvio Berlusconi can be considered a 'populist' in terms of style, but his parties are more readily associated with conservative counterparts in terms of programmes and policies (Raniolo 2006; Verbeek and Zaslove 2015; Tarchi 2016).

As regards the other parties, the configuration of the Christian democratic component, and its relationship with the mainstream right, has varied over time,[1] but small parties such as the CCD, CDU and UDC can safely be located in the centre-right of the political spectrum. On the far right, the tension between the values of the silent revolution and silent counter-revolution emerges with respect to AN – the successor of the extreme right *Movimento Sociale Italiano* (Italian Social Movement; MSI). Scholars in fact categorize AN alternatively as radical right (Norris 2005; van der Brug and Fennema 2009) or conservative, recognizing its progressive abandonment of nativism and populism in favour of liberal values (Griffin 1996; Ignazi 2005; Mudde 2007). The drift ultimately led AN to merge into PDL in 2009, completing the shift towards conservatism, but a splinter of the right-wing faction of the new party formed the populist radical right

---

[1] On the relationship between the mainstream right and the Catholic Church in Italy see Ozzano and Giorgi (2015).

FdI. Different categorization issues concern the *Lega Nord*. Due to its heterogeneous ideological stances, scholars have long disagreed on whether it configured a far-right party (Zaslove 2004; Norris 2005), an 'anti-political' force (Mastropaolo 2005) or a 'regionalist populist' actor (McDonnell 2006), even though the recent ideological and organizational developments seem to confirm its transition away from regionalism and towards radical right populism (Giovannini, Albertazzi and Seddone 2018). Since these issues reflect the key challenges presented by the interaction between radical and mainstream components of the political right, we consider that *Alleanza Nazionale* (until its merger with PDL) and FdI, as well as the Northern League (and its rebrand *Lega*) are generally located to the right of the above-mentioned parties, albeit with important variations over time.

This leaves us with four groups of parties active from 1994 to 2018. Figure 7.1 below, reporting each party's right–left position scores using the RILE index of party manifestos (Budge and Laver 1992), confirms how difficult it is to classify the various components of the Italian centre-right. On the one hand, the Northern League does not appear to be more right-wing than the other parties. On the other, party scores tend to converge during government (2001–2008), and disperse in the early and late periods. This raises the question of the continuity of these parties over time, outlined earlier in this section.

To look at the evolution of the Italian mainstream right, we identify three main phases: breakthrough (1994–2001), government (2001–2011) and decline (2011–2018). The first phase corresponds to the foundation of FI, its first electoral success and experience in office

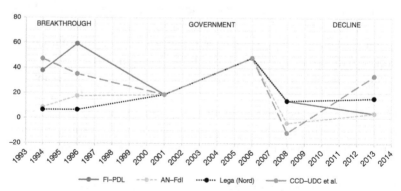

Figure 7.1 Right–left position of right-wing parties in Italy, 1994–2013

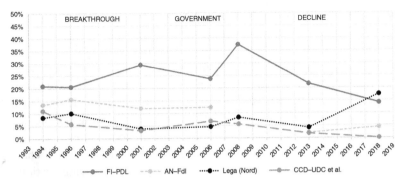

Figure 7.2 Electoral scores of right-wing parties in Italy, 1994–2018
Source: Ministry of Internal Affairs, data from the Lower Chamber.

(1994) and its first electoral defeat in a general election (1996). The second phase comprises three elections: two of them saw the victory of the centre-right led by Berlusconi's parties (2001 and 2008), whereas the intermediate one marked the short centre-left interregnum (2006). The third phase opens with the replacement of Berlusconi's government by the technocratic government led by Mario Monti, and includes the general elections which marked the decay of FI (2013) and the triumph of the League and the coalition government with the M5S (2018).

As illustrated by Figure 7.2, the electoral scores of the mainstream right in the lower house of Parliament varied considerably across the seven general elections that took place during this period. These years were also characterized by major changes in the morphology and dynamics of the Italian party system, because of semi-systematic party and parliamentary group switching, and a seemingly endless process of electoral law reform. After forty years using a proportional electoral system, the 1994, 1996 and 2001 elections were in fact run using a mixed system with single-member constituencies and a compensatory proportional formula (Mattarellum). The law was reformed in 2005 in favour of a proportional system (without preferences) compensated by a majority bonus (Porcellum), which sparked much criticism but remained in place for the following three general elections in 2006, 2008 and 2013. After a first reform of this electoral law was deemed unconstitutional, a new law was ultimately passed prior to the 2018 general elections, reintroducing a mixed system with part of the seats allocated through a first-past-the-post system and part through a proportional system (Rosatellum).[2]

The distinction of these four group of parties, with FI–PDI playing the role of mainstream right, and three phases of recent Italian politics allow us to map the Italian centre-right over the past twenty-five years. The unsuccessful federative attempts of the political right and the decay of its mainstream right component might reflect growing fragmentation triggered by the silent revolution and silent counter-revolution in the Italian centre-right. To further elaborate on the key policy challenges associated with this political dynamic, the following sections present information on the demand-[3] and supply-side profile[4] of each group of parties. Based on this data, the next sections trace the main

---

[2] While for reasons of space these reforms will only be addressed marginally in this chapter, we will nevertheless consider the crucial role they played in structuring the alliance and conflict patterns in the Italian party system. For a detailed analysis of the politics of institutional and electoral reform in Italy, see, for example, Bardi (2007); Bull (2016); Bedock (2017); Regalia (2018).

[3] Demand-side data uses the Italian National Election Study (ITANES) post-electoral survey for all elections from 1994 to 2013. This includes demographic information on age, gender, education and class. Education was measured by means of a three-point scale, using lower education (International Standard Classification of Education (ISCED), level 1–2) as a reference, whereas class distinguishes between 'upper' and 'working' classes, and two intermediate categories for the 'middle' and 'lower middle' class. Furthermore, we look at the geographic distribution of voters in terms of the urban–rural divide (with rural identifying voters in cities with less than 10,000 inhabitants), and the divide between regions in the north, centre and south of Italy (based on the categories of the Italian National Institute of Statistics, ISTAT). Finally, we account for voters' left–right self-placement on a ten-point scale, and for the issues they consider as the most pressing problems for their countries at the time of interviews. In line with the premises of this volume, we focus on four issue areas/problems: taxes and welfare; immigration; EU integration; and corruption and justice.

[4] The supply-side of centre-right parties is based on the Comparative Manifesto Project (CMP), now MARPOR. The CMP data allows the measurement of the right–left positions of parties presented in Figure 7.1, and the relative salience of different issue areas in their electoral programmes. In this regard, our analysis focuses on seven policy areas. Four correspond to the key policy challenges outlined in the introduction of this volume: welfare, European integration, immigration (see Alonso and da Fonseca 2012) and moral issues (using categories for traditional morality and corruption). The three additional issue areas include decentralization, which has been a key theme for the Italian centre-right, and notably for the former regionalist League. We include a category measuring positive incentives for business since this has been a recurring message for Berlusconi's parties. Finally, we focus on governmental efficiency because the improvement of bureaucratic and administrative procedures in Italy has been at the core of party competition at least since the 1990s.

developments taking place during the phases of breakthrough, government and the decay of Berlusconi's personalistic parties, comparing the profiles of the different components of the centre-right coalition in terms of key demand- and supply-side factors.

3. Berlusconi and the Construction of the Italian Centre-Right, 1994–2001

The 'foundational phase' of FI (Raniolo 2006: 440) began with Silvio Berlusconi's entry into politics in January 1994 and his first success in a general election. In just two months, the newly born FI capitalized on the transformation of the Italian party system (Morlino and Tarchi 1996) to win a 21 per cent vote share and over 8 million votes. FI managed to set the agenda of the elections through the support of Berlusconi's personal business and television group, intensive campaigning and effective electoral marketing. To cope with the highly volatile electoral context of the early 1990s, Berlusconi was also successful in building an asymmetrical coalition comprising the LN in the north and AN in the south, as well as former Christian Democrats. This unprecedented coalition, however, contained some structural weaknesses, and the first Berlusconi executive soon collapsed amidst disagreements with the League over the financial law in December 1994. The governmental crisis triggered political uncertainty and favoured the electoral success of the centre-left coalition led by Romano Prodi at the 1996 general elections. While FI confirmed its predominance over the Italian right (with more than 20 per cent and over 7.5 million votes) and while AN increased its support at the national level, their coalition crucially lacked the League, which stood as an independent party. The results thus favoured a reconstitution of the alliance with the northern party on the opposition benches, and its confirmation at the following European (1999) and regional elections (2000). Overall the composition of the centre-right proved to be relatively stable over these years, as FI strengthened its internal organization and consolidated the alliances on its right and in the centre (Raniolo 2006). This allowed FI, AN and LN to lay down the foundations of an alliance that would last, albeit with some ups and downs, over the following twenty years.

In this political phase, the centre-right alliance was primarily motivated by the backlash against the pre-existing Italian political system. Yet each party in the coalition defined this in its own terms: FI focused on Italy's statism and promised a 'liberal revolution', the LN opposed the country's centralism, whereas the AN challenged the post-1948 constitutional regime. The supply-side programmatic profile of the four components of the centre-right is thus clearly distinguishable, as illustrated in Figure 7.3. In terms of the four key policy challenges, while *Lega* and FI focused more attention on welfare issues than AN and the Christian democrats, they also supported less state intervention in the economy than their allies, who instead tried to strike a balance between support for the free market and calls for social justice. All parties devoted considerable importance to migration, generally in negative terms; indeed, this is the policy area in which the four centre-right actors score the lowest mean difference. Yet, while AN and, to a lesser extent, LN were very critical of migration and minority rights in the years in which Italy was turning into a destination country for international migrants, FI and the Christian democrats backed some mildly pro-immigration proposals. While only the Christian democrats invested in advocating traditional moral values, only AN campaigned against the EU, all other parties being generally favourable to integration. Finally, decentralization was the core issue of LN, reflecting the importance attributed by this party to regional autonomy in the early years – whereas the agenda of FI focused on business support and on governmental efficiency.

Overall, the analysis of the supply side suggests that the basis of the centre-right alliance over these years had to do with its (mild) opposition to immigration and state interventionism. This is partly confirmed

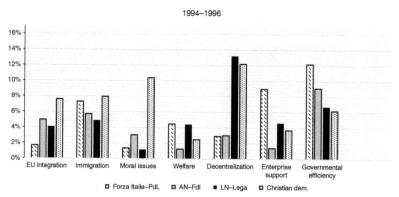

Figure 7.3 The supply side of right-wing politics in Italy, 1994–1996

Table 7.1 *The demand side of right-wing politics in Italy, 1994–1996*

				Parties		
1994–1996		FI–PdL	AN–FdI	LN–Lega	Christian democrats	*Mean diff.*
Demographics	Gender (f)	52.9	44.4	42.5	41.3	*6.1*
	Education (low)	50.1	38.4	51.8	29.2	*13.2*
	Class (work)	43.0	37.1	48.0	25.8	*12.1*
	Age (>50)	57.4	28.2	27.1	43.6	*17.7*
Geography	U–R divide (rural)	30.5	31.8	42.8	40.8	*7.6*
	N–S divide (north)	51.0	35.0	97.2	49.1	*31.4*
	N–S divide (south)	34.3	41.2	0.5	34.5	*20.3*
Attitudes (MIP)	Taxes & welfare	34.5	32.4	27.6	19.3	*8.4*
	Immigration	12.1	15.9	25.0	6.5	*9.9*
	EU integration	0.0	0.0	0.0	0.0	*0.0*
	Corruption & Justice	43.8	43.9	48.1	53.2	*5.4*
Self-placement	Right-wing	61.0	83.5	37.5	36.5	*27.4*
	Centre	20.0	6.5	26.5	41.5	*18.6*

if we look at the demand side of centre-right politics, reported in Table 7.1. While the electorates of the four actors present some sociodemographic differences, notably in terms of age, class and territorial distribution, the attitudinal profile is coherent across the centre-right alliance. Corruption and justice stand out as the most important problem for about half of all respondents, which is not surprising considering the corruption scandals that tore apart the Italian political system over those years. Similarly, about one-third of the electorate of FI, AN and LN, like a fifth of the Christian democratic electorate, are concerned with taxes and welfare issues. Migration is most important for the LN voters (25 per cent), less so for FI and AN (12 and 15 per cent, respectively), and quite marginal for the Christian democrats

(6 per cent). Meanwhile, the EU does not appear to be a concern for any right-wing voter. Partisan ideological differences also emerge if we look at the left–right orientation of voters. With over 85 per cent of the AN voters identifying as right-wing, there is no doubt about the location of this party on the spectrum. FI follows with 60 per cent of its voters identifying as right-wing and 20 per cent as centrists. While the plurality of the Christian democratic electorate identifies as centrist (40 per cent), the LN stands out as a hybrid with a split electorate out of which about a third does not identify as either centrist (26 per cent) or right-wing (37 per cent).

Overall, during the breakthrough, then, parties in the right-wing coalition shared concerns about immigration and a mildly liberal economic agenda. Their electorates recognize these issues as priorities despite important ideological variation across parties.

4. The 'Short' Decade of Centre-Right Government, 2001–2011

The second phase comprises three general elections (2001, 2006 and 2008) and constitutes a 'short' decade during which centre-right coalitions were in office for more than eight out of ten years (2001–2006 and 2008–2011). The phase opened with the success of Berlusconi's centre-right coalition *Casa delle Libertà* (House of Freedom) at the May 2001 elections. FI alone won more than 29 per cent or 11 million votes, thirteen percentage points ahead of the main centre-left party, the second largest in the country. Berlusconi's second cabinet would become the longest serving in Republican history, but was also challenged by growing popular unrest and had to cope with multiple conflicts between FI and its partners (Andrews 2006) that undermined governmental popularity and its stability. The House of Freedom suffered a severe vote loss at the European and regional elections in 2004, and the tensions within the government led to the formation of a new Berlusconi cabinet in 2005. Yet, in the 2006 general election, apart from the addition of some small lists from the centre and minor extreme-right formations, the main members of the coalition did not change. The strategy involved differentiating what was on offer so that each actor could catalyse the support of its own electorate (Tarchi 2018). Furthermore, Berlusconi took on the leadership of the campaign himself, with a series of last-minute promises, controversial statements and attacks on the opposition of which his allies were given little (if any) prior notice. The electioneering outcome of this strategy was partly successful: the centre-right managed to stem any loss of votes and obtained 49 per cent of the vote, suffering only the narrowest of defeats in the closest election in Italian history. Yet this strategy also exacerbated the conflict between FI and the rest of the centre-right, as coalition partners became increasingly dissatisfied with Berlusconi's leadership style.

In response, Berlusconi upped the stakes and launched a campaign to federate the centre-right within a new unitary party *Popolo della Libertà* (People of Freedom; PDL). If the project was initially met with diffidence, the collapse of the second Prodi government accelerated the merger of FI and AN, albeit amidst tension among sections of the latter, personal disputes and disagreement over policy directions (Tarchi 2018). The 2008 elections rewarded this strategy: the PDL won over 37 per cent of the vote and its allies LN about 8 per cent, seizing a solid parliamentary majority even without the support of the Christian democrats, who had left the coalition ahead of the elections. The new Berlusconi government, however, suffered a new set of problems. First, different components of PDL argued over the management of the party, its territorial organization, and its programmatic profile on crucial economic issues and civil rights. Second, the LN backed an increasingly radical agenda on migration and security, escalating tensions with the moderate wing of the government. Third, a series of sex scandals involving Berlusconi leaked into the media, exacerbating the conflict between the government, the media and the judiciary. The overall effect of these tensions was the progressive loss of parliamentary support for the government, especially after the formation of a splinter parliamentary group by former AN members. Ultimately, the outbreak of the economic crisis and the pressures by the European Commission to reduce public debt left Berlusconi with no parliamentary majority. His resignation in November 2011 paved the way for Mario Monti's technocratic executive, effectively ending the 'short' decade of Italy's centre-right governments.

This phase is thus characterized by the consolidation of the centre-right alliance in its various configurations but also by persistent turbulence. This is partly reflected in Figure 7.4 below, reporting the supply side of centre-right politics during 2001–2008. The issue attention profiles of the four parties are very similar, as a result of their running

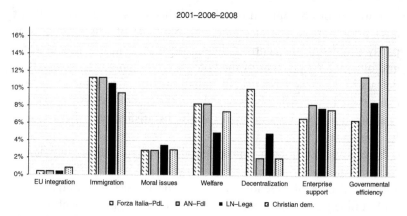

Figure 7.4 The supply side of right-wing politics in Italy, 2001–2008

consistently on joint electoral programmes, with a few exceptions concerning the enhanced importance attributed by FI to decentralization, and by the Christian democrats and AN to government efficiency. The four parties campaigned predominantly on welfare and, even more so, on immigration. Consistent with the findings outlined above, moral and EU integration issues did not play a major role in the political platforms of the Italian centre-right, which generally expressed support for traditional values and mildly pro-European tones. Welfare issues included provisions aimed at families and younger people, accompanied by economic incentives and the expected benefits of a sharp decline in taxation on specific economic sectors and housing. Once more, therefore, the various parties combined a neoliberal economic view with mild pro-welfare provisions, mainly focused on taxation. Similarly, migration tops the agenda of the four parties. Under the initiative of AN and the LN, the coalition found common ground on an illiberal approach, framing immigrant settlement as corrosive of social order, and successfully reforming migration law with the ambition of creating a guest-worker style of recruitment. Over time, this approach was progressively softened in response to calls from the Christian democrats and the increasingly permissive approach of AN, which allowed for profession-specific and generalized regularizations of illegal migrants (Geddes 2008). In short, while migration is at the core of centre-right politics, its treatment is linked to coalition dynamics, so that the illiberal rhetoric and restrictive policies promoted by the radical wing of the coalition were repeatedly watered down by the more moderate components of the centre-right.

The idea that compromises on the migration agenda kept the centre-right coalition together over these years is confirmed by demand-side data reported in Table 7.2. Concerns about migration, in fact, topped the agenda of most centre-right voters. About half of the LN electorate (46 per cent), more than a third of those who voted FN and AN, and 28 per cent of Christian democrats saw immigration as the most urgent problem facing Italy during these years. In general, notwithstanding substantial sociodemographic and territorial differences in the composition of the vote for the centre-right, the four parties' voters display considerable attitudinal coherence. Akin to what we noted in the previous political phase, the ranking of the most important problems

Table 7.2 *The demand side of right-wing politics in Italy, 2001–2008*

		Parties				
2001–2006–2008		FI–PdL	AN–FdI	LN–Lega	Christian democrats	*Mean diff.*
Demographics	Gender (f)	53.3	42.9	45.1	46.6	*5.4*
	Education (low)	55.2	44.0	55.2	38.0	*10.5*
	Class (work.)	46.0	22.4	48.2	36.5	*14.5*
	Age (>50)	48.0	37.9	43.9	51.8	*7.7*
Geography	U–R divide (rural)	37.6	34.4	49.0	45.3	*8.6*
	N–S divide (north)	43.4	36.6	97.9	40.5	*31.1*
	N–S divide (south)	39.8	39.7	0.4	44.3	*22.0*
Attitudes (MIP)	Taxes & welfare	16.1	18.6	21.9	14.7	*4.0*
	Immigration	35.6	35.2	46.0	27.6	*9.2*
	EU integration	0.4	0.6	0.0	0.5	*0.3*
	Corruption & Justice	10.7	11.1	12.1	9.2	*1.5*
Self-placement	Right-wing	67.3	79.0	69.0	33.8	*22.9*
	Centre	18.7	12.7	20.0	54.3	*21.1*

in the country is the same across the coalition, although migration replaces corruption and justice as the most pressing issue, followed by taxes and welfare (again, especially so among voters of LN and least so for the Christian democrats). Demand-side data also illustrate the progressive transformation of the four centre-right actors along the left–right continuum. Despite the evolution of AN towards mainstream conservative politics, its electorate remains the most right-wing of the coalition, with 79 per cent identifying with this category. Similarly, the Christian democrats display a moderate profile, counting on over 50 per cent of centrist and 33 per cent of right-wing voters. Compared with the previous political phase, however, the electorate of FI and in particular of LN shifts considerably to the right. If for FI the change over time is moderate (from 60 to 67 per cent of right-wing voters), the tendency is significant for the LN, which now counts on an overwhelmingly right-wing electorate (69 per cent).

In sum, this phase during which centre-right governments loomed large marked important developments for the coalition. All parties improved their electoral support and experienced organizational and ideological change. FI started consolidating its party organization and kept the balance in the coalition; the LN moved further to the right, progressively detaching itself from regionalism; and AN pursued its transition towards conservatism. In this period, the coalition was kept together by a primary focus on migration issues. While this renewed political agenda arguably matched the preferences of an increasingly right-wing electorate, it also required compromise with societal actors (the Church and business interests) that were close to the moderate wing of the centre-right coalition.

5. Mainstream Right Decline, 2011–2018

The year 2011 marked a juncture in the coalition politics of the Italian centre-right for a number of reasons. The first disturbance concerned whether or not to support Monti's technocratic government. While the former AN and the PDL were willing, albeit with some hesitation, to do so, the LN strongly opposed the idea and moved to the opposition. Second, a serious scandal involving electoral reimbursement fraud hit LN and its founder Umberto Bossi, eventually leading to the moderate wing of Roberto Maroni taking over the party in 2012. Third, the leadership of PDL and the centre-right coalition came under pressure due to Berlusconi's ongoing legal problems and to the tensions between supporters and opponents of the Monti government. In the light of the 2013 elections, conflicts intensified over the choice of the candidate for prime minister, with Berlusconi first agreeing to hold primary consultations and then suddenly changing his mind and imposing himself as leader. This prompted the departure of a group of MPs originating from the AN, who founded the new radical right party *Fratelli d'Italia* (FdI) led by former minister Giorgia Meloni.

Despite disagreements on many issues, including government participation, PDL, LN and FdI eventually established a formal alliance for the 2013 general election – primarily in order to cope with the prevailing electoral law, which provided a majority bonus to coalitions rather than parties. With the breakthrough of Beppe Grillo's *Movimento 5 Stelle* (Five Star Movement, M5S), the elections marked the parliamentary downsizing of the centre-right, but confirmed its internal power distribution, with the PDL being the main party, the LN suffering a steep electoral decline, and FdI scoring less than 2 per cent of the vote. As shown in Figure 7.5, the political supply of the coalition partners reflected this pattern of forced alliance: PDL and LN ran with a common electoral platform emphasizing decentralization, efficiency and mild support for welfare provision. If the coalition's positions on immigration were largely negative, the issue received considerably less attention than in previous years. The same applies to moral issues, although PDL and LN proposed family-oriented welfare benefits as well as the protection of life and the heterosexual family. On the right, FdI ran an aggressive campaign on migration, which stands out as the most important issue in an election programme strongly focused on security, border control, and the cultural and religious assimilation of migrant residents.

In showing that the attitudes of Christian democrat voters differ from those of people who voted for the other three parties, demand-side data reported in Table 7.3 illustrates the breakaway of the moderates from the centre-right coalition in 2013. For the first time, the ranking of perceived problems differs markedly across parties. In a context deeply affected by the consequences of the global recession, voters of all parties prioritized taxes and welfare, even if issues of corruption and justice (45 per cent) were the primary concern of the Christian democratic electorate. Unlike previous years, only the

Table 7.3 *The demand side of right-wing politics in Italy, 2013*

2013		FI–PdL	AN–FdI	LN–Lega	Christian democrat	*Mean diff.*
				Parties		
Demographics	Gender (f)	57.6	45.3	48.3	66.7	*12.2*
	Education (low)	13.4	3.8	10.9	3.0	*6.4*
	Class (work.)	7.6	8.0	10.2	6.1	*2.1*
	Age (>50)	59.5	54.6	47.8	45.4	*8.1*
Geography	U–R divide (rural)	20.4	26.4	23.9	30.3	*5.4*
	N–S divide (north)	46.7	47.6	92.3	54.5	*23.9*
	N–S divide (south)	36.4	37.7	2.2	30.3	*18.7*
Attitudes (MIP)	Taxes & welfare	48.9	35.8	41.3	30.3	*10.2*
	Immigration	11.5	11.3	21.7	18.2	*6.3*
	EU integration	10.5	11.9	7.5	3.0	*4.9*
	Corruption & Justice	33.4	32.1	33.7	45.4	*6.7*
Self-placement	Right-wing	80.2	67.8	70.6	15.1	*33.0*
	Centre	11.0	22.6	9.8	57.6	*25.8*

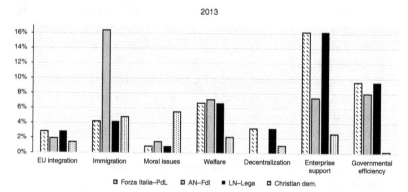

Figure 7.5 The supply side of right-wing politics in Italy, 2013

electorate of LN (and to a lesser extent the moderates) attributed substantial importance to immigration (over 20 per cent). However, EU integration now is addressed as a problem by about 10 per cent of the electorate of both FI and FdI. The loosening of the centre-right alliance is further confirmed by voters' self-placement on the left–right scale. On the one hand, while a majority of the FdI's voters were right-wing (68 per cent), this is considerably less than was the case for FI voters (80 per cent). On the other hand, while the LN carried on its journey to the right (over 70 per cent of voters identifying as right-wing), the right-wing base of the Christian democrats was now down to just 15 per cent – or 50 per cent lower than in the previous phase. Overall, the mean differences for the electorates of the four parties of Italy's centre-right are higher in 2013 than ever before, whether we are looking at the perception of most important problems or voters' self-placement on the left–right scale.

Divisions within the centre-right, however, did not end with the 2013 elections and the electoral alliance proved to be short-lived once the contest had taken place. In the new parliament, the LN and FdI joined the opposition, whereas the PDL initially opted to participate in a grand coalition government with the mainstream left and the moderates. Over the following months, partly because of this, the PDL experienced a new split: a group of MPs led by Angelino Alfano adopted the name *Nuovo Centrodestra* (New Centre-Right; NCD) with the goal of establishing a more durable relationship with the mainstream left, whereas the rest of Berlusconi's PDL moved to the opposition and started calling themselves *Forza Italia* once again. Meanwhile the LN had begun the process that would lead to a change in the party leadership, ultimately resulting in the election, in December 2013, of Matteo Salvini as new federal secretary.

The divisions within the centre-right continued in the months preceding the 2014 European Parliament elections. Berlusconi showed some sympathy towards the constitutional reforms proposed by the centre left, especially under the new leadership of Matteo Renzi. The former AN engaged in a legal battle with FdI over the use of the old party's symbols. The LN set out to stretch its reach beyond northern regions, putting aside its traditional focus on federalism to emphasize anti-establishment rhetoric, restless anti-immigrant campaigning, and opposition to the EU and the banking system. FI's ambiguous position towards the government and the weakness of its leadership was severely sanctioned at the 2014 elections (at which it took only 16 per cent). While FdI failed to pass the threshold, the vote showed some small progress for the LN (6 per cent), indicating that Salvini's strategy had the potential to reverse the party's vote losses and to reconstruct its identity within the centre-right. In the new EU Parliament, FI seated itself with the European People's Party group, holding to pro-EU positions alongside the MEPs of NCD and other centrist parties who had left the centre-right alliance. Despite the formal alliance with FI at home, the LN seated itself in Brussels and Strasbourg with the Eurosceptic group of Europe of Nations and Freedom, alongside the French Front National.

The marginalization of FI, the intensification of the conflict between PD and M5S, and the clouding of the political leadership of Berlusconi further allowed the LN to take charge of the opposition in the years that followed. The leader of LN upped its media profile, focusing primarily on criticizing the government's economic agenda and its policy on immigration. It set up short-lived electoral alliances with the extreme right *CasaPound Italia*,[5] as well as FdI, to campaign on these issues, showing its willingness to move the centre of gravity of the centre-right towards the right. Finally, it created the electoral list '*Noi con Salvini*' ('We with Salvini') to take advantage of the party's increasing popularity in the south, thus challenging FI's leadership role in that region. That decision was rewarded at regional elections in 2015, as LN did better than FI in most of the regions that held elections. Even though the rift between the mainstream right (represented by FI) and the radical right (LN and FdI) continued, the defeat of the December 2016 Constitutional referendum offered a new opportunity to re-launch the project of a unified centre-right, which was confirmed by the success of the centre-right coalition at the 2017 local elections.

To sum up, the last few years have witnessed the effective collapse of the mainstream right in Italy. This resulted notably from the weakening of *Forza Italia* and the rise of the LN that is today the dominant party of the centre-right. After the 2018 parliamentary elections, the LN pursued a new strategy of 'asymmetric' coalitions. In fact, while the *Lega* formed a coalition government with the M5S at the national level, at

---

[5] On the relationship between the LN and the extreme right in Italy, see Froio et al. (2020).

the local level it maintains its alliances with *Forza Italia*. At the European level today, the *Lega* is close to the French *Rassemblement National* (previously Front National).

6. Comparative Findings and Concluding Remarks

The chapter offered an account of the transformation of the Italian centre-right over the past twenty-five years. In line with the premises of this volume, it examined how the dominant mainstream right actor, that is, Berlusconi's personalistic parties, coped with the tensions associated with the silent revolution and silent counter-revolution. While the reasons behind the collapse of the Italian party system in the early 1990s had little to do with the emergence of new political cleavages, the following decades were largely shaped by the interaction between mainstream right parties and the populist radical right. Notably, migration stands out as the key policy challenge shaping mainstream right politics in Italy. Triggering discussions over security, welfare and cultural protectionism, this policy field cemented the centre-right alliance that would dominate Italian politics for most of the early 2000s (Fella and Ruzza 2013; Castelli Gattinara 2016). Yet the subsequent migration 'emergencies' that culminated in the 2015 asylum policy crisis, which tapped into the crisis of political legitimacy at the national and EU level (Castelli Gattinara 2017), progressively spooked government parties of the mainstream right – much to the advantage of their populist radical competitors. With the relevant exception of migration policy, Berlusconi's personalist parties can be categorized as vote-seeking and/or office-seeking, but not as policy-seeking. This absence of emphasis on the policy-seeking dimension helps to explain the decay of these parties. In this regard, our analysis allows us to draw general conclusions on four aspects of right-wing politics in Italy: the structure of the coalitions between the mainstream and radical component; the electoral strength of the mainstream right; and both the programmatic positions (political supply) and the sociological profile of its voters (political demand).

In the last twenty-five years, the composition of the centre-right displays considerable discontinuity in terms of party organization and labelling, but a substantial stability in terms of coalition-building. With few exceptions, all four components of the centre-right have been involved in broad centre-right coalitions for most of the period under observation. In this respect, Italy's fragmented bipolarism (D'Alimonte 2005) does not display the signs of polarization and fragmentation triggered by the contrasting forces of the silent revolution and silent counter-revolution. This owes a great deal to the federative efforts of Berlusconi and to electoral systems that, despite changing over time, have generally favoured the formation of broad alliances at the national level. Yet the concentration of most decision-making power in the hands of Berlusconi has had negative consequences on the stability of the centre-right, too. On the one hand, it hampered the institutionalization of the mainstream right parties, which remained organizationally weak and overly dependent on their charismatic leaderships. On the other, it favoured the emergence of factionalism due to the presence of scarcely coordinated local potentates and, lacking a shared worldview, the development of currents and party factions within both the mainstream and far-right components.

Organizational instability and coalition continuity have consequences for the supply side of right-wing politics. We observed substantial over-time change. While all parties pay sporadic attention to moral issues and EU integration, the relative importance accorded to welfare and, in particular, to immigration, increases. Furthermore, the results show that the difference in the programmatic profiles of the four components of the centre-right were lowest during the years 2001–2008. The four actors focused on similar issues in the period in which they held office jointly, as compared with earlier years and the post-2011 phase, when their policy preferences tended to diverge more conspicuously. It is difficult to tell from this data whether the mainstream right radicalized its programmatic positions, although it appears that the joint government experience fostered adaption in centre-right policy preferences. As for the sociodemographic profile of centre-right voters, this displayed both stability and change over time. While the level of education increased and the working-class vote decreased, the figures for gender, geography and age remained relatively stable. Additionally, the findings point to attitudinal changes for voters of the centre-right, with increasing importance put on immigration, taxes and welfare. In this regard, voters of mainstream right parties stand out because their average level of education decreased over time and because they accorded more importance to European integration. In sum, even if more fine-grained data are needed to further examine demand-side factors, our study suggests that the sociological profile of mainstream right electorates in Italy did not change substantively, whereas voters' issue priorities did.

As for electoral strength, power relations remained relatively stable within the centre-right coalition, despite changes to the electoral system. From the 1994 until the 2008 general election, right-wing parties could together count on about half of the active electorate. The mainstream right took the lion's share obtaining 20 per cent to almost 30 per cent of the votes, whereas AN scored systematically above 10 per cent. The LN was generally below this threshold, and the Christian democrats played the role of minor partners. In this period, all parties and factions that departed from Berlusconi's coalition suffered tremendous electoral defeats and rapidly fell into political irrelevance. But things changed considerably after the failure of PDL (2009–2013) and the dramatic 2011 change of government. While this was partly due to Berlusconi's weakening leadership, the increasing salience of issues like immigration, law and order, and EU integration seems to suggest that the political right has increasingly turned towards electorates sympathizing with authoritarian and nativist ideals associated with the silent counter-revolution. Similarly, the transformation of the League under Salvini means that the party now pursues a radical right populist agenda.

In the aftermath of the Great Recession, Salvini turned the League into a credible radical right party at the national level. Salvini's hegemony, which effectively ended Berlusconi's dominance over the centre-right, means that the League may become the voice not just of the radical right but of the most conservative parts of the mainstream right, too. In 2018, the League obtained its best result ever in a general election, becoming the primary party of the centre-right with 17 per cent of the votes. In the following months, the League defeated FI again, striking a government deal with the M5S without officially disrupting the centre-right alliance at the local level. From a position of strength, the League could drain votes from its government allies M5S as well as from the minor partners in the right-wing bloc, as confirmed by the 2019 European Parliament elections where the League obtained a stunning 34 per cent share of the vote (an increase of 28 per cent from 2014). While enduring disputes led to the collapse of the government and the formation of a new (and unlikely) coalition cabinet between the 5-Star Movement and PD, by 2019 the League was not only the main party in the right-wing bloc but also the largest party in Italy.

With the return of the League to opposition, however, centre-right parties found themselves once more in a situation of forced coalition. And with immigration losing importance in the wake of the Covid-19 crisis, the dormant conflict between the mainstream and radical components of the Italian political right became manifest again. On the one hand, the new scenario gave the survivors of *Forza Italia* the opportunity to break away from Salvini's hard-line strategy, attempting to appeal to moderate voters and potential allies in parliament. On the other, it marked the increasing popularity of Giorgia Meloni, exposing the double nature of Brothers of Italy as both an experienced government ally for the League and a radical competitor for Salvini's leadership.

The transformations within Italy's right are thus far from settled. The permanent state of emergency associated with migration in Italy will soon restore the issue to centre-stage in national public debate. And as the Eurozone economy heads towards more financial trouble, the legitimacy crisis of national and EU institutions might further strengthen the predominance of radical parties over the Italian mainstream right, posing some serious challenges over the fundamentals of liberal democracy in Italy.

8 The Netherlands: How the Mainstream Right Normalized the Silent Counter-Revolution

STIJN VAN KESSEL

1. Introduction

Both the silent revolution and the silent counter-revolution have left their marks on the Dutch political landscape. A considerable number of new parties entered parliament in the decades following the Second World War, some of which, albeit from different ideological perspectives, expressed ideas that can be associated with the post-materialist values of the silent revolution (Ingehart 1977). A few of these parties still survive. Democrats 66 (*Democraten 66*; D66), a culturally and economically liberal party founded in 1966, was initially known for its call for institutional renewal and democratization. The more socioeconomically left-wing Green party, 'Green Left' (*GroenLinks*), was formed in 1989 after the merger of four small parties, which between them propagated post-materialist values such as environmentalism, international solidarity, demilitarization and gender equality.[1] Whilst D66, known for its electoral ebbs and flows, managed to establish itself as a regular governing coalition partner, post-materialist parties remained relatively modest in terms of size. Moreover, the silent revolution did not radically alter competition for government, which was still dominated by the three traditional party families: the Christian democrats, united since 1980 in a single party (*Christen Democratisch Appel*; CDA); the social democrats (*Partij van de Arbeid*; PvdA); and the conservative liberals (*Volkspartij voor Vrijheid en Democratie*; VVD).

---

[1] More recently, the environmentalist and fauna-friendly Party for the Animals (*Partij voor de Dieren*; PvdD) made its parliamentary debut in 2006. DENK, a party founded by two former social democrat MPs of Turkish origin, won three parliamentary seats in 2017, and preached values of tolerance, equality and societal pluralism – although its liberal credentials have been questioned. Given their relative electoral weakness, neither party will be further discussed here.

More recently, however, the Dutch party system has become far more fragmented, election results more volatile and competition for government more unstructured. Although these trends were already visible in the 1990s, they became stronger after the genuine break-through of the populist right after the turn of the twenty-first century. This marked the relatively late dawn in the Netherlands of the silent counter-revolution (Ignazi 1992) – if one disregards the two far right parties led by Hans Janmaat in the 1980s and 1990s (the Centre Party, *Centrumpartij*, and Centre Democrats, *Centrumdemocraten*), which achieved only limited and short-lived electoral success. In the election of 2002, the List Pim Fortuyn (*Lijst Pim Fortuyn*; LPF), fared consid-erably better. After a brief stint in government and an extended period of infighting, however, the party soon lost support. In its place came Geert Wilders' Freedom Party (*Partij voor de Vrijheid*; PVV), which developed into a more unmistakable and durable populist radical right (PRR) party.

This chapter will argue that the entrance of these 'counter-revolution parties' had the most profound impact on the contemporary Dutch party system. They have driven the politicization of the themes of immigration and cultural integration of minorities, and also pressed both the CDA and, especially, VVD to take less immigrant-friendly positions and to explicitly question the merits of multiculturalism. Increased efforts by the Dutch centre-right to appeal to voters con-cerned about these issues, however, have not done much to dent the success of the PRR in the Netherlands. While this accommodative strategy may have led to momentary success for the VVD, both in vote- and office-seeking terms, the PRR has established itself as a key force in Dutch politics. The 2017 parliamentary election even saw the modest breakthrough of a second such party, Forum for Democracy (*Forum voor Democratie*; FvD), which grew to rival the PVV in terms of electoral appeal. In the provincial election of March 2019, FvD even finished ahead of all other parties, albeit in a highly fragmented field. Instead of stemming the 'populist tide', CDA and VVD have thus contributed to the normalization and legitimization of radical right discourse and positions. Given the joint majority of the right-wing 'bloc', this has pushed culturally liberal parties onto the defensive, even though recent years have also seen substantive support for parties, such as the Greens and D66, characterized by more cosmopolitan and immigration-friendly positions.

The remainder of this contribution discusses in more detail the impact of the silent revolution and, especially, the silent counter-revolution on the Dutch centre-right. It starts by discussing which Dutch parties can be considered 'centre-right', and describing key electoral developments in the Netherlands, with a particular emphasis on the period since the 1990s. Second, it touches on the profiles of Dutch voters and the (potential for) vote-switching between the various parties. Third, it considers recent ideological and discursive developments of centre-right parties. Finally, it discusses the position of the centre-right as far as government formation is concerned.

2. The 'Centre-Right' in the Netherlands and Key Electoral Developments

In contemporary Dutch politics, two parties can unmistakably be considered centre-right parties: the Christian democratic CDA and the conservative-liberal VVD. D66, at least as far as its position on socioeconomic positions is concerned, may also be considered a centre-right party. The party is comparable to the UK's Liberal Democrats in terms of its ideological positions. In addition, its participation in eight governing coalitions to date arguably attests to its 'mainstream' character. Yet, in terms of origin and founding principles, D66 is more an exponent of the silent revolution than a traditional centre-right mainstream party. Its current positions on issues such as gender equality, LGBTQ rights and euthanasia also place the party clearly on the 'progressive' side of the sociocultural debate. Dutch parties that are, on the other hand, clearly culturally conservative are the Christian Union (*ChristenUnie*; CU) and the Reformed Political Party (*Staatkundig Gereformeerde Partij*; SGP). The latter party, in particular, adheres to orthodox Protestant values and has long opposed active participation of women in politics. The SGP has remained a marginal electoral force and never joined a governing coalition, although it has in recent years provided ad-hoc parliamentary support when the government lacked a parliamentary majority in the lower house (*Tweede Kamer*) and/or Senate (*Eerste Kamer*). The CU, on the other hand, has been in government with CDA and PvdA between 2007 and 2010, and also joined the four-party coalition which emerged from the 2017 election (alongside the VVD, CDA and D66). Following the conceptual framework of this volume and given their 'niche' character, however, neither the CU nor the SGP are typical 'centre-right' parties, and are therefore excluded from further consideration.

When we consider the electoral strength of the Dutch centre-right, the Christian democrats have long been the largest party family in the Netherlands, while the VVD was traditionally the third largest electoral force behind the centre left PvdA. As Figure 8.1 indicates, two of the traditional mainstream party families (the Christian democrats and social democrats) have experienced serious electoral setbacks in recent years. This is part of a longer-term process: as in other West European countries, processes of economic change and secularization eroded the natural support base of these party families. A variety of new parties gained parliamentary representation from the late 1950s onwards. In the case of the Christian democrats, electoral decline was already under way in the 1960s. Despite a few modest revivals in the 1980s and early 2000s, the general trend has been unmistakably downward, and the Christian democrats have lost their dominant position. While the electoral trajectory of the PvdA is marked by a less evident long-term decline, the party suffered a devastating loss in the 2017 election, receiving merely 5.7 per cent of the vote. The party bounced back in the May 2019 European elections with 19 per cent of the vote, benefiting from its high-profile *Spitzenkadidat*, Frans Timmermans (Ipsos 2019a: 11). Yet in national parliamentary elections, the VVD has been the only

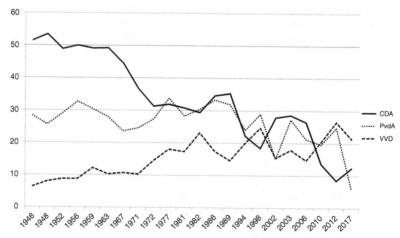

Figure 8.1 Vote share of three traditional mainstream parties

traditional mainstream party to extend its support in recent years, even becoming the largest party from 2010 onwards.

Where the mainstream parties saw an erosion of their collective support in recent years, D66 and the Greens – parties with a culturally liberal silent revolution profile – performed well in the parliamentary election of 2017 (see Table 8.1). In comparison with previous contests, the Greens also extended their support in the March 2019 provincial elections (10.8 per cent of the nationwide vote),[2] as well as the European Parliament elections two months later (10.9 per cent of the vote). D66, on the other hand, suffered losses in both elections, with 7.8 and 7.1 per cent of the vote, respectively.

The rise (and fall) of parties associated with the silent counter-revolution has been more spectacular. The populist (radical) right has established itself as a regular part of the Dutch political landscape ever since the election of 2002. In February of that year, former sociology professor Pim Fortuyn founded the LPF after being expelled from another newly founded party. Fortuyn's political programme was characterized by a populist anti-establishment message, economic liberalism, and restrictive positions on immigration and cultural integration (Lucardie and Voerman 2012; van Kessel 2015). The LPF's positions on the latter issues were relatively moderate in comparison with PRR parties in other countries, leading some scholars to classify the LPF as a 'neoliberal' populist party (e.g., Mudde 2007). After Fortuyn's assassination, nine days prior to the 2002 election, the LPF secured an unprecedented victory for a newcomer, winning 17 per cent of the vote, and the political heirs of Fortuyn went on to join a short-lived government. Without Fortuyn, however, the party lacked appealing leadership, and continuous infighting contributed to the party's electoral demise (de Lange and Art 2011).

When the LPF disappeared from parliament in 2006, its position on the populist right was filled by the PVV of Geert Wilders, a former MP for the VVD. A party strictly controlled by its leader, the PVV was initially similar to the LPF in terms of ideological and populist profile. Over the years, Wilders notably radicalized his discourse on Islam and European integration – since 2012, the PVV has even proposed ending Dutch EU membership (Vossen 2017; Pirro and van Kessel 2018). While the PVV grew to be the dominant PRR force in the

---

[2] Provincial elections also determine the composition of the Dutch Senate.

Table 8.1 *Dutch parliamentary election results, 1989–2017, in % of the vote*

Party	1989	1994	1998	2002	2003	2006	2010	2012	2017
Christian Democrats (CDA)	35.3	22.2	18.4	27.9	28.6	26.5	13.6	8.5	12.4
Social democrats (PvdA)	31.9	24.0	29.0	15.1	27.3	21.2	19.6	24.8	5.7
Liberals (VVD)	14.6	20.0	24.7	15.4	17.9	14.7	20.5	26.6	21.3
Democrats 66 (D66)	7.9	15.5	9.0	5.1	4.1	2.0	7.0	8.0	12.2
GreenLeft (GL)	4.1	3.5	7.3	7.0	5.1	4.6	6.7	2.3	9.1
Christian Union (CU)	2.2[*]	3.1[*]	3.3[*]	2.5	2.1	4.0	3.2	3.1	3.4
Reformed Party (SGP)	1.9	1.7	1.8	1.7	1.6	1.6	1.7	2.1	2.1
Centre Democrats (CD)	0.9	2.5	0.6						
Socialist Party (SP)	0.4	1.3	3.5	5.9	6.3	16.6	9.8	9.7	9.1
List Pim Fortuyn (LPF)				17.0	5.7	0.2			
Freedom Party (PVV)						5.9	15.5	10.1	13.1
Forum for Democracy (FvD)									1.8
Others	0.8	6.2	2.4	2.4	1.3	2.7	2.4	4.8	9.8

Data: Döring and Manow (2019).

[*] The percentage for the Christian Union (CU) prior to 2002 is the combined percentage of two Protestant parties that merged in 2000.

Netherlands for over a decade, the modest breakthrough of the FvD in 2017, and its steady growth in opinion polls afterwards, indicated there was space for an additional family member and suggested Wilders' political shelf life might be coming to its end. Indeed, with 14.5 per cent of the vote, FvD outperformed the PVV (as well as all other parties) in the March 2019 provincial elections. Wilders' party received less than 7 per cent. In the May 2019 European Parliament elections, FvD finished fourth with almost 11 per cent of the vote, well ahead of the PVV (3.5 per cent), which suffered a large defeat. In terms of style, FvD figurehead Thierry Baudet, who holds a doctorate in law, has made an effort to present himself as an intellectual well-versed in Latin, political philosophy and other highbrow areas. In this regard, he distinguished himself from Wilders, who is known for his cruder hard-hitting rhetoric. In addition to its nativist and hard Eurosceptic positions, which are broadly comparable with those of the PVV, the FvD has also called for democratization in order to break the traditional 'party cartel' supposedly (mis)ruling the Netherlands.

Although a variety of 'new' parties have eaten into the vote share of traditional parties, the mainstream right has retained an important place in the increasingly fragmented Dutch party landscape. Certainly, the CDA is a shadow of its former self and has achieved historically dismal results in recent years, but it was one of the winners of the 2002 earthquake election, and the largest party until 2010. The VVD, meanwhile, has arguably experienced its heyday in the past decade. This suggests that centre-right and PRR parties may flourish in tandem – at least when their results are compared with the left-wing 'bloc' (Bale 2003), which has traditionally found it hard to gain a majority in the Netherlands.

3. The Demand Side: Electoral Interchange and Voter Profiles

In addition to the fragmentation of the Dutch party system, voting behaviour has become increasingly volatile. The decline of traditional cleavages meant that citizens' social background became an increasingly poor predictor for voting behaviour, at least as far as support for the traditional mainstream parties is concerned (Andeweg and Irwin 2009). Aggregate volatility levels have also reached record highs in the past decades (Mair 2008): party identification has weakened and voters are increasingly inclined to alter their vote choice from election to election (Otjes 2018). It is going too far to claim, however, that the Dutch electorate has become entirely footloose: voters tend to switch between relatively like-minded parties, and most vote-switching can therefore be characterized as 'bounded' or 'bloc' volatility (van der Meer et al. 2012).

More specifically, in recent years, most voters considered voting for parties within partially overlapping and roughly defined, 'left-wing' (SP, PvdA, GL, D66), 'right-wing' (PVV, VVD, CDA, D66) and religious (CDA, CU, SGP) blocs (van der Meer et al. 2012; Otjes 2018). Given D66's economically liberal ('right-wing') and culturally liberal ('left-wing') position, it has been able to attract voters from the left-wing bloc, as well as former CDA and VVD – but not PVV – supporters. There has also been a limited degree of interchange between the PVV and the radical left Socialist Party (*Socialistische Partij*; SP), which both share anti-establishment, Eurosceptic and welfare chauvinist positions. There is, on the other hand, little evidence suggesting that the PVV has been able to attract a large share of former PvdA supporters. Indeed, a study by de Lange, Harteveld and Rooduijn (2018) found that, in 2017, the PvdA primarily lost voters to the 'cosmopolitan' parties GL and D66, followed by the SP, and then the mainstream right parties VVD and CDA. Under 6 per cent of PvdA defectors opted for the PRR. Generally speaking, then, centre-right parties and radical right parties have been fishing in a similar electoral pond, although D66 acted as an alternative for less culturally conservative centre-right voters. In line with this observation, a survey by Ipsos (2019b: 17) showed that half of the supporters of the new PRR party FvD in the 2019 provincial elections had previously voted for a different right-wing party in the 2017 parliamentary election: 31 per cent voted PVV, 15 per cent VVD and 10 per cent CDA.

When we consider voter profiles, a composite picture emerges. On the basis of Dutch Parliamentary Election Studies, Otjes (2018) provided an impression of different party supporters. In terms of socio-economic profile, PVV voters have more in common with PvdA and SP supporters, typical working-class parties. D66 and VVD, on the other hand, are typical 'middle-class parties'. In terms of positions on cultural issues, however, PVV voters have more in common with CDA and VVD voters; all three parties attracted voters who favoured a restriction of immigration and multiculturalism. D66, PvdA, as well as GL, on the other hand, appealed to voters with culturally liberal views. Unlike the CDA and PvdA, which attracted pro-EU voters, populist right-wing parties in the Netherlands have won support from Eurosceptic voters. Finally, in contrast to the centre-right parties, the PVV has mobilized supporters who are against welfare state reform – which is consistent with the party's welfare chauvinist positions. When PVV supporters are compared with those who supported the PRR newcomer FvD, there is some evidence that the latter tend to be better educated, less sympathetic towards measures to reduce income inequality, less nativist, and more liberal concerning moral–cultural issues related to gender, marriage and family (Otjes 2020). On the basis of different data, Harteveld (2019) similarly observed the difference in education levels, but concluded that PVV and FvD voters are relatively similar in their negative attitudes towards, inter alia, immigration, Islam and European integration (see also Ipsos 2019b).

The above findings suggest that Dutch politics is marked by several dimensions that are relevant in explaining party support and voting behaviour. In particular, Dutch politics, like the politics of other European countries, is increasingly characterized by both a 'cosmopolitan–parochial' and an economic left–right divide (de Vries 2018b). When we consider voter exchanges, it becomes clear that, aside from those who previously abstained, most PRR votes have come from the two traditional centre-right parties: VVD, in particular, but also CDA. The next section discusses in more detail the positions the Dutch centre-right parties have taken on PRR signature issues in the past few decades.

4. The Supply Side: Mainstream Parties' Programmatic and Discursive Developments

PRR parties typically blame established parties for ignoring pressing societal problems, not least those related to immigration and multiculturalism. These issues have become increasingly salient in many West European countries, and the Netherlands is no exception. Aarts and Thomassen (2008: 217) found that issues related to minorities and refugees had gained in importance for many Dutch voters in the 1990s. It is not the case that centre-right parties in the Netherlands were completely unresponsive to voters caring about such issues. Although the far right – in the form of the CD – was ostracized during the 1990s, VVD leader Frits Bolkestein attracted controversy for voicing concern that minority groups' lack of cultural integration would threaten (secular) Western liberal achievements (Prins 2002). Furthermore, a study by van Heerden et al. (2013) found that, in the same decade, centre-right parties were already paying increased attention in their manifestos to immigration and integration. The position of the CDA, however, remained relatively generous in terms of admitting more immigrants. Moreover, prior to the election of 2002 – the year that saw the breakthrough of the LPF – most parties devoted less attention to immigration than they had in their previous electoral programmes. Only the VVD adjusted its manifesto prior to the election in response to Pim Fortuyn joining the electoral race (van Heerden et al. 2013: 127).

At this time, then, there was considerable scope for the populist right-wing argument that established parties failed to recognize citizens' concerns about immigration and the multicultural character of society. Following Pellikaan, van der Meer and de Lange (2007: 294), Fortuyn introduced a new 'cultural' line of political conflict which 'had been ignored by the political elite, but was highly salient to the electorate'. What is more, neither Fortuyn, nor Wilders and Baudet in later years, faced the same level of stigmatization that the Dutch radical right had faced in the past (van Kessel 2015; de Lange 2018). These conditions combined go a long way to explaining the somewhat belated breakthrough of the populist right in the Netherlands.

This breakthrough has had limited impact on mainstream party positions on the already established socioeconomic conflict dimension. The VVD has always adopted a laissez faire position on economic issues, whilst the CDA, in line with its Christian democratic ideology, has taken a more centrist stance. The Dutch populist right has supported entrepreneurship and favoured lower taxation; policies not genuinely at odds with those of the traditional centre-right parties. The PVV has become notably more positive about the Dutch welfare state over the years, adopting more explicit 'welfare chauvinist' rhetoric (Abts et al. 2021). Accordingly, Wilders came to cherish the welfare state but argued that it was under financial pressure due to the influx of undeserving welfare-scrounging foreigners, who ought to be excluded from benefits. On this specific issue – which brings together the themes of welfare and immigration – the Dutch centre-right actually moved towards the PVV (Schumacher and van Kersbergen 2016). In terms of their more general welfare state agenda, however, CDA and

VVD remained more 'welfare reformist', as opposed to the PVV, whose more recent position could better be described as 'anti-reform' (Otjes 2018).

The impact of the populist right in other areas was more noticeable. To use the words of van Kersbergen and Krouwel (2008: 400), 'the epicenter of political competition has shifted from economic or left–right issues to non-material issues such as national identity, immigration, asylum, law and order, and the future of European integration'. It therefore makes sense to concentrate specifically on how mainstream parties (re-)positioned themselves regarding more 'cultural' themes.

In the years since Fortuyn's breakthrough, the traditional centre-right parties, in particular, could be seen to take more restrictive immigration stances, and to adopt more 'monoculturalist' positions (van Kersbergen and Krouwel 2008; Oosterwaal and Torenvlied 2010; van Heerden et al. 2013). These shifts can safely be interpreted as a direct response to electoral competition, and a vote-seeking strategy on the part of centre-right mainstream parties hoping to 'lure back' voters from the populist right (Akkerman 2021). After the demise of the LPF, however, it was the PVV that managed to gain ownership of issues related to immigration and cultural integration (Lucardie and Voerman 2012: 166). It was also Wilders' party that placed most emphasis on these issues – not least in relation to the supposed threat of 'Islamization'.

While the PVV was free to take unambiguous anti-immigration and monoculturalist positions, mainstream right parties had to tread more carefully in order not to lose their more moderate voters (van Kersbergen and Krouwel 2008). In addition, the CDA, more so than the VVD, has faced internal disagreements about its ideological course and a potential accommodative strategy vis-à-vis the radical right in particular (van der Meer 2019; Valk 2020). Thus, neither CDA nor VVD copied the PVV's radical Islamophobic frames and proposals – outlined in a single-page manifesto for the 2017 election – to 'de-Islamize' the Netherlands, allow zero further asylum seekers and no further immigrants from Islamic countries, denaturalize and deport criminals with dual nationality, close all mosques and Islamic schools, and ban the Quran (PVV 2016).

Nevertheless, both traditional centre-right parties have taken restrictive positions on immigration in their 2017 parliamentary election manifestos (see Figure 8.2). The VVD considered the current

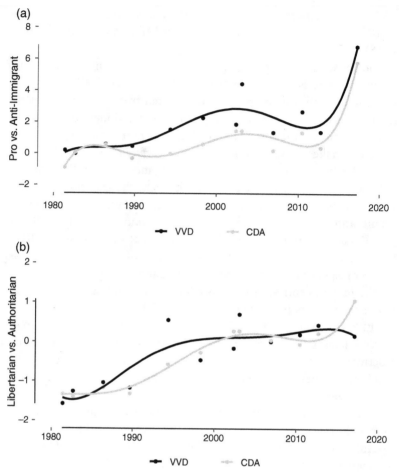

Figure 8.2 Dutch centre-right parties' movements on immigration; the cultural conflict dimension; traditional morality; and European integration, 1980–2017

migration system to be 'untenable', and proposed to keep refugees nearer to their country of origin (to provide 'shelter in the region') (VVD 2017a: 18–19). The party took a tough line on the need to deport immigrants who unsuccessfully applied for refugee status, and proposed to criminalize illegal residence, and the facilitation thereof. The CDA struck a less adversarial tone, showing compassion to those genuinely in need, but also stressed the need to provide shelter outside Europe to manage increasing 'migration pressure', and proposed

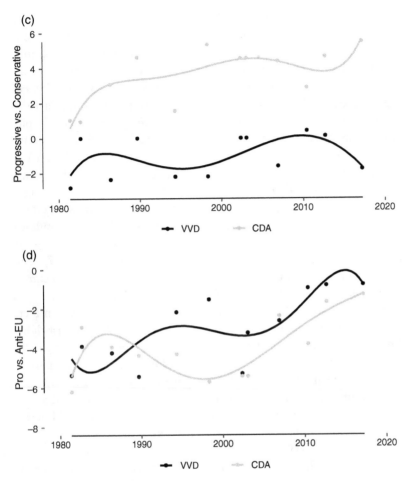

Figure 8.2 *cont.*
Notes: based on MARPOR data (Volkens et al. 2018). See Abou-Chadi and Krause (this volume) for the policy items that were used to calculate the scores. Higher values indicate, respectively, more anti-immigrant, authoritarian, conservative moral and anti-EU positions

a 'strict policy of admission and integration' for 'regular' migrants (CDA 2017: 39–40). Both VVD and CDA expressed concern about Islamic-extremist terrorism, though in much less alarmist terms than Wilders (and FvD leader Baudet).

Both centre-right parties also referred extensively to the need to protect Dutch norms and values. In the run-up to the 2017 parliamentary election, Prime Minister and VVD leader Mark Rutte wrote an open letter, published in Dutch newspapers, lamenting the abuse of liberty by people 'who came to our country precisely because of that freedom' (VVD 2017b). He urged those people to accept Dutch norms (to 'act normal') or to leave the country. In terms of symbolism, CDA leader Buma possibly found inspiration in previous PVV manifestos, proposing that schoolchildren should learn and sing the national anthem in class. It appears that both the VVD and CDA subscribed to the idea of a Dutch *Leitkultur* to which citizens, particularly those with a foreign background, are to adapt. The messages of the two centre-right parties were nevertheless framed somewhat differently, in line with their ideological roots. The CDA's 2017 manifesto emphasized the importance of 'values and traditions', and rejected indecency, indulgence and excessive individualism (CDA 2017: 7). The VVD, on the other hand, typically described Dutch values as being centred on liberalism and individual freedom (e.g., VVD 2017a: 6).

References to the 'liberal' character of Dutch society have, in fact, also been quite prominent in the discourse of the Dutch populist right. This appears peculiar at first sight, given that liberalism is typically associated with the values of the silent revolution, and not with parties that advocate monoculturalism. References to liberal values are not uncommon among PRR parties in (Northern) Europe, however, and it has been observed that such parties often rhetorically defend liberty, free speech and Enlightenment values, and even present themselves as guardians of LGBTQ rights and gender equality (Akkerman 2015a; Moffitt 2017). They appear to do so, however, mainly for instrumental reasons and as part of their anti-Islam discourse; Islam, in this context, is portrayed as a misogynistic and homophobic religion, incompatible with Western civilization. At the same time, whilst they often present themselves as defenders of freedom of speech, many PRR parties are quite happy to restrict the religious freedom of Muslims.

The Dutch case also presents us with populist right-wing parties characterized by such 'liberal illiberalism' (Moffitt 2017). Despite their rejection of anything they branded as 'left-wing', both the LPF and PVV placed notable emphasis on their presumed liberal principles (see van Kessel 2016; Vossen 2017). Pim Fortuyn, himself openly gay, supposedly had a personal motivation to stand up for LGBTQ rights. The LPF also voiced liberal ideas where gender equality was concerned, for instance in terms of labour market participation and equal pay, and supported legalization of certain recreational drugs. Like the LPF, the PVV also made explicit references to values of enlightenment, humanism and modernity (de Lange and Mügge 2015), but came to frame its 'liberalism' more exclusively in terms of its anti-Islam discourse. In its 2010 manifesto, for instance, 'Islamization' was argued to 'drive out Jews and gays, and flush the century-long emancipation of women down the toilet' (PVV 2010: 6). While Akkerman (2015a) found the PVV to be less conservative than other PRR parties in Europe on gender issues, these issues per se have never been very salient for Wilders' party (de Lange and Mügge 2015). The PVV's position on abortion has been ambiguous, and its parliamentary motion in June 2019 – which was supported by VVD and FvD – pleading for the reintroduction of 'grid girls' at the 2020 Dutch Formula 1 grand prix was hardly evidence of any feminist disposition on the party's part. The FvD's position on moral–cultural issues has been somewhat ambiguous, but party leader Baudet has attracted controversy on multiple occasions with misogynistic remarks, including in a review essay of Michel Houellebecq's novel *Sérotonine*, in which the emancipation of women was linked to the 'demographic decline of Europe' and other adverse societal consequences (Baudet 2019).

The position of Dutch populist right-wing parties on moral–cultural themes has thus been somewhat varied and ambiguous. Such issues, however, have not been very crucial in terms of electoral competition with the centre-right. The official positions of VVD and CDA on traditional morality are more clearly informed by their liberal and Christian democratic roots, respectively (see Figure 8.2). Liberal principles featured prominently in the introduction of the 2017 VVD manifesto: 'Our history is one of curiosity, of trade and guts. Of freedom of expression, freedom of religion and equal rights for gays and heterosexuals, already at a time when other countries in the world were not ready for that' (VVD 2017a: 6). The party has also taken liberal positions on the topics of euthanasia and abortion. The CDA struck a more conservative tone in these areas, and also proposed stricter anti-drugs policies. Its manifesto said little about specific LGBTQ and gender issues, though the party rejected discrimination on the basis of sex and sexual orientation, and noted that freedom in Dutch society implies 'respect for mutual differences, room for those with different opinions and the dignity of each human being' (CDA 2017: 16, 22).

Finally, European integration is a potentially relevant theme in terms of party competition between mainstream and PRR parties, given that the latter typically adopt pronounced Eurosceptic positions (see Meijers 2017). Both the LPF and PVV have expressed criticism of the European Union, and Wilders' Euroscepticism even took a hard turn in 2012. Since then, the PVV has proposed leaving the EU, which it described as a costly threat to national sovereignty, and an agent of multiculturalism and more immigration. Both VVD and CDA have voiced Eurosceptic arguments in recent years, taking a 'Europe where necessary' approach and, as was very visible during the Covid-19 crisis, opposing pan-European debt mutualization. Yet all Dutch mainstream parties remained far-removed from Wilders' hard-Eurosceptic position (see Figure 8.2). As a case in point, in a one-to-one televised election debate, VVD leader Rutte accused Wilders of acting irresponsibly by defending a Dutch withdrawal from the EU (NOS 2017). Only the FvD joined the PVV in voicing support for revoking Dutch EU membership, and attracting voters on the basis of this (Otjes 2020; see also van Kessel et al. 2020). After the election, the party's position became more ambiguous, and FvD downplayed its desire for a Dutch departure from the EU (a 'Nexit').

Ultimately, then, while centre-right parties in the Netherlands have moved closer to the ideological territory of the PRR, most likely driven by vote-seeking motives, they have not quite adopted its radical policy positions or framing regarding typical PRR issues such as immigration, Islam and European integration. This, however, does not need to stand in the way of cooperation in office, which invariably requires compromise and toning down campaign rhetoric. The following section focuses on the centre-right's lasting presence in office, and discusses further the (potential for) governmental cooperation between the centre-right and PRR.

5. The Dutch Centre-Right in Government

The centre-right has been a permanent feature of Dutch post-war cabinets. Prior to 1994, Christian democrats were always represented in government. Depending on election results and formation talks, Christian democratic parties ended up in coalitions including either the PvdA or, more often, the VVD. Between 1994 and 2002, the Christian Democrats were excluded from office for the first time, when their traditional adversaries PvdA and VVD twice formed a coalition that also included D66 (see Table 8.2). Yet also after the turn of the twenty-first century the CDA was in office more often than not (between 2002 and 2012, and since October 2017). In 2010, however, it was electorally overtaken by the VVD, which has provided the prime minister since then. Despite their dominance in office, centre-right parties were not always in the 'driving seat' in terms of coalition-building, and the formation of stable governments has become an increasingly challenging puzzle in recent years.

In terms of cabinet dominance, the centre-right was arguably weakest in the period of the PvdA-led Den Uyl government (1973–1977). In the preceding decade, the Christian democrats saw a steep electoral decline and in 1972 the PvdA received, for the first time, more votes than the Christian democratic parties combined. The Labour Party was subsequently able to form a coalition with two Christian democratic parties, in addition to two exponents of the silent revolution: D66 and the Political Party of Radicals (*Politieke Partij Radikalen*; PPR), a party founded by progressive former Christian democrats that would eventually merge into the Greens. The Den Uyl government is generally dubbed the 'most progressive' cabinet ever in Dutch history. Yet, even though D66 has become a regular coalition partner since, the silent revolution did not fundamentally alter competition for office, or break the dominance of the centre-right in this regard. Despite its 1977 electoral victory, the PvdA was relegated to opposition, and the Christian democrats would again take charge as the largest governing party until 1994. Between 1982 and 1989, two cabinets were formed consisting only of the CDA and VVD.

A Dutch government without at least one of the centre-right parties remains just as difficult to imagine in the twenty-first century. Nevertheless, the fragmentation of Dutch party politics has complicated the formation process: votes and parliamentary seats have in recent years been distributed among a relatively large number of medium-sized parties. The parliamentary election of 2017 provides a striking illustration: the largest party (VVD) gained no more than 21.3 per cent of the vote, followed by five parties with between 9.1 and 13.1 per cent. The mechanics of the Dutch electoral system dictate that seats are distributed almost in perfect proportion to the vote share, doing little to safeguard the position of traditional parties or to conveniently limit coalition options. In addition, not least because of the rise of new radical parties and the ideological repositioning of old ones, Dutch party competition has become more polarized and centrifugal, and the CDA has lost its traditional core position (Pellikaan, van der Meer and de Lange 2018). The above trends have contributed to party competition in the Netherlands becoming highly unstructured. The past decades have seen many so-called 'innovative' governing coalitions (Mair 2002), including parties that never governed before in the same configuration (see Table 8.2). That said, government alternation has always been 'partial': two of the three traditional party families have still been represented in every government (de Lange 2018).

Increased fragmentation has made mainstream parties more reliant on other parties to form parliamentary majorities. This also included, in two governing periods, populist right-wing parties. The silent counter-revolution has thus also left its mark on government formation in the Netherlands. Prior to the twenty-first century, the far right was excluded from office, due both to its electoral weakness and to its ostracization. Pim Fortuyn's rise was also met with considerable hostility from the side of most other parties. However, there was a broad consensus that the LPF deserved representation in government after its resounding electoral victory (de Lange 2018). CDA and VVD, whose policies and priorities were relatively similar to those of the LPF, were logical coalition partners from both an office- and policy-seeking perspective. The fact that the government would only last for eighty-seven days – thereby making it the shortest incumbent in Dutch history – was not so much caused by ideological differences as by continuous LPF infighting (de Lange and Art 2011; van Kessel 2015).

In the next two elections, the populist right's results were less impressive, but the 'return to normality' proved to be short-lived. In 2010, Geert Wilders' PVV came close to the initial vote share of the LPF, making the party hard to ignore in the subsequent coalition-formation process. By this time, critical opinions about Islam and multiculturalism had become normalized, and excluding parties was generally seen as counterproductive and anti-democratic (de Lange 2018). The 2010 coalition-formation process was complicated nevertheless; after several rounds of negotiations, the VVD and CDA formed a minority coalition that relied on the parliamentary support of the PVV. Collaboration with the PVV proved to be a bone of contention for many CDA members in particular. The centre-right parties therefore shunned a fully fledged coalition with the PVV for ideological reasons; notably, they refused to acknowledge the PVV's position that Islam was an 'ideology' rather than a religion. The three parties also agreed to

Table 8.2 *Cabinets in the Netherlands from 1989*

Start date	Name	Composition
7 November 1989	Lubbers III	CDA; PvdA
22 August 1994	Kok I	PvdA; VVD; D66
3 August 1998	Kok II	PvdA; VVD; D66
22 July 2002	Balkenende I	CDA; LPF; VVD
27 May 2003	Balkenende II	CDA; VVD; D66
7 July 2006	Balkenende III	CDA; VVD
2 February 2007	Balkenende IV	CDA; PvdA; CU
23 February 2010	Balkenende V	CDA; CU
14 October 2010	Rutte I	VVD; CDA
5 November 2012	Rutte II	VVD; PvdA
26 October 2017	Rutte III	VVD; CDA; D66; CU

Source: based on Otjes (2018).
Notes: Balkenende III and V were minority caretaker governments. Rutte I relied on the parliamentary support of the PVV

disagree on policies related to European integration. Nevertheless, the two centre-right parties' office-seeking inclinations once again resulted in collaboration with the populist right.

While the minority coalition proved to be more durable than the short-lived right-wing coalition of 2002, it would also come apart prematurely. In April 2012, Wilders refused to sign up to newly drafted austerity measures in response to the economic crisis, and withdrew his support from the coalition. This triggered new elections, in which the PVV suffered a loss and returned to opposition. What is more, Wilders' party also appeared to have isolated itself in the longer run: all the main contenders in the 2017 parliamentary election ruled out forming a coalition with the PVV. The official reason was Wilders' continued use of polarizing and xenophobic language. It is also likely that personal relationships had soured and trust had waned after the 2012 cabinet crisis, reducing the appetite among CDA and VVD for future collaborations with the PVV. Given that the VVD ruled out collaboration with Wilders' party at a relatively late stage, it has also been suggested that strategic vote- and office-seeking consideration were at play (Akkerman 2021). For a long time, pre-election polls indicated the PVV was vying (with the VVD) to become the largest party. By excluding the PVV, the VVD arguably hoped to win the horse race, attracting potential PVV voters who would rather vote for a party with a greater chance of ending up in office, as well as voters eager to prevent Wilders' party from finishing first.

The PRR party family may, however, earn a seat in Dutch government again one day, even if 'silent revolution parties' like D66 and, potentially, the Greens are more palatable partners for the Dutch mainstream. Given the profound fragmentation of Dutch party politics, it becomes increasingly difficult to form coalitions without including parties outside the traditional mainstream. The coalition formed in 2017 is a case in point: the collaboration of no less than four parties – with evident ideological differences – was required to secure a parliamentary majority. Such awkward partnerships are unlikely to contribute to the stability of Dutch politics, and potentially fuel further PRR success when sympathizers feel the 'establishment' is colluding and excluding populist challengers at all costs.

Recent developments at the subnational level have, in fact, illustrated the continued coalition potential between mainstream and radical right. In April 2020, CDA, VVD, FvD and a local party agreed to jointly form the provincial executive of Noord-Brabant. Both PVV and FvD politicians were already represented in neighbouring Limburg's 'extra parliamentary' executive. As in 2010, these collaborations sparked more of a debate within CDA ranks than among VVD members and figureheads (Valk 2020). This once more suggested that seeking office by coalescing with the radical right appears a more controversial strategy for the Christian Democrats than for the conservative-liberals. History does not repeat itself, but it often rhymes.

6. Conclusion

As in many other West European countries, Dutch mainstream parties have collectively seen an erosion of their electoral support. This development is related to the silent revolution, which notably hit the

Christian democrats in the 1960s and 1970s, as well as the silent counter-revolution and the associated rise of right-wing populist parties. At the same time, however, the centre-right VVD experienced its electoral heyday in recent years, and became the largest party in parliament after the three subsequent elections since 2010. It is important, however, not to overestimate its recent strength: the Dutch party system has become so fragmented that the question of 'who finishes first' is increasingly irrelevant. Given that voters also easily switch to ideologically like-minded parties, Dutch parties need to work hard to retain their electoral base.

Recent elections have shown that many voters can be swayed by 'silent revolution parties' with a liberal sociocultural agenda, such as D66 and the Greens, and 'silent counter-revolution' parties, like the PVV and FvD, expressing discontent with immigration and multiculturalism. The latter have recently left the greatest mark on the positions and discourse of centre-right parties. It is safe to assume that the electoral pressure from populist right-wing parties has inspired the centre-right competitors, VVD and CDA, to take a more nationalist and immigration-sceptic turn (see Abou-Chadi and Krause 2020). We can see the clearest influence of the populist right when we consider mainstream parties' shifts on issues related to immigration, cultural diversity and, albeit to a lesser extent, European integration. Socioeconomic policies and issues related to traditional morality have played less of a role in present-day party competition between mainstream and radical right.

Given that they face the greatest electoral competition from PRR contenders, the VVD and CDA have consciously aimed to woo voters sceptical about immigration and multiculturalism. For the VVD, this vote-seeking strategy may have worked out relatively well in the short run, but the party cannot afford to move too sharply to the cultural right if it seeks to retain more culturally liberal supporters who might otherwise be tempted to defect, for instance, to D66. For the CDA, the increased focus on national traditions and values seems to have done little to stem its long-term decline, and not all of its members are content with the shift towards PRR ideological territory. What is more, populist radical right parties have hardly disappeared as a result of the accommodative strategies of the Dutch mainstream right; instead, the latter have contributed to the normalization of at least parts of the PRR agenda. The Dutch case suggests, therefore, that accommodative strategies of mainstream parties do not automatically lead to a vote loss for the insurgent parties (cf. Meguid 2008; Krause, Cohen and Abou-Chadi 2019; Spoon and Klüver 2020). Moreover, both centre-right parties will have to consider whether seeking support from potential PVV and FvD supporters makes legitimizing the PRR's agenda, and venturing too far from their ideological origins, worthwhile.

For the moment, the Dutch centre-right remains a permanent feature of governing coalitions. It is typically in the driving seat as far as the quest for 'office' is concerned, although the participation of the Christian Democrats has become much less certain than before. Yet the ongoing fragmentation of the Dutch party system has meant that the inclusion of non-traditional parties is required in order to obtain workable parliamentary majorities. D66 has become a regular feature of Dutch cabinets, but the populist right has also been involved in two governments, once as a full coalition member (LPF, 2002–2003) and once providing parliamentary support for a VVD–CDA minority government (PVV, 2010–2012). If the centre-right parties stick to their accommodative strategies, and if they are keen to prevent awkward partnerships, we may indeed see more coalitions between them and the PRR in the future. Indeed, developments after the March 2019 provincial elections showed that both the VVD and CDA can still be tempted to partner up with the PRR – although internal opposition to this within the CDA remains considerable.

At the time of writing, following the March 2021 general election, the prospects of a collaboration of a similar kind at the national level appear relatively slim. The CDA and VVD have both signalled their reluctance to engage in a new coalition with the PVV or FvD. The Covid-19 crisis has instigated a seemingly durable 'rally around the flag' effect, and a surge of Prime Minister Rutte's VVD in opinion polls. It is unclear how much political capital the PVV and FvD have gained by criticizing the government's imperfect response to the crisis. The pandemic has also decreased the salience of their core sociocultural themes. Irrespectively, the Dutch PRR parties retained their combined popularity. Several months ahead of the election, the electoral landscape in fact looked similar to the one of four years before. In the course of 2020, the PVV had again surged in opinion polls, at the cost of FvD. The latter party suffered from severe intra-party disagreements and defections, and there surfaced evidence of widespread racist attitudes and discourse within the FvD youth branch and amongst senior FvD politicians, including Baudet himself. Nevertheless, both parties returned to the lower house in March 2021. For the foreseeable future, then, Dutch politics will continue to bear witness to all the complexities of the relationship between mainstream and radical right.

9 Spain: The Development and Decline of the Popular Party[1]

SONIA ALONSO AND BONNIE N. FIELD

1. Introduction

The main argument of this book is that the mainstream right in Western Europe is under pressure from two primary trends: the silent revolution (Inglehart 1977) and the silent counter-revolution (Ignazi 1992). This holds true for the Spanish case, but there are some important peculiarities one has to consider to better understand the evolution and fate of the Spanish mainstream right. Spain was not immune to the societal changes that Inglehart predicted. Yet these changes were not an obstacle to Spain's mainstream right party, the *Partido Popular* (Popular Party; PP), becoming hegemonic on the right for a quarter of a century. The party moderated to capture centrist voters in the 1990s without losing far right voters and did not face competition from a far right party until recently. First, it confronted a new challenger on the centre-right, *Ciudadanos* (Citizens; Cs), which entered parliament in 2015, then on the far right, from *Vox*, in 2018.

Today, in 2020, PP is severely weakened and ideologically sandwiched between two right-wing party challengers. It now confronts dilemmas similar to those of many of its European counterparts. Instead of a straightforward story explained by demand or supply, PP's decline (and political fragmentation) is due to a favourable opportunity structure for the rise of new parties – one related to the Great Recession, political corruption and the push for independence in Catalonia. In this context, PP was unable to retain the diverse electorate that had previously stood it in such good stead.

[1] This research was partly funded by the Qatar Foundation/GUQ-sponsored Faculty Research Grant. We thank Matthias Scantamburlo for his invaluable research assistance.

The party's initial response to the rise of the far right was to move rightward and accommodate *Vox* as a potential, then actual, ally. PP prioritized governing, where possible, in the short term, while retaining the hope that it could reunite the political right under its leadership over the longer term. PP's willingness to ally with Citizens and *Vox* allowed it to govern in several regions in 2019, including in the populous regions of Madrid and Andalusia, at a time of severe electoral decline. It is too early to assess whether PP will successfully adjust to the new competitive environment. Its performance in the April 2019 parliamentary elections was its worst since the 1970s. With stiff competition on the right, PP regained some lost electoral ground in the new parliamentary elections in November 2019. Yet the challenge of the silent counter-revolution heightened; those same elections catapulted the far right *Vox* to prominence, making it the third largest party in Spain.

2. The Silent Revolution in Spain

With Spain's transition to democracy in the late 1970s, political parties encountered a society that was changing. Having lagged behind its Western European neighbours in economic and social modernization, the transformation of Spain between 1978 and 2019 was dramatic. It became a service-based economy, with 76 per cent of the workforce employed in services in 2018, compared with 43 per cent in 1978.[2] The infant mortality rate declined nearly fivefold, to 3 per cent. Life expectancy increased by eight years for women and nine for men, to eighty-six and eighty years, respectively. The place of women in society changed fundamentally. Women with higher education degrees increased threefold, from 10 per cent in 1978 to 37 per cent in 2018. Female labour force participation grew from 28 per cent in 1978 to 53 per cent in 2018 (the EU average was 66 per cent in 2017, according to Eurostat). The age at first marriage increased from twenty-four years in 1978 to thirty-three years in 2018. The number of children per woman also fell from 2.54 to 1.31, while the age at which women had their first child increased from twenty-five to thirty-one.

Spain's deep and relatively rapid transformation may help to account for why the prevalence of post-materialist values began to match that seen in other Western European countries. Inglehart's four-item

---

[2] All data in this paragraph come from Spain's National Institute for Statistics.

materialist–post-materialist index shows that Spanish citizens were comparatively materialist at the beginning of democracy but by the first half of the 1990s had reached the Western European average.[3] The silent revolution had arrived in Spain (Torcal 1989; Díez 1994).

Nonetheless, there is variation across the value areas that constitute the post-materialist dimension. Regarding moral values, including attitudes towards homosexuality, abortion, divorce and gender equality, Spaniards have been comparatively tolerant and progressive since the early days of democracy in the 1980s, and they have only grown more so, as European and Spanish survey data consistently show.[4] Secularization also changed behaviour and attitudes dramatically.[5] In 1979, nearly 89 per cent of Spaniards defined themselves as Catholic; in 2018, only 68 per cent did so.[6] Church attendance also declined from levels that were already quite modest.[7]

In contrast, environmentalist and anti-immigration attitudes among the population increased in the late 1990s and early 2000s.[8] Yet no significant Green or far right party emerged (Alonso and Rovira Kaltwasser 2015). Instead, the existing parties absorbed these preferences. In the 2000s, *Partido Socialista Obrero Español* (Spanish Socialist Workers' Party; PSOE) emphasized post-materialist issues and the Rodríguez Zapatero government approved several measures, including same-sex marriage and adoption, a sweeping gender equality act, a law that made divorce easier and reformed education law to remove religion as an obligatory course, among others (Encarnación 2009; Field 2009). And PP took a harder line on immigration (Alonso and da Fonseca 2012). Comparatively speaking, however, Spaniards' attitudes towards immigrants were, and still are, highly tolerant.

The intensity of Spanish nationalism among Spaniards has declined over time. Yet national identity issues were (and are) prevalent and often dominant in party competition. Asked how proud they were of being Spanish, 91 per cent of respondents to a 1987 CIS survey answered that they felt very or quite proud; only 7 per cent said that they were not proud at all or only a little proud. These numbers

---

[3] GESIS Study No. ZA4804 v. 3, available at: https://europeanvaluesstudy.eu.
[4] 1987 Special Eurobarometer 'Men and Women in Europe'; 1993 Special
     Eurobarometer 'Europeans and the family'; European Values Studies, waves 1–4;
     CIS series: F.1.06.02.001, F.1.07.01.001.
[5] CIS series: F.1.03.01.001–009.   [6] CIS series: F.1.04.01.007.
[7] CIS series: F.1.04.01.004.   [8] CIS series: E.4.01.04.025–038.

have consistently decreased ever since. In 2016, 79 per cent of respondents were very or quite proud while 17 per cent said they were not or were only a little proud. Other indicators are consistent with this picture.[9]

Ideologically, in the late 1990s and early 2000s, very large majorities placed themselves at and around the centre of the left–right scale (see Figure 9.1). In the 2010s, however, there has been a twofold increase in Spaniards identifying with the far left (as defined by positions 1–2 on a left–right scale) in comparison with the early 1980s, as well as a declining number of voters in the centre and centre left.[10] This shift presented more of a challenge for PSOE than for PP. And yet, new parties have emerged to the left of the Socialists and to the right of PP.

Thus, demand-side explanations of party system change cannot fully explain the evolution of party competition on the right. When space first opened up on the demand side for challengers to the right and the left of the mainstream parties, no serious challengers emerged and mainstream parties were able to absorb the public's changing preferences. In the second half of the 2010s, however, when immigration and environmentalism were not salient, when very large majorities held progressive moral values, when nationalist feelings were weaker, and

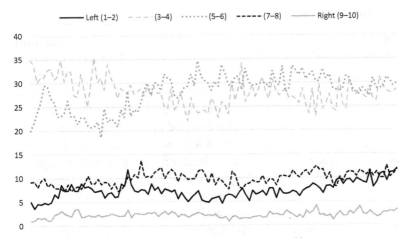

Figure 9.1 Spaniards' ideological positions, 1983–2019[11]

---

[9] CIS series: A.2.02.03.024–A.2.02.05.006.
[10] The only other time when the far left was as large was in March 1993.
[11] CIS series: A.3.06.01.004 From July 1983 to March 2019 (every March, July and December).

when the number of voters on the far left was four times greater than the number on the far right, two challengers on the right emerged and quickly attracted sizeable support. As Art (2011) demonstrated for other Western European countries, demand-side explanations are insufficient.

3. The Evolution of Party Competition on the Right

This section traces the Popular Party's competitive circumstances since Spain's re-democratization. During this period, the PP made a singular journey from a right-wing party tainted by its Francoist origins to a successful governing party that was hegemonic on the right: no other Western European party successfully pursued a similar trajectory. But things changed and that hegemony ended. Why? We argue that a series of crises changed the opportunity structure, leading to the success of new parties in the 2010s and helping to account for PP's decline. To do that, we divide the analysis into three stages: (1) PP's journey to the mainstream in the 1970s and 1980s; (2) its hegemony on the political right in the 1990s until 2015; and (3) the current scenario of tripartite competition on the right.

3.1 Mainstreaming a Party with Tainted Origins

The origins of the PP lie in a segment of the Francoist political elite who launched the right-wing *Alianza Popular* (Popular Alliance; AP) during Spain's transition to democracy in the mid-1970s (López Nieto 1988). During the 1970s and early 1980s, the more centrist *Unión de Centro Democrático* (Union of the Democratic Centre; UCD) dominated the political right. The UCD was also founded in part by a segment of the Francoist political elite, including Adolfo Suárez – the head of government during the transition. Yet moderates from the democratic opposition also joined in launching it. This gave it stronger democratic credentials than AP (Gunther, Sani and Shabad 1988: 96–8).

Because of its origins, rhetoric and political leadership, AP struggled to gain credibility as a mainstream party of the right (Gunther, Sani and Shabad 1988). In the 1970s, it averaged only 7 per cent of the vote compared with the UCD's 35 per cent. And those who most ardently opposed political liberalization joined the extreme right *Fuerza Nueva* or other, smaller far-right parties (Rodríguez 1994). *Fuerza Nueva* gained only one seat in parliament in 1979, as part of the National

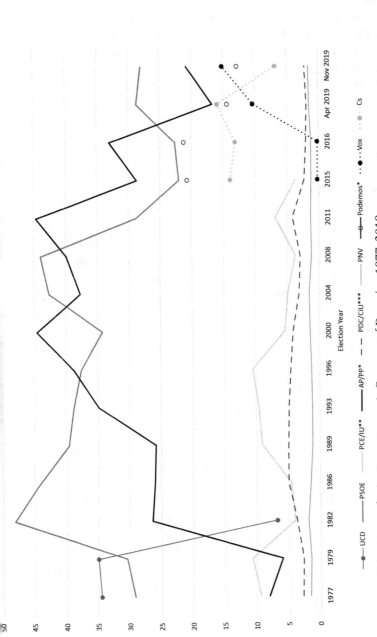

Figure 9.2 Election results (vote percentages), Congress of Deputies, 1977–2019

Party acronym key: AP (*Alianza Popular*); CDS (*Centro Democrático y Social*); CDC (*Convergència Democràtica de Catalunya*); CiU (*Convergència i Unió*); Cs (*Ciudadanos*); ERC (*Esquerra Republicana de Catalunya*); IU (*Izquierda Unida*); JxCat (*Junts per Catalunya*); PCE (*Partido Comunista de España*); PDC (*Pacte Democràtic per Catalunya*); PNV (*Partido Nacionalista Vasco*); PP (*Partido Popular*); PSOE (*Partido Socialista Obrero Español*); UCD (*Unión de Centro Democrático*); UN (*Unión Nacional*); UPyD (*Unión, Progreso y Democràcia*).

Notes: *Includes election allies. **Allied with Podemos in 2016. ***CDC in 2015, 2016; JxCat in 2019. Does not include other small parties.

Source: Ministry of Interior, Spain (valid votes).

Union (UN) alliance, which it lost in 1982 and never returned to parliament.

AP became the largest party on the right in 1982 when it benefited from the electoral collapse of the UCD. Hovering around 26 per cent of the vote, it took another decade for AP to become a serious electoral threat to the centre left PSOE. AP still struggled to convince a large share of the electorate that it was a party of the moderate right, despite considerable programmatic and leadership renewal (López Nieto 1988; Montero 1988). Moreover, during this period, it competed with centre-right parties, such as the *Centro Democrático y Social* (Social and Democratic Centre; CDS).

By the early 1990s, however, the party had transformed itself into a 'big tent', catch-all party. It incorporated the national, centre-right into the re-named Popular Party in 1989. It accomplished generational turnover of its leadership, with José María Aznar in 1990, and further moderated its electoral appeals (Ramiro-Fernández 2005; Astudillo and García-Guereta 2006). By this point, it was best characterized as a conservative party, combining rightist socioeconomic policies with conservative moral positions and nationalism. Instead of doctrinaire economic liberalism, PP under Aznar 'proposed a policy mix of liberal economic policies and sustainable welfare social policies' and developed a '"nationalistic" policy profile' (Astudillo and García-Guereta 2006: 411, 413), particularly in relation to Spain's peripheral national identities. That did not, however, prevent PP from being a staunch supporter of the European Union.

3.2 Popular Party Hegemony on the Right, 1990s–2015

Party competition in Spain occurs primarily along the left–right and centre–periphery (national identity) dimensions. Between 1990 and 2015, PP dominated on the right. It averaged 40 per cent of the vote, and won the elections for the first time in 1996. It governed between 1996 and 2004 under Aznar, and again between 2011 and 2018 under Mariano Rajoy. However, its hegemony was not absolute. The national right always competed with centre-right regional parties that advocate greater political autonomy and recognition of a distinct cultural or national identity. These parties have been the dominant mainstream parties in some regions, such as the Catalan CiU (*Convergència i Unió*) and the Basque PNV (*Partido Nacionalista Vasco*). In these and other regions, PP represents typically more right-wing and pro-centre positions, particularly with regard to

Spanish national identity (Alonso 2012). Nonetheless, PP was pragmatic when it needed political support to govern in minority, reaching agreements with centre-right peripheral nationalist parties, including CiU, PNV and the Canary Island Coalition (Field 2016).

During this period, new parties could take little encouragement from the prevailing political opportunity structure – defined as 'the degree of "openness" or "accessibility" of a given political system for would-be political entrepreneurs' (Arzheimer and Carter 2006: 422). Spain's electoral system for the Congress of Deputies tended to favour the large parties (PP, PSOE), discouraging challengers and encouraging voters to vote strategically. Public financing of parties and elections tied to parliamentary representation also favoured insiders. The Popular Party had a large membership base, which doubled between 1989 and 1996 (Astudillo and García-Guereta 2006: 407), as well as a significant institutional presence at the local, regional and national level, which provided organizational, media and patronage benefits. Aznar, as party leader, also built a cohesive and efficient party organization (Ramiro-Fernández 2005; Astudillo and García-Guereta 2006). While Spain and PP certainly faced challenges, it was, generally speaking, also an era of social and economic progress. Party challengers that emerged, such as *Unión, Progreso y Democracia* (Union, Progress and Democracy; UPyD) and Citizens gained little traction.

3.3 Crises and New Challengers on the Right, 2015–2019

The opportunity structure for the success of new parties began to change in the 2010s because of three interrelated developments: the Great Recession; a series of political corruption scandals; and the push for independence in Catalonia. Satisfaction with democracy and trust in political institutions plummeted – only 22 per cent of Spaniards indicated they were satisfied with democracy in 2013, down from 77 per cent in 2007.[12] This would have enormous consequences for Spanish mainstream parties, left and right. Focusing on the political right, the crises opened a window for challengers, first from the centre-right Citizens and then from the far right *Vox*.

After Greece, Spain was probably the West European country hardest hit by the 2008 financial crisis, and the subsequent sovereign

---

[12] Eurobarometer data.

debt crisis.[13] Using World Bank data, the GDP annual growth rate of 3.8 per cent in 2007 declined to 1.1 per cent in 2008, and turned negative in 2009 (–3.6 per cent). Growth would not return until 2014. Per capita income fell nearly 9 per cent in real terms between 2007 and 2010, and nearly 22 per cent of households fell below the poverty line in 2011, among the highest proportions in Europe (Field and Botti 2013). Inequality increased. Spain's GINI index increased from 34 in 2008 to 36 in 2013, according to the World Bank. Unemployment reached 26 per cent in 2013, according to Eurostat. In 2018, Spain was at the same level of convergence with Western Europe as in 2003.

In 2011, the public punished PSOE, which was in power at the onset of the crisis and implemented austerity measures. This initially benefited PP, which won the elections and a majority in parliament. Once in power, however, the PP government of Mariano Rajoy only heightened austerity measures. Furthermore, a series of corruption scandals wracked Spain, several of which implicated the PP, the most prominent being the Gürtel case, which involved influence trafficking, illegal party financing, kickback and bribes. While known previously, in early 2013, the scandal exploded when newspapers published the PP party treasurer's secret ledgers that showed money coming in from business donors and payments to PP party leaders.[14] Five years later, in 2018, Spain's High Court legally sanctioned the party for benefiting financially from Gürtel, leading to a successful vote of no confidence in the Rajoy government.[15]

In the 2015 parliamentary elections, electoral support for PP dropped to 29 per cent from 45 per cent in the prior election. While PP was still the lead party, Citizens entered parliament with 14 per cent of the vote, attracting many former PP voters (Rodríguez and Barrio 2018). Cs placed itself in the centre of the left–right ideological spectrum, emphasized Spanish national identity (in opposition to peripheral nationalism), and campaigned for political renewal. The 2015 elections transformed a party system dominated by two main national parties to one comprising four: Podemos, PSOE, Citizens and PP.

---

[13] European Commission's *European Economy*, several issues.
[14] Francisco Mercado et al., 'Las cuentas secretas de Bárcenas', *El País*, 31 January 2013.
[15] Fernando J. Pérez, 'Governing Popular Party and its ex-treasurer, sentenced in massive corruption case', *El País*, 24 May 2018.

Unable to form a government, Spain held new elections in 2016, with broadly similar results. Studies demonstrate that economic and political dissatisfaction, particularly in relation to corruption, help to explain the transformation of the party system (see, e.g., Vidal 2018). While there is still debate about the precise impact of economic assessments on the vote for Citizens in 2015/16, the effect of political disaffection is clearer (Rodríguez and Barrio 2018; Vidal 2018).

Additionally, Catalan nationalists began calling for a referendum on independence from Spain, particularly after 2012. This came on the heels of a constitutional court ruling that declared aspects of Catalonia's 2006 autonomy law unconstitutional. Along with other regions, Catalonia's autonomy law had been revised during the Socialist government of PM Zapatero, which stressed post-materialist issues and centre–periphery relations. In 2006, PP had lodged a constitutional challenge against the autonomy law.

The independence push occurred while the PP governed Spain, and, between 2015 and 2018, while PP and Cs competed for hegemony in the Spanish nationalist identity space. The independence drive came to a head in 2017. In defiance of a court ruling, the Catalan government (in the hands of pro-independence parties) went ahead with an independence referendum – a decision which met with police repression. Based on the result of the referendum, boycotted by many opponents of a breakaway, the pro-independence parties in parliament declared independence. In response, the PP-led Spanish government, with support from Spain's Senate, temporarily suspended Catalonia's autonomy and disbanded the Catalan government and parliament. Several Catalan independence leaders were imprisoned, pending trial for charges including rebellion. The Spanish government's handling of the crisis generated a range of criticisms. To some, it was an authoritarian thug that had trampled on the legitimate rights of citizens. To others, particularly on the right, it was a weakling that had allowed the defiance of Catalan independence leaders to go too far, culminating in a 'coup' against Spain.

In this context, *Vox* made an electoral breakthrough in the 2018 regional elections in Andalusia, with 11 per cent of the vote. Based on an analysis of exit polls, *Vox* supporters were former PP voters (48 per cent), former Cs voters (21 per cent) and those who had previously abstained (10 per cent), with few of the party's supporters coming from former left party voters (Turnbull-Dugarte 2019). The same study found that individual support for *Vox* stemmed from political conflict related to the independence push in Catalonia and the central government's inability to solve it.

Vox went on to win 10 per cent of the vote in Spain's parliamentary election five months later in April 2019, and representation in numerous regional and local parliaments in elections the subsequent month. *Vox* emphasized Spanish nationalism – particularly in relation to Spain's own peripheral national identities and the independence push in Catalonia – the reversal of political decentralization, conservative values and rightist economic positions. *Vox* is staunchly anti-feminist, putting centre-stage its opposition to what the far right refers to as 'gender ideology'.[16] This challenges a convergence on gender equality of the two largest parties, PP and its stronger advocate, PSOE.[17] Similar to other European far right parties, it is nativist and anti-Islam. However, immigration and populism were less prominent than they are in many European far right parties (Anduiza 2018; Acha 2019).

New parliamentary elections, which took place in November 2019 after the failure to form a national government, allowed PP to recover some lost ground, increasing from 16.7 to 20.8 per cent of the vote. However, the perceived winner was *Vox*, whose vote share increased from 10.3 to 15.1 per cent and parliamentary representation from 6.9 to 14.9 per cent of seats. The major loser was Cs, which plummeted from 15.9 per cent of the vote to 6.8 per cent. Notably, the vote share for the national right and left did not change substantially – competition was mainly intra-bloc.

4. Hegemony on the Right: PP's Programmatic Offer and Voters, 1993–2011

The Popular Party became the hegemonic party on the right after moderating its programmatic offer, thereby attracting a wider spectrum of Spanish voters. By the early 1990s, PP had become a European-style conservative party capable of competing with the Socialist Party for the median voter. This section analyses separately the evolution of the party's programmatic offer and the enlargement of its voter pool.

---

[16] Luis Fernando López and Rafael J. Álvarez, 'Politólogos y sociólogos: "A Vox, el antifeminismo le funciona electoralmente; aún tiene margen"', *El Mundo*, 2 February 2019.

[17] Margarita León, 'El voto de las mujeres', *El País*, 5 February 2019.

4.1 The Offer: Political Moderation[18]

We examine PP's programmatic offer primarily using Manifesto Project data (Volkens et al. 2018), as well as the secondary literature.[19] Manifestos convey the party's policy promises to the citizens – the 'contract' on which the relationship of democratic representation is based. We compare the manifestos of PP and PSOE to contextualize PP's strategic positioning in the Spanish party system.[20] We show that partisan conflict was limited regarding the welfare state, fiscal consolidation, European integration and post-materialist values, in part because of PP's attempt to attract the median voter. Partisan conflict occurred, instead, around issues of national identity and political decentralization, though polarization was less visible during this period because of its lower salience.

In Spain's two-dimensional electoral space, all parties convey positions along the left–right and centre–periphery dimensions (Alonso 2012; Queralt 2012). The left–right dimension includes two main components, economic and sociocultural.[21] The centre–periphery dimension contains a territorial component related to issues of political

---

[18] Graphs in this section include the entire period of analysis. The discussion is limited to 1993–2011.

[19] Manifesto data are obtained from the manual content analysis of electoral manifestos. The text unit of analysis is the (quasi-)sentence. Every quasi-sentence of a manifesto is coded into one of fifty-six issue categories that refer to a wide variety of policy matters. The dataset calculates the percentage of each issue category over the total number of manifesto sentences. For more information on this methodology, please visit the project's website at: https://manifesto-project.wzb.eu/.

[20] In order to test the robustness of our findings, we also analysed party positioning based on the Chapel Hill Expert Survey (CHES, n.d.). The results did not differ in any substantive way.

[21] The left–right economic dimension is calculated as follows: first, all the left and all the right economic categories are added up to produce the overall saliency scores of economic left and right issues, respectively; second, the saliency score of left issues is subtracted from the saliency score of right issues; finally, the resulting figure is divided by the total saliency of both left and right issues ((right saliency – left saliency)/(right saliency + left saliency)). Theoretically, this position score ranges from –1 for a fully left manifesto to +1 for a fully right manifesto. Empirically, it goes from –1 to 0.19. The same calculation applies to the left–right sociocultural dimension, using only the sociocultural categories. Empirically, it goes from –0.83 to 0.70.

decentralization, and a cultural one, about cultural nationalism (Alonso 2012; Alonso, Gómez and Cabeza 2013).[22]

Left–right competition in Spain is more about social and cultural issues than economic ones. During the 1990s and 2000s, PP devoted three times more attention (salience) to sociocultural issues than to economic issues (Figure 9.3), PSOE likewise. PP manifestos dedicated around 10 per cent of their sentences to strictly economic issues, compared with 30–40 per cent that dealt with sociocultural ones, including moral issues. PP moved rightward on sociocultural values in 1996 and 2004; yet turned back leftward in 2000 and 2008 (Figure 9.4).

On economic issues, partisan conflict was limited. PP offered a centrist programme (Figure 9.3) to attract a wide spectrum of the electorate and thus maintain its electoral hegemony from the centre to the far right. This was conveyed through its pro-welfare stances and absence of anti-welfare ones. Between 7 and 12 per cent of PP manifesto sentences were dedicated to pro-welfare issues (the range in PSOE's manifestos was 11 and 16 per cent). There was little partisan conflict around the welfare state (Fernández-Albertos and Manzano 2012; Del Pino 2013). Regarding macro-economic policy, the degree of convergence across both parties was remarkable, at least from the early 2000s onwards (Royo 2009). Following the sovereign debt crisis of 2010, PSOE and PP agreed on an 'express' reform of the constitution to include fiscal consolidation as a constitutional duty of Spanish governments.

PP's moderation was also visible on topics related to post-materialism and European integration. The party gave moderate and positive attention to post-materialist issues (environmentalism, anti-militarism, gender equality, multiculturalism). Salience remained stable at between 7 and 10 per cent of manifesto sentences (twice as

---

[22] The centre–periphery territorial dimension is calculated as follows: first, all the pro-centre and all the pro-periphery territorial categories are added up to produce the overall saliency scores of the pro-centre issues and pro-periphery issues, respectively; second, the saliency score of pro-periphery issues is subtracted from the saliency score of pro-centre issues; finally, the resulting figure is divided by the total saliency of both pro-centre and pro-periphery issues ((centre saliency – periphery saliency)/(centre saliency + periphery saliency)). Theoretically, this position score ranges from –1 for a fully pro-periphery manifesto to +1 for a fully pro-centre manifesto. Empirically, it goes from –1 to 0.87. The calculation of the centre–periphery cultural dimension is the same, using cultural categories. Empirically, it goes from –1 to +1.

(a)

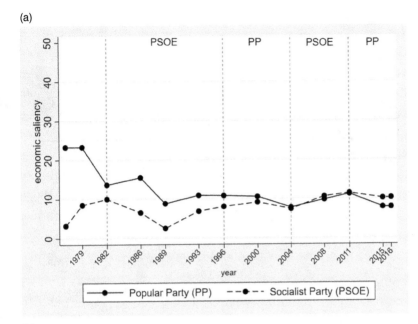

(b)

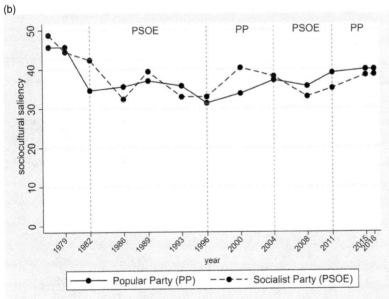

Figure 9.3 The salience of economic and sociocultural issues, PP and PSOE manifestos, 1979–2016 (% of sentences)

Notes: *Own calculation based on Manifesto categories and left–right categorization by Franzmann (2009).

*Vertical reference lines and party names at the top indicate the party in office.

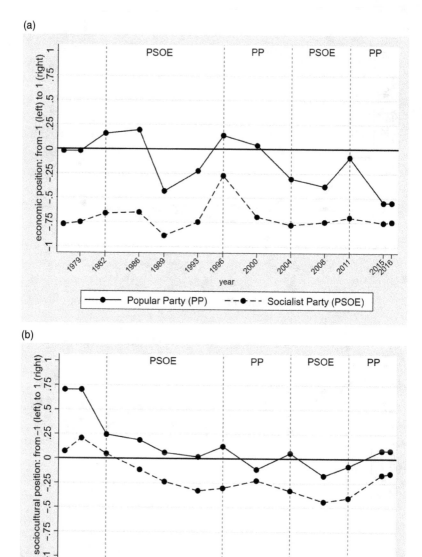

Figure 9.4 Economic and sociocultural left (negative) and right (positive) positions, PP and PSOE, 1979–2016
Notes: See notes, Figure 9.3.

much in PSOE's manifestos) until the 2008 elections, the mid-point of Socialist PM Zapatero's tenure (2004–2011), when both parties' attention to post-materialist issues peaked at 15 per cent, becoming more salient than economic issues. European integration was one of the most important policy agendas of Spain from the 1980s to the 2000s. Yet the entire political establishment agreed on this. PP was consistently and strongly pro-EU for the two decades under analysis.

The issue of immigration, for a few years, diverted PP from its moderation path. PP did not pay attention to or mobilize on it in the 1990s, when immigration was not prevalent in Spanish society. In 2000, however, and for the next five years, immigrants started to arrive in Spain in large numbers. The El Ejido events, where violent clashes occurred between immigrant workers and locals in this southern Spanish town shortly before the election, featured in the 2000 elections. PP used the riots to play the anti-immigration card for the first time in a national election (Zapata-Barrero 2003). This began a trend that continued in subsequent elections. Indeed, the party's most anti-immigrant manifestos were those produced for the 2004 and 2008 elections.

Yet partisan conflict was still more evident around the centre–periphery dimension, particularly Spanish nationalism vis-à-vis peripheral nationalisms (and, as shown earlier, immigration). Its relevance in the manifestos of PP and PSOE (between 1 and 2 per cent of PP manifesto sentences) might appear modest compared with the left–right dimension (Figure 9.5). However, aside from the fact that it is measured by including a smaller number of categories and therefore less salient by design, the centre–periphery dimension of competition had the potential to polarize Spanish partisan conflict (Orriols and Balcells 2012).

Indeed, examining the positions of PP and PSOE, there is a high level of polarization on this dimension (Figure 9.6). PP's programmatic moderation, so visible in all the previous issue dimensions, is less consistent here. After a decade of relative moderation in the 1990s, after 2004 it took a dramatic turn towards pro-centre positions on the territorial dimension, when PSOE, under PM Zapatero, returned to office. Previously, after 1996, when PP won the elections and governed for the first time, PSOE had repositioned itself towards the pro-periphery side of Spanish cultural nationalism. The result was a large gap between the parties on the territorial and cultural-national identity subdimensions (Figure 9.6). This

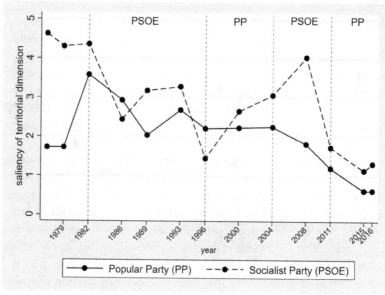

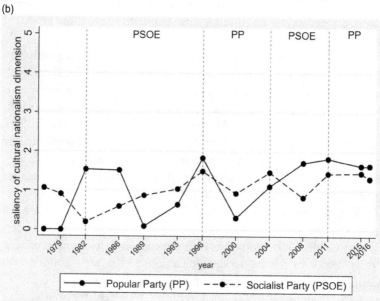

Figure 9.5 Salience of centre–periphery territorial and cultural nationalist issues, PP and PSOE manifestos, 1979–2016 (% of sentences)

Notes: *Own calculation based on Manifesto categories and centre–periphery categorization by Alonso (2012).

*Vertical reference lines and party names at the top indicate the party in office.

(a)

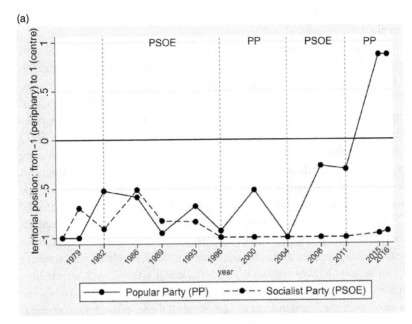

(b)

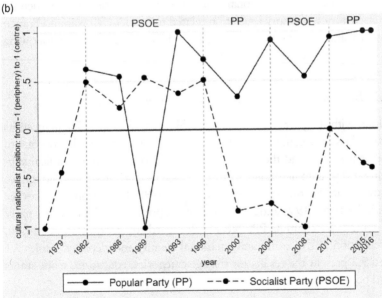

Figure 9.6 Pro-periphery (negative) and pro-centre (positive) territorial and cultural nationalist positions, PP and PSOE, 1979–2016
Note: See notes on Figure 9.5.

polarization would intensify after the emergence of credible challengers on the right.

Clearly, programmatic positioning and behaviour did not always match. This occurred particularly when PP was in opposition after 2004. Although the 2008 PP manifesto suggests a leftward turn on moral issues, PP had adamantly opposed the novel progressive social policy agenda of the Socialist government of PM Zapatero. This agenda focused on post-materialist issues, such as the promotion of gender equality and LGBTQ rights, and the regularization of some immigrants, as well as advocating policies with significant moral and religious content, such as stem cell research and removing religion as a compulsory subject in schools. The Socialist agenda met with fierce opposition from the Spanish Catholic Church, which regularly took to the streets in protest and voiced its concerns through aligned media outlets. While the Church's relationship with PP was complex and at times critical – indeed, Berrettini characterizes it as a 'tension between proximity and blackmail' – the Church nonetheless 'appealed for votes for the Popular Party' (Berrettini 2013: 169). The parties polarized around these issues, and those related to territorial accommodation (e.g., regional autonomy reforms) and national identity (e.g., historical memory legislation related to Spain's civil war and Franco dictatorship) – a polarization that would continue into the following decade (Encarnación 2009; Field 2009).

4.2 Becoming a Catch-all Party: PP Voters

Along with the party's moderation until the mid-2000s, PP enhanced its cross-class appeal, making inroads into the ideologically moderate voter of the centre-right and the centre left, without losing its more radical supporters. The data here come from CIS post-electoral surveys. Although we present data for the whole period (1993–2019), this section discusses the period between 1993 and 2011, the election prior to the change of the party system.[23] We examine PP voters with regard to age, gender, education, occupation, size of community, national identity and ideology. Tables 9.1 and 9.2 present the results for the age categories, education, work status and occupation.

---

[23] Election years: 1993 (CIS 2061), 1996 (CIS 2210), 2000 (CIS 2384), 2004 (CIS 2559), 2008 (CIS 2750), 2011 (CIS 2920), 2015 (CIS 3126), 2016 (CIS 3145).

Table 9.1 Age and education of PP voters compared with survey sample

	Age				Education				
	18–25	26–35	66–75	76+	No education	Primary	Secondary	Vocational	Higher education
1993	19.1 (18.6)	17.4 (20.3)	9.8 (11.0)	3.3 (4.0)	36.9 (22.2)	22.6 (46.0)	25.9 (15.8)	7.61 (9.0)	7.7 (6.5)
1996	17.6 (18.0)	18.2 (20.4)	11.5 (11.2)	4.8 (5.0)	12.5 (17.1)	29.0 (26.8)	33.1 (33.0)	8.6 (10.6)	16.5 (12.8)
2000	12.3 (16.0)	19.0 (20.0)	14.8 (13.3)	6.9 (6.0)	7.9 (9.3)	47.8 (45.0)	17.5 (16.8)	9.4 (11.9)	17 (16.7)
2004	10.4 (15.9)	16.7 (20.1)	17.2 (13.1)	7.7 (6.5)	12.1 (12.3)	44.6 (45.6)	14.4 (13.0)	12.2 (13.8)	16.7 (16.3)
2008	10.3 (12.2)	20.2 (20.4)	14.5 (11.9)	7.0 (7.8)	6.6 (8.6)	49.4 (47.0)	12.0 (11.9)	13.7 (15.6)	18.3 (16.7)
2011	9.1 (10.5)	16.5 (18.7)	14.3 (10.7)	9.1 (8.2)	6.0 (6.5)	50.8 (47.7)	12.6 (11.4)	14.05 (15.9)	16.6 (18.5)

Table 9.1 (*cont.*)

	Age				Education				
	18–25	26–35	66–75	76+	No education	Primary	Secondary	Vocational	Higher education
2015	4.6 (9.3)	7.5 (14.2)	**21.9** (12.6)	**16.9** (9.2)	**10.2** (7.2)	**24.6** (18.3)	33.6 (35.8)	13.3 (17.9)	17.8 (20.2)
2016	5.3 (9.7)	9.5 (14.3)	**20.4** (12.1)	**16.9** (10.0)	**9.3** (7.0)	**25.3** (18.3)	35.2 (37.2)	10.1 (16.1)	19.7 (21.2)
2019	3.3 (8.9)	9.8 (13.2)	**18.6** (13.3)	**17.9** (10.0)	**6.2** (5.7)	**22.5** (16.8)	33.0 (36.5)	15.0 (18.0)	23.1 (22.7)

* *Note:* In bold, over-represented categories among PP voters. Survey sample in parentheses.

Table 9.2 Work status and occupation of PP voters compared with survey sample

	Work status				Occupation						
	Retired	Unemployed	In education	Unpaid domestic work	Managers and professionals	Technicians	Small business	Agricultural workers	White-collar workers	Skilled blue-collar workers	Unskilled blue-collar workers
1993	15.3 (17.4)	7.5 (10.7)	10.5 (7.5)	23.4 (22)	4.6 (3.0)	6.1 (5.0)	8.3 (6.5)	2.4 (1.4)	7.6 (7.0)	6.4 (8.9)	3.4 (6.4)
1996	19.6 (20.6)	9.9 (12.8)	9.0 (7.3)	20.7 (19.9)	4.0 (2.5)	5.7 (5.8)	7.2 (5.6)	2.6 (1.5)	6.5 (6.5)	4.7 (6.9)	6.6 (6.9)
2000	27.2 (23.4)	6.1 (7.8)	5.5 (7.3)	19.1 (17.3)	3.9 (2.9)	5.5 (6.1)	5.9 (4.9)	1.5 (1.2)	8.5 (7.6)	6.0 (9.1)	7.6 (8.9)
2004	26.2 (22.2)	6.6 (8.3)	5.6 (6.3)	18.0 (15.3)	5.5 (3.7)	7.4 (7.5)	4.8 (4.3)	2.6 (1.4)	7.6 (9.1)	6.7 (10.3)	6.4 (9.5)
2008	25.6 (24.0)	7.3 (9.3)	4.0 (4.2)	12.8 (11.1)	7.0 (4.5)	8.0 (9.5)	5.2 (4.4)	1.3 (1.0)	7.5 (8.3)	9.8 (10.3)	9.4 (11.2)
2011	26.5 (23.6)	19.0 (19.7)	4.3 (4.8)	10.3 (8.8)	4.9 (3.6)	6.5 (8.6)	5.1 (4.1)	1.3 (1.1)	6.2 (6.9)	5.9 (6.7)	7.7 (9.8)

Table 9.2 (*cont.*)

	Work status				Occupation						
	Retired	Unemployed	In education	Unpaid domestic work	Managers and professionals	Technicians	Small business	Agricultural workers	White-collar workers	Skilled blue-collar workers	Unskilled blue-collar workers
2015	**41.5**	12.3	2.3	**10.3**	**4.4**	7.1	**4.2**	**1.5**	3.4	3.5	**8.2**
	(27.2)	(18.1)	(4.6)	(7.3)	(3.8)	(10.6)	(4.1)	(1.1)	(4.7)	(6.1)	(11.0)
2016	**39.1**	10.1	2.8	**11.4**	**4.5**	8.2	**4.5**	**1.7**	4.3	4.1	7.5
	(26.2)	(16.1)	(4.4)	(7.6)	(4.0)	(11.7)	(4.0)	(0.8)	(5.5)	(6.6)	(11.5)
2019	34.2	6.9	1.7	9.7	5.3	11.2	2.8	0.9	4.5	5.5	9.4
	(28.1)	(11.2)	(4.6)	(6.2)	(4.7)	(13.8)	(3.3)	(0.6)	(6.2)	(7.4)	(12.1)

* *Note:* In bold, over-represented categories among PP voters.

During the 1990s, PP incrementally attracted the votes of a representative sample of Spanish society. The internal renewal of the party's cadres and ideology was reflected in the changed profile of its electorate. PP opened up to new sociodemographic and occupational groups – students, younger generations, less educated and lower income populations, and large-city dwellers. In 2000, when the party obtained a majority of seats in parliament, the sociodemographic profile of PP's electorate was a close reflection of the Spanish electorate at large. By 2011, however, the elderly, less educated and pensioners were over-represented among PP's voters, and the party had begun to lose students, the young, the highly educated, white-collar workers and high-level technicians.

The ideological profile of PP voters also changed quite dramatically during the 1990s and 2000s. Figure 9.7 shows their ideological distribution. During the 1990s, the share of far right voters gradually declined and, by 2000, it had halved. In that year, 7 per cent of PP voters were on the far right, while 58 per cent were centrists.

Figure 9.8 examines the vote share PP received from each group of voters. PP monopolized the far right electorate for the whole period. In most elections, over 90 per cent of far right voters chose it. Simultaneously,

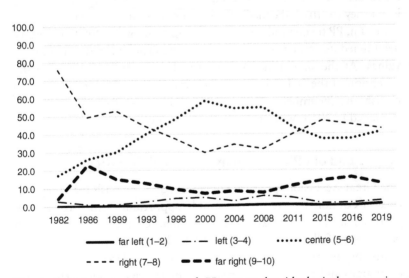

Figure 9.7 Ideological position of PP voters by ideological categories, 1982–2019

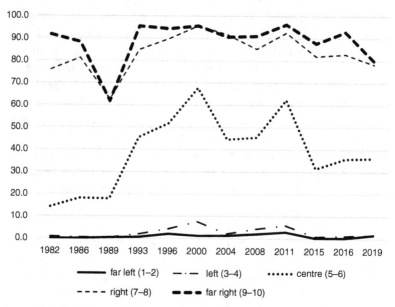

Figure 9.8 Percentage of PP voters by ideological categories, 1982–2019

the support of centrist voters for PP grew during the 1990s and peaked in the elections of 2000, at 68 per cent. This, in effect, was the culmination of its journey to attract the median voter without losing the far right.

In sum, PP turned right after the Socialist victory in 2004. The party heightened its emphasis on Spanish nationalism and traditional moral values. At the same time, it started to lose centrist voters, with the exception of the 2011 election which was decided by voters' desire to punish the incumbent PSOE for the economic crisis. These trends deepened in 2015, when new challengers emerged.

5. The End of PP's Hegemony on the Political Right

The Great Recession, political corruption and the push for independence in Catalonia created a favourable opportunity structure for new party challengers. The 2015 elections marked the entry of Cs into parliament, followed by *Vox* in 2019. In the post-2015 elections, centre–periphery issues and in particular the Catalan crisis dominated campaigns and politics more broadly, with the right-wing parties competing for votes in the Spanish nationalist, pro-centre space. PP voters in 2015 and 2016 were less representative of the Spanish public at large, with more centrists voting for Cs and far right voters supporting *Vox* in 2019.

PP and PSOE conveyed centre-left economic positions in their 2015 and 2016 manifestos, but this centrism was of little significance given the modest relevance accorded to economic issues in a country that was confronting the worst period of economic hardship since the establishment of democracy (8 and 10 per cent respectively, Figures 9.3 and 9.4). In spite of its rhetorical commitment to the centre-ground, however, the PP government actually implemented a harsh fiscal adjustment programme between 2011 and 2016. Simultaneously, the sociocultural dimension gained relevance: indeed, both of the two main parties dedicated half of all their manifesto sentences to social values and cultural issues. Immigration and European membership, on the other hand, were not relevant issues.

Polarization along the centre–periphery dimension reached very high levels in 2015 and 2016. This is when PP advocated its strongest Spanish nationalist position to date, and its weakest pro-decentralization position since 1979. This reflects competition with Cs, which stressed Spanish identity and opposition to Catalan nationalism. Cs' manifesto in 2016 shows a pro-centre position, that is, political recentralization (0.6) and Spanish nationalism (0.75), close to PP's (Figure 9.6), although somewhat less extreme. It is also in line with the finding that elites in Spain divert attention to territorial conflicts when the economy is performing poorly (Pardos-Prado and Sagarzazu 2019). While manifesto data are not yet available for 2019, centre–periphery competition dominated the campaigns and radicalized with the rise of *Vox*.

The long-dominant Spanish mainstream parties paid a high electoral price for the economic crisis and corruption scandals. This is evident in the profile of their respective voters. CIS post-electoral surveys for 2015 and 2016 show that the profile of PSOE and PP voters changed in the same direction: they were older, with a high concentration among those older than sixty-six, had lower education levels, lived in smaller towns and rural areas, and were more likely to be pensioners or unpaid domestic workers (for PP, see Tables 9.1 and 9.2). In clear contrast, younger people, students, the more highly educated, and large-city dwellers were over-represented among voters of the new challenger parties on the left (Podemos) and the right (Citizens).

As for the ideological composition of PP's electorate, by 2016, 61 per cent self-identified as right or far right, and only 37 per cent as centrists. This is a remarkable contrast to 2000, when the corresponding figures were 37 and 58 per cent, respectively. PP had lost the centrist space and, with it, the median voter.

The contrast between the electorates of Citizens and the Popular Party in 2016 was noteworthy, too. The former attracted younger (11 per cent of Citizens' vs. 5 per cent of PP voters are aged between eighteen and twenty-five), better educated (32 per cent vs. 20 per cent have a university degree), more urban (12 per cent vs. 9 per cent live in cities of more than 1 million inhabitants) voters. Also, students (6 per cent vs. 3 per cent) and the unemployed (17 per cent vs. 10 per cent) were more prevalent among Cs' voters. Interestingly, the Spanish socioeconomic elite (those at the top of the salary and the occupational ladders), who until 2011 were over-represented among PP's electorate, started to migrate to Citizens, while PP retained the farmers and the lower middle classes (Table 9.2).

Ideologically, Citizens' electorate in 2016 was much more moderate than that of the Popular Party: 70 per cent of its voters identified as centrists and only 17 per cent placed themselves on the right or far right (in comparison with 61 per cent and 37 percent, respectively, in PP). The only characteristic that the voters of both parties shared in 2016 was national identity: voters that felt only Spanish or more Spanish than the various peripheral identities were over-represented among PP's and Citizens' voters. Interestingly, the share of the far right vote PP won in 2015 – the year the Spanish party system transformed to include Citizens and Podemos (see Figure 9.8) – declined to its lowest level since 1989 (87 per cent).

Vox's breakthrough in the April 2019 parliamentary elections did not change these trends in any significant way, although it served to pull far right voters away from PP (93 per cent of self-identified far right voters cast their vote for PP in 2016 as opposed to 79 per cent in April 2019) and to reduce the number of self-identified far right voters within PP's electorate (from nearly 16 per cent in 2016 to 12 per cent in 2019).

6. Contemporary Challenges

Unlike most European mainstream right parties, PP has begun only recently to face the strategic dilemmas of both revolutions, with competition from the far right *Vox* (as well as from the centre-right Citizens that labels itself liberal). PP's initial response to *Vox* was to move rightward and accommodate it as a potential ally. PP prioritized office goals and governing, where possible, in the short term, while hoping it could reunite the right under its leadership as time went on.

    Vox first became a relevant institutional actor in the region of Andalusia in 2018, where it was the lynchpin of a potential right-wing government that could displace the Socialist Party that had been in power since 1982. PP wasted no time in spearheading the formation of a rightist government under its leadership, despite a decline in vote- and seat-share, and even though it performed worse than PSOE. To do so, it negotiated agreements, separately, with Cs and *Vox* to secure a PP–Cs minority coalition government with the external support of *Vox*. Cs attempted to keep its distance from *Vox*, refusing to directly negotiate with it so as not to damage its more centrist brand. However, this quickly proved difficult to manage in practice. The three parties jointly led a rally against the Socialist government of Pedro Sánchez in February 2019, and governing in Andalusia requires cooperation between PP, Cs and *Vox*.

    Prior to the April 2019 national parliamentary elections, in which polls indicated that a right-wing majority (PP, Cs and *Vox*) might result, PP and Cs moved rightward and competed with one another (and with *Vox*) on their Spanish nationalist credentials. PP transparently expressed its willingness to negotiate with Citizens and *Vox* in the April 2019 national election, and the May 2019 regional, local and European elections. PP's general secretary bluntly stated that there would be no *cordon sanitaires* (*cordones sanitarios, ninguno*).[24] While remaining rather more ambiguous, Cs did not rule out post-election deals with *Vox*. Instead, the party voted unanimously against negotiating with the Socialists, in part because it accused the Socialists of cosying up to secessionists.[25] PP ultimately did poorly in the April 2019 elections. While it remained the largest party of the right,

---

[24] P. Montesinos, 'García Egea asegura que "cualquier candidato del PP" puede suscribir el pacto con Vox en Andalucía', *Libertad digital*, 5 February 2019.
[25] Paloma Esteban, 'El no de Rivera a Sánchez golpe de efecto y "mensaje claro" para cortar la ofensiva del PP', *El Confidencial*, 19 February 2019.

it had its worst showing since the 1970s, and parliamentary arithmetic did not allow for a right-wing government.

PP also performed poorly in the subsequent local, regional and European elections in May 2019. It was not the first-placed party in any of the regions that held elections. Yet it was ultimately able to head up several regional (and local) governments due to its alliance strategies. PP took the lead to forge a majority coalition with Cs in Castile and Leon, and to broker agreements with Cs and *Vox* in Madrid (city and region) and Murcia to form PP+Cs minority coalitions with *Vox*'s parliamentary support. Therefore, by the end of 2019, PP led governments in five regions (Galicia, as a single-party majority government since 2016, Andalusia, Madrid, Murcia, and Castile and Leon) in spite of its poor electoral performance. Cs' refusal to negotiate with PSOE was a cornerstone of this outcome. The November 2019 national elections reshuffled party prominence on the right, with *Vox* replacing Cs as PP's largest competitor on the that side of the political spectrum.

7. Conclusion

Of the two revolutions analysed in this volume – the silent revolution and silent counter-revolution – the Popular Party in Spain confronted only the former for several decades. In general, it adapted to a more liberal society by moderating to capture centrist voters in the 1990s without losing far right voters. However, midway through the follow-ing decade, Spain's two main parties moved further apart on post-materialist and centre–periphery issues, with the Socialists becoming more socially liberal and pro-periphery, and PP emphasizing conserva-tive moral stances and Spanish nationalism.

Unlike most European mainstream right parties, PP has only recently begun to face the strategic dilemmas of both revolutions, with compe-tition from the far right *Vox*, as well as from the centre-right Citizens that labels itself liberal. PP's initial response was to move rightward and accommodate both parties as allies. It is too early to tell how and how successfully PP will adapt to the new competitive environment in which it faces challengers on the centre and far right – and a very crowded field in the Spanish national identity space. It is unlikely that there is the room on the right in the long run for three relevant parties. Predictions are always risky; but, the PP's history of adaptability suggests that it will not be the one to disappear.

More broadly, Spain now has a party system with two significant parties on the left, PSOE and Podemos, who are now governing Spain jointly in a minority coalition, with precarious support from the pro-Catalan independence party ERC. In addition to being Spain's first coalition government since the transition, government and opposition are also occurring in the context of the Coronavirus pandemic, which hit Spain particularly hard and will have severe economic consequences. While predictions are, again, very risky, initial developments indicate that, of the four policy challenges highlighted comparatively in this volume – EU integration, immigration, moral issues and welfare – welfare may be the most daunting challenge for the mainstream right in the coming years.

10 | Sweden: The Difficult Adaptation of the Moderates to the Silent Counter-Revolution

ANDERS RAVIK JUPSKÅS

1. Introduction

'The silent revolution' had a significant impact on Swedish culture and policy regime (Jamison, Eyerman and Cramer 1990; Knutsen 1990; Inglehart and Norris 2003). Since the mid-1980s, established parties have rarely emphasized traditional morality in their manifestos and 'green issues' have become increasingly salient. In 1988, the Greens became the first new party to enter the Swedish parliament in the post-war period (Bennulf and Holmberg 1990). The World Value Survey suggests that Sweden, in fact, is the most post-materialist country in the world, as indicated by strong support for values such as freedom and self-expression, as well as high levels of subjective well-being, interpersonal trust and tolerance of out-groups (Inglehart and Baker 2000: 29). Indeed, more recent studies indicate that Sweden has comparatively low levels of hostility and scepticism towards immigration and immigrants (Demker 2014: 103).

At the same time, however, Sweden is no longer 'an exceptional case' as regards the presence or absence of a successful populist radical right party (Rydgren and van der Meiden 2018). The Sweden Democrats (SD) entered parliament in 2010 and the party has increased its electoral support in all subsequent elections. The 'immigration issue' has rapidly become one of the most salient issues in Swedish politics – largely among a minority that (still) hold sceptical and xenophobic views. Although this 'silent counter-revolution' came later in Sweden than most others countries, the SD has already affected the political agenda and patterns of coalition formation (Jupskås 2018). In 2018, it became the third largest party in the Swedish parliament.

In this chapter, I assess the evolution of the Moderates, the key catch-all party on the mainstream right, within the context of an embedded post-materialist political culture and an emboldened populist radical

246

right party. More specifically, the chapter looks at how the Moderates have developed electorally, ideologically and strategically since the 1990s. The key argument is that the 'silent counter-revolution' – the 'immigration issue' in particular – has been quite challenging for the Moderates across different arenas (i.e., electoral, governing and internal arena) and that the party has had major difficulties in adapting to a new political landscape. At the same time, the party seems increasingly willing to sacrifice policy purity in order to (re-)gain voters and form possible governing coalitions, which means that it might once again assume its role as the dominant party of the right.

In the 1990s, the Moderates – founded in 1904 as a traditional conservative party – were mainly policy-driven focusing on economic liberalism. Within a stable yet increasingly fragmented multiparty system, the party was the leading party on the right – a position it won in the early 1980s.[1] In 1991, the party entered office as part of a centre-right minority coalition and, for the first time in post-war Sweden, the prime minister was from the Moderates. However, this government only lasted one term; the Social Democrats continued to dominate in both the electoral and governing arena.

After a decade in opposition and an electoral setback in the early 2000s, the Moderates adopted a more office- and vote-seeking strategy, moving towards economic pragmatism. Their electoral support increased significantly and, in 2010, the party even gained more than 30 per cent of the votes, challenging the Social Democrats' position as the largest party for the first time since 1914. The party was also able to form a credible pre-electoral centre-right coalition called 'The Alliance', which governed Sweden between 2006 and 2014. Not since 1936 had the Social Democrats been out of office for so long.[2]

After the electoral breakthrough of the SD in 2010 and the growing salience of the immigration issue, however, the Moderates gradually began losing electoral support. Moreover, despite a clear right-wing majority in parliament since 2014, the party was unable to enter office due to profound disagreement within 'the Alliance' regarding whether or not to form a (minority) government that would rely on tacit support

---

[1] Until the mid-1960s, the Liberals were the largest party on the right. Between the mid-1960s and the late 1970s, the agrarian Centre Party was biggest.

[2] The only exception is six years of centre-right governments between 1976 and 1982.

from the SD. On top of this, the leadership has struggled to reconcile the different views internally on the immigration issue, as well as on how the party should relate to the SD.

Faced with an increasing trade-off between a vote-seeking strategy, on the one hand, and a policy-seeking and office-seeking strategy, on the other hand, the party initially seemed to prioritize the latter two. In fact, rather than moving towards the SD, sacrificing policy purity and jeopardizing the relationship with the centrist parties, the party reinforced its cosmopolitan position. However, the combination of further electoral strengthening of the SD, growing internal pressure and a changing public discourse in the wake of the refugee crisis, provided a strong impetus for the adoption of new strategies. First, as part of a vote-seeking strategy, the party replaced its moralizing cosmopolitan discourse with a more technocratic-informed social conservatism. By this I mean, in short, that the Moderates stopped challenging the nativist and authoritarian problem description of immigration and integration put forward by the SD, but instead argued that it was more capable of solving 'the problem'. Second, as part of a new office-seeking strategy, after seeing that two of its former allies decided to support the incumbent Social Democratic prime minister after the elections in 2018, the party no longer rules out future formal collaboration with the SD.

In what follows, the chapter elaborates upon these three phases – economic liberalism, economic pragmatism and technocratic social conservatism. I discuss the party's ideology, its coalition preferences, the electoral strength and the sociological profile of its electorate. The chapter combines data from electoral surveys, party leader debates, campaign material and media reports.

2. Economic Liberalism: from 1990 to 2002

The ideological profile of the Moderates in the 1990s was one of economic liberalism, internationalism and sociocultural conservatism (see Figure 10.2). The latter, however, was not particularly salient and almost exclusively related to their emphasis on law and order. Most scholars agree that liberalism replaced conservatism as the core ideology of Moderates throughout the twentieth century (Hylén 1991), although they disagree whether it happened in the 1950s (Ljunggren 1992), in the 1970s as part of the Anglo-Saxon wave of neoliberalism

(Lewin 1994) or in the 1980s (Boréus 1994).[3] In any case, the Moderates clearly advocated economic liberalism in the early 1990s, focusing on 'deregulation, privatization and tax reductions, primarily for small-scale entrepreneurs' (Wörlund 1992: 140). The nationalist aspects that characterized the Moderate's ideology at least until the 1950s became gradually less salient and by the end of the 1970s, the party had largely replaced nationalism with internationalism (Ljunggren 1992: 308; Nilsson 2004). In the 1990s, the Moderates were strongly in favour of Swedish membership in the EU and 'the moderate person' was a global and internationalized citizen transcending the borders of the nation state (Ekengren and Oscarsson 2015: 159). On socio-cultural issues, the party combined law and order with progressive policies related to gay rights, gender equality and cultural diversity, but these issues were not particularly salient (Nilsson and Reiterskiöld 2016: 36).

This ideological profile seemed electorally beneficial. In 1991, Sweden experienced its first 'earthquake election' in the post-war period. The Social Democratic Party, which had received well above 40 per cent in elections since 1932, due to a strong labour movement and an almost exclusive ownership of the welfare state, was struggling with de-industrialization and the rise of the middle class (Therborn 1992; Lindström 2005). On top of this, there were signs of growing unemployment, as well as increased dissatisfaction with the established parties due to political 'scandals' and 'affairs' in the late 1980s and early 1990s (Wörlund 1992: 139–40). After an electoral campaign in which the size and growth of the public sector was the key issue, the Social Democrats suffered their worst result since 1920, two new parties entered parliament, the Christian Democrats and the right-wing populist New Democracy, and the centre-right gained a majority of the seats in parliament for the first time since 1979 (Wörlund 1992). As the most clear-cut right-wing party, the Moderates were the only established party able to capitalize on increased volatility among voters and a growing demand for privatization and de-regulation of the Swedish economy. With 21.9 per cent of the votes, the party had its second best electoral result since 1928 (see

---

[3] Part of the disagreement seems to be related to what kind of data they use to interpret ideological change and whether they emphasize change rather than continuity.

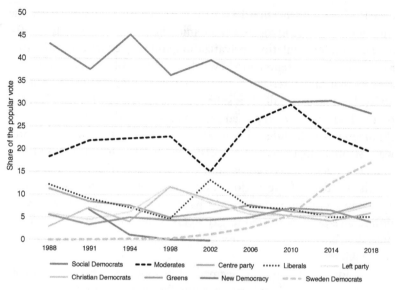

Figure 10.1 Electoral support of parliamentary parties in Sweden, 1991–2018
Source: SCB/Valmyndigheten.

Figure 10.1). To be sure, the party did lose voters to New Democracy – voters who were distrustful of politics and who wanted stricter immigration policies (Oscarsson and Holmberg 2016: 165). At the time, Sweden experienced large numbers of refugees fleeing from the war in the former Yugoslavia, and New Democracy was the only party mobilizing on xenophobia. Yet the Moderates more than compensated for the electoral loss to New Democracy not only by 'stealing' voters from the Liberals, but also by unprecedented gains among voters who had previously supported the Social Democrats (Gilljam and Holmberg 1993: 74).

As the largest party on the right, the party leader of the Moderates, Carl Bildt, became prime minister. Although only the Liberals campaigned on a common platform with the Moderates prior to the elections, the Center Party and the Christian Democrats agreed to join Bildt's centre-right government. The latter party had initially refused to take a position on the traditional left–right cleavage, but an electoral alliance with the Center Party in 1985 'made it adamantly clear that the Christian Democratic Union was a party of the right' (Wörlund 1992: 138). As the enfant terrible of Swedish politics, New Democracy was not part of the coalition, but being a minority government, Bildt had to rely on its tacit support to remain in power.

In the 1994 election, the Moderates increased their votes, but the other coalition partners and New Democracy did not. The latter even fell out of parliament largely due to organizational weaknesses and internal factionalism. Consequently, the centre left regained the majority in parliament, and the Social Democrats returned to power. Support for the Moderates increased further in 1998, but there was still no centre-right majority. Bildt, who became increasingly popular as party leader throughout the 1990s (Holmberg 2000: 165), stepped down and was succeeded by a much less popular leader, Bo Lungren. His first and only election as party leader in 2002 proved to be disastrous (see Figure 10.1). On the one hand, many voters viewed the party as dogmatically (economically) right-wing, almost exclusively campaigning on extensive tax cuts. And when the Liberals politicized the immigration issue by suggesting a language test to get Swedish citizenship, a significant share of those who voted for the Moderates in 1998 switched to the Liberals. On the other hand, the Moderates also suffered from a scandal in which a journalist from SVT revealed racist and xenophobic attitudes among politicians in different parties at the local level – seventeen from the Moderates, far more than in any other party – using hidden cameras. While we should not overestimate the electoral damage done by this scandal (Holmberg and Oscarsson 2004: 125), it received a great deal of attention and the Moderates certainly had problems getting their political message across towards the end of the campaign.

In the 1990s, the Moderates' sociological profile was urban middle class with higher education and high income (see Table 10.1). The party gained around 30 per cent in the three largest cities (Stockholm, Gothenburg and Malmö). In terms of education, the support was twice as high among those with higher education compared with those with lower education. Among the top 15 per cent of the income bracket, 35 per cent or more voted for the Moderates. The party had no consistent age profile, but did get significant support from first-time voters in 1991 and 1998. In this period, the support was usually about five percentage points higher among men compared with women, and about ten percentage points higher in the private sector compared with the public sector. Finally, electoral support was particularly strong among self-employed with employees (almost

50 per cent in 1994 and 1998) and higher-grade officials (more than 40 per cent).

The party's electoral reverse in 2002 does indicate, however, that the electorate in the 1990s was actually a combination of what we might call 'the liberal–conservative right' and the 'authoritarian right'. These two groups differ mainly in terms of sociocultural political orientation: the latter being, among other things, more xenophobic, more in favour of stricter sentences, and more opposed to Swedish membership of the EU (Holmberg and Oscarsson 2004: 120).[4] However, they also seem to differ with regard to gender and income. After a significant share of the 'authoritarian right' defected to the Liberals, the Moderates became less male-dominated and more over-represented among affluent groups (see Table 10.1).

3. Economic Pragmatism: from 2003 to 2014

Not surprisingly, the setback in 2002 contributed to a re-orientation of the party. In 2003, Lungren stepped down and the party elected Fredrik Reinfeldt as its party leader. Together with a few other strategists, Reinfeldt developed a new political profile – one of economic pragmatism (see Figure 10.2). More specifically, the 'New Moderates' drifted towards a more centrist position, putting less emphasis on large tax cuts, deregulation of labour legislation and the need for a strong nightwatchman state (Ekengren and Oscarsson 2015: 159). In other words, the party largely accepted key elements of the (social democratic) welfare state (Lindbom 2010). Key strategists within the Moderates believed that the party had criticized welfare arrangements too much, resulting in fear among voters that the party would dismantle the welfare state altogether (Ekengren and Oscarsson 2015: 160). As noted by Jensen (2014), welfare policies tend to be a valence issue in the Scandinavian countries meaning that right-wing parties cannot afford to be seen as anti-welfare parties. The voters quickly noticed the party's re-orientation as the mean perception of the party on a 0 (left) to 10 (right) point scale decreased from being close to 9 in

---

[4] Holmberg and Oscarsson do not specifically analyze the composition of the Moderate electorate, but they show that new and old voters of the Liberal Party differ from each other on various political issues. Given that most of the new voters came from the Moderates, it seems reasonable to interpret this as the views of those who defected from the Moderates.

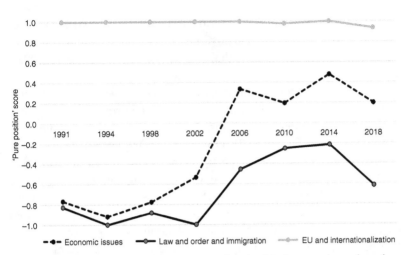

Figure 10.2 Laver's 'pure position' score for the Moderates along three key ideological dimensions, 1991–2018

Source: MARPOR data and Bergman, Hellström and Sandström (2018) for 2018 (for data collection, see Hellström, Bergman and Bäck 2018). Notes: –1 refers to 'right-wing economics', 'authoritarian positions on law and order and immigration' and 'anti-EU and opposition towards internationalism', respectively. 1 refers to 'left-wing economics', 'liberal positions on law and order and immigration' and 'pro-EU and internationalism'. Between 2006 and 2014, the Moderates did not present their own manifesto, but campaigned on a joint manifesto with the other three centre-right parties as part of 'The Alliance'. This may explain part of the shift towards a more centrist position along the economic and sociocultural (law and order and immigration) dimension. It should also be noted that the extreme scores on 'law and order and immigration' and 'EU and internationalization' dimensions are based on very few statements in the manifestos.

Operationalization: The three dimensions are defined as follows. The economic right: 303 (decentralization positive), 401 (free enterprise positive), 402 (incentives positive), 407 (protectionism negative), 414 (economic orthodoxy positive), 505 (welfare state limitation positive), 702 (labour groups negative) and 704 (middle-class and professional groups positive). The economic left: 404 (economic planning positive), 406 (protectionism positive), 409 (Keynesian demand management), 412 (controlled economy), 413 (nationalization positive), 415 (Marxist analysis positive), 503 (social justice positive), 504 (welfare state expansion positive) and 701 (labour groups positive). The authoritarian position on the 'law and order and immigration' dimension: 605 (law and order), 601 (national way of life: positive) and 608 (multiculturalism: negative). The liberal position: 602 (national way of life: negative), 607 (multiculturalism: positive) and 705 (underprivileged minority groups: positive). Pro-EU and internationalism: 107 (internationalism: positive) and 108 (European Community/Union: positive). Anti-EU and nationalism: 109 (internationalism: negative) and 110 (European Community/Union: negative).

1979–2002 to 8.4 in 2006 (Oscarsson and Holmberg 2008: 131). Even after the Moderates entered government (see below) and levels of taxation were reduced more than the party had promised in 2002, voters viewed the party as increasingly centrist.

In terms of sociocultural profile, the party continued its commitment to internationalism and liberal values. Most importantly, throughout this period the Moderates put more emphasis on progressive immigration policies (see Figure 10.2). However, the Moderates also became more liberal on moral issues, partly as the result of pressure from the youth wing. To be sure, the party had de-emphasized the role of Christianity already in the early 1970s (Nilsson 2004: 205–13) and gradually accepted free abortion legislation. Yet, in the 1990s, the party continued to promote traditional family values, most notably by opposing same-sex marriage, even if these issues, according to the party manifestos, were never particularly salient. In the early 2000s, particularly after Reinfeldt became party leader, however, the party started drifting towards a more liberal position. While all MPs, except two (one of them being Reinfeldt), had voted against same-sex marriage in 1994, a large majority of the party congress in 2007 supported gender-neutral marriage legislation (Eriksson and Nilsson 2007). The congress also voted in favour of publicly funded insemination for gay and lesbian couples and same-sex adoption. Furthermore, in terms of gender equality, the party has gradually adopted the (radical) feminist notion of structural discrimination of women, even arguing in 2009 that gender quotas might be necessary if gender-power relations do not improve (Wottle and Blomberg 2011: 111).

Fredrik Reinfeldt's project was not only related to policies, it also involved the formation of a pre-electoral alliance – simply called the Alliance – together with the other centre-right parties: the Liberals, the Center and the Christian Democrats. The formation of the Alliance marked an important departure from established patterns of inter-party interaction on the centre-right. The main explanation seems to be a marked shift among party elites in the Moderate party from a strategy of policy purity towards office-seeking in response to the profound electoral shock of 2002 (Allern and Aylott 2009).

The ideological re-orientation of the Moderates, as well as the formation of a pre-electoral alliance, seemed to pay off electorally. In 2006, only four years after the electoral setback, the Moderates increased their support significantly. Indeed, with 26.2 per cent of the votes, the party experienced its best result since 1928.[5] The electoral gain was particularly strong among those who had previously voted for the Liberals and the Social Democrats (see Table 10.2), and the increase may well have been related to materialist concerns and a right-wing turn among the voters. Those who switched from the Social Democrats to the centre-right parties mentioned jobs, education and taxation as the three most important issues (Oscarsson and Holmberg 2008: 58–9). For those who switched from the Social Democrats to the Moderates, jobs seemed to be the most important issue, followed by taxation and then the economy. More voters than ever before self-identified as right-wing. The Moderates' coalition partners also did quite well. Together they controlled a majority of seats in parliament, and for the first time since 1928, the Moderates were leading a centre-right majority government.

The electoral success continued in the 2010 election. Contrary to the general trend of losing support as the governing party, though less for the largest party in a governing coalition (Hjermitslev 2018), the Moderates increased their support receiving 30.1 per cent of the vote. Surveys suggest that the party not only continued to attract a significant number of voters who had previously voted for the Social Democrats (see Table 10.2). It also gained some votes from the Liberals and lost relatively few voters to the radical right SD, which passed the electoral threshold for the first time after receiving 5.7 per cent of the votes (see Figure 10.1). The election result in 2010 was also symbolically important as the Moderates were now seriously challenging the Social Democrats as Sweden's largest party. While the Social Democrats and the Moderates had been polling around 45 per cent and 21–22 per cent, respectively, about two years before the elections, the latter was actually ahead of the former during the campaign. In the end, the Social Democrats gained a few decimal points more than the Moderates, partly because of Moderate sympathizers tactically voting for other centre-right parties in order to help them stay above the electoral threshold of 4 per cent (Oscarsson and Holmberg 2013: 175; Fredén 2014).

---

[5] SCB (2008), *Allmänna valen 2006*. Del 4. Specialundersökningar. Stockholm: SCB.

The ideological turn towards economic pragmatism and growing electoral support made the sociological profile of the Moderate electorate less distinct, but perhaps in a different way than expected based on the party's rebranding as the 'New Labour Party'.[6] Although the party did increase its vote share among workers compared with the 2002 election, the support was not much higher than it had been in the 1990s, and the party continued to be rather unpopular among this group with 15 per cent support (see Table 10.1). Instead, the party seemed to be increasingly popular among what we might call 'purple pragmatists' – that is, highly educated middle-class voters living in urban areas who are rather centrist in their views on the economy. The Moderates got as much as 57 per cent among higher-grade officials and 36 per cent among lower- and middle-grade officials. There was no longer a difference between their support in metropolitan areas (where their support had always been high) and the other big cities (where their support had been somewhat lower).

Moreover, and perhaps most importantly, the Alliance was re-elected and Reinfeldt continued as prime minister. Although the electoral support of the three smaller parties in the coalition decreased somewhat, the Alliance gained more support and received more seats in parliament compared with the three parties of the red–green bloc (i.e., the Social Democrats, the Greens and the Left). However, due to the electoral breakthrough of the SD, the Alliance parties no longer controlled a majority of the seats. Hence, they would need support from at least one of the red–green parties in order to pass legislation. In contrast to New Democracy, the SD were not only considered organizationally unreliable but also politically beyond the pale.

Neither the established parties, including the Moderates, nor the mainstream media perceived the SD as a legitimate political actor. Confronted with its increasing support, mainstream actors resorted to a moral frame in which they were 'the good guys' while the SD was considered 'a devil in disguise' (Hellström and Nilsson 2010). Arguably, the most important reason for the unanimous attacks on the SD is the origin of the party. Contrary to many other successful right-wing populist parties in Western Europe, the SD emerged from the neo-Nazi subculture. Although the party had modernized

---

[6] It is important to note that in Sweden, the re-branding was about being a party for work rather than the party for workers.

Table 10.1 *Electoral support for the Moderates for different groups,*
1991–2018

	1991	1994	1998	2002	2006	2010	2014	2018
Women	19	17	20	12	25	27	20	17
Men	24	24	27	15	28	35	26	21
Age 18–22[1]	30	18	30	15	28	26	24	19
Age 23–30[2]	27	21	24	13	25	24	19	18
Age 31–40	19	18	24	15	28	38	27	18
Age 41–50	22	22	23	12	29	33	31	23
Age 51–60	18	18	26	13	23	32	20	20
Age 61–70	21	21	18	14	27	24	19	16
Age 71–80	18	24	19	13	26	33	19	18
Income 0–15%	23	20	25	12	27	20	21	16
Income 15–35%	19	16	16	10	19	24	15	19
Income 35–65%	19	16	19	8	22	25	19	16
Income 65–85%	19	19	22	13	26	35	22	20
Income 85–100%	33	37	38	28	43	47	38	29
Private sector	26	24	26	16	29	34	27	22
Public sector	15	15	19	8	21	23	13	15
Rural areas	20	18	19	12	23	28	22	16
Towns	19	17	21	10	21	33	23	17
Cities	20	21	23	12	29	29	22	21
Metropolitan areas	33	27	33	17	30	34	27	20
Higher education	28	28	33	16	30	33	22	20
Medium education	26	24	24	12	26	30	21	21
Lower education	14	12	14	8	17	21	21	11
Workers	14	8	12	6	15	21	14	12
Lower-grade officials	25	26	26	13	26	30	22	20
Middle-grade officials	27	31	32	17	36	38	26	24
Higher-grade officials	41	41	47	28	57	51	38	30
Self-employed without employees	32	43	42	28	40	35	26	28

Table 10.1 (*cont.*)

	1991	1994	1998	2002	2006	2010	2014	2018
Self-employed with employees	46	49	48	45	52	60	43	35
Farmers	25	20	13	7	12	25	33	25

Notes: 1. Until 1998, the youngest cohort includes only those aged between 18 and 22.
2. Until 1998, the second youngest cohort includes those aged between 22 and 30.
Sources: Hedberg (2020). *Note*: Occupation is based on subjective assessments by the respondent. Figures might deviate somewhat from more objective measures.

throughout the 2000s (Widfeldt 2008), it very much lacked a 'reputational shield' (Ivarsflaten 2006) in order to fend off criticism of racism and extremism. Time and again, the mainstream parties, the media and civil society reminded voters about the extreme right legacy of the party. Moreover, numerous scandals in which representatives at the local, as well as the national level, made blatant racist statements did not make the transition towards a more respectable party any easier.

Consequently, any collaboration with the SD was off the table. In fact, already a year prior to the election, Reinfeldt concluded that he would rather resign than work with the SD. In an interview with Swedish Radio, he argued as follows: 'We will not be dependent upon the SD, which is a party that has been brutalized with its "us and them" rhetoric. It would be impossible for me to collaborate with such a party' (cited in Aftonbladet 2009). Instead, he suggested that the Alliance might collaborate with the Greens because of their pro-EU position and a more centrist position on labour migration. On the eve of the election, Reinfeldt restated his interest in cross-bloc collaboration with the Greens in order to neutralize the SD. While the Greens were initially sceptical about becoming a support party, they eventually agreed to collaborate on specific issues such as asylum and immigration.

During the Alliance's second term in office, the support for the Moderates started declining – and the development seemed closely connected to the growing influence of the SD, on the one hand, and the party's strategic response, on the other hand. In short, informed by both an office-seeking and policy-seeking strategy, the Moderates seemed profoundly committed to their cosmopolitan position on immigration. Only a few months after the election, in March 2011, the Alliance and the Greens presented a new immigration policy. Through this cross-bloc agreement, the official immigration policy remained liberal and conservative voters who were hoping for a more restrictive policy were disappointed (Ekengren and Oscarsson 2015: 155). For example, the electoral survey from 2010 suggests that just above one-third of the Moderate voters (36 per cent) wanted Sweden to accept fewer refugees (Oscarsson and Holmberg 2013: 228).

The SD initially had limited impact upon public discourse, and its support hovered around 5 per cent, partly because of several political scandals. However, its key issue – immigration – became increasingly salient after the summer of 2012. The national broadcasting company SVT even introduced the issue during a party leader debate using a much-criticized radical right framing: 'how much immigration can Sweden take?' (SVT, Agenda, 12 October 2012). This change seemed beneficial for the SD and damaging for the Moderates. While support for the SD increased to almost 10 per cent, the Moderates' support gradually fell, dropping about five percentage points every year: from around 35 per cent in late 2011 to 30 per cent in late 2012 and 25 per cent in late 2013 (Oscarsson and Holmberg 2016: 28).

However, despite the increased salience of the immigration issue, as well as declining support in the polls, the Moderates did not move closer to the position of the SD – either politically or rhetorically. Indeed, on the contrary, the Moderates, as well as the other parties, eventually adopted even more liberal policies and discourse (see Figure 10.2). During the 2014 election campaign, Prime Minister Reinfeldt asked the voters to 'open their hearts for those vulnerable people who we see around the world' (Aylott and Bolin 2015: 733). However, throughout the first term after the SD entered parliament, the established parties seemed increasingly willing to discuss challenges related to immigration and integration using a political rather than moral framing. When the SVT gathered all party leaders in May 2013, integration was one of the four main topics in the debate. While the host (again) framed integration mainly as a problem by pointing to challenges in Malmö, all party leaders except the SD's Jimmie Åkesson explained challenges of segregation as the result of either economic inequalities, racism and/or the lack of skills needed to function in an advanced capitalist economy. Moreover, they argued that the debate on integration had become too 'problem-oriented' and that most immigrants are, or soon would be, well integrated. Although hardly participating in the debate on this topic, Fredrik Reinfeldt's main message was that immigration had been good for Sweden thus far and that the country would still need (more) migrants to maintain its welfare system.

The electoral results largely confirmed what the polls had been showing. The Moderates were the losers, going down from 30.1 per cent to 23.3 per cent, and the SD was the clear winner increasing its support from 5.7 per cent to 12.9 per cent. The support for other parties remained rather stable. In terms of parliamentary seats, the Moderates lost twenty-three and the SD gained twenty-nine. Individual-level data from several surveys suggest the Moderates lost most voters to the SD, but also to other parties, including the Social Democrats and its coalition partners, particularly the more liberal Centre Party (Oscarsson and Holmberg 2016: 155; see also Table 10.2). To be sure, a significant part of those switching to the SD still viewed the Moderates as the 'best party', yet they voted as they did presumably because they wanted a stricter immigration policy (Oscarsson and Holmberg 2016: 165). Certainly, surveys do indicate that those who defected to the SD had lower trust in politicians and were far more sceptical of immigration than those who continued to vote for the Moderates (Ekengren and Oscarsson 2015: 155).

In terms of sociological profile, those voters defecting from the Moderates to the SD were mainly elderly men (see also Table 10.1), which in turn significantly altered the age composition of the SD's electorate. Furthermore, and in contrast to the analysis put forward by Moderate strategists, they were not former Social Democrats who had switched to the Moderates in 2010, before further switching to the SD in 2014. On the contrary, panel data suggest that they were long-standing supporters of the Moderates, voting Moderate in 2006 as well as in 2010 (Ekengren and Oscarsson 2015). In other words, the SD seemed to tap into the voter segment previously referred to as the 'authoritarian right'. On top of that, the party seemed less popular among the 'purple pragmatists' who returned to the Social Democrats (see Table 10.2). The support among voters in the public sector decreased from 23 per cent in 2010 to only 13 per cent in 2014 (see Table 10.2).

Table 10.2 *Net loss and gain for the Moderates, 2006–2018*

	2002–2006	2006–2010	2010–2014	2014–2018
Left Party	9,000	−6,000	−4,000	−2,000
Social Democrats	154,000	102,000	−97,000	53,000
Green Party	12,000	6,000	−37,000	11,000
Liberals	273,000	22,000	−53,000	−10,000
Centre Party	17,000	0	−69,000	−94,000
Christian Democrats	71,000	0	−45,000	−105,000
Sweden Democrats	0	−17,000	−156,000	−165,000
Non-voters	100,000	96,000	−32,000	N/A

Source: Swedish Electoral Surveys 2006, 2010 and 2014. I have calculated the figures for 2014–2018 based on exit poll data from the Swedish Television (SVT VALU 2018).

The setback for the Moderates was governmental as well as electoral. The Alliance also ended up with fewer seats than the red–green bloc. Fredrik Reinfeldt announced that he would resign as party leader and prime minister. Realizing that the SD would probably gain blackmail potential after the election, the centre-right coalition stated in the campaign that it would not oppose the formation of a centre-left government if it constituted the largest bloc after the election. However, the weaknesses of the new centre-left government, which was headed by Stefan Lövfen from the Social Democrats, became evident when the SD decided to break the (non-formalized) parliamentary code of conduct by supporting the budget proposed by the centre-right coalition rather than its own budget. Demonstrating its newly acquired blackmail potential, the SD argued that it would vote against any government that did not significantly limit the number of immigrants.

The result was a crisis of government, and, for the first time since the 1950s, the prime minister announced that he might call for early elections if the situation remained unresolved. However, most of the parties were not particularly interested in yet another election campaign and the Alliance agreed to strike a deal with the red–green government. In order to maintain the *cordon sanitaire* against the SD and continue with existing 'bloc politics', this agreement would allow the largest bloc to govern even without a parliamentary majority, and there would be cross-bloc collaboration on issues such as defence, pensions and energy (Larsson 2014).

The agreement quickly became unpopular within some of the right-wing parties, most notably the Moderates and the Christian Democrats. In fact, some politicians viewed the agreement as fundamentally undemocratic. Not only did it effectively depoliticize major issues in Swedish politics, it also allowed the Social Democrats to govern despite the large right-wing majority in parliament. In this sense, the agreement became a problem for the Moderates' vote-seeking, policy-seeking and, perhaps most importantly, office-seeking strategy. In October 2015, a majority of the delegates at the party convention of the Christian Democrats abandoned the agreement. The Moderates immediately did the same.

4. Technocratic Social Conservatism: from 2015 Onwards

After the poor election result in 2014, there was a growing feeling among activists and representatives that the party needed to act pro-actively by adopting a more vote-seeking strategy. Immigration was now one of the three most important issues for Swedish voters. Moreover, for those who had switched from the Moderates to the SD, or even those who still voted for the Moderates, it was the most important issue. Only 26 per cent of the Moderate electorate believed that society was moving in the right direction – as many as 59 per cent did not (Novus 2018). Addressing issues associated with the 'silent counter-revolution' (i.e., immigration and law and order) became a key feature of a new party strategy (see Figure 10.2). However, on moral issues, the party reinforced its liberal position, most recently by attacking one of its political allies – the Christian Democrats – for not being unconditionally in favour of free abortion.

The leadership succession from Reinfeldt to Anna Kinberg Batra made the transition away from the initial dismissive strategy towards a more socially conservative position easier, even if Batra was also part of the liberal wing of the party. At the convention in 2015, the party created an internal working group dealing with the integration issue. Batra was particularly concerned with integration. During the long-established and symbolically important political festival Almedalsveckan in 2016, Batra's speech was all about the importance of 'Swedish values'. However, many activists believed that the party also needed to develop a new position on immigration issues (Stenberg and Eriksson 2016). According to Batra's successor, Kristersson, the

Moderates would not allow the SD to monopolize the issue of immigration (Micu 2018). When the number of refugees increased dramatically in September and October 2015 (162,877 applied for asylum in Sweden that year), the Moderates re-stated their commitment to a stricter immigration policy, demanding a return to provisional residence permits for asylum seekers. As noted by two journalists in *Dagens Nyheter*, the party's public discourse rapidly changed from appealing to 'open hearts' to emphasizing the need for 'closed borders' (Stenberg and Eriksson 2016).

Furthermore, the Moderates adopted what might be labelled a strategy of 'technocratic confrontation', arguing that they had 'real solutions' to the problems pointed out by the populist radical right. While the Moderates had previously confronted the SD using a moral framework, the main criticism now was the radical right's alleged inability to 'fix' challenges related to immigration and integration. As argued by Batra in Malmö in 2015, after presenting a stricter immigration policy, 'SD is a party that makes Sweden suffer. They exploit societal problems instead of solving them' (Stenberg and Eriksson 2016). According to the party secretary, this was part of a deliberate electoral strategy in which the party emphasized its comparative advantage vis-à-vis the radical right, namely, its governing experience and competence (Stenberg and Eriksson 2016). Batra's successor, Ulf Kristersson, repeated the argument when he met Jimmie Åkesson in a televised debate for the first time some months before the elections. While Kristersson acknowledged that the SD had been 'good at identifying problems', he maintained that the radical right 'never presented concrete proposals that would really solve those problems' (SVT, Agenda, 29 April 2018).

Although the party moved closer to the SD in terms of policy proposals and even discursive framing (and some representatives wanted to move even closer), the Moderates did not yet adopt the ideology of the SD. In the televised duel between Ulf Kristersson and Jimmie Åkesson, the former repeatedly emphasized that the Moderates believed in different values from the radical right, most notably openness and international cooperation. And their support for a stricter immigration policy was presented as a question of necessity in view of the rapid increase in the number of refugees rather than as a matter of ideological conviction. As argued by an influential politician in the party, 'If someone is going to close the border, it should be us. We really hate it. We do it because we are forced to' (Stenberg and Eriksson 2016). In other words, it was not so much that the Moderates had changed their ideology, but that the party perceived the 'reality' as fundamentally different.[7] An analysis of the manifesto presented by the Moderates in 2018 provides additional support for this argument. Despite it being the most comprehensive manifesto produced by any of Sweden's parties prior to the 2018 election, the text was largely lacking ideological features (Demker 2018: 71). Instead, the party focused on being able to deliver high-quality services and public goods, which resemble the technocratic turn on immigration and integration issues observed previously. Finally, the explicit aim of dealing with the immigration issue through cross-bloc collaboration with the Social Democrats also points in the direction of a pre-emptive consensus strategy, which mainstream parties to the left and right have adopted successfully in the Norwegian context (Bale et al. 2010).

In terms of coalition strategies, the Moderates seemed to struggle with a changing political landscape. The rise of the SD had made the prospects of regaining a majority together with the three other centre-right parties highly unrealistic. Moreover, the abandonment of the December agreement implied that the Moderates would not necessarily enter office even if the Alliance ended up with more seats than the red–green bloc. It all depended upon whether or not the other centre-right parties would join or support any government that relied also on the support of the SD. While the Christian Democrats said yes, the Centre Party and the Liberals said no. Although they too promised to replace Stefan Lövfen as prime minister after the election, they were not willing to grant the SD any kind of blackmail potential. After all, it was very unlikely that the SD would act as a reliable support party without significant concessions on immigration policies. According to Jimmie Åkesson, a new 'Alliance government' should give 'influence in proportion to (SD's) size and on the issues SD think are most important, such as immigration policy and security issues' (Forsberg 2018). The hitherto successful Alliance was disintegrating. In contrast to every election since 2006, the centre-right did not put forward a common platform in the 2018 campaign, fighting instead on individual party manifestos.

---

[7] Interestingly, both Batra and Kristersson belong to the cosmopolitan faction of the party. And both have previously defended the policies of open borders.

The Moderates were either profoundly uncertain or deliberately vague about how to deal with the diverging preferences among centre-right parties. While Batra initially argued that 'collaboration with the SD is not a basis for building a government' even after moving towards some of the SD's policy positions, she changed position in early 2017 suggesting that the Moderates would indeed be willing to collaborate with the SD in parliament. Several surveys had suggested that support for the isolation strategy was fading among voters and politicians at the local level, particularly within the Moderates and the Christian Democrats (SVT, 11 December 2014; Kärrman 2015). However, Batra's new strategy backfired massively. After being heavily criticized, by other centre-right parties also, she resigned and was succeeded by Ulf Kristersson. Kristersson returned to the isolationist strategy, yet during the campaign it was not entirely clear whether or not the Moderates would seek office by relying on support from the SD (Bergman, Hellström and Sandström 2018: 22).

The election result in 2018 reinforced the emergence of a new political landscape characterized by three blocs rather than two. In fact, the Moderates barely received more votes than the SD (see Figure 10.1). However, while the party lost a significant number of voters to the Social Democrats in 2014, most of its voters this time were defecting either to more socially conservative parties of the right (SD and Christian Democrats) or liberal parties of the right (Centre and the Liberals) (see Table 10.2). Most important in terms of numbers was the SD's ability to attract previous Moderate voters associated with the 'authoritarian right'. Those who switched from Moderate to SD had similar right-wing and welfare chauvinist views on economic issues to those who still voted for the Moderates, but they were much more hostile to immigration (Jylhä, Rydgren and Strimling 2019). Moreover, in contrast to those who switched from the Social Democrats to the SD, these voters did not seem to switch party due to economic insecurity or deprivation. As suggested by Jÿlha et al. (2019), protection of one's privileges might be a more important explanation. Electoral survey data suggest that the vote loss was high both among social groups associated with the radical right, such as those with lower education and in more rural areas, and among more affluent groups, such as the top-income groups, self-employed with employees and those in the Metropolitan areas (see Table 10.1).

Perhaps even more important than losing voters, the new landscape with three rather than two blocs had a significant impact on the potential capacity of the Moderates to govern. The party seemed far away from achieving its office-seeking goals. The four parties of the Alliance coalition only held about 40 per cent of the parliamentary seats, and one seat less than the red–green bloc. However, neither a leftwards or rightwards expansion of the coalition seemed feasible. On the one hand, including the Greens would be politically acceptable to all of the Alliance parties, but would not result in a majority of the seats. The Greens were also campaigning on a continuation of the red–green governing coalition with the Social Democrats. Furthermore, and in contrast to countries like Austria, the Netherlands and Germany, a grand coalition between the Moderates and the Social Democrats was for historical reasons a non-option. Moreover, even if it was, it would not control a majority of the seats. Moving rightwards and collaborating formally or informally with the SD would, on the other hand, result in a majority of the seats, but this was completely unacceptable for two of the centrist parties (the Centre Party and the Liberals). Without these two centrist parties, this alternative would also fall short of a majority in parliament.

During the campaign, the two centrist parties had made two promises that, due to the electoral results, were difficult to combine: continue the isolation of the SD, on the one hand, and replace Lövfen as prime minister, on the other hand. Not surprisingly, which of the two promises they would violate had been subject to massive speculation during the campaign. The uncertainty continued for a long time after the election as the two centrist parties voted against both Kristersson and Lövfen as prime minister. However, after lengthy negotiations with the Social Democrats and the Greens, in which the centre left agreed to implement several economically right-wing policies, they eventually decided to support the incumbent government. Consequently, the Alliance's days were numbered. The Moderates had lost the election and now also two of their coalition partners.

5. Concluding Remarks

Prior to the 'silent counter-revolution' in Sweden, the Moderates were increasingly successful. Even if the first Moderate-headed government was not re-elected after three years in office in 1994, the Moderates continued to grow in the subsequent elections, consolidating their position as the dominant opposition party to the ruling Social democratic party. Its electorate seemed to be a coalition of the 'liberal–conservative right' and the 'authoritarian right'. After a temporary setback in 2002, in which parts of the 'authoritarian right' defected to the Liberals, the party moved towards the centre – from economic liberalism to economic pragmatism – and won the 2006 election as part of a formalized centre-right coalition called 'the Alliance'. The party's electorate now also included a significant share of 'purple pragmatists'.

The emergence of a 'silent counter-revolution', however, proved difficult for the Moderates. As most other issues related to the 'silent counter-revolution', such as Euroscepticism and traditional morality, have had low salience in Swedish politics in recent decades, the difficulties were almost exclusively related to the 'immigration issue'. To be sure, the Moderates have always consisted of both more cosmopolitan and progressive representatives and voters, on the one hand, and nationalist and traditional representatives and voters, on the other hand. Tensions between these groups were particularly visible in 1991 and 2002 when New Democracy and the Liberals, respectively, politicized the immigration issue. Yet this politicization turned out to be short-lived and traditional left–right issues rapidly returned to the public agenda – fortunately for the Moderates. As long as politics revolved around economic issues, the Moderates did well, particularly after moving towards the centre and successfully challenging the Social Democrats as the credible guarantor for (the survival of) the Swedish welfare state.

When the SD entered parliament and immigration became one of the key issues on the agenda, the situation certainly became more complex. As noted by van Kersbergen and Krouwel (2008), adopting a sociocultural conservative agenda in general and stricter immigration policies in particular is certainly 'a double-edged sword' for the mainstream right. On the one hand, they may benefit from connecting immigration to an issue where they hold strong ownership such as law and order. On the other hand, 'too harsh a law and order profile, nationalistic and anti-foreigner profile run the risk of ripping the centre-right apart' (van Kersbergen and Krouwel 2008: 399). On top of that, by emphasizing sociocultural issues, the party would be less capable of appealing to the 'purple pragmatists'.

There is no easy way out of this strategic dilemma. Recent developments, however, suggest that the Moderates once again are sacrificing their policy position, though this time on cultural rather than economic issues, in order to re-gain voters, as well as forming a credible governing right-wing alternative. After all, now that the liberal centrist parties have aligned with the centre left, the centre-right is already 'ripped apart', and although the current debate is more about health than immigration due to the Covid-19 crisis, there is no reason to believe that the latter will become less important in Sweden in the years to come. In this sense, the Swedish case provides more empirical evidence suggesting that if the only way to power goes through the radical right, catch-all mainstream right parties will eventually adjust their policies and strategies accordingly, even in cases where the radical right has a clear-cut undemocratic legacy.

While the discursive move towards a more socially conservative position has been noted in this chapter already, the Moderates also no longer oppose the emergence of a cultural conservative bloc, which includes the small but stable Christian Democrats and the rising SD. In fact, in late 2019, only a few months after the leader of the Christian Democrats met with the SD leader to discuss politics for the first time, the leader of the Moderates did the same, effectively ending the long-standing *cordon sanitaire* against the radical right. In June 2020, the Moderate party leader even explicitly stated that he would not rule out future formal cooperation with the SD. Given that the two parties have agreed to collaborate not only on immigration and integration, but also on law and order, as well as on energy policies (i.e., defending nuclear power), Sweden might end up witnessing a more comprehensive 'silent counter-revolution' than first expected.

11 The United Kingdom: The Conservatives and their Competitors in the post-Thatcher Era

RICHARD HAYTON

1. Introduction

The Conservative Party is the most successful political party in British electoral history. Since 1886 – the start of what Seldon and Snowdon (2001: 27) labelled the 'long Conservative century' – the Conservatives have governed for 101 years and been out of office for just thirty-three. No wonder then, that a self-image as the 'natural party of government' has become deeply embedded in the Conservative Party's psyche. Much of the academic work on the party consequently emphasizes its capacity for effective statecraft and political renewal. Following the end of the premiership of Margaret Thatcher, however, the Conservatives struggled to regain the hegemonic position they enjoyed under her leadership. Not until 2019 did the party once again win a general election with a majority comparable to those achieved under Thatcher. This chapter analyses these travails in relation to the silent revolution and the silent counter-revolution, both of which have presented difficulties to parties on the right across Western Europe. It argues that, as a classic catch-all party, the Conservatives have had to battle to hold together a sufficiently broad electoral coalition, challenged in the political centre by the Liberal Democrats and (for a time) New Labour, and on the right by Eurosceptic populists in the UK Independence Party (UKIP) and (albeit briefly) the Brexit Party. As the chapter explores, the Conservatives in opposition after the 1997 general election responded initially to the silent counter-revolution, attempting to shore-up their support on the right. Ongoing electoral defeat saw the party under David Cameron embrace modernization in an effort to signal catch-up with the process of value change identified in Inglehart's (1977) 'silent revolution' thesis. In more recent years, and especially since the 2016 vote for Brexit, the Conservatives have sought once again to contain, and arguably have embraced, the silent counter-revolution of the populist right.

In 2010, David Cameron led his party back to power after thirteen years in opposition, but, lacking an overall majority, formed a coalition government with the Liberal Democrats (Hayton 2014). The widely anticipated result of the 2015 general election was another hung parliament, but Cameron defied expectations to secure a small majority of twelve seats. This slender majority evaporated, however, in the 2017 general election called by Cameron's successor, Theresa May, in the aftermath of the Brexit referendum. Even as the Conservatives' vote share rose to 42.4 per cent (its highest level since 1983) a surge in support for Labour caused a net loss of thirteen seats for the governing party, leaving them dependent on a confidence and supply arrangement with the Democratic Unionist Party (DUP) of Northern Ireland (Tonge 2017). In December 2019, however, the Conservatives (now led by Boris Johnson) triumphed in the 'Brexit election', winning a majority of eighty seats on 43.6 per cent of the vote, the party's best performance since Thatcher's third election victory in 1987 (Figure 11.1).

As we enter the third decade of the twenty-first century, the Conservatives find themselves once again in the driving seat, with the opportunity to profoundly reshape British politics and society through the 2020s. Departing the European Union in early 2020 finally put to bed the most divisive issue in Conservative Party politics in recent decades, namely, the question of European integration. Yet the Conservatives face considerable challenges, not least the ongoing Covid-19 crisis that consumed the new Johnson administration in spring 2020, and navigating the complex post-Brexit policy terrain around issues such as immigration, the economy and trade. This chapter explores this in the following way. The first section considers the electoral challenge that faced the Conservatives in the post-Thatcher period, arguing that in opposition after 1997 the party's response was primarily driven by the silent counter-revolution. The second section looks at the process of adaptation towards a more centrist 'liberal conservatism' under David Cameron, which is interpreted as a response to the silent revolution, which succeeded in returning the Conservatives to office. The third section argues that in seeking to see off the challenge posed by UKIP and the Brexit Party, the Conservatives once again framed their response in relation to the silent counter-revolution.

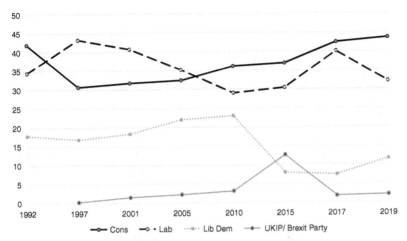

Figure 11.1 Vote share (%) at UK general elections, 1992–2019

2. The Conservative Crisis

Under the leadership of Margaret Thatcher, the Conservatives returned to power with a forty-three-seat majority in 1979 and went on to secure landslide re-elections in 1983 (majority of 144) and in 1987 (majority of 102). Few would have predicted then that not for another thirty-two years would the Conservatives enjoy a general election victory on that scale. In the seven general elections that fell between the premierships of Thatcher and Johnson, they secured small overall majorities twice (21 in 1992, and 12 in 2015) and finished as the largest party on two other occasions, in 2010 and 2017. Landslide defeats were inflicted by New Labour in 1997 (majority 179) and 2001 (majority 167), and Tony Blair secured a third term (majority 66) in 2005. No wonder, then, that the period after 1992 was widely characterized as one of Conservative crisis (Garnett and Lynch 2003).

The puzzle regarding the electoral performance of the Conservative Party after 1992 is not why they lost the election in 1997. After a record eighteen years in office the electoral pendulum was already well overdue to swing back in Labour's favour, a fate made inevitable by the loss of any semblance of governing competence in the dying years of the Major government, and the emergence of a charismatic leader of a modernized opposition in the shape of Tony Blair and New Labour. Rather, the intriguing question is why it took the Conservatives so long to recover power, or even begin to make a credible move back in that direction. A key aspect of the answer is the extent to which the Conservatives were disorientated by the New Labour project, which simultaneously seized the centre-ground of British politics in left–right terms and embraced the post-materialist values of the silent revolution. Labour's shift to the political centre is captured by the left–right scale of the Manifesto Project (Volkens et al. 2018) which illustrates the dramatic rightward shift the party took in 1997 (Figure 11.2). Although there was a slight leftward drift in the three manifestos that followed, Labour, and the Liberal Democrats, on this measure retained centrist positions, with the Conservatives noticeably further to the right. For a time, this effectively neutered the traditional Conservative appeal to the electorate as the anti-socialist party.

Furthermore, New Labour effectively tapped into the progressive sensibilities of (often middle-class) voters on post-material questions such as climate change and environmental protection, women's rights, minority rights, an 'ethical' foreign policy and international aid. In the Conservative Party, where the ideological legacy of Thatcherism remained potent, many of these developments were ones that much of the party found disagreeable, even if (perhaps sensing the shifting public mood) the leadership was sometimes unwilling to strongly

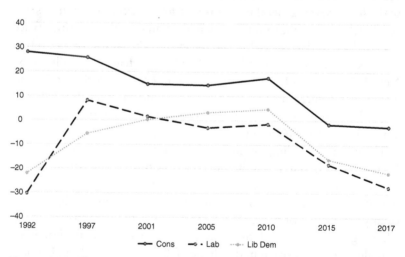

Figure 11.2 Changes in parties' left–right scores 1992–2017 (MARPOR)
Source: Volkens et al. (2018).

attack them. In essence, the Conservatives faced a strategic choice. Should they seek to neutralize New Labour's electoral advantage by sticking closely to the political centre, and presenting themselves as a viable, moderate alternative administration when the sheen of the new government inevitably began to wear off? Or should the Conservatives seek instead to put 'clear blue water' between themselves and Labour, by reinforcing the appeal to their own 'core vote'? Otto Kirchheimer's (1966) catch-all party thesis implies that the former strategy would be pursued, to the detriment of 'meaningful political opposition and of ideology' (Williams 2009: 539). However, academic analyses of the Conservatives between 1997 and 2005 concur that efforts to reach out to the median voter were, at best, severely limited (Garnett and Lynch 2003; Seldon and Snowdon 2005; Bale 2010; Hayton 2012). Successive party leaders – William Hague 1997–2001; Iain Duncan Smith 2001–2003; and Michael Howard 2003–2005 – either rapidly retreated to a core-vote strategy after encountering resistance to other approaches, or, in Howard's case, made barely even a token gesture in the direction of the centre-ground. Central to explaining this political choice, but something so far only implicit in the existing literature, was the Conservatives' understanding of and response to the silent counter-revolution (Ignazi 1992).

In part, the choices made by Hague, Duncan Smith and Howard reflected the party management constraints that each faced. The priority for Hague, elected to the leadership in the aftermath of a crushing electoral defeat, was to hold the party together and to attempt some organizational reform, rather than to start the painful task of confronting some of the Conservatives' core beliefs. Iain Duncan Smith suffered from the twin handicaps of his own ineptitude as a political leader and communicator, and a narrow support base within the parliamentary party, which gave him little in the way of political capital with which to drive forward the agenda of 'change' which he had at least identified as necessary (Hayton and Heppell 2010). Succeeding Duncan Smith less than eighteen months out from a general election, effectively as an interim leader, Michael Howard's only concern was to restore a sense of discipline, unity and credibility to his party, and he regarded a core-vote strategy as the only way to do that (Hayton 2012: 54–8). Critics were therefore justified in suggesting that even after eight years in opposition, the Conservatives had failed to learn 'the major lesson, that power will only be gained and retained by capturing and retaining the centre-ground of the electorate, rather than merely courting the Conservative core vote, however ideologically satisfying and pleasing to the right-wing press that might be' (Seldon and Snowdon 2005: 740).

The analytical frame of the silent counter-revolution helps us provide a fuller explanation of why this was the case. In the original formulation of the thesis, Piero Ignazi (1992) argued that a conservative backlash against the revolution in post-material values on the left was facilitating the (re)emergence of extreme right-wing parties. However, this shift towards party competition along primarily cultural rather than economic lines had implications for the mainstream right too. Ignazi highlighted 'the rise of a new "neo-conservative" cultural mood' (1992: 16) as an essential ingredient in the emergence of the silent counter-revolution, and the United Kingdom had been at the forefront of this in the form of Thatcherism. While the Thatcherite project is best remembered for its radical programme of neoliberalism in the economic sphere, as a hegemonic project it was also engaged in an ideological battle to counter the rise of leftist post-material values. Characterized by Stuart Hall (1983) as 'authoritarian populism', Thatcherism consequently emphasized the importance of law and order, social discipline and tradition, and limiting immigration. This restricted the political space available for the extreme right in Britain, where the fascist National Front and British National Party were squeezed to the very margins. However, over the space of two decades Thatcherism had a transformative effect on the outlook of the Conservative Party itself, critically influencing the strategies adopted in opposition from 1997.

The Conservatives' 'continued adherence to Thatcherism' was, critics suggested, an 'obstacle' to adaptation (Heppell 2014: 103). This was perhaps most starkly illustrated by the party leadership elections, where on Europe in particular ideological acceptability overrode other considerations such as public appeal, experience or leadership skills. The most well-known and well-liked Conservative MP, Ken Clarke, was consequently passed over for the leadership on three separate occasions. The ideological grip of Thatcherism on the party in the 1990s was similarly demonstrated by the fact that its default core-vote position was firmly Thatcherite, whether that be on Europe, immigration, taxation and the role of the state, or social issues. Unfortunately, in electoral terms on salient issues such as spending on public services, this left the Conservatives as the party furthest from the median voter (Norris and Lovenduski 2004: 85). An important driver of this seemingly irrational positioning by an office-seeking party was 'selective perception', which left Conservative politicians more likely to 'miss the target' when attempting to locate the political centre-ground (Norris and Lovenduski 2004: 85). Indeed, 'To those in charge before David Cameron, change was not merely difficult, it was by no means clear to them that it was even rational' (Bale 2010: 367).

Given the scale of the defeat they suffered, and the damage done to the party's image and reputation by factional infighting and governance problems in the 1992–1997 Parliament, they may have had a point. With New Labour occupying the political centre-ground, the Conservatives were 'forced into a strategy of promoting a narrow range of their traditional strengths, representing a limited issue domain on which they have a chance of being rated more positively' (Green 2011: 738). As such, the focus on core-vote issues such as taxation, immigration and Europe should be understood not as the path of least resistance for a party overly attached to Thatcherite shibboleths, but can be understood as an attempt to exploit the 'party's remaining "best issues" or their perceived "owned issues"' (ibid.). Certainly, in the case of Michael Howard's relentless focus on reducing immigration in the 2005 election campaign, the high salience of the issue, and the Conservatives' substantial lead over Labour as the party best able to deal with it, provided a logical basis for the strategy. However, as Howard acknowledged, it also ran the risk of reinforcing negative perceptions of the party as 'pandering to the right' (quoted in Green 2011: 760). Given the extent of the Conservatives' party image problem it ultimately probably did as much harm as good, and the party duly went down to a third successive defeat. Previous excuses, such as the charisma and popularity of Prime Minister Tony Blair, could no longer be plausibly thought to account for the Conservatives' continued troubles. Howard had 'tested to destruction' the theory that an insistent and pugnacious core-vote campaign would bend the electorate's preferences to fit those of the Conservatives, and persuaded more of them to give 'preference accommodation' a go (Bale 2010: 376).

3. Catching-up with the Silent Revolution: Party Change through Modernization

David Cameron was elected Conservative Party leader on an explicitly modernizing platform. His pitch for the job stressed that the Conservatives must 'change to win', and he diagnosed the necessary process of adaptation as one that would take the party firmly towards more moderate stances on a range of issues, relocating it on the political centre-ground. He articulated this strategy in relation to Thatcherism, from which he sought to distance himself rhetorically. He pointedly refused, for example, to describe himself as a Thatcherite, and in a symbolic counterblast to Thatcher's oft-quoted mantra insisted that 'there is such a thing as society, it's just not the same thing as the state' (Cameron 2005).

Cameron's modernization agenda encompassed a wide-ranging policy review, a concerted effort to improve party image and the Conservative 'brand', and ideological repositioning towards the centre-ground. Mindful of the problem acknowledged above by Howard, Cameron chose instead to downplay the habitual Conservative concerns of Europe, taxation, immigration, and law and order, and attempted to advance into Labour territory by focusing on issues such as the NHS (Bale 2010: 315–16). Non-traditional issues such as the environment and climate change, poverty and social justice, and feminization became central planks of Cameron's modernization strategy, as did a positive attitude towards gay rights and racial equality. The focus on matters such as these was an explicit effort to signal Conservative catch-up with the process of value change identified in Inglehart's (1977) 'silent revolution' thesis, and to detoxify the Conservative brand so that it no longer repelled middle-class professional voters who might be the party's natural constituency in economic terms, but were uneasy with its positioning in relation to their post-material values. Cameron and his fellow advocates of modernization argued that their 'liberal conservatism' was the ideological and policy prescription the Conservatives needed to adapt to this context and compete successfully in elections in the twenty-first century. Even if many in their own party did not like it, they insisted that public opinion had moved in a socially liberal direction, and that this was in many ways consistent with the individualistic economic liberalism the Conservatives had championed since the 1980s.

In the early years of David Cameron's leadership, some observers accordingly argued that it had brought about a substantial shift in Conservative Party ideology, policy and electoral strategy. Writing in 2007, Peter Dorey, for example, noted that: 'Cameron has toiled tirelessly during his first year as Conservative leader to reposition the Party ideologically, and revive the "one nation" strand which atrophied during the 1980s and 1990s. In so doing, he has explicitly eschewed Thatcherism, and effectively apologized for many aspects of it, while explicitly abandoning many of the policies implemented during the Thatcher–Major premierships' (Dorey 2007: 162).

However, the consensus amongst academic evaluations of Cameron's modernization agenda is that although there were clearly identifiable initial efforts to steer the Conservatives back towards the centre-ground, these foundered relatively quickly, and proved insufficiently substantial to prevent a turn back towards an essentially neoliberal programme in the context of the worsening economic circumstances from 2008 onwards. As one comprehensive assessment put it, 'lacking a sufficiently robust and coherent core' Conservative modernization 'proved insubstantial in both ideational and policy terms' (Kerr and Hayton 2015: 129). This is explored here in relation to the four major policy challenges that mainstream right parties face today, namely, European integration, immigration, moral issues and welfare.

One of the most striking aspects of Cameron's leadership of the Conservative Party was his unwillingness to challenge its approach to the European issue. Clearly conscious of the fact that Euroscepticism was the biggest determinant of voting in the 1997 and 2001 party leadership elections, Cameron sought to burnish his own anti-integrationist credentials by pledging in his own bid for the job to withdraw Conservative MEPs from the main centre-right grouping in the European Parliament, the European People's Party (EPP), if elected. Analysis by Heppell and Hill (2009: 396) suggested that 181 of the 198 MPs eligible to participate in the election could be classified as Eurosceptic, and that 78 of these backed Cameron. Given this depth of Euroscepticism in both the parliamentary party and wider membership by 2005, it seems questionable that as the least Eurosceptic candidate on offer he would have secured the leadership without offering this assurance (which was duly fulfilled in 2009). However, as explored in the section on Brexit below, this Eurosceptic positioning would leave Cameron with little room for manoeuvre once in government.

On immigration, in their analysis of the Conservatives' unsuccessful 2005 general election campaign, Philip Cowley and Jane Green (2005: 61) argued that the party 'had little choice' but to focus heavily on the topic, as it was one of the few issues where they had a clear lead over Labour, and its salience had risen substantially since 2001. Nevertheless, determined to learn the lessons of that failed campaign, Cameron, at least initially, sought to significantly downplay core-vote issues such as Europe, crime and immigration. On the latter, he appointed the liberal-minded Damian Green as the shadow minister responsible for policy development and modulated the party's rhetoric so that at least some forms of economic migration were discussed in much more positive language, stressing its benefits to society (Partos and Bale 2015). This change of tone was part of a wider effort, central to the modernization strategy, to combat the 'nasty party' image identified as a problem in 2002 by the then Party Chairman Theresa May. Given the wider societal value shift towards more widespread acceptance of multiculturalism, Cameron argued that by sticking to their traditional positions the Conservatives 'had lost touch with the country' (Cameron and Jones 2010: 292). The sense that the Conservative brand was toxic and in need of decontamination was also reinforced by evidence suggesting that in a number of areas, including immigration, policy positions lost support when voters learned they were Tory ones (Partos and Bale 2015: 171). But, as with the European issue, the substance of modernization in this area was very limited, with the party retaining a relatively hard-line stance aimed at significantly reducing the overall level of net inward migration. Furthermore, the change of tone proved temporary, with 'tough' talk returning from late 2007 onwards (Partos and Bale 2015: 172).

If the embrace of liberal values by Conservative modernizers on immigration was rather qualified, it was on moral issues, especially gay rights and gender equality, that they chose to engage in a full-frontal confrontation with traditionalists in the party. Most dramatically and symbolically, Cameron personally drove forward the introduction of equal marriage for same-sex couples in 2013, to the fury of Thatcherite social conservatives. Some 136 Conservative MPs voted against the legislation at second reading, with only 127 voting for it, meaning that it was carried only with the support of opposition parties (Hayton 2018: 227). On gender equality, Cameron took steps as leader of the opposition to prioritize the selection of female (and ethnic minority) parliamentary candidates through a priority list mechanism, which helped to raise the number of Conservative women in the House of Commons from seventeen to forty-nine in 2010. In 2009, Cameron also pledged that by the end of his first term in office a third of his government would be female, although he ultimately failed to meet this target (Campbell and Childs 2015: 154–5). This in itself is a reminder that Cameron's policy record in this area was mixed. On the one hand, championing 'the family' and marriage (albeit including for same-sex couples) demonstrated 'the limits of Conservative feminism in the social sphere' (Campbell and Childs 2015: 163); on the other hand, liberal feminist policies were promoted in areas such as women's participation in the workplace, for example, flexible working and shared parental leave (Campbell and Childs 2015: 159). In short, while Cameron's approach was undoubtedly driven in significant part by a desire to change the face of his party for electoral reasons, it also marked a shift towards more open-minded positions on sociocultural issues such as gay rights and gender equality. Although the party (both in Parliament and in the country) remains deeply divided on moral matters, the appetite for refighting battle issues such as same-sex marriage where legislative changes have been made seems limited, as other issues have risen to the fore.

If advocates of 'progressive conservatism' could feel comfortable with, or even proud of, the record of the Conservative-led Coalition government on moral issues, it is unlikely the same could be said in relation to welfare, where, with an individualist outlook consistent with Thatcherism, it downgraded the role of the state in reducing material inequalities (Griffiths 2014). The welfare state became the target for genuinely significant spending cuts as part of the austerity agenda aimed at eliminating the deficit in the public finances, which was enshrined as the number one objective of the government in the 2010 Coalition Agreement (Hayton 2014). In opposition, Cameron had appeared to distance himself from Thatcherite welfare policy through an emphasis on 'social justice' (a Social Justice Policy Group was established), and explicit recognition of the need to tackle relative as well as absolute poverty (Hayton and McEnhill 2015: 140). However, as with immigration, in office this shift proved to be more rhetorical than substantive, with the Treasury-driven priority of reducing expenditure overriding the (often conflicting) policy ambitions of the Department for Work and Pensions.

Critics also accused the government of using welfare policy to create divisions for electoral advantage rather than to promote social cohesion (e.g., the relative protection afforded to pensioner benefits, received by older people who are more likely to be Conservative voters) and as a way of masking a wider programme of neoliberal retrenchment (Taylor-Gooby 2016). In short, the bleak economic outlook from 2008 onwards prompted a return by the Conservatives to their default Thatcherite position of scepticism regarding the need to use welfare policies to proactively reduce inequality, with a focus on individual responsibility (e.g., to seek work) remaining absolutely central to the party's approach. In spite of the pressure on the government finances, large sums were committed to reducing income tax for lower and middle earners. So, rather than giving precedence to post-material value concerns, the Conservatives used welfare policy as an aspect of an electoral strategy based on defending the material interests of the party's core electoral blocs, namely, middle-class and older voters.

Cameron's leadership of the Conservative Party can therefore be credited with modernizing its appeal sufficiently to return it to power after thirteen years in opposition in 2010. But there are caveats. It marked a significant alteration of leadership strategy from that pursued by his predecessors, predicated as it was on enthusiastically accepting, rather than bemoaning, the post-material value change which New Labour had for a period effectively represented. And this shift enabled Cameron to form the Coalition government with the centrist Liberal Democrats, which would have been almost unimaginable prior to his leadership. It also helped Cameron to cannibalize Liberal Democrat support at the following general election in 2015, capturing twenty-seven seats from his partners in government to secure an unexpected overall majority. However, Cameron's modernization strategy lacked ideological coherence, was at times inconsistently applied, and left the leadership exposed to party management difficulties (Kerr and Hayton 2015). To a notable degree these limitations reflected not only the continued attachment to the core tenets of Thatcherism within the Conservative Party, but the unceasing challenge of holding together an electoral coalition appealing to centre-ground swing voters, while retaining core supporters sympathetic to (indeed part of) the silent counter-revolution. The difficulties of doing so, in the face of intensifying party competition on the right, are analysed in the following section.

4. Not So Silent: Brexit and the Divide on the Right

The origins of UKIP lie in the divide on the right over the issue of European integration that opened up in British politics over the Maastricht Treaty in the early 1990s. Growing Euroscepticism in the Conservative Party under Thatcher exploded into internecine warfare over the ratification of the treaty, pushing John Major's government to the brink of collapse. UKIP was formed in 1993 as a hard-Eurosceptic party committed to withdrawal from the EU, mainly by disaffected Conservatives many of whom had been involved in the Bruges Group (Tournier-Sol 2015: 142). However, most Conservative Eurosceptics remained in their party, and UKIP struggled to break through from the fringes of British politics. Most obviously it was constrained by the first-past-the-post electoral system, but it also faced numerous difficulties in terms of its strategy, internal organization and leadership (Usherwood 2008). Although some Conservatives became increasingly concerned about the potential split in the centre-right vote, the party leadership 'consistently rebuffed' any suggestion of forming an electoral pact with UKIP (Usherwood 2008: 259).

The shift, in 1999, to proportional representation for elections to the European Parliament facilitated UKIP's breakthrough onto the national political stage, winning three seats that year, twelve in 2004, thirteen seats (and finishing second) in 2009, and twenty-four (putting them in first place) in 2014. As David Cutts et al. (2019: 3) highlight, the long-term trend of declining vote-share for the two main parties since the 1970s was intensified at European elections by the change of electoral system, to the extent that 'by 2004 fewer than half of all voters were voting for one of the two main parties'. This trend continued, with the Conservatives and Labour receiving just 22.4 per cent of the vote between them in 2019. UKIP's rise was also undoubtedly assisted by increasing immigration, particularly following the 2004 enlargement of the EU and the decision by the UK government not to impose immigration controls on citizens from the ten new member states (Evans and Mellon 2019). This facilitated the fusion of Euroscepticism with the issue of immigration as the salience of the latter rose.

However, arguably at least as important to the rise of UKIP was the strategy of the Conservatives in opposition from 1997 onwards, who, driven by the silent counter-revolution as discussed above, 'first fused populism and Euroscepticism' (Bale 2018: 263). As Bale argues, Hague 'moved the party onto unashamedly populist territory' with unmistakably nativist, authoritarian and Eurosceptic refrains such as his infamous 'foreign land' speech (Bale 2018: 266). With New Labour sweeping up voters who identified with centrist, liberal and progressive values, it is perhaps unsurprising that the Conservatives orientated themselves towards an audience more receptive to the silent counter-revolution (Ignazi 1992). These values were, after all, already ingrained in the ideology of the party in the form of Thatcherism, which combined a neoliberal approach to economic issues with social authoritarianism and nationalism. However, the about-turn in strategy marked by Cameron's election as party leader 'created a vacuum that a skilfully led, out-and-out populist party could rush in to fill' (Bale 2018: 265). Moreover, as discussed above, although this modernization strategy was not sustained for as long or with the vigour of its early promise, the 'hiatus proved to be a critical juncture: by the time the Tories tried to return to that strategy after 2007, they had lost their monopoly on it' (Bale 2018: 274). The fact that early in his leadership Cameron had dismissed UKIP as 'a bunch of fruitcakes, loonies and closet racists, mostly'[1] set the tone for the future difficulties he would have convincing voters inclined to give UKIP a hearing that even when he talked tough on the issues of Europe and immigration he could be trusted to deliver.

If the early years of Cameron's leadership made countering UKIP more problematic for the Conservatives, the formation of the Coalition government with the centrist Liberal Democrats reinforced the opportunity structure for the radical right party to exploit. UKIP presented itself as the obvious home for traditionalist Tories disgruntled with their party's drift in a more socially liberal direction, and sought to capitalize on dissatisfaction with the government's failure to meet its promises to reduce immigration, and used the issue of free movement of people as a way to link this with the question of EU membership. A 2013 survey of Conservative Party members found that more than half of them were willing to contemplate voting UKIP,

[1] BBC News, 4 April 2006.

with 28.9 per cent describing themselves as likely UKIP voters (Webb and Bale 2014: 964). Ideologically, that section of the Conservative membership viewed themselves as closer to UKIP than to David Cameron, strongly favouring lower immigration, withdrawal from the EU and opposing their leader's support for gay marriage (Webb and Bale 2014: 965). The expression of such sentiments in local associations, and the general rise in support for UKIP in the opinion polls, only increased the motivation for Conservative MPs to demonstrate their own Eurosceptic credentials by backing calls for a referendum on EU membership. Cameron gave in to this pressure in January 2013, announcing that the Conservatives would legislate for a referendum if re-elected with a majority enabling them to do so. It is almost inconceivable that he would have conceded to this vote without the presence of UKIP on the populist right, which was a powerful weapon for those within the Conservative Party arguing for a hard Eurosceptic position.

If Cameron hoped this promise would take the wind out of UKIP's sails and diffuse the pressure in his own party, he would soon be disappointed. Accompanied as it was by an undertaking to renegotiate the terms of British membership of the EU, it effectively legitimized the complaints about it that had long been advanced by UKIP and Eurosceptics in his own party. For Copsey and Haughton (2014: 79) this represented the culmination of what they term 'issue capture' – whereby the terms of the debate came to be 'determined by the vocal, Eurosceptic minority'. Cameron consequently set himself up to fail in the renegotiations, where whatever he proved able to achieve (which in the end was not a great deal) would never be sufficient to satisfy the hard Eurosceptics. UKIP's prominence continued to increase as its support rose, leading to its victory in the 2014 European Parliament elections and the defection of two Conservative MPs, who both then went on to win back their seats in by-elections as UKIP candidates. Under Cameron, despite his desire to play down the issue, the Conservative Party followed a path of 'Eurosceptic radicalization' (Alexandre-Collier 2018). The referendum pledge fuelled rather than quelled this, as it forced Conservative Eurosceptics to confront the choice of remaining or leaving in the EU. In the end, some 140 Conservative MPs, among them high-profile MPs like Boris Johnson and Michael Gove, backed Vote Leave – a significantly larger number than had been anticipated by the leadership.

In the UK case, the silent counter-revolution thus found its voice in the form of opposition to membership of the EU, culminating in the vote for Brexit in 2016. Both UKIP and the Conservative strategy discussed above fermented and facilitated this outcome. One reading of the Conservatives' handling of UKIP is that in the face of surging support for the radical right the governing party gave ground, seeking to adopt elements of its position to diminish its support. However, of at least as much importance to understanding the Conservatives' approach to the European question, and UKIP, is the extent to which Euroscepticism had become ingrained in the party's post-Thatcherite DNA. As UKIP and a series of external factors helped to raise the salience of the issues of Europe and immigration, the Conservative response was inevitably framed through a Eurosceptic lens. Further evidence for this can be found in the continued Eurosceptic radicalization of the Conservative Party, including the leadership, in the aftermath of the referendum (Alexandre-Collier 2018: 213–16). However, the risks with this approach were highlighted at the 2017 general election. While support for UKIP collapsed, and was largely folded into that for the Conservatives, support for the main parties became more sharply divided on Remain versus Leave lines. With Leave voters being more likely to be older, white and socially conservative, moving in this direction risked undoing the progress Cameron had made in adapting to the silent revolution and appealing to the median voter.

The 2017 general election provided an unexpected return to two-party politics, with the Conservatives and Labour winning their highest combined vote share (82.4 per cent) since 1970. The overall 6 per cent rise in Conservative vote share was not, however, evenly distributed, with the party actually losing ground amongst the under 45s and BME voters (Table 11.1). Liberals who had moved towards the party under Cameron also dropped away, while support amongst more authoritarian voters increased (Figure 11.3). The precariousness of the support for the two main parties was brutally exposed by the elections to the European Parliament in 2019. In that ballot, Labour received 13.6 per cent, and the Conservatives just 8.8 per cent, the worst result in the latter's history (Cutts et al. 2019: 2). The election was won by the Brexit Party, which had been formed just six weeks earlier by the former leader of UKIP, Nigel Farage. This new outfit, which advocated a no-deal 'hard' Brexit from the EU, secured twenty-nine seats and 30.5 per cent of the vote. Remain voters meanwhile flocked to the

Table 11.1 *Profile of 2017*
Conservative voters

All voters	44 (+6)
Gender	
Male	44 (+6)
Female	43 (+6)
Age	
18–24	27 (–1)
25–34	27 (–6)
35–44	33 (–2)
45–54	43 (+7)
55–64	51 (+14)
65+	61 (+14)
Social class	
AB	47 (+2)
C1	44 (+2)
C2	45 (+13)
DE	38 (+12)
Ethnic group	
White	45 (+6)
Black and Minority Ethnic	19 (–4)
Education	
No qualifications	52
Other qualifications	46
Degree or higher	33

Source: Bale and Webb (2018: 54).

resurgent Liberal Democrats (sixteen seats, 19.6 per cent) and the Greens (seven seats, 11.8 per cent). Analysis of vote-switching at the 2017 general election attributed the rise in support for the Conservatives to their 'compelling appeal' to Leave voters after the referendum, which 'removed the main obstacle to a credible Conservative policy on immigration' (Mellon et al. 2018: 727, 733–4). The failure to deliver Brexit by the long-promised (and self-imposed) deadline of 29 March 2019 destroyed this credibility, and drove the surge in support for Farage's new party. Faced with destruction, the Conservatives reached for the emergency lever: the man who had led Vote Leave to victory, Boris Johnson.

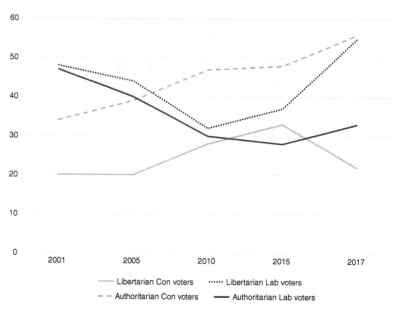

Figure 11.3 Conservative and Labour vote choice by libertarian–authoritarian position
Source: reproduced from British Social Attitudes 35: Voting (2017: 1).

5. 'Do or Die': The Conservatives under Boris Johnson

Unable to secure parliamentary support for the withdrawal agreement she had negotiated with the EU, and faced with electoral humiliation, Theresa May, Conservative Prime Minister since Cameron's post-referendum departure in the summer of 2016, resigned. Boris Johnson, who had led the Leave campaign in the 2016 referendum, won the leadership election that followed, becoming the first Conservative leader to be elected with the support of a majority of both the Conservative MPs (51.1 per cent) and party members (66.4 per cent). Key to this victory was his insistence that for him Brexit was 'do or die' and would be elevated above every other governing priority. This chimed with the views of the party membership, who prioritized it not only over the very survival of the Conservative Party itself, but even over the unity of the United Kingdom (YouGov 2019). Like Johnson, the party members also believed that failing to deliver Brexit would condemn the Conservatives to crushing electoral defeat and threaten the party's very survival. For an office-seeking party, the decision to elect Johnson therefore made sense, even if it came with significant attendant risks, given his status as a divisive political figure and doubts about his suitability for high office.

Boris Johnson's strategy was to position himself, and the Conservative Party, as the standard bearer for the silent counter-revolution symbolized by Brexit. However, the position of Brexit at any cost was not one all of the Parliamentary Conservative Party was willing to stomach, and in early September twenty-one Conservative MPs joined forces with opposition parties to force the government to request a further extension to Article 50 if a deal was not reached by 19 October. Johnson's response was to expel the rebels, leaving his government with a majority of minus forty-three. Pitching himself as the voice of the people against Parliament, Johnson called for a general election to be held, but this was resisted by Labour on the grounds that the threat of a 'No Deal' Brexit remained, and Johnson was consequently unable to reach the supermajority stipulated by the Fixed-Term Parliaments Act for an early dissolution. However, to the surprise of many observers a revised Withdrawal Agreement was struck with the EU on 17 October, which Johnson insisted could be pushed through Parliament in three days, to enable a departure at the end of the month. Parliament again voted for an extension to Article 50 (to 31 January 2020), which meant that Labour's opposition to a general election crumbled, and a date of 12 December was agreed.

Johnson's renegotiation of the Brexit deal provided him with a simple message for the general election: vote Conservative to 'get Brexit done'. Although Johnson's deal was criticized by Nigel Farage as a sell-out, he was able to marginalize the Brexit Party and effectively unify much of the Leave vote behind the Conservatives, while the Remain vote was much more fragmented. At the 2019 general election, around three-quarters of the 2016 Leave vote backed the Conservatives, enabling the party to capture Labour seats in the so-called 'red wall' of working-class, Leave-voting Labour heartlands in the North and Midlands (Cutts et al. 2020). In short, Johnson effectively mobilized the political cleavage of the silent revolution and silent counter-revolution that had been crystallized by the Brexit vote. Johnson's election triumph, winning a majority of eighty seats, meant that the Withdrawal Agreement legislation could be quickly passed, and the United Kingdom departed the EU at the end of January 2020, seven months after Boris Johnson became prime minister.

6. Conclusion

If the UK's departure from the EU was a cause for Conservative celebration, any sense of triumph was short-lived. The Johnson administration was rapidly consumed by an altogether more deadly crisis of a different magnitude, as the United Kingdom was engulfed by the Covid-19 pandemic a few weeks later, and in April 2020 the prime minister found himself battling the disease in intensive care. While we can readily assume that the likely economic, social and political impacts will be profound, ascertaining what form these might take over the long term is all but impossible. The level of government intervention into British economic and social life is unprecedented in peace time and throws into question many of the neo-Thatcherite shibboleths that have shaped Conservative politics over the past three decades. Rebuilding the economy, and dealing with the profound societal consequences of the pandemic are challenges which put the (as yet still unresolved) question of the nature of the UK's future relationship with the EU in the shade. Nonetheless, it will be a Conservative government that confronts these tasks, and which will approach them from the viewpoint identified in this chapter. As we have seen, the post-Thatcher era was one of crisis for the Conservative Party, which struggled to rebuild its electoral credibility in the face of New Labour's occupation of the political centre-ground. Initially, the Conservatives responded to the silent counter-revolution, attempting to shore-up their support on the right, before modernization under David Cameron saw the party adapt to the silent revolution. The limits of party change achieved by Cameron were, however, exposed by austerity politics and the continued hard-line policy positions on immigration and European integration. This left open a clear pathway to the populist embrace of the silent counter-revolution typified by Johnson.

Johnson's success in getting Brexit over the line in 2020 – something which looked far from certain at various points in the preceding three years – left the coalition of cosmopolitan, liberal and progressive forces that had gathered to resist Britain's departure from the EU scattered and weakened. It also took off the table the issue of European integration which had dogged the mainstream right in Britain since the early 1990s. Yet it is likely that liberal opponents of Johnson's politics will muster once again around other issues and test the coherence and potency of the Conservative Party's approach. Perhaps the most likely site of discord on the mainstream right will be on the issue of immigration, which has been a consistent headache for the Conservatives in recent decades and – although it became intertwined with the question of European integration – has not disappeared with Brexit. The opportunity to 'take back control' of immigration was trumpeted by Leavers as a key benefit of leaving the EU, and in February 2020 the government published a policy statement on its plan to introduce a 'points-based system' that would treat EU and non-EU citizens equally (HM Government 2020). The overall intention would be to reduce the overall level of migration, whilst also attracting 'the high-skilled workers we need to contribute to our economy, our communities and our public services' (HM Government 2020). The potential conflict here between the demands of business and the economy, and the desire of many voters to see immigration significantly reduced, is obvious. Previous form would suggest that the Conservatives will lean towards the objective of vote-seeking, but the trade-off could be costly for a party that traditionally liked to see itself as the voice of business.

Over the coming years and decades, the mainstream right in the United Kingdom will therefore face immense challenges as the Conservatives in government seek to navigate the uncharted waters of life after coronavirus and post-Brexit. Although the Labour Party faces an uphill task recovering from its worst defeat since the 1930s, the first seeds of recovery may have been sown by the election in April 2020 of Kier Starmer as leader, who has signalled his intention to rebuild Labour's credibility as an opposition by more effectively holding the government to account. And while the Brexit Party and UKIP were seemingly vanquished at the December 2019 general election, the prospect of another radical right challenger party emerging to take on the Conservatives can certainly not be discounted. Nonetheless, the Conservative Party enters the 2020s holding the levers of power and with the cushion of its largest majority since the 1980s. On balance, a further decade of Conservative dominance looks more likely than not.

12 The Mainstream Right in Western Europe in the Twenty-First Century

TIM BALE AND CRISTÓBAL ROVIRA
KALTWASSER

1. Introduction

An awful lot of ink has been spilled in recent years on the decline of social democracy and the rise of the populist radical right – and for good reason. Both developments represent major shifts in the political landscape of Western Europe even if, contrary to conventional wisdom in the media and even among politicians themselves, the one is not necessarily the cause of the other. But we need to be careful lest the attention devoted to them leads us to ignore something equally import-ant, namely, the fate of those parties that sit somewhere between the centre left and the far right. Conservative, Christian democratic and liberal parties may seem less 'sexy' than their more progressive and more regressive counterparts – at least in the eyes of academic and journalistic observers of politics. But they continue to matter to many voters, even if the socioeconomic changes associated with de-industrialization, feminization and mass migration have helped to trigger widespread fragmentation and polarization across Western European party systems, and led in many (though not quite all) cases to a significant and worrying loss of vote share. Moreover, and not-withstanding that loss of vote share, parties of the mainstream right continue – in some countries at least – to form the backbone of many of the administrations that govern them, giving those parties a crucial role both in public policy and in the maintenance (and maybe even the survival) of democracy. By overlooking the evolution and fate of the mainstream right, scholars are forgetting that the latter is a crucial actor when it comes to thinking about the preservation of the liberal order in Western Europe. Where the mainstream right '... holds fast in its commitment to democratic norms, it hinders far-right extremists from winning majorities and governing'. (Grzymala-Busse 2019: 41). However, as Donald Trump's presidency in the United States revealed, mainstream right forces are not immutable and under certain circumstances can end up being colonized by populist radical right actors, who gradually subvert the liberal democratic regime from within (Mudde and Rovira Kaltwasser 2017; Levitsky and Ziblatt 2018).

This in itself would make our effort to look more closely at Western Europe's mainstream right parties a worthwhile exercise. But our intention was to do more than that. First, we wanted to provide some conceptual clarity as to which parties could be usefully labelled as such and a guide to the differences and similarities between them, as well as the differences and similarities between them and the far right, whether of the populist or the extreme variants of the latter (Mudde 2019). Mainstream right parties, we concluded, drawing on the work of other scholars, share with their more radical counterparts a belief that the main inequalities within society are natural and largely outside the purview of the state. However, they are distinct from them in proffering more moderate policies, and they generally support existing norms and values as well as refrain from calling for the overthrow of the political system as currently constituted. Put briefly, and to use the concepts coined by Juan Linz (1978), while the mainstream right is a loyal supporter of the liberal democratic model, the far right should be seen rather as semi-loyal – and in some cases even disloyal.

Mainstream right parties, then, are drawn from one of three party families: the Christian democrats, the conservatives and the liberals – or at least the liberals of the market rather than the social variety. The first of the three party families – the Christian democrats – is characterized not only by the promotion of European integration, class compromise, accommodation and pluralism, but also by the development of a particular welfare regime that, amongst other things, privileges families over individuals and is based on the principle of subsidiarity. Members of the second party family – the conservatives – generally promote a rather more residual welfare state, and take a more nationalistic line, being noticeably less enthusiastic, for instance, about European integration. By contrast, members of the third party family – the liberals – are generally more internationalist as well as more concerned with the promotion and protection of pluralism and individual rights (and not just property rights) rather than the preservation of traditional values.

Having established these definitions, we then sought to improve our understanding of the current situation of, and the challenges faced by, the mainstream right in Western Europe. These, we argued, are profitably understood as its need to cope, both sequentially and simultaneously, with the silent revolution outlined by Inglehart (1977, 1990) and the silent counter-revolution predicted by Ignazi (1992). The very appearance of these two revolutions means managing the trade-off between office-seeking, policy-seeking and vote-seeking objectives (Strøm and Müller 1999) is becoming harder and harder for the mainstream right across the region. In effect, mainstream right parties face a tension between, on the one hand, their need to attract better-off and better-educated voters, many of whom express the liberal and progressive values associated with the silent revolution and, on the other, their desire – for some of them a desire that borders on desperation – to attract often (but not always) less well-off and less well-educated voters sympathetic to the authoritarian and nativist appeals associated with the silent counter-revolution. That tension, of course, potentially occurs across a range of policy domains, but we chose to focus on those where it seemed to us most likely to flare up, namely, European integration, immigration, moral issues and welfare.

In this conclusion, we aim to summarize the lessons learned both from our eight country case studies and the two comparative chapters that preceded them – one looking at the supply side (the parties of the mainstream right) and one looking at the demand side (their voters – whether actual, potential or now lost). The rest of this final contribution is structured in four parts. First, we assess the extent to which the general argument of the book holds true for all the country cases included in our analysis. After this, we turn our attention to the three party families of the mainstream right – Christian democrats, conservatives and liberals – and examine the ways in which each of them has been coping with the tension between the silent revolution and silent counter-revolution. In part three, we look at four policy dimensions that have been and will continue to be key for the electoral profile of the mainstream right, namely, European integration, immigration, moral issues and welfare. Finally, we close by advancing some ideas on the future research agenda on the mainstream right in Western Europe and beyond.

2. Does the Framework Work for All Countries?

Framing the dilemmas and difficulties experienced by mainstream right parties in Western Europe as the consequence of the challenges of both the silent and the silent counter-revolution has, we would argue, proved a fruitful approach in nearly all of the countries on which we have chosen to focus. In fact, the two large N studies that examine the demand side (Chapter 2) and the supply side (Chapter 3) of mainstream right parties in Western Europe, confirm the validity of the main argument of this book. However, when we carry out a more in-depth analysis of the country cases considered in this edited volume, it would appear that, in two instances – Italy and Spain – our theoretical framework applies only with some caveats.

As Castelli Gattinara and Froio note in their chapter, the Italian party system was rather unusual in that it had been dominated for decades by a centre-right, Christian democratic party that was always in office and by a Communist party (the PCI) that was effectively prohibited from participating in government – at least at the national level. It was also unusual in that, from very early on and notwithstanding its association with violence, an out-and-out far right party (albeit a small one – the MSI) received a sufficient share of the vote in Italy's then very permissive electoral system to count in what was already a fairly fragmented environment. Then, most unusual of all, that party system imploded almost overnight in the early 1990s as the Christian Democrats and the small (nominally) Socialist Party was mired in scandal and the PCI was left beached by the collapse of Soviet-sponsored Communism throughout the continent, east and west (Morgan 2012). The vacuum – at least on the right – was then filled not by a representative of any of the three familiar mainstream right party families (conservatives, Christian democrats and liberals), but by a personalist, populist party created by Silvio Berlusconi, largely, it so often seemed, to satisfy his vanity and to protect his extensive and often rather murky business interests (McDonnell 2013). Indeed, the authors of the Italian chapter emphasize that Berlusconi's political parties should be thought of as vote-seeking and/or office-seeking but not really as policy-seeking machines.

Berlusconi's *Forza Italia* was helped to govern by the MSI or rather the supposedly 'post-fascist', more mainstream conservative party, *Alleanza Nazionale*, into which it rapidly transformed itself – before, that is, eventually merging with *Forza Italia* to form *Il Popolo della Libertà*. It was also helped into government by the *Lega Nord* – originally a regionalist party campaigning for more autonomy, only later becoming the populist radical right party (and now very much the standard-bearer for the silent counter-revolution) that is the *Lega* today. Its popularity, along with the waning of Berlusconi's, means that, for the moment at least, the mainstream right, even if it has not quite disappeared from Italy, has only a minor presence there. In summary, although it is true that the tension between the silent revolution and silent counter-revolution is present in contemporary Italy, the right-wing bloc does not contain an electorally strong representative of any of the three mainstream party families; and it is therefore no coincidence that the populist radical right is performing so well today. Indeed, Italy is the country in Western Europe in which the chances of far right success are probably greatest – something that, of course, represents a major challenge to the liberal democratic regime.

The second case study where the theoretical framework would seem to apply only with caveats is Spain. As Alonso and Field rightly point out in their chapter, the Popular Party (PP) was able to entrench itself as the hegemonic player in the right-wing bloc for more than twenty years. This success story is related to the capacity of this conservative party, first, to adapt itself to the silent revolution that manifested itself so powerfully after years of repression in post-transition Spain, and, second, to adopt pragmatic positions that allowed the party to form governments with different political actors relevant at the regional level. As a consequence, for a long stretch of time, the PP did not find it too difficult to maintain a balance between its office-seeking, policy-seeking and vote-seeking objectives. However, the PP has recently lost its dominant position owing to the rise of two right-wing competitors: on the one hand, a liberal (albeit strongly nationalist) party (*Ciudadanos*), and, on the other hand, a populist radical right party (*Vox*).

Interestingly, the origins of this transformation of the right-wing bloc in contemporary Spain have little to do with the tension between the silent revolution and silent counter-revolution, but rather with three phenomena that deeply altered the country's political system: the Great Recession; corruption scandals affecting the PP in particular; and the push for independence in Catalonia (Orriols and Cordero 2015; Bosch and Durán 2019; Roberts 2017). In these circumstances, the PP is increasingly struggling to maintain its catch-all profile. For the moment, the PP appears to be prioritizing office goals at the expense of policy goals, accommodating some of the demands of the far right with the aim of building governments at the regional level. Nevertheless, it remains to be seen if this strategy can work at the national level and whether there is sufficient electoral space in Spain for the consolidation of all three right-wing political parties.

By looking at the cases of Italy and Spain, one can observe that the tension between the silent revolution and silent counter-revolution is certainly important to understand the fate of the mainstream right in these two countries today. Nevertheless, the collapse of the Italian Christian Democrats in the early 1990s and the recent electoral defeats of the PP in Spain are related to country-specific problems, such as corruption scandals, economic performance and the salience of centre–periphery cleavage. This means that, although nowadays the mainstream right in these countries is, as it is in other countries, caught between the silent revolution and silent counter-revolution, the roots of its electoral decay primarily lie elsewhere. Whether this argument may hold true for other Southern European countries too should be examined by future studies, but some evidence already points to this possibility (e.g., Hutter and Kriesi 2019; Roberts 2019b).

By contrast, in all the other country cases considered in this book (Austria, Germany, France, the Netherlands, Sweden and the United Kingdom), it is clear that the silent revolution and silent counter-revolution are having a deep impact on the political system in general and on the right-wing bloc in particular. While in some countries the backlash against increasing immigration and the cultural changes began as far back as the 1980s due to the early consolidation of the populist radical right (e.g., Austria and France), in other countries this backlash is rather a more recent phenomenon due to the late arrival of the populist radical right (e.g., Germany and Sweden). Despite differences in the timing of the latter, however, all mainstream right parties in Western Europe have been (or at least felt) obliged do something to ride, if not to resist, the populist radical right wave – one that threatens their ability to maintain both their electoral footing and a halfway coherent ideological profile. Nevertheless, as we will discuss in the next section, although all of the party families of the mainstream right in Western Europe have been adapting in the face of electoral pressure from the populist radical right, they have adopted different strategies to cope with the backlash against the silent revolution.

3. How the Different Party Families are Caught between the Silent Revolution and Silent Counter-Revolution

Another way of exploring the utility of the framework is to move away from the country cases *qua* country cases and to look instead, and in turn, at the three party families that, make up the mainstream right: the Christian democrats, the conservatives and the liberals. Does their shared need to cope with the challenges of the revolutions in question tell us something about how each of them has fared and which might be best positioned to cope (see Gidron, 2020)? As we will explain below, all three have been trying to ride the populist radical right wave in different ways, but they tend to share an important similarity – namely, a tendency to adopt harsher stances on immigration without necessarily taking negative positions on other dimensions associated with the liberal and progressive values of the silent revolution.

Clearly, in some ways things have been hardest for Christian democratic parties – at least across Western Europe as a whole. In effect, the data presented at the beginning of this book (Chapter 1) reveal that this party family has been suffering a gradual electoral decline since the 1980s onwards. The silent revolution brought a decline not just in religiosity but in adherence to the traditional values associated with it, both of which are associated with support for the Christian democrats. Meanwhile, the silent counter-revolution – and in particular the nationalism, xenophobia and antipathy to immigration associated with it – represents a direct challenge to Christian democracy's support for internationalism (typified by its role in encouraging European integration) and its traditional commitment to charity and 'turning strangers into friends'.

Certainly, it would appear that the Austrian, Dutch and German Christian democrats have suffered as expected. In these three cases, we find important commonalities, such as decreasing electoral support over time and growing trouble in maintaining a catch-all profile. In spite of this, Christian democratic parties continue to play a key role in Austria, Germany and the Netherlands, since they have been able to form a government on several occasions, either as junior partners in the case of the Netherlands or as the main partner that provides the prime minister in the cases of Austria and Germany. This confirms that Christian democracy in Western Europe puts special emphasis on its office-seeking dimension but, as we will explain below, this has important consequences on its policy-seeking and vote-seeking dimensions.

Stijn van Kessel shows in Chapter 8 that even though the Dutch Christian Democrats (CDA) have still been able to get into government recently, their electoral support has been declining over time – and at a fairly fast pace. Part of the reason for this lies in the increasing fragmentation of the Dutch political system and the emergence of different populist radical right parties that attract some of the voters that in the past voted for the Christian democrats. Not by chance, the CDA has been adopting a harsher discourse on immigration while at the same time maintaining a centrist position on economic issues. Whether, however, that can provide it with a clear ideological profile that is attractive to the electorate and facilitates its continued participation in government remains to be seen. The more the party is willing to accommodate anti-immigrant discourse, the more it legitimizes the agenda of the populist radical right and the less capacity it will have to develop a distinctive and attractive programmatic profile.

In the German case, the electoral decline of the CDU/CSU has been gradual and constant. In fact, three of the four governments headed by Chancellor Angela Merkel (2005–2009, 2013–2017 and 2017–present) have been *große Koalitionen* between Christian and Social Democrats. As Sarah Wiliarty argues in Chapter 6, while the problems caused to the party by the need to adapt to the country's growing social liberalism have made for some awkward moments, the challenges presented both by the presence of a large ethnic minority population and, even more so, by the refugee/migration crisis have proved to be more difficult still. Indeed, were it not for the weakness of its traditional centre-left opponent, the CDU/CSU would, one assumes, be in much greater trouble than it currently seems to be (or at least was prior to the pandemic), not least owing to the rise of the increasingly populist and increasingly radical right AfD. Nevertheless, the CDU/CSU remains an extremely pragmatic party that has enough ideological flexibility to form government coalitions with different political parties, demonstrating the priority it places on office-seeking. The only option in that respect that appears to remain off the table is counting on the formal or informal support of the populist radical right, since this

would damage the capacity of the CDU/CSU to present itself as
a *mainstream* right party capable of adapting to the silent revolution
rather than adopting the values of the silent counter-revolution.

In Austria, as in Germany, the Social Democrats have experienced
a much steeper electoral decline than the Christian democrats. But in
contrast to Germany, the Austrian Christian democrats have decided to
assume office with the support of the far right. Heinisch and Werner
convincingly argue in Chapter 4 that two interrelated factors help us to
understand the willingness of the Austrian Christian democratic party
(ÖVP) to cooperate with and adapt to the agenda of populist radical
right. First, when the ÖVP has been polling behind the populist radical
right, it shows more inclination to accommodate and even support
a backlash against increasing immigration and the cultural changes of
the silent revolution. Second, whenever its hard-line conservative and
market liberal factions grow stronger within the party, the possibility
of building a governing coalition with the populist radical right
becomes much stronger. In effect, as we will go on to discuss in more
detail below, the apparent rude health of the party under Sebastian
Kurz seems to have come at the cost of it moving a very long way from
(and critics might even say abandoning) some, if not all, of its Christian
democratic principles. In other words, the rise of Kurz epitomizes the
defence of office-seeking and vote-seeking strategies at the cost of
Christian democracy's ability to advance a clear and coherent policy-
seeking profile – or at least one that accords with what we have
traditionally understood as its ideological underpinnings.

Western Europe's conservative parties should, on the face of it,
have been better able to cope with the silent counter-revolution
since nationalism, as well as, for instance, a penchant for 'law and
order', was already very much part of who they were. Their respect
for traditional hierarchies and so-called 'family values', on the other
hand, admittedly made the silent revolution a slightly trickier prospect, although what, in most cases, were rather looser links with the
Church offered them a little more flexibility than their Christian
democrat counterparts. An additional problem for conservatives is
the difficult – if not impossible – reconciliation of liberal economic
positions with opting to closing borders to foreigners. When riding
the populist radical right wave, conservative parties should in theory
have difficulty in advocating harsh anti-immigration policies which
could end up alienating one of its main core constituencies – the

business community. After all, the latter is normally in favour of immigration as a way to maintain access to cheap and/or skilled labour and thereby remain competitive.

The British Conservative Party, save for a brief (albeit quite costly) hiatus during the early years of David Cameron's leadership between 2005 and 2016, has indeed found little difficulty in moving to the right on the cultural dimension, in particular by politicizing immigration (not least by tapping into welfare chauvinism) and the issue of national sovereignty. Some, however, would argue that the strategy was taken too far in response to the rise of the populist radical right party, UKIP, and its successor, the Brexit Party, resulting in the United Kingdom leaving the EU. When it comes to growing social liberalism, on the other hand, the Conservative Party initially found things trickier: what was acceptable up until the early 1990s (such as its lack of support for equalities legislation covering race, gender and sexuality) became far less so as the twentieth century turned into the twenty-first. As Richard Hayton maintains in Chapter 11, until David Cameron took over in 2005 with a mandate to modernize the party's appeal in the wake of three successive general election losses, many worried that it had effectively passed its sell-by date. In fact, any move towards what he billed 'liberal Conservatisim' proved only temporary and partial, and it enjoyed relatively narrow support at the party's grassroots. However, there seems little chance that some of its headline policy consequences – equal marriage and at least a superficial commitment to environmental and overseas aid targets – will be reversed. Nor has the party worried too much about the supposed inconsistency between them and the highly restrictive stance it has pursued on immigration since re-entering government in 2010.

As a result, at least in the short to medium term, then, the Conservatives in the United Kingdom can claim to have weathered both the silent revolution and silent counter-revolution relatively well. As with the Austrian Christian democrats, however, it is possible to argue that it has been able to do so only by coming awfully close, particularly in the post-Cameron era to turning itself into an *ersatz* populist radical right party. Certainly, for some Tories who retain their belief in the small-state market liberalism that for so long distinguished the United Kingdom from many other European countries (and drove a decade of unprecedented austerity after 2010), that is a serious concern – not least as they observed the potent combination of nationalism, law and order, hostility to immigration, and the large spending increases promised by the party at the 2019 general election. Whether, though, such an agenda has long-term appeal in a country that is becoming more socially liberal and ever more multicultural will be interesting to see in the coming years. As Hayton rightly points out, the party has united behind Boris Johnson not because of his ability to advance a convincing policy platform, but rather because of the success of his office-seeking and vote-seeking strategy. In other words, it remains to be seen if the Conservatives can develop a coherent ideological agenda in post-Brexit (and indeed post-pandemic) Britain.

But by no means every West European conservative party, however, has been able to cope as well as its British counterparts (so far anyway) with the challenges posed by the two revolutions. As Anders Ravik Jupskås shows in Chapter 10, Sweden's conservative party, the Moderates, was – more than most conservative parties – relatively comfortable with the silent revolution. Although taking a slightly tougher line on law and order than its Swedish rivals, that was not a big part of its platform. Moreover, it seemed relatively in tune with the welfare regime that characterizes most Nordic countries and was notably less nationalist than its sister parties in other European countries, being strongly in favour – in marked contrast to the British Conservatives – of European integration. Its enthusiasm for globalization also meant it was, for some years anyway, reluctant to adopt the concerns of the silent counter-revolution in spite of rising evidence of a backlash against increasing immigration and the cultural changes that accompanied it. Any losses to other parties more prepared to tap into those concerns, however, were more than compensated for by increased support from voters disillusioned with the economic governance of the Social Democrats and reassured by the Moderates' move to distance themselves from neoliberalism and instead pursue seemingly pragmatic positions to nurture its office-seeking and vote-seeking objectives. Nevertheless, as anxiety about immigration has mounted, the Moderates appear to have suffered losses to the far right Sweden Democrats, prompting a move on the party's part to the authoritarian right in order to stem those losses – a move that so far seems to be proving largely ineffectual and may have prompted losses to liberal parties on the other flank.

A similar, but probably more dramatic, tale is perhaps unfolding in France. Evans and Ivaldi maintain in Chapter 5 that the Gaullist right, in its various formations, for a long time did little to adapt itself to the silent revolution: it retained its small-c conservative stance and paid little attention to the environmental concerns that helped to contribute to the rise, on the other side of the fence, of *la gauche plurielle*, relying perhaps (whether consciously or otherwise) on the more liberal UDF to pick up mainstream right voters, many of whom have become disillusioned as a consequence of its inertia. It proved more alive to the concerns of the silent counter-revolution, especially when they began to be expressed by voters switching to the Front National (FN), with Chirac and especially Sarkozy talking (and sometimes acting) tough on immigration and integration as a vote-seeking strategy. Arguably, however, their successors overshot, doubling down on a conservative cultural agenda that extended beyond migration and multiculturalism to issues like equal marriage – a move that was both symptom and cause of liberal voters (and politicians) becoming alienated from the party. Nor in any case did it do the Gaullists much good: working-class, authoritarian voters to whom that cultural agenda may have appealed were put off by the so-called neoliberal, austerity policies advocated by them in response to the global financial crisis and instead were attracted by the anti-globalist, welfare chauvinist appeal of the FN. On the other flank, and as a consequence of the increasing adoption of tougher positions on the cultural dimension of competition, many liberal mainstream right voters defected (along with some politicians) to Macron's *En Marche!*, which developed a policy-seeking strategy based on the articulation of liberal positions on both sociocultural and socioeconomic issues, effectively stranding the Gaullists between the proverbial devil and the deep blue sea.

In Spain, the *Partido Popular* was (as a result of its *Franquista* heritage and unusually for a conservative rather than a Christian democratic party) closely associated with a highly traditionalist Catholic Church – an association that effectively prevented its politicians (even assuming they had wanted to) from embracing the cultural concerns of the silent revolution. However, as Alonso and Field reveal in Chapter 9, the PP was able to moderate over time, to the point that by the 1990s it had become catch-all party. Nor did its church links loom large – certainly not when compared with its aggressive defence of Spanish nationalism – until, that is, the party's socialist rival began, after it returned to power in 2004, to turn its increasing social liberalism into government policy, provoking a religiously inspired backlash. Even then, however, it seems clear that what cost the party most support was its fiscally orthodox, austerity-based response to the Great Recession, which hit Spain hard – especially when that response was combined with the corruption scandals that engulfed its representatives at all levels and with the moves towards separatism in Catalonia. Even worse for PP, that crisis gave rise to a seemingly more socially liberal (and corruption-free) new entrant on the right, *Ciudadanos*. It also (together with some, albeit limited, concerns about immigration and Islamism) fuelled the rise on the far right of what was effectively the belated, and highly nationalist, standard-bearer of the silent counter-revolution, *Vox* – an insurgency whose legitimacy and popularity PP only served to increase by ramping up its own rhetoric in an attempt to avoid being outflanked. For the moment, it seems that the Spanish conservatives appear to have been saved – at least at the November 2019 general election – from the fate suffered by their French counterparts, who did the same thing, by the decision of *Ciudadanos* to shift markedly to the nationalist right over the course of that year rather than following Macron's example and cleaving to the more liberal centre.

In summary, conservative parties in Western Europe have been deeply affected by the silent revolution and silent counter-revolution, to the point that most of them are searching for what might ultimately be an impossible electoral profile, namely, one that can simultaneously attract right-wing moderate and right-wing radical voters. As the French case study reveals, by trying to develop this sort of chameleonic electoral profile, mainstream right parties risk alienating rather than attracting voters, paving the way for a twofold process: the formation of a new political party that can represent centre-right voters; and the consolidation of a populist radical right that can give voice to far right voters. The Conservative Party in the United Kingdom might be the only exception to this critical trend, but caveats remain: this may in part be due to the peculiarities of the British electoral system, and the party's success in holding together its liberal and authoritarian factions may be more apparent than real in the long term.

In most of Western Europe, of course, mainstream right voters have long had an alternative to conservative and Christian democratic parties – namely, the liberals (see Close and van Haute 2019). In some countries, that alternative has traditionally been relatively marginal. Indeed, France, where the UDF (in spite of providing some prominent individual politicians and even, in the 1970s, a president) has served (depending on one's point of view) as an irritant or an adjunct to the Gaullists, is a good example of one such party. As Evans and Ivaldi's chapter shows, by failing to hold together despite its already small size, it can hardly be said to have effectively seized the opportunity presented by the Gaullists' move towards a culturally conservative agenda. The situation for Macron's *En Marche!* is different, since this is a new liberal political party that so far has been able to combine the defence of the values of the silent revolution with the endorsement of relatively pro-business positions. Should Macron's experiment endure and entrench itself in the French party system, it may become a success story for the liberal party family and a role model to be imitated by its counterparts across the continent. If, instead, it crashes and burns electorally, it will be a different story.

Liberal parties in other West European countries may have avoided French-style fragmentation. However, some have struggled either to retain a legislative and executive foothold or (partly in order to retain such a foothold) have moved away (at least in some aspects) from the cultural liberalism that used to distinguish them from their conservative and Christian democratic rivals on the centre-right. When one looks at Germany, for instance, it is clear that the liberal party (FDP) has been rapidly losing weight within the political system. Even when it achieves respectable results in federal elections, it finds it increasingly difficult to leverage them into a successful office-seeking strategy. But it is also struggling to find a programmatic profile that effectively attracts those voters who favour the free market and those who also hold progressive cultural values, some of whom may defect to the Greens, raising the possibility that the FDP might not make it into future parliaments – something that already actually happened in 2013.

Further West, in the Netherlands, however, the liberals have, as van Kessel's chapter shows, effectively ditched those values – at least as they relate to migration and multiculturalism if not to, say, sexuality – in an attempt to retain sufficient support to stay in government and further stem the flow of Dutch voters to the far right. In fact, under the leadership of Mark Rutte, the VVD in the Netherlands has at least for the moment succeeded in terms of office-seeking and vote-seeking, but at the cost of supporting ideas and policies that are at odds with key aspects of the silent revolution and therefore the agenda that, in theory at least, one would expect from a liberal party. Seen in this light, it could be argued that Rutte is following a similar approach to the one that the Austrian Christian democrats adopted under Kurz and that the Conservatives have followed in the post-Cameron era, namely, to build an *ersatz* populist radical right party.

Turning southwards, a much newer liberal party can be found in Spain. As Alonso and Field show in Chapter 9, the Great Recession and the corruption scandals that affected the two mainstream parties of the country (PP and PSOE) opened up the electoral opportunity structure – one that was exploited by *Ciudadanos*, which entered parliament in 2015. *Ciudadanos* is a liberal party, promoting mild pro-market reforms and progressive values; but it nevertheless adopts a harsh stance against regionalist parties – particularly against the pro-independence forces from Catalonia. Indeed, the reluctance of *Ciudadanos* to form a government with the social democratic PSOE or tolerate a minority government headed by the latter, has arguably moved the party into the silent counter-revolution camp championed by *Vox*. This has certainly eroded its liberal credentials and it remains to be seen if it can recover. But even if it can, it remains difficult to know whether, given Spain's relatively unforgiving electoral system, there is really room for three significant parties on the right.

As this brief overview of the three different party families that make up the mainstream right in Western Europe shows, all of them are caught between the silent revolution and the silent counter-revolution. By taking one side or the other, mainstream right parties risk alienating voters who back the other revolution and vice versa. When confronting this dilemma, there are some parties that have succeed in achieving office-seeking and vote-seeking objectives, but at the expense of the policy-seeking dimension. Therefore, this sort of 'winning formula' is deeply problematic because it implies neglecting some of the key features that differentiate the mainstream right from the far right. There may be no better example of this problematic situation than the Conservative Party in the post-Cameron era in the United Kingdom, the Christian democratic party in Austria under the leadership of Sebastian Kurz and the liberal party in the Netherlands headed by Mark Rutte. All these instances are marked by the acceptance and even endorsement of some of the values of the silent counter-revolution, to the point that – as we will argue below – scholars should seriously assess the extent to which these parties can be categorized as mainstream right cases.

4. Four Key Policy Challenges for the Mainstream Right in Western Europe

As we stated in Chapter 1, because they are caught between the silent revolution and silent counter-revolution, mainstream right parties in Western Europe are finding it increasingly hard to develop programmes and agendas that might allow them to represent large factions of the electorate. There are four policy dimensions where this challenge is particularly evident: European integration, immigration, moral issues and the welfare state. While in theory these four key policy challenges are of equal magnitude, in practice the contributions to this edited volume reveal that immigration is certainly the most salient and daunting. As the analysis on the evolution of Western Europe's mainstream right policy positions shows (Chapter 3), there is clear evidence that Christian democratic, conservative and liberal parties have increasingly adopted anti-immigration positions with the aim of countering the competition from the populist radical right.

Nevertheless, when analysing these four challenges in comparative perspective, there is considerable variation across both countries and party families, although there are clear patterns visible on EU integration and on immigration, with inertia characterizing the overwhelming majority of mainstream right parties on the former and a shift towards both greater emphasis and increasingly restrictive positions on the latter. On what we might term moral issues and the welfare state, however, it is less easy to discern clear patterns across all cases, suggesting that not all the issues that are normally associated with the silent revolution have equal relevance across Western Europe. In the following, we examine how the mainstream right in Western Europe is dealing with each of these four policy challenges.

On the EU, there is one clear outlier – the UK's Conservative Party. True, there have been some expressions of what might be termed 'soft Euroscepticism' from the ÖVP in Austria, the VVD in the Netherlands and from some Gaullist politicians in France. However, no West European mainstream right party has shown serious signs of wanting to follow the example set by their British counterpart – perhaps not surprisingly given the myriad difficulties Brexit has thrown up in the

United Kingdom. Although the results of Brexit will take years to properly assess, there is good reason to think that the example set by the UK's Conservative Party will not be seen as something to be imitated by their Western European brethren. After all, the Brexit referendum did little or nothing to unite the Conservative Party and its currently strong electoral position has a lot to do with the weakness of the centre left, an electoral system that is not present in any other Western European country, and the presence of a leader (Boris Johnson), who so far has succeeded in terms of office-seeking and vote-seeking but has arguably done so to the detriment of advancing a coherent policy-seeking strategy.

That notwithstanding, the majority of West European mainstream right parties, albeit at different speeds, have made significant moves towards more restrictive positions on immigration – even if those moves have rarely, if ever, achieved what seems to have been their main aim, namely, to kill off (or at least reduce) the electoral threat posed by the far right. The British Conservative Party, of course, has a long history, stretching back well over half a century, of passing restrictive legislation and talking tough in this area. In Italy, under the aegis of Berlusconi, in part because he was in an alliance with a post-fascist conservative party (AN) and the *Lega* (*Nord*), what passed for that country's mainstream right did the same in the 1990s. The French centre-right, after placing little emphasis on the issue in that decade, then moved to harden its line under Sarkozy and has done so even more under his successors. The PP in Spain began to do the same, although its attempt to do so stalled when the Great Recession hit the country hard. In contrast, in the Netherlands, both the Christian democratic CDA and the liberal VVD have placed more rather than less emphasis on immigration and integration in recent times, especially in the wake of the so-called migration crisis, although it is important not to forget that the VVD's record on both issues actually stretches back beyond the spectacular entry of Pim Fortuyn into Dutch politics in the early 2000s and the rise of the populist radical right PVV, founded by Geert Wilders, himself a defector from the VVD. In Sweden, despite the liberals there flirting with the *inte*gration (if not necessarily the *immi*gration) issue, the conservatives (the Moderates) resisted the temptation – until, that is, they began to lose significant numbers of voters to the Sweden Democrats, at which point they have moved to highlight migration as a problem, even if (for the moment at least) they differ from the far right on how best to tackle it.

Over in Germany, the country's Nazi past was long seen as a constraint on both support for the far right and the advocacy of anything resembling a far right message on immigration by the mainstream right (Art 2011). Yet CDU and especially CSU politicians have over the years made interventions on the issue, in part, some would argue, to prevent the rise of a serious rival on their right flank. Not surprisingly, then, many look upon Angela Merkel's generous response to the refugee crisis as a historic mistake that will help the party that now qualifies as such – the *Alternative für Deutschland* (AfD) – to win even more support. And it is noticeable that the CDU/CSU has made a lot of effort since then to stress that it is no soft touch. So far, however, we have not seen Germany's mainstream right (or indeed any country's mainstream right, apart from perhaps the UK's) come anything like as close, even in the wake of the external shock wrought by the 'migrant crisis', as the ÖVP in Austria and the VVD in the Netherlands have to promoting the kind of xenophobic (and even Islamophobic) policies and rhetoric most often associated with Europe's far right parties.

Things look more complicated when one examines the position of the mainstream right on moral issues, one of the key aspects – if not the key aspect – of the silent revolution according to Inglehart's (1977, 1990) early work. The absence of a clear pattern across the continent is probably related to the fact that the salience of moral issues hinges much more on national than on continental developments. While immigration is usually perceived and framed as a European problem, discussions about issues such as abortion, divorce, gay rights and gender equality become more or less relevant due to debates occurring at the national level. As a result, whether and how mainstream right parties decide to politicize moral issues depends on the public debate on them in each country. For instance, the ÖVP's move to the right on immigration and willingness to govern with the populist radical right FPÖ has gone hand in hand with a general move to the right on almost all cultural issues. But what some would see as a rejection of the concerns and values of the silent revolution is not necessarily par for the course everywhere.

Indeed, making that wider move is risky in terms of the vote-seeking strategy of mainstream right parties because – as appears to have been the case, for instance, for the French conservatives – it can trigger a loss of support from the more liberal (and often more affluent) voters on whom some of them rely. One reason for the Dutch VVD's relative electoral success, for example, may well be that it maintains a liberal position on virtually everything else apart from immigration and integration. The Dutch Christian Democrats, on the other hand, have maintained a more traditional position on moral issues, although, like their sister party in Germany, they have to some extent moved with the times with the aim of achieving their office-seeking and vote-seeking objectives. The same cannot, however, be said for the conservative PP in Spain, whose links to the country's Catholic Church seemed to oblige it to take a much more traditionalist line when the PSOE began to pass liberal legislation after it assumed office in 2004. This, however, contrasts markedly with the Swedish conservatives who (unlike the Swedish Christian Democrats) moved to a pro-choice position relatively early and who, by the turn of the century, were on their way to accepting same-sex marriage and adoption. The British Conservative Party followed a similar trajectory, albeit a little later, with any internal dissent soon fading away once the Cameron government's permissive legislation was passed after 2010.

If the picture presented by Western Europe's mainstream right on moral issues is a mixed one, the same can be said with respect to the welfare state, although the range of positions is rather narrower – perhaps because the parties involved recognize (as Chapter 2 shows) that relatively affluent, economically right-wing voters continue to make up a large proportion of their electorates. This means that the more socioeconomically heterogeneous the voting profile of the mainstream right, the more it should be keen on defending the welfare state. By contrast, when those who support the mainstream right are mainly well-off citizens, the easier it is for the party to develop policies in favour of reduced state intervention in the economy. Here, the UK Conservatives, who have always favoured as residual and as cheap a system as possible, are not so much an outlier as positioned at one end of the (mainstream right) spectrum, although that may change, first, in the wake of an election victory in 2019 that relied heavily on picking up voters in less affluent, so-called 'left-behind' areas of the country, and, second, in the wake of the huge rise in government intervention necessitated by Covid-19. At the other end lie the German Christian Democrats, who seem (especially after the strong approval for Angela Merkel's pro-welfare measures in the wake of the

Covid-19 crisis) to retain their belief (like their Dutch sister party) in the social market, and the Swedish Moderates, who seem to be sticking to the more centrist stance established by their 'modernizing' leader, Fredrik Reinfeldt, in the mid-2000s.

Rather closer to the British Conservatives – at least in terms of flirting with welfare chauvinism and an ambition to cut the size of the state and weaken organized labour – is the Austrian ÖVP, notwithstanding the party's desire to appeal to 'blue-collar' workers with the aim of stealing the traditional electorate of the Social Democratic party. The conservatives in France and Spain have also moved in a direction their opponents would characterize as 'neoliberal' and 'pro-austerity', which has had a negative impact in terms of the vote-seeking dimension since it alienated less well-off citizens who are strong supporters of the welfare state. Meanwhile, the Dutch VVD and the German FDP continue to position themselves as market liberals, something that is not difficult for them given their desire to appeal to affluent voters. Berlusconi's formations were generally pro-business but also pro a welfare system that supported families in particular rather than demonstrating any desire to restructure the welfare state as a whole.

5. Future Research Agenda

Mainstream right parties in Western Europe have had to cope with multiple challenges, two of which – the silent revolution and the silent counter-revolution – we have focused on. Some have coped better than others. In one country, Italy, it has disappeared altogether and in another, France, the conservative Gaullists may find it difficult to recover from the squeeze they are now facing not just from the far right (led by Le Pen) but from the liberal centre (led by Macron). In contrast, parties – each of them originally from a different party family – in the United Kingdom, Austria and (albeit in a far more fragmented party system) the Netherlands can claim to have discovered something of a 'winning formula' consisting of a (mild) neoliberal economic policy and a distinctly illiberal stance on immigration, along with a dash (or, in the UK Conservatives' case, considerably more than a dash) of Euroscepticism.

The fact that they have done so arguably has a lot to do with leadership, as well as with the victory (not always permanent) of one party faction over another. For instance, before David Cameron won the Conservative leadership in the United Kingdom in 2005, the party was very much the standard bearer of the silent counter-revolution; he – at least on moral issues – forced it to confront the concerns of the silent revolution rather than, as he put it, 'banging on' about Europe and immigration; however, he soon found himself forced by his party to do so, and his successors, Theresa May and Boris Johnson, have continued in the same vein. Or take Austria: it is clear that both Wolfgang Schüssel and Sebastian Kurz, and the factions that have supported them, have made a big difference to the ÖVP's ideological emphasis, its policy direction and its coalition decisions. The same can be said of the influence of Angela Merkel on the CDU in Germany, although it is sometimes easy to forget because her predominance was so often marked – unlike, say, Berlusconi's – by her simply holding the ring rather than creating some sort of spectacle. Failure of leadership can also be crucial, the French Gaullists being the obvious case in point, with that failure being thrown into even sharper contrast by the dark charisma of Marine Le Pen and the emergence of a politician who may or may not turn out to be on the mainstream right but who some see as a once-in-a-generation (albeit potentially temporary) phenomenon, Emmanuel Macron.

Institutions, or at least electoral systems, however, do not seem to matter so much. The Conservatives in the United Kingdom, for example, cannot simply dismiss the populist radical right because it cannot seem to win seats in the legislature as a result of Britain's first-past-the-post electoral system; the Tories still have to (and do) worry about the radical right costing them seats – indeed, perhaps all the more so because the Conservatives know support for it will be effectively 'wasted' since it will not produce a potential right-wing coalition partner for them in Parliament. The French centre-right also has to worry because of the possibility of being knocked out of the presidential contest. More acute is the pressure produced by highly per-missive electoral systems, like that used in the Netherlands, where no party – let alone a mainstream right party – can develop a catch-all profile, and in consequence, political competition is becoming increasingly harsh as parties compete to demonstrate to voters the differences between them.

All in all, it seems that mainstream right parties in Western Europe are facing a critical situation and their prospects can hardly be called bright. The evidence presented in this collection shows that they are finding it increasingly difficult to adequately manage the trade-off between the office-seeking, policy-seeking and vote-seeking objectives theorized by Strøm and Müller (1999). The unfolding of the Covid-19 crisis makes prediction even more difficult than it might be otherwise, but in any case, we, no more than anyone else, can claim to possess a crystal ball that can tell us for sure how the mainstream right will evolve in years to come. What we can do, however, to better understand where things might be going, is to close by flagging up three possibilities that comparative scholars might profitably explore when undertaking future comparative studies.

The first relates to the 'winning formula' that some mainstream right parties have sought to develop in order to remain electorally competitive. As the Conservatives in the post-Cameron era in the United Kingdom, the Christian democrats in Austria under the leadership of Sebastian Kurz and the liberal party in the Netherlands headed by Mark Rutte reveal, one possible way forward for them is to adapt to the silent counter-revolution on issues such as immigration/integration with the aim of closing the space available for the populist radical right. However, it is debatable whether this strategy represents a successful approach in the long term. There is no clear evidence that the radicalization of the mainstream right implies that the far right will disappear from the electoral scene. Given that populist radical right parties often succeed in owning the immigration issue, mainstream right parties can only partially please those citizens with strong xenophobic tendencies, many of whom will continue, to coin a phrase, to prefer the original to a copy.

Moreover, by adopting an anti-immigration profile, mainstream right parties risk alienating their moderate voters. Indeed, they might find it valuable to recall that in the late 1990s social democratic parties like Labour in the United Kingdom and the SPD in Germany also claimed to have discovered a 'winning formula' – in their case 'modernizing' the welfare state and adopting certain market-friendly policies. While this approach appeared to be a smart move in the short term, it is clear that in the long term it was a counterproductive strategy, helping to account for the difficult, even dire, situations that both currently face. If mainstream parties adopt policies that go against the ideas and interests of some of their core constituencies (e.g., the unionized working class in the case of social democratic parties and middle-class citizens with progressive values in the case of mainstream right parties), this can have a devastating long-term effect (Grzymala

Busse 2019). While blurring its policy profile and imitating some aspects of the populist radical right might be a useful short-term strategy for the mainstream right to deal with the office-seeking and vote-seeking dimensions, it generates a major problem in the long term for the policy-seeking dimension as voters find it increasingly difficult to understand not only what distinguishes the mainstream from its far right competitor but what it stands for at all.

The second aspect worth exploring is the extent to which the modification of the programmatic profile of the mainstream right should lead us to rethink and/or be more cautious about the concepts that we use to define and understand this group of parties. As we stated at the outset of our study, conservative, Christian democratic and liberal parties are considered *mainstream* because they not only take relatively moderate positions, but also (and perhaps more importantly) because they are committed to respecting liberal democracy. Yet several of our case studies suggest that, caught between the silent revolution and the silent counter-revolution, mainstream right parties sometimes end up adopting extreme positions and also deviating from the liberal democratic rules of the game. Just think about the increasingly illiberal tone of the Austrian Christian democrats under Sebastian Kurz, as well as some of the aggressively populist language, constitutional short-cuts and flouting of international law pursued by the Conservative Party under the leadership of Boris Johnson, and the harsh discourse on integration and immigration advanced by Mark Rutte's liberal party in the Netherlands. Will we always be able to classify such parties as *mainstream* right? Clearly, it would be far too premature right now to group them along with the Trump-era Republican Party and Orban's FIDESZ in Hungary. But in the future, who knows?

As a result, scholars would do well to analyse the programmatic evolution of mainstream right parties in Western Europe so as to determine whether they are still defenders of the liberal democratic order or not. Answering this question is important not only because, as scholars, we should always strive to employ the right labels if we are to draw useful comparisons, but also because it has important consequences for the prospects of democracy in the region. Scholarship on the populist radical right has shown that this party family has a difficult relationship with liberal democracy and that under certain circumstances it can trigger a process of 'democratic backsliding' (Mudde 2007, 2013, 2019; Wodak 2015; Mudde and Rovira Kaltwasser

2017; Levitsky and Ziblatt 2018; Rydgren 2018). But if mainstream right parties end up evolving to the point that they transform themselves into an *ersatz* version of the populist radical right, then scholars and policy-makers alike should start seriously worrying about the health of democracy and the liberal order in Western Europe. In turn, this could have dramatic consequences for both democracy and liberalism worldwide, since both have historically been promoted and defended by Western European countries.

The third and last topic that we consider worthy of further exploration is negative partisanship – the fact that, just as voters can feel closer to particular political parties, they can also routinely recoil from others – a phenomenon to which scholars are paying increasing attention in different parts of the world (e.g., Caruana, McGregor and Stephenson 2015; Abramowitz and Webster 2016; Samuels and Zucco 2018; Meléndez and Rovira Kaltwasser 2019). By examining the nature and extent to which mainstream right and far right voters feel negatively about the parties involved, we may be able to gauge the potential for crossover.

As far as we know, the only empirical study that provides some information about this is a recent report by the Bertelsmann Foundation (Rovira Kaltwasser, Wratil and Vehrkamp 2019) that was conducted before the 2019 elections for the European Parliament. The evidence presented there shows that almost 50 per cent of the electorate in Western Europe feels negatively about the far right. Additional analyses of this empirical dataset reveal that those Western European citizens with either positive or negative attitudes towards the populist radical right are very different from each other and constitute two contrary constituencies (Meléndez and Rovira Kaltwasser forthcoming). On the one hand, those who are positively inclined towards the populist radical right are at odds with European integration and immigration; are inclined to socially conservative values; endorse an illiberal understanding of democracy; and do not see democracy as the most preferable political regime. On the other hand, those who take a negative view of the populist radical right are in favour of both European integration and immigration; show preferences for the electoral, liberal and social democratic dimensions of democracy; and are supportive of the democratic regime despite their dissatisfaction with it.

Crucially, the relative size of these two different constituencies could change in the near future, particularly if mainstream right parties prove increasingly willing to cooperate with the populist radical right and/or transform themselves into *ersatz* versions (see Twist 2019). This could lead to profound structural transformations in the political landscapes of Western European societies. If mainstream right and far right parties become increasingly similar and eager to join forces, we may very well see the formation of a strong right-wing bloc bent on bold reforms that could shift the post-war West European consensus on what democracy actually means. As a response, opponents of this right-wing bloc would presumably try to mobilize negative partisanship against it with the aim of defending liberal democracy and the ideas associated with the silent revolution, thereby polarizing politics still further – not a happy note to end on but a necessary one all the same.

References

Aarts, K. and Thomassen, J. (2008). 'Dutch Voters and the Changing Party Space 1989–2006', *Acta Politica* 43(2/3): 203–34.

Abou-Chadi, T. (2016). 'Niche Party Success and Mainstream Party Policy Shifts: How Green and Radical Right Parties Differ in Their Impact', *British Journal of Political Science* 46(2): 417–36.

Abou-Chadi, T. and Finnigan, R. (2019). 'Rights for Same-Sex Couples and Public Attitudes toward Gays and Lesbians in Europe', *Comparative Political Studies* 52(6): 868–95.

Abou-Chadi, T. and Krause, W. (2020). 'The Causal Effect of Radical Right Success on Mainstream Parties' Policy Positions: A Regression Discontinuity Approach', *British Journal of Political Science* 50(3): 829–47.

Abou-Chadi, T. and Wagner, M. (2019). 'The Electoral Appeal of Party Strategies in Post-Industrial Societies: When Can the Mainstream Left Succeed?' *Journal of Politics* 81(4): 1405–19.

Abramowitz, A. and Webster, S. (2016). 'The Rise of Negative Partisanship and the Nationalization of U.S. Elections in the 21st Century', *Electoral Studies* 41: 12–22.

Abts, K., Dalle Mulle, E., van Kessel, S. and Michel, E. (2021): The welfare agenda of the populist radical right in Europe: Combining chauvinism, producerism, and populism. *Swiss Political Science Review*, published online, DOI: 10.1111/spsr.12428

Acha, B. (2019). 'No, no es un partido (neo)fascista', *Agenda Pública*, 6 January, available at: http://agendapublica.elpais.com/no-no-es-un-partido-neofascista, last accessed 7 February 2019.

Afonso, A. (2015). 'Choosing Whom to Betray: Populist Right-Wing Parties, Welfare State Reforms and the Trade-Off between Office and Votes', *European Political Science Review* 7(2): 271–92.

Akkerman, T. (2015a). 'Gender and the Radical Right in Western Europe: A Comparative Analysis of Policy Agendas', *Patterns of Prejudice* 49(1/2): 37–60.

(2015b). 'Immigration Policy and Electoral Competition in Western Europe: A Fine-Grained Analysis of Party Positions over the Past Two Decades', *Party Politics* 21(1): 54–67.

(2021). 'The Netherlands', in D. Albertazzi and D. Vampa (eds), *Populism and New Patterns of Political Competition in Western Europe*, Abingdon: Routledge, pp. 120–42.

Akkerman, T., de Lange, S. and Rooduijn, M. (2016). *Radical Right-Wing Populist Parties in Western Europe: Into the Mainstream?* Abingdon: Routledge.

Alexandre-Collier, A. (2018). 'From Soft to Hard Brexit: UKIP's Not So Invisible Influence on the Eurosceptic Radicalisation of the Conservative Party Since 2015', in L. Herman and J. Muldoon (eds), *Trumping the Mainstream*, London: Routledge, pp. 204–21.

Allern, E. H. and Aylott, N. (2009). 'Overcoming the Fear of Commitment: Pre-electoral Coalitions in Norway and Sweden', *Acta Politica* 44(3): 259–85.

Alonso, S. (2012). *Challenging the State: Devolution and the Battle for Partisan Credibility*, Oxford University Press.

Alonso, S. and da Fonseca, S. C. (2012). 'Immigration, Left and Right', *Party Politics* 18(6): 865–84.

Alonso, S., Gómez, B. and Cabeza, L. (2013). 'Measuring Centre–Periphery Preferences: The Regional Manifestos Project', *Regional & Federal Studies* 23(2): 189–211.

Alonso, S. and Rovira Kaltwasser, C. (2015). 'Spain: No Country for the Populist Radical Right?', *South European Society and Politics* 20(1): 21–45.

Andersen, R. and Evans, J. (2003). 'Values, Cleavages and Party Choice in France, 1988–1995', *French Politics* 1(1): 83–114.

Andeweg, R. and Irwin, G. (2009). *Governance and Politics of the Netherlands*, 3rd edn, Houndmills: Palgrave Macmillan.

Andrews, G. (2006). 'The Italian General Election of 2006', *Representation* 42(3): 253–60.

Anduiza, E. (2018). 'El discurso de Vox', *Agenda Pública*, 6 December, available at: http://agendapublica.elpais.com/el-discurso-de-vox, last accessed 7 February 2019.

Art, D. (2007). 'Reacting to the Radical Right: Lessons from Germany and Austria', *Party Politics* 13(3): 331–49.

(2011). *Inside the Radical Right: The Development of Anti-Immigrant Parties in Western Europe*, Cambridge University Press.

Arzheimer, K. (2009). 'Contextual Factors and the Extreme Right Vote in Western Europe, 1980–2002', *American Journal of Political Science* 53(2): 259–75.

(2013). 'Working Class Parties 2.0? Competition between Centre Left and Extreme Right Parties', in J. Rydgren (ed.), *Class Politics and the Radical Right*, London: Routledge, pp. 75–90.

Arzheimer, K. and Carter, E. (2006). 'Political Opportunity Structures and Right-Wing Extremist Party Success', *European Journal of Political Research* 45(3): 419–43.

(2009). 'Christian Religiosity and Voting for West European Radical Right Parties', *West European Politics* 32(5): 985–1011.

Astudillo, J. and García-Guereta, E. (2006). 'If It Isn't Broken, Don't Fix It: The Spanish Popular Party in Power', *South European Society and Politics* 11(3/4): 399–417.

Aylott, N. and Bolin, N. (2015). 'Polarising Pluralism: The Swedish Parliamentary Election of September 2014', *West European Politics* 38(3): 730–40.

Bale, T. (2003). 'Cinderella and Her Ugly Sisters: The Mainstream and Extreme Right in Europe's Bipolarising Party Systems', *West European Politics* 26(3): 67–90.

(ed.) (2008). *Immigration and Integration Policy in Europe: Why Politics – and the Centre-Right – Matter*, Abingdon: Routledge.

(2010). *The Conservative Party from Thatcher to Cameron*, Cambridge: Polity Press.

(2013). 'More and More Restrictive – But Not Always Populist: Explaining Variation in the British Conservative Party's Stance on Immigration and Asylum', *Journal of Contemporary European Studies* 21(1): 25–37.

(2018). 'Who Leads and Who Follows? The Symbiotic Relationship between UKIP and the Conservatives – and Populism and Euroscepticism', *Politics* 38(3): 263–77.

Bale, T., Green-Pedersen, C., Krouwel, A., Richard Luther, K. and Sutter, N. (2010). 'If You Can't Beat Them, Join Them? Explaining Social Democratic Responses to the Challenge from the Populist Radical Right in Western Europe', *Political Studies* 58(3): 410–26.

Bale, T. and Krouwel, A. (2013). 'Down but Not Out: A Comparison of Germany's CDU/CSU with Christian Democratic Parties in Austria, Belgium, Italy and the Netherlands', *German Politics* 22(1–2): 16–45.

Bale, T. and Szczerbiak, A. (2008). 'Why is There No Christian Democracy in Poland – And Why Should We Care?', *Party Politics* 14(4): 479–500.

Bale, T. and Webb, P. (2018). '"We Didn't See It Coming": The Conservatives', *Parliamentary Affairs* 71(S1): 46–58.

Bardi, L. (2007). 'Electoral Change and Its Impact on the Party System in Italy', *West European Politics* 30(4): 711–32.

Bartolini, S. (1984). 'Institutional Constraints and Party Competition in the French Party System', *West European Politics* 7(4): 103–27.

Bartolini, S., Chiaramonte, A. and D'Alimonte, R. (2004). 'The Italian Party System between Parties and Coalitions', *West European Politics* 27(1): 1–19.

Bauböck, R. and Perchinig, B. (2006). 'Migrations-und Integrationspolitik', in H. Dachs et al. (eds), *Politik in Österreich: Das Handbuch*, Vienna: MANZ Verlag, pp. 726–42.

Baudet, T. (2019). 'Houellebecq's Unfinished Critique of Liberal Modernity', *American Affairs* 3(2): 213–24.

Bedock, C. (2017). *Bundling the Bundles: Coalition Dynamics and Institutional Reforms in Italy, 2003–2006*, Oxford University Press.

Bell, D. (1976). 'The Extreme Right in France', in M. Kolinsky and W. Paterson (eds), *Social and Political Movements in Western Europe*, London: Croom Helm, pp. 91–105.

Bennulf, M. and Holmberg, S. (1990). 'The Green Breakthrough in Sweden', *Scandinavian Political Studies* 13(2): 165–84.

Beramendi, P., Häusermann, S., Kitschelt, H. and Kriesi, H. (2015). 'Introduction: The Politics of Advanced Capitalism', in P. Beramendi, S. Häusermann and H. Kitschelt (eds), *The Politics of Advanced Capitalism*, Cambridge University Press, pp. 1–64.

Bergman, T., Hellström, J. and Sandström, C. (2018). 'Regeringsbildningen efter riksdagsvalet 2018', in L. Nord, M. Grusell, N. Bolin and K. Falasca (eds), *Snabbtänkt: Reflektioner från valet 2018 av ledande forskare*, Sundsvall: Mittuniversitetet Demicom, rapport nr 38.

Berrettini, M. (2013). 'The Spanish Catholic Church from the Zapatero Era to the Rajoy Government', in B. Field and A. Botti (eds), *Politics and Society in Contemporary Spain: From Zapatero to Rajoy*, New York: Palgrave Macmillan, pp. 161–78.

Betz, H. G. (1994). *Radical Right-Wing Populism in Western Europe*, London: Macmillan.

Betz, H. G and Johnson, C. (2004). 'Against the Current – Stemming the Tide: The Nostalgic Ideology of Contemporary Radical Populist Right', *Journal of Political Ideologies* 9(3): 311–27.

Bischof, D. (2017). 'Towards a Renewal of the Niche Party Concept: Parties, Market Shares and Condensed Offers', *Party Politics* 23(3): 220–35.

Bobbio, N. (1996). *Left and Right: The Significance of a Political Distinction*, London: Polity Press.

Boix, C. (2007). 'The Emergence of Parties and Party Systems', in C. Boix and S. Stokes (eds), *The Oxford Handbook of Comparative Politics*, Oxford University Press, pp. 499–521.

Boréus, K. (1994). *Högervåg. Nyliberalismen och kampen om språket i svensk debatt 1969–1989*, Stockholm: Tidens förlag.

Bornschier, S. (2010). *Cleavage Politics and the Populist Right: The New Cultural Conflict in Western Europe*, Philadelphia, PA: Temple University Press.

Bösch, F. (2002). *Macht und Machtverlust: Die Geschichte der CDU*, Stuttgart: Deutsche Verlags-Anstalt.

Bosch, A. and Durán, I. M. (2019). 'How Does Economic Crisis Impel Emerging Parties on the Road to Elections? The Case of the Spanish Podemos and Ciudadanos', *Party Politics* 25(2): 257–67.

Brubaker, R. (2017). 'Between Nationalism and Civilizationism: The European Populist Moment in Comparative Perspective', *Ethnic and Racial Studies* 40(8): 1191–226.

Buchanan, T. and Conway, M. (1996). *Political Catholicism in Europe, 1918–1965*, Oxford University Press.

Budge, I. and Laver, M. (1992). *Party Policy and Government Coalitions*, London: Palgrave Macmillan.

Bull, M. (2016). 'A "Perfect Storm": Institutional Reform in Italy after the 2013 National Elections', in J. Edelmann and R. Kaiser (eds), *Crisis as a Permanent Condition?: The Italian Political System between Transition and Reform Resistance*, Baden-Baden: Nomos Verlag, pp. 81–98.

Bustikova, L. (2014). 'Revenge of the Radical Right', *Comparative Political Studies* 47(12): 1738–65.

Cameron, D. (2005). 'Cameron Victory Speech', BBC News, 6 December, available at: http://news.bbc.co.uk/1/hi/uk_politics/4504722.stm, last accessed 20 February 2020.

Cameron, D. and Jones, D. (2010). *Cameron on Cameron: Conversations with Dylan Jones*, London: Fourth Estate.

Campbell, R. and Childs, S. (2015). 'Conservatism, Feminisation and the Representation of Women in UK Politics', *British Politics* 10(2): 148–68.

Caramani, D. (2008). 'Party Systems', in D. Caramani (ed.), *Comparative Politics*. Oxford University Press, pp. 224–44.

Caruana, N., McGregor, R. M. and Stephenson, L. B. (2015). 'The Power of the Dark Side: Negative Partisanship and Political Behaviour in Canada', *Canadian Journal of Political Science/Revue canadienne de science politique* 48(4): 771–89.

Castelli Gattinara, P. (2016). *The Politics of Migration in Italy*, London: Routledge.

(2017). 'The Refugee Crisis in Italy as a Crisis of Legitimacy', *Contemporary Italian Politics* 9(3): 318–31.

CDA (2017). 'Keuzes voor een beter Nederland. Verkiezingsprogramma 2017-2021', CDA parliamentary election manifesto, Netherlands.

Charalambous, G. (2015). *The European Far Right: Historical and Contemporary Perspectives*, Oslo: Peace Research Institute Oslo.

Clemens, C. (2013). 'Beyond Christian Democracy? Welfare State Politics and Policy in a Changing CDU', *German Politics* 22(1/2): 191–211.

Close, C. and van Haute, E. (2019). *Liberal Parties in Europe*, Abingdon: Routledge.

Copsey, N. and Haughton, T. (2014). 'Farewell Britannia? "Issue Capture" and the Politics of David Cameron's 2013 EU Referendum Pledge', *Journal of Common Market Studies* 52(S1): 74–89.

Cowley, P. and Green, J. (2005). 'New Leaders, Same Problems: The Conservatives', in A. Geddes and J. Tonge (eds), *Britain Decides: The UK General Election 2005*, Basingstoke: Palgrave Macmillan, pp. 46–69.

Cutts, D., Goodwin, M., Heath, O. and Milazzo, C. (2019). 'Resurgent Remain and a Rebooted Revolt on the Right: Exploring the 2019 European Parliament Elections in the United Kingdom', *Political Quarterly* 90(3): 496–514.

Cutts, D., Goodwin, M., Heath, O. and Surridge, P. (2020). 'Brexit, the 2019 General Election and the Realignment of British Politics', *The Political Quarterly* 91(1): 7–23.

Czernin, H. (2000). *Wofür ich mich meinetwegen entschuldige: Haider, beim Wort genommen*, Vienna: Czernin Verlag.

D'Alimonte, R. (2005). 'Italy: A Case of Fragmented Bipolarism', in M. Gallagher and P. Mitchel (eds), *The Politics of Electoral Systems*, Oxford University Press, pp. 253–76.

Davidson-Schmich, L. (2018). 'LGBTI Rights and the 2017 German National Election', *German Politics and Society* 36(2): 27–54.

Debus, M. and Müller, J. (2013). 'The Programmatic Development of CDU and CSU since Reunification: Incentives and Constraints for Changing Policy Positions in the German Multi-Level System', *German Politics* 22(1/2): 151–71.

de Lange, S. (2012). 'New Alliances: Why Mainstream Parties Govern with Radical Right-Wing Populist Parties', *Political Studies* 60(4): 899–918.

(2018). 'From Limited Multipartism to Extended Multipartism? The Impact of the Lijst Pim Fortuyn, the Partij voor de Vrijheid and the Socialistische Partij on the Dutch Party System', in S. Wolinetz and A. Zaslove (eds), *Absorbing the Blow: Populist Parties and their Impact on Parties and Party Systems*, Colchester: ECPR Press, pp. 55–82.

de Lange, S. and Art, D. (2011). 'Fortuyn versus Wilders: An Agency-Based Approach to Radical Right Party Building', *West European Politics* 34(6): 1229–49.

de Lange, S. and Mügge, L. (2015). 'Gender and Right-Wing Populism in the Low Countries: Ideological Variations Across Parties and Time', *Patterns of Prejudice* 49(1/2): 61–80.

de Lange, S., Harteveld, E. and Rooduijn, M. (2018). 'Social Democratic Parties Caught between a Rock and a Hard Place. Explaining the Decline of the Dutch PvdA', paper presented in the '(Yet another) crisis of social democracy', Berlin, 29–30 November.

Del Pino, E. (2013). 'The Spanish Welfare State from Zapatero to Rajoy: Recalibration to Retrenchment', in B. Field and A. Botti (eds), *Politics and Society in Contemporary Spain: From Zapatero to Rajoy*, New York: Palgrave Macmillan, pp. 197–216.

Demker, M. (1997). 'Changing Party Ideology: Gaullist Parties Facing Voters, Leaders and Competitors', *Party Politics* 3(3): 407–26.

Demker, M. (2014). *Sverige åt svenskarna. Motstånd och mobilisering mot invandring och invandrare i Sverige*, Stockholm: Atlas förlag.

(2018). 'Valmanifest och ideologiska föreställningar', in L. Nord, M. Grusell, N. Bolin and K. Falasca (eds), *Snabbtänkt. Reflektioner från valet 2018 av ledande forskare*, Sundsvall: Mittuniversitetet Demicom, rapport nr 38.

Der Bundeswahlleiter (2018). 'Ergebnisse Früherer Bundestagswahlen', 8 November, Der Bundeswahlleiter database viewed 5 October 2020.

de Vries, C. (2007). 'Sleeping Giant: Fact or Fairytale? How European Integration Affects National Elections', *European Union Politics* 8(3): 363–85.

(2018a). *Euroscepticism and the Future of European Integration*, Oxford University Press.

(2018b). 'The Cosmopolitan–Parochial Divide: Changing Patterns of Party and Electoral Competition in the Netherlands and Beyond', *Journal of European Public Policy* 25(11): 1541–65.

de Vries, C., Hakhverdian, A. and Lancee, B. (2013). 'The Dynamics of Voters' Left/Right Identification: The Role of Economic and Cultural Attitudes', *Political Science Research and Methods* 1(2): 223–38.

Díez, J. (1994). 'Postmaterialismo y desarrollo económico en España', in J. Díez and R. Inglehart (eds), *Tendencias mundiales de cambio en los valores sociales y políticos*, Madrid: FUNDESCO, pp. 125–55.

Dokumente (2018). 'Angela Merkel mit 364 Stimmen zur Bundeskanzlerin gewählt', Dokumente, available at: www.bundestag.de/dokumente/textarchiv/2018/kw11-de-kanzlerwahl-546336, last accessed 14 March 2018.

Dorey, P. (2007). 'A New Direction or Another False Dawn? David Cameron and the Crisis of British Conservatism', *British Politics* 2(2): 137–66.

Döring, H. and Manow, P. (2019). 'Parliaments and Governments Database', ParlGov Information on Parties, Elections and Cabinets in Modern Democracies, development version, viewed 22 March 2019.

Dostal, J. (2017). 'The German Federal Election of 2017: How the Wedge Issue of Refugees and Migration Took the Shine off Chancellor Merkel and Transformed the Party System', *Political Quarterly* 88(4): 589–602.

Dupoirier, E. and Sauger, N. (2010). 'Four Rounds in a Row: The Impact of Presidential Election Outcomes on Legislative Elections in France', *French Politics* 81(1): 21–41.

Eatwell, R. (2003). *Fascism: A History*, London: Pimlico.

(2014). 'Fascism', in M. Freeden et al. (eds), *The Oxford Handbook of Political Ideologies*, Oxford University Press, pp. 474–92.

(2017). 'Populism and Fascism', in C. Rovira Kaltwasser et al. (eds), *The Oxford Handbook of Populism*, Oxford University Press.

Eger, M. and Valdez, S. (2015). 'Neo-nationalism in Western Europe', *European Sociological Review* 31(1): 115–30.

Ekengren, A.-M. and Oscarsson, H. (2015). 'Ett liv efter nya Moderaterna?' *Statsvetenskaplig Tidskrift* 117(2): 153–68.

Elgie, R. (2006). 'France: Stacking the Deck', in M. Gallagher and P. Mitchell (eds), *The Politics of Electoral Systems*, Oxford University Press, pp. 70–87.

Encarnación, O. (2009). 'Spain's New Left Turn: Society Driven or Party Instigated?', *South European Society and Politics* 14(4): 399–415.

Engeli, I., Green-Pedersen, C. and Larsen, L. (2012). *Morality Politics in Western Europe: Parties, Agendas and Policy Choices*, Basingstoke: Palgrave Macmillan.

Engler, F., Bauer-Blaschkowski, S. and Zohlnhöfer, R. (2019). 'Disregarding the Voters? Electoral Competition and the Merkel Government's Public Policies, 2013–17', *German Politics* 28(3): 312–31.

Ellinas, A. A. (2013). 'The Rise of Golden Dawn: The New Face of the Far Right in Greece', *South European Society and Politics* 18(4): 543–65.

Eriksson, G. and Nilsson, D. (2007). 'M säger ja til homoäktenskap', *Svenska Dagbladet*, 27 October, available at: www.svd.se/m-sager-ja-till-homoaktenskap, last accessed 20 June 2019.

European Social Survey Cumulative File (2018). 'ESS 1-8', Data file edition 1.0. NSD – Norwegian Centre for Research Data, Norway, data archive and distributor of ESS data for ESS ERIC, viewed 5 September 2020.

Evans, G. and Mellon, J. (2019). 'Immigration, Euroscepticism, and the Rise and Fall of UKIP', *Party Politics* 25(1): 76–87.

Evans, J. (2000). 'Le vote gaucho-lepéniste: le masque extrême d'une dynamique normale', *Revue Française de Science Politique* 50(1): 21–51.

Evans, J. and Ivaldi, G. (2017). 'An Atypical "Honeymoon" Election? Contextual and Strategic Opportunities in the 2017 French Legislative Race', *French Politics* 14(4): 493–504.

(2018). *The 2017 French Presidential Elections: A Political Reformation?* Basingstoke: Palgrave Macmillan.

Fella, S. and Ruzza, C. (2013). 'Populism and the Fall of the Centre-Right in Italy: The End of the Berlusconi Model or a New Beginning?', *Journal of Contemporary European Studies* 21(1): 38–52.

Fernández-Albertos, J. and Manzano, D. (2012). 'The Lack of Partisan Conflict over the Welfare State in Spain', *South European Society and Politics* 17(3): 427–47.

Field, B. (2009). 'A "Second Transition" in Spain? Policy, Institutions and Interparty Politics under Zapatero (2004–8)', *South European Society and Politics* 14(4): 379–97.

(2016). *Why Minority Governments Work: Multilevel Territorial Politics in Spain*, New York: Palgrave Macmillan.

Field, B. and Botti, A. (2013). 'Introduction: Political Change in Spain, from Zapatero to Rajoy', in B. Field and A. Botti (eds), *Politics and Society in Contemporary Spain: From Zapatero to Rajoy*, New York: Palgrave Macmillan, pp. 1–19.

Forsberg, B. (2018). 'Vi kan komma överens med C om flyktingpolitiken', *Svenska Dagbladet*, 23 August, available at: www.svd.se/vi-kan-komma-overens-med-c-om-flyktingpolitiken, last accessed 20 June 2019.

Forschungsgruppe Wahlen (n.d.). 'Wenn am nächsten Sonntag Bundestagswahl wäre', available at: www.wahlrecht.de/umfragen/polit barometer.htm, last accessed 5 October 2020.

Fossati, F. and Häusermann, S. (2014). 'Social Policy Preferences and Party Choice in the 2011 Swiss Elections', *Swiss Political Science Review* 20(4): 590–611.

Franzmann, S. (2009). 'The Change of Ideology: How the Left–Right Cleavage Transforms into Issue Competition: An Analysis of Party Systems Using Party Manifesto Data', PhD thesis, University of Cologne.

(2015). 'Towards a Real Comparison of Left–Right Indices: A Comment on Jahn', *Party Politics* 21(5): 821–8.

Fredén, A. (2014). 'Threshold Insurance Voting in PR Systems: A Study of Voters' Strategic Behaviour in the 2010 Swedish General Election', *Journal of Elections, Public Opinion & Parties* 24(4): 473–92.

Freeden, M. (2015). *Liberalism: A Very Short Introduction*, Oxford University Press.

Freeden, M. and Stears, M. (2014). 'Liberalism', in M. Freeden et al. (eds), *The Oxford Handbook of Political Ideologies*, Oxford University Press, pp. 329–47.

Frey, T. (2009). *Die Christdemokratie in Westeuropa: der schmale Grat zum Erfolg*, Baden-Baden: Nomos.

Froio, C., Castelli, P., Bulli, G. and Albanese, M. (2020). *CasaPound Italia: Contemporary Extreme Right Politics*, London: Routledge.

Galli, G. (1966). *Il bipartitismo imperfetto: comunisti e democristiani in Italia*, Bologna: Il Mulino.

Garnett, M. and Lynch, P. (2003). *The Conservatives in Crisis*, Manchester University Press.

Garritzmann, J., Busemeyer, M. and Neimanns, E. (2018). 'Public Demand for Social Investment: New Supporting Coalitions for Welfare State Reform in Western Europe?', *Journal of European Public Policy* 25 (6): 844–61.

Geddes, A. (2008). 'Il Rombo Dei Cannoni? Immigration and the Centre-Right in Italy', *Journal of European Public Policy* 15(3): 349–66.

Gidron, N. (2020). 'Many Ways to be Right: Cross-Pressured Voters in Western Europe', *British Journal of Political Science*, 1–16. doi:10.1017/S0007123420000228.

Gidron, N. and Ziblatt, D. (2019). 'Center-Right Political Parties in Advanced Democracies', *Annual Review of Political Science* 22: 17–35.

Gilljam, M. and Holmberg, S. (1993). *Väljarna inför 90-talet*, Stockholm: Norstedts.

Gingrich, J. (2017). 'A New Progressive Coalition? The European Left in a Time of Change', *Political Quarterly* 88(1): 39–51.

Gingrich, J. and Ansell, B. (2015). 'The Dynamics of Social Investment: Human Capital, Activation and Care', in P. Beramendi et al. (eds), *The Politics of Advanced Capitalism*, Cambridge University Press, pp. 282–304.

Gingrich, J. and Häusermann, S. (2015). 'The Decline of the Working-Class Vote, the Reconfiguration of the Welfare Support Coalition and Consequences for the Welfare State', *Journal of European Social Policy* 25(1): 50–75.

Giovannini, A., Albertazzi, D. and Seddone, A. (2018). '"No Regionalism Please, We Are Leghisti!" The Transformation of the Italian Lega Nord under the Leadership of Matteo Salvini', *Regional & Federal Studies* 28(5): 645–71.

Green-Pedersen, C. (2007). 'The Growing Importance of Issue Competition: The Changing Nature of Party Competition in Western Europe', *Political Studies* 55(3): 607–28.

(2012). 'A Giant Fast Asleep? Party Incentives and the Politicisation of European Integration', *Political Studies* 60(1): 115–30.

Green, J. (2011). 'A Test of Core Vote Theories: The British Conservatives, 1997–2005', *British Journal of Political Science* 41(4): 735–64.

Green, S. (2013). 'Societal Transformation and Programmatic Change in the CDU', *German Politics* 22(1/2): 46–63.

Green, S. and Turner, E. (2014). *Understanding the Transformation of Germany's CDU*, London: Routledge.

Griffin, R. (1996). 'The "Post-Fascism" of the Alleanza Nazionale: A Case Study in Ideological Morphology', *Journal of Political Ideologies* 1(2): 123–45.

Griffiths, S. (2014). 'What was Progressive in "Progressive Conservatism"?' *Political Studies Review* 12(1): 29–40.

Grunberg, G. (2008). 'Vers un espace politique bipartisan?' in P. Perrineau (ed.), *Le vote de ruptura*, Paris: Presses de Sciences Po, pp. 253–70.

Grunberg, G. and Haegel, F. (2007). *La France vers le bipartisme? La présidentialisation du PS et de l'UMP*, Paris: Presses de Sciences Po.

Grzymala-Busse, A. (2013). 'Why There Is (almost) no Christian Democracy in post-Communist Europe?' *Party Politics* 19(2): 319–42.

Grzymala-Busse, A. (2019). 'The Failure of Europe's Mainstream Parties', *Journal of Democracy* 30(4): 35–47.

Gunther, R., Sani, G. and Shabad, G. (1988). *Spain after Franco: The Making of a Competitive Party System*, Berkeley: University of California Press.

Hafez, F. and Heinisch, R. (2018). 'Breaking with Austrian Consociationalism: How the Rise of Right-Wing Populism and Party Competition have Changed Austria's Islam Politics', *Politics and Religion* 30(11): 649–78.

Hall, S. (1983). 'The Great Moving Right Show', in S. Hall and M. Jacques (eds), *The Politics of Thatcherism*, London: Lawrence & Wishart, pp. 19–39.

Han, K. J. (2015). 'The Impact of Radical Right-Wing Parties on the Positions of Mainstream Parties Regarding Multiculturalism', *West European Politics* 38(3): 557–76.

Harmel, R. and Janda, K. (1994). 'An Integrated Theory of Party Goals and Party Change', *Journal of Theoretical Politics* 6(3): 259–87.

Harteveld, E. (2016). 'Winning the "Losers" but Losing the "Winners"? The Electoral Consequences of the Radical Right Moving to the Economic Left', *Electoral Studies* 44: 225–34.

(2019). 'Stuivertje wisselen: neemt FvD de electorale plek van PVV over?' Stuk Rood Vlees, 22 March, available at: http://stukroodvlees.nl/stuivertje-wisselen-neemt-fvd-de-electorale-plek-van-pvv-over, last accessed 22 March 2019.

Harteveld, E., van der Brug, W., Dahlberg, S. and Kokkonen, A. (2015). 'The Gender Gap in Populist Radical-Right Voting: Examining the Demand Side in Western and Eastern Europe', *Patterns of Prejudice* 49(1/2): 103–34.

Harvey, D. (2005). *A Brief History of Neoliberalism*, Oxford University Press.

Häusermann, S., Picot, G. and Geering, D. (2013). 'Rethinking Party Politics and the Welfare State: Recent Advances in the Literature', *British Journal of Political Science* 43(1): 221–40.

Hayton, R. (2012). *Reconstructing Conservatism? The Conservative Party in Opposition, 1997–2010*, Manchester University Press.

(2014). 'Conservative Party Statecraft and the Politics of Coalition', *Parliamentary Affairs* 67(1): 6–24.

(2018). 'British Conservatism after the Vote for Brexit: The Ideological Legacy of David Cameron', *British Journal of Politics and International Relations* 20(1): 223–38.

Hayton, R. and Heppell, T. (2010). 'The Quiet Man of British Politics: The Rise, Fall and Significance of Iain Duncan Smith', *Parliamentary Affairs* 63(3): 425–45.

Hayton, R. and McEnhill, L. (2015). 'Cameron's Conservative Party, Social Liberalism and Social Justice', *British Politics* 10(2): 131–47.

Hedberg, P. (2020). *Väljarnas partier 1956–2018. Valforskningsprogrammets rapportserie 2020:3*, Gothenburg: Statsvetenskapliga institutionen/ Göteborgs universitet.

Heinisch, R. (2002). *Populism, Proporz, and Pariah – Austria Turns Right: Austrian Political Change, its Causes and Repercussions*, Huntington, NY: Nova Science.

(2003). 'Success in Opposition – Failure in Government: Explaining the Performance of Right-Wing Populist Parties in Public Office', *West European Politics* 26(3): 91–130.

Heinisch, R. and Hauser, C. (2015). 'The Mainstreaming of the Austrian Freedom Party: The More Things Change', in T. Akkerman, S. de Lange and M. Rooduijn (eds), *Radical Right-Wing Populist Parties in Western Europe: Into the Mainstream?* London: Routledge, pp. 73–93.

Hellström, A. and Nilsson, T. (2010). 'We Are the Good Guys', *Ethnicities* 10(1): 55–76.

Hellström, J., Bergman, T. and Bäck, H. (2018). 'Party Government in Europe Database (PAGED)', unpublished database, open-access in 2020, Umeå University.

Hemerijck, A. (2013). *Changing Welfare States*, Oxford University Press.

Heppell, T. (2014). *The Tories: From Winston Churchill to David Cameron*, London: Bloomsbury.

Heppell, T. and Hill, M. (2009). 'Transcending Thatcherism? Ideology and the Conservative Party Leadership Mandate of David Cameron', *Political Quarterly* 80(3): 388–99.

Hjermitslev, I. B. (2018). 'The Electoral Cost of Coalition Participation: Can Anyone Escape?', *Party Politics* 26(4): 510–20.

Hjertén, L. (2009). 'Reinfeldt: Jag avgår hellre än samarbetar med SD', *Aftonbladet*, 23 October, available at: www.aftonbladet.se/nyheter/a/ 9mB4wl/reinfeldt-jag-avgar-hellre-an-samarbetar-med-sd, last accessed 20 June 2019.

HM Government (2020). 'The UK's Points-Based Immigration System: Policy Statement', HM Government (GOV.UK), 19 February, available at: www .gov.uk/government/publications/the-uks-points-based-immigration-system-policy-statement/the-uks-points-based-immigration-system-policy-statement, last accessed 14 May 2020.

Hobolt, S. and Tilley, J. (2016). 'Fleeing the Centre: The Rise of Challenger Parties in the Aftermath of the Euro Crisis', *West European Politics* 39(5): 971–91.

Hobolt, S. and de Vries, C. (2016). 'Public Support for European Integration', *Annual Review of Political Science* 19(1): 413–32.

Hofinger, C., Jenny, M. and Ogris, G. (2000). 'Steter Tropfen höhlt den Stein. Wählerströme und Wählerwanderungen 1999 im Kontext der 80er und 90er Jahre', in F. Plasser, P. Ulram and F. Sommer (eds), *Das österreichische Wahlverhalten*, Vienna: Signum Verlag, pp. 117–40.

Holmberg, S. (2000). *Välja parti*, Stockholm: Norstedts Juridik AB.

Holmberg, S. and Oscarsson, H. (2004). *Väljare. Svenskt väljarbeteende under 50 år*, Stockholm: Norstedts Juridik AB.

Hooghe, L. and Marks, G. (2009). 'A Postfunctionalist Theory of European Integration: From Permissive Consensus to Constraining Dissensus', *British Journal of Political Science* 39(1): 1–23.

(2018). 'Cleavage Theory Meets Europe's Crises: Lipset, Rokkan, and the Transnational Cleavage', *Journal of European Public Policy* 25(1): 109–35.

Hooghe, L., Marks, G. and Wilson, C. J. (2002). 'Does Left/Right Structure Party Positions on European Integration?' *Comparative Political Studies* 35(8): 965–89.

Hutter, S. and Kriesi, H. (2019). *European Party Politics in Times of Crisis*, Cambridge University Press.

Hylén, J. (1991). *Fosterlandet främst?: konservatism och liberalism inom högerpartiet 1904–1985*, Stockholm: Norstedts juridikförl.

Ignazi, P. (1992). 'The Silent Counter-Revolution: Hypotheses on the Emergence of Extreme Right-Wing Parties in Europe', *European Journal of Political Research* 22(1): 3–34.

(2003). *Extreme Right Parties in Western Europe*, Oxford University Press.

(2005). 'Legitimation and Evolution on the Italian Right Wing: Social and Ideological Repositioning of Alleanza Nazionale and the Lega Nord', *South European Society and Politics* 10(2): 333–49.

Immerzeel, T., Jaspers, E. and Lubbers, M. (2013). 'Religion as Catalyst or Restraint of Radical Right Voting?', *West European Politics* 36(5): 946–68.

Inglehart, R. (1971). 'The Silent Revolution in Europe: Intergenerational Change in Post-Industrial Societies', *American Political Science Review* 65(4): 991–1017.

(1977). *The Silent Revolution: Changing Values and Political Styles among Western Publics*, Princeton University Press.

(1990). *Culture Shift in Advanced Industrial Society*, Princeton University Press.

Inglehart, R. and Baker, W. E. (2000). 'Modernization, Cultural Change, and the Persistence of Traditional Values', *American Sociological Review* 65(1): 19–51.

Inglehart, R. and Norris, P. (2003). *Rising Tide: Gender Equality and Cultural Change Around the World*, Cambridge University Press.

Inglehart, R. and Rabier, J.-R. (1986). 'Political Realignment in Advanced Industrial Society: From Class-Based Politics to Quality-of-Life Politics', *Government & Opposition* 21(4): 456–79.

Inglehart, R. and Welzel, C. (2005). *Modernization, Cultural Change, and Democracy. The Human Development Sequence*, Cambridge University Press.

(2010). 'Changing Mass Priorities: The Link between Modernization and Democracy', *Perspectives on Politics* 8(2): 551–67.

Invernizzi-Accetti, C. (2020). *What is Christian Democracy? The Forgotten Ideology*, Cambridge University Press.

Ipsos (2019a). 'EP19. Verkiezingsonderzoek Ipsos in opdracht van de NOS', Research Report, 29 May, available at: www.ipsos.com/sites/default/fi les/ct/news/documents/2019-05/19020845_ipsos_ep19_v1.3.pdf, last accessed 29 May 2020.

Ipsos (2019b). 'PS19. Verkiezingsonderzoek Ipsos in opdracht van de NOS', Research Report, 1 April, available at: www.ipsos.com/sites/default/files/ct/ news/documents/2019-04/18063768_ipsos_ps19_v1.0.pdf, last accessed 1 April 2020.

Ivaldi, G. (2015). 'Towards the Median Economic Crisis Voter? The New Leftist Economic Agenda of the Front National in France', *French Politics* 13(4): 346–69.

(2018a). 'No Longer a Pariah? The Front National and the French Party System', in A. Zaslove and S. B. Wolinetz (eds), *Absorbing the Blow: Populist Parties and their Impact on Parties and Party Systems*, London: Rowman & Littlefield/ECPR Press, pp. 171–96.

(2018b). 'Contesting the EU in Times of Crisis: The Front National and Politics of Euroscepticism in France', *Politics* 38(3): 278–94.

Ivaldi, G. and Gombin, J. (2015). 'The Front National and the New Politics of the Rural in France', in D. Strijker, G. Voerman and I. Terluin (eds), *Rural Protest Groups and Populist Political Parties*, Wageningen: Wageningen Academic Publishers, pp. 35–62.

Ivarsflaten, E. (2006). 'Reputational Shields: Why Most Anti-Immigrant Parties Failed in Western Europe, 1980-2005', paper prepared for the Annual Meeting of the American Political Science Association, Philadelphia, 31 August–3 September.

Ivarsflaten, E., Blinder, S. and Bjånesøy, L. (2020). 'How and Why the Populist Radical Right Persuades Citizens', in E. Suhay, B. Grofman and A. H. Trechsel (eds), *The Oxford Handbook of Electoral Persuasion*, Oxford University Press, pp. 815–38.

Jahn, D. (2011). 'Conceptualizing Left and Right in Comparative Politics: Towards a Deductive Approach', *Party Politics* 17(6): 745–65.

(2014). 'What is Left and Right in Comparative Politics? A Response to Simon Franzmann', *Party Politics* 20(2): 297–301.

Jamison, A., Eyerman, R. and Cramer, J. (1990). *The Making of the New Environmental Consciousness: A Comparative Study of the Environmental Movements in Sweden, Denmark and the Netherlands*, Edinburgh University Press.

Jensen, C. (2014). *The Right and the Welfare State*, Oxford University Press.

Jupskås, A. R. (2018). 'Shaken, but not Stirred: How Right-Wing Populist Parties have Changed Party Systems in Scandinavia', in S. B. Wolinetz and A. Zaslove (eds), *Absorbing the Blow: Populist Parties and their Impact on Parties and Party Systems*, London: Rowman & Littlefield/ECPR Press, pp. 103–44.

Jylhä, K. M., Rydgren, J. and Strimling, P. (2019). 'Radical Right-Wing Voters from Right and Left: Comparing Sweden Democrat Voters Who Previously Voted for the Conservative Party or the Social Democratic Party', *Scandinavian Political Studies* 42(3/4): 220–44.

Kaiser, W. (2007). *Christian Democracy and the Origins of European Union*, Cambridge University Press.

Kalyvas, S. (1996). *The Rise of Christian Democracy in Europe*, London: Cornell University Press.

Kalyvas, S. and van Kersbergen, K. (2010). 'Christian Democracy', *Annual Review of Political Science* 13: 183–209.

Kärrman, J. (2015). 'Väljarstödet för att isolera SD luckras upp', *Dagens Nyheter*, 5 May, available at: www.dn.se/nyheter/politik/valjarstodet-for-att-isolera-sd-luckras-upp, last accessed 20 June 2019.

Kerr, P. and Hayton, R. (2015). 'Whatever Happened to Conservative Party Modernisation?', *British Politics* 10(2): 114–30.

Kim, J. (2018). 'The Radical Market-Oriented Policies of the Alternative for Germany (AfD) and Support from Non-Beneficiary Groups: Discrepancies between the Party's Policies and Its Supporters', *Asian Journal of German and European Studies* 3(6): 1–24.

Kirchheimer, O. (1966). 'The Transformation of the Western European Party Systems', in J. LaPalombara and M. Weiner (eds), *Political Parties and Political Development*, Princeton University Press, pp. 177–200.

Kirchner, E. (1988). 'Introduction', in E. Kirchner (ed.), *Liberal Parties in Western Europe*, Cambridge University Press, pp. 1–15.

Kitschelt, H. (1994). *The Transformation of European Social Democracy*, Cambridge University Press.

(2007). 'Party Systems', in C. Boix and S. Stokes (eds), *The Oxford Handbook of Comparative Politics*, Oxford University Press, pp. 522–54.

(2012). 'Social Class and Radical Right: Conceptualizing Political Preference Formation and Partisan Choice', in J. Rydgren (ed.), *Class Politics and the Radical Right*, London: Routledge, pp. 224–51.

Kitschelt, H. and Mcgann, A. J. (1997). *The Radical Right in Western Europe: A Comparative Analysis*, University of Michigan Press.

Kitschelt, H. and Rehm, P. (2014). 'Occupations as a Site of Political Preference Formation', *Comparative Political Studies* 47(12): 1670–706.

Knapp, A. and Wright, V. (2006). *The Government and Politics of France*, Abingdon: Routledge.

Knutsen, O. (1990). 'Materialist and Postmaterialist Values and Social Structure in the Nordic Countries: A Comparative Study', *Comparative Politics* 23(1): 85–104.

Krause, W., Cohen, D. and Abou-Chadi, T. (2019). 'Does Accommodation Work? Mainstream Party Strategies and the Success of Radical Right Parties', unpublished manuscript, working paper.

Krause, W. and Giebler, H. (2020). 'Shifting Welfare Policy Positions: The Impact of Radical Right Populist Party Success Beyond Migration Politics', *Representation* 56(3): 331–48.

Kriesi, H. (1998). 'The Transformation of Cleavage Politics: The 1997 Stein Rokkan Lecture', *European Journal of Political Research* 33(2): 165–85.

Kriesi, H., Grande, E., Lachat, R., Dolezal, M., Bornschier, S. and Frey, T. (2008). *West European Politics in the Age of Globalization*, Cambridge University Press.

Krouwel, A. and Bale, T. (2013). 'Down but Not Out: A Comparison of Germany's CDU/CSU with Christian Democratic Parties in Austria, Belgium, Italy and the Netherlands', *German Politics* 22(1/2): 16–45.

Laponce, J. (1981). *Left and Right: The Topography of Political Perceptions*, Toronto University Press.

Larsson, M. J. (2014). 'Så fungerar decemberöverenskommelsen', *Dagens Nyheter*, 27 December, available at: www.dn.se/nyheter/politik/sa-fungerar-decemberoverenskommelsen, last accessed 20 June 2019.

Laubenthal, B. (2019). 'Refugees Welcome? Reforms of German Asylum Policies between 2013 and 2017 and Germany's Transformation into an Immigration Country', *German Politics* 28(3): 412–25.

Levitsky, S. and Ziblatt, D. (2018). *How Democracies Die*, New York: Crown.

Lewin, L. (1994). 'Om falukorv, sakinflytande och ideologisk livskraft', *Statsvetenskaplig Tidskrift* 97(3): 279–83.

Lieberman, R., Mettler, S., Pepinsky, T., Roberts, K. and Valelly, R. (2019). 'The Trump Presidency and American Democracy: A Historical and Comparative Analysis', *Perspectives on Politics* 17(2): 470–9.

Lindbom, A. (2010). 'Moderaterna och välfärdsstaten', *Statsvetenskaplig Tidskrift* 112(2): 143–52.

Lindström, U. (2005). 'De socialdemokratiska partierna', in M. Demker and L. Svåsand (eds), *Partiernas århundrade. Fempartimodellens uppgång och fall i Norge og Sverige*, Stockholm: Santérus förlag, pp. 80–104.

Linz, J. (1978). *The Breakdown of Democratic Regimes: Crisis, Breakdown and Reequilibration. An Introduction*, Baltimore, MD: Johns Hopkins University Press.

Lipset, S. and Rokkan, S. (1967). *Party System and Voter Alignments: Cross-National Perspectives*, New York: Free Press.

Ljunggren, S. B. (1992). *Folkhemskapitalismen: högerns programutveckling under efterkrigstiden*, Stockholm: Tiden.

López Nieto, L. (1988). *Alianza Popular: Estructura y evolución electoral de un partido conservador (1976–1982)*, Madrid: Centro de Investigaciones Sociológicas.

Lowe, W., Benoit, K., Mikhaylov, S. and Laver, M. (2011). 'Scaling Policy Preferences from Coded Political Texts', *Legislative Studies Quarterly* 36(1): 123–55.

Lucardie, P. and Voerman, G. (2012). *Populisten in de Polder*, Amsterdam: Boom.

Luther, K. R. (2010). 'Governing with Right-Wing Populists and Managing the Consequences: Schüssel and the FPÖ', in G. Bischof and F. Plasser (eds), *The Schüssel Era in Austria*, New Orleans and Innsbruck: New Orleans University Press and Innsbruck University Press, pp. 79–103.

Mair, P. (2002). 'Comparing Party Systems', in L. LeDuc, R. Niemi and P. Norris (eds), *Comparing Democracy 2: New Challenges in the Study of Elections and Voting*, London: Sage, pp. 88–107.

(2008). 'Electoral Volatility and the Dutch Party System: A Comparative Perspective', *Acta Politica* 43(2/3): 235–53.

Mair, P. and Mudde, C. (1998). 'The Party Family and its Study', *Annual Review of Political Science* 1: 211–29.

Markovits, A. S. and Gorski, P. S. (1993). *The German Left: Red, Green, and Beyond*, Oxford University Press.

Marks, G. and Wilson, C. (2001). 'The Past in the Present: A Cleavage Theory of Party Response to European Integration', *British Journal of Political Science* 30(3): 433–59.

Martin, C. 2018. 'Electoral Participation and Right Wing Authoritarian Success: Evidence from the 2017 Federal Elections in Germany', SSRN, 26 April, available at: http://dx.doi.org/10.2139/ssrn.3159320, last accessed 5 October 2020.

Mastropaolo, A. (2005). *La Mucca Pazza Della Democrazia: Nuove Destre, Populismo, Antipolitica*, Torino: Bollati Boringhieri.

Mayer, N. (2002). *Ces Français qui votent Le Pen*, Paris: Flammarion.

McDonnell, D. (2006). 'A Weekend in Padania: Regionalist Populism and the Lega Nord', *Politics* 26(2): 126–32.

(2013). 'Silvio Berlusconi's Personal Parties: From Forza Italia to the Popolo Della Libertà', *Political Studie* 61(S1): 217–33.

McGann, A. J. and Kitschelt, H. (2005). 'The Radical Right in the Alps: Evolution of Support for the Swiss SVP and Austrian FPÖ', *Party Politics* 11(2): 147–71.

Meguid, B. M. (2008). *Party Competition between Unequals: Strategies and Electoral Fortunes in Western Europe*, Cambridge University Press.

Meijers, M. (2017). 'Contagious Euroscepticism: The Impact of Eurosceptic Support on Mainstream Party Positions on European Integration', *Party Politics* 23(4): 413–23.

Meléndez, C. and Rovira Kaltwasser, C. (2019). 'Political Identities: The Missing Link in the Study of Populism', *Party Politics* 25(4): 520–33.

(forthcoming). 'Negative Partisanship towards the Populist Radical Right and Democratic Resilience in Western Europe', *Democratization* (DOI: 10.1080/13510347.2021.1883002).

Mellon, J., Evans, G., Fieldhouse, E., Green, J. and Prosser, C. (2018). 'Brexit or Corbyn? Campaign and Inter-Election Vote Switching in the 2017 UK General Election', *Parliamentary Affairs* 71(4): 719–37.

Micu, P. (2018). 'Ulf Kristersson: SD var de enda som talade om problem med invandringen', *Expressen*, 26 January, available at: www .expressen.se/nyheter/ulf-kristersson-sd-var-de-enda-som-talade-om-problem-med-invandringen, last accessed 20 June 2019.

Moffitt, B. (2017). 'Liberal Illiberalism? The Reshaping of the Contemporary Populist Radical Right in Northern Europe', *Politics and Governance* 5(4): 112–22.

Montero, J. R. (1988). 'More than Conservatism, Less than Neoconservatism', in B. Girvin (ed.), *The Transformation of Contemporary Conservatism*, London: Sage, pp. 145–63.

Montgomery, K. A. and Winter, R. (2015). 'Explaining the Religion Gap in Support for Radical Right Parties in Europe', *Politics & Religion* 8(2): 379–403.

Morgan, J. (2012). *Bankrupt Representation and Party System Collapse*, University Park, PA: Pennsylvania State University Press.

Morlino, L. and Tarchi, M. (1996). 'The Dissatisfied Society: The Roots of Political Change in Italy', *European Journal of Political Research* 30(1): 41–63.

Mudde, C. (2000). *'The Republikaner': The Ideology of the Extreme Right*, Manchester University Press, pp. 31–59.

(2004). 'The Populist Zeitgeist', *Government & Opposition* 39(4): 541–63.

(2007). *Populist Radical Right Parties in Europe*, Cambridge University Press.

(2010). 'The Populist Radical Right: A Pathological Normalcy', *West European Politics* 33(6): 1167–86.

(2013). 'Three Decades of Populist Radical Right Parties in Western Europe: So What?', *European Journal of Political Research* 52(1): 1–19.

(2014). 'Fighting the System? Populist Radical Right Parties and Party System Change', *Party Politics* 20(2): 217–26.

(2019). *The Far Right Today*, Cambridge: Polity.

Mudde, C. and Rovira Kaltwasser, C. (2012). *Populism in Europe and the Americas: Threat or Corrective for Democracy?* Cambridge University Press.

(2013). 'Exclusionary vs. Inclusionary Populism: Comparing Contemporary Europe and Latin America', *Government & Opposition* 48(2): 147–74.

(2017). *Populism: A Very Short Introduction*, Oxford University Press.

Müller, J.-W. (2006). 'Comprehending Conservatism: A New Framework for Analysis', *Journal of Political Ideologies* 11(3): 359–65.

(2011). *Contesting Democracy: Political Ideas in Twentieth-Century Europe*, Princeton University Press.

(2018). 'Europe Forgot What "Conservative" Means', *Foreign Policy*, 21 March, available at: https://foreignpolicy.com/2018/03/21/europe-forgot-what-conservative-means, last accessed 5 September 2020.

Müller, W. C. (2002). 'Evil or the "Engine of Democracy"? Populism and Party Competition in Austria', in Y. Mény and Y. Surel (eds), *Democracies and the Populist Challenge*, London: Palgrave Macmillan, pp. 155–75.

Müller, W. C., Plasser, F. and Ulram, P. A. (2004). 'Party Responses to the Erosion of Voter Loyalties in Austria: Weakness as an Advantage and Strength as a Handicap', in P. Mair, W. C. Müller and F. Plasser (eds), *Political Parties and Electoral Change*, London: Sage, pp. 145–78.

Müller, W. C. and Strøm, S. (1999). *Policy, Office, or Votes? How Political Parties in Western Europe Make Hard Decisions*, Cambridge University Press.

Nilsson, T. (2004). *Mellan arv och utopi – moderata vägval under hundra år, 1904–2004*, Stockholm: Santérus förlag.

Nilsson, T. and Reuterskiöld, A. (2016). 'Moderat I spagat', Fokus, 1 July, available at: www.fokus.se/2016/07/moderat-i-spagat/?fbclid=IwAR3a TQ2eKeAp-o8_B9FHUOLXhqAhC0EO17DBP5qaJw8TP1hhgG R237AgL-w, last accessed 20 June 2019.

Noël, A. and Thérien, J. (2008). *Left and Right in Global Politics*, Cambridge University Press.

Norris, P. (2005). *Radical Right: Voters and Parties in the Electoral Market*, Cambridge University Press.

Norris, P. and Inglehart, R. (2019). *Cultural Backlash: Trump, Brexit, and Authoritarian Populism*, Cambridge University Press.

Norris, P. and Lovenduski, J. (2004). 'Why Parties Fail to Learn: Electoral Defeat, Selective Perception and British Party Politics', *Party Politics* 10(1): 85–104.

NOS (2017). 'NOS Nederland Kiest: Het Debat', televised election debate, NOS, Amsterdam.

Novus (2018). 'Moderaternas väljare juni 2018', Novus, available at: https:// novus.se/wp-content/uploads/2018/06/2ae4e982a85ef46c77e736a0d103 0368.pdf, last accessed 20 June 2019.

Odmalm, P. and Bale, T. (2015). 'Immigration into the Mainstream: Conflicting Ideological Streams, Strategic Reasoning and Party Competition', *Acta Politica* 50(4): 365–505.

Oesch, D. (2006a). 'Coming to Grips with a Changing Class Structure: An Analysis of Employment Stratification in Britain, Germany, Sweden and Switzerland', *International Sociology* 21(2): 263–88.

(2006b). *Redrawing the Class Map: Stratification and Institutions in Britain, Germany, Sweden and Switzerland*, Houndmills: Palgrave Macmillan.

Oosterwaal, A. and Torenvlied, R. (2010). 'Politics Divided from Society? Three Explanations for Trends in Societal and Political Polarisation in the Netherlands', *West European Politics* 33(2): 258–79.

Orriols, L. and Balcells, L. (2012). 'Party Polarisation and Spatial Voting in Spain', *South European Society and Politics* 17(3): 393–409.

Orriols, L. and Cordero, G. (2015). 'The Breakdown of the Spanish Two-Party System: The Upsurge of Podemos and Ciudadanos in the 2015 General Election', *South European Society and Politics* 21(4): 469–92.

Oscarsson, H. and Holmberg, S. (2008). *Regeringsskifte. Väljarna och valet 2006*, Stockholm: Norstedts Juridik AB.

(2013). *Nya svenska väljare*, Stockholm: Norstedts Juridik.

(2016). *Svenska väljare*, Stockholm: Wolters Kluwer.

O'Sullivan, N. (2014). 'Conservatism', in M. Freeden et al. (eds), *The Oxford Handbook of Political Ideologies*, Oxford University Press, pp. 293–311.

Otjes, S. (2018). 'The Phoenix of Consensus Democracy: Party System Change in the Netherlands', in M. Lisi (ed.), *Party System Change, the European Crisis and the State of Democracy*, Abingdon: Routledge, pp. 171–93.

(2020). 'The Fight on the Right: What Drives Voting for the Dutch Freedom Party and for the Forum for Democracy?', *Acta Politica*, 1–33.

Ozzano, L. and Giorgi, A. (2015). *European Culture Wars and the Italian Case: Which Side Are You On?*, Abingdon: Routledge.

Panebianco, A. (1988). *Political Parties: Organization and Power*, Cambridge University Press.

Paolucci, C. (2008). 'From Democrazia Cristiana to Forza Italia and the Popolo Della Libertà: Partisan Change in Italy', *Modern Italy* 13(4): 465–80.

Pardos-Prado, S. (2015). 'How Can Mainstream Parties Prevent Niche Party Success? Center-right Parties and the Immigration Issue', *Journal of Politics* 77(2): 352–67.

Pardos-Prado, S. and Sagarzazu, I. (2019). 'Economic Performance and Center–Periphery Conflicts in Party Competition', *Party Politics* 25(1): 50–62.

Partij Voor de Vrijheid (2010). 'De agenda van hoop en optimism Een tijd om te kiezen: PVV 2010–2015', *Verkiezing van de Tweede Kamer der Staten-Generaal*, 9: 301–59.

Partos, R. and Bale, T. (2015). 'Immigration and Asylum Policy Under Cameron's Conservatives', *British Politics* 10(2): 169–84.

Patton, D. (2011). *Out of the East: From PDS to Left Party in Unified Germany*, New York: State University of New York Press.

Pellikaan, H., van der Meer, T. and de Lange, S. (2007). 'Fortuyn's Legacy: Party System Change in the Netherlands', *Comparative European Politics* 5(3): 282–302.

(2018). 'The Centre Does Not Hold: Coalition Politics and Party System Change in the Netherlands, 2002–12', *Government and Opposition* 52(2): 231–55.

Perrineau, P. (2014). *La France au front*, Paris: Fayard.

Pierson, P. and Hacker, J. S. (2010). *Winner-Take-All Politics: How Washington Made the Rich Richer and Turned its Back on the Middle Class*, New York: Simon & Schuster.

Pirro, A. and van Kessel, S. (2018). 'Populist Eurosceptic Trajectories in Italy and the Netherlands during the European Crises', *Politics* 38(3): 327–43.

Poguntke, T. (1994). *Alternative Politics: The German Green Party*, Edinburgh University Press.

Politico (2017). 'Angela Merkel, Chancellor of Germany: The New Leader of the Free World', *Politico*, 27 October, available at: www.politico.com/i nteractives/2017/politico50/angela-merkel, last accessed 28 May 2020.

Polk, J., Rovny, J., Bakker, R., Edwards, E., Hooghe, L., Jolly, S. and Steenbergen, M. (2017). 'Explaining the Salience of Anti-Elitism and Reducing Political Corruption for Political Parties in Europe with the 2014 Chapel Hill Expert Survey Data', *Research & Politics* January/March: 1–9.

Pridham, G. (1977). *Christian Democracy in Western Germany: The CDU/CSU in Government and Opposition, 1945–1976*, London: Croom Helm.

Prins, B. (2002). 'The Nerve to Break Taboos: New Realism in the Dutch Discourse on Multiculturalism', *Journal of International Migration and Integration* 3(3/4): 363–80.

PVV (2010). 'De agenda van hoop en optimisme. Een tijd om te kiezen: PVV 2010–2015', PVV parliamentary election manifesto, Amsterdam.

PVV (2016). 'Nederland weer van ons! Concept-verkiezingsprogramma PVV 2017–2021', PVV parliamentary election manifesto, Amsterdam.

Queralt, D. (2012). 'Spatial Voting in Spain', *South European Society and Politics* 17(3): 375–92.

Ramiro-Fernández, L. (2005). 'Programmatic Adaptation and Organizational Centralization in the AP–PP', *South European Society and Politics* 10(2): 207–23.

Raniolo, F. (2006). 'Forza Italia: A Leader with a Party', *South European Society and Politics* 11(3/4): 439–55.

Regalia, M. (2018). 'Electoral Reform as an Engine of Party System Change in Italy', *South European Society and Politics* 23(1): 81–96.

Regierungsprogramm (2017). 'Zusammen. Für unser Österreich', Regierungsprogramm 2017–2022, 2017, available at: www.oeh.ac.at/ sites/default/files/files/pages/regierungsprogramm_2017-2022.pdf, last accessed 30 September 2020.

Rekker, R. (2018). 'Growing Up in a Globalized Society: Why Younger Generations are More Positive about the European Union', *Young* 26: 56S–77S.

Richter, P. (1998). 'Die Außerparlamentarische Opposition in der Bundesrepublik Deutschland 1966 bis 1968', *Geschichte Und Gesellschaft, Sonderheft* 17: 35–55.

Roberts, K. (2017). 'State of the Field. Party Politics in Hard Times: Comparative Perspectives on the European and Latin American Economic Crises', *European Journal of Political Research* 56(2): 218–33.

(2019a). 'Parties, Populism, and Democratic Decay: A Comparative Perspective on Political Polarization in the United States', in K. Weyland and R. L. Madrid (eds), *When Democracy Trumps Populism: European and Latin American Lessons for the United States*, Cambridge University Press, pp. 132–53.

(2019b). 'Bipolar Disorders: Varieties of Capitalism and Populist Out-Flanking on the Left and Right', *Polity* 51(4): 641–53.

Rodríguez, J. L. (1994). *Reaccionarios y golpistas. La extrema derecha en España: del tardofraquismo a la consolidación de la democracia (1967–1982)*, Madrid: Consejo Superior de Investigaciones Científicas.

Rodríguez, J. and Barrio, A. (2018). 'Ciudadanos: el asalto al centro', in F. Llera, M. Baras and J. Montabes (eds), *Las elecciones generales de 2015 y 2016*, Madrid: Centro de Investigaciones Sociologicas, pp. 249–71.

Rooduijn, M. (2018). 'What Unites the Voter Bases of Populist Parties? Comparing the Electorates of 15 Populist Parties', *European Political Science Review* 10(3): 351–68.

Rooduijn, M., de Lange, S. and van der Brug, W. (2012). 'A Populist Zeitgeist? Programmatic Contagion by Populist Parties in Western Europe', *Party Politics* 20(4): 563–75.

Röth, L., Afonso, A. and Spies, D. (2018). 'The Impact of Populist Radical Right Parties on Socio-Economic Policies', *European Political Science Review* 10(3): 325–50.

Rovira Kaltwasser, C. (2014). 'The Responses of Populism to Dahl's Democratic Dilemmas', *Political Studies* 62(3): 470–87.

Rovira Kaltwasser, C., Wratil, C. and Vehrkamp, R. (2019). 'Europe's Choice: Populist Attitudes and Voting Intentions in the 2019 European Election', Gütersloh: Bertelsmann Foundation.

Rovny, J. (2013). 'Where Do Radical Right Parties Stand? Position Blurring in Multidimensional Competition', *European Political Science Review* 5(1): 1–26.

Royo, S. (2009). 'Reforms Betrayed? Zapatero and Continuities in Economic Policy', *South European Society and Politics* 14(4): 435–51.

Rueda, D. (2007). *Social Democracy Inside Out: Partisanship and Labour Market Policy in Advanced Industrialized Democracies*, Oxford University Press.

Ruzza, C. and Fella, S. (2011). 'Populism and the Italian Right', *Acta Politica* 46(2): 158–79.

Rydgren, J. (2005). 'Is Extreme Right-Wing Populism Contagious? Explaining the Emergence of a New Party Family', *European Journal of Political Research* 44(3): 413–37.

(2007). 'The Sociology of the Radical Right', *Annual Review of Sociology* 33: 241–62.

(2013). *Class Politics and the Radical Right*, London: Routledge.

(2018). *The Oxford Handbook of the Radical Right*, Oxford University Press.

Rydgren, J. and van der Meiden, S. (2018). 'The Radical Right and the End of Swedish Exceptionalism', *European Political Science* 18(3): 439–55.

Samuels, D. and Zucco, C. (2018). *Partisans, Antipartisans, and Nonpartisans Voting Behavior in Brazil*, Cambridge University Press.

Sánchez-Cuenca, I. (2017). 'From a Deficit of Democracy to a Technocratic Order: The Post-Crisis Debate on Europe', *Annual Review of Political Science* 20: 351–69.

Sartori, G. (1970). 'Concept Misformation in Comparative Politics', *American Political Science Review* 64(4): 1033–53.

(1976). *Parties and Party Systems: A Framework for Analysis*, Cambridge University Press.

(1982). *Teoria dei partiti e caso italiano*, Milan: Sugarco Edizioni.

Sauger, N. (2007). 'Le vote Bayrou. L'échec d'un succès', *Revue Française de Science Politique* 57(3): 447–58.

Schain, M. (2006). 'The Extreme-Right and Immigration Policy-Making: Measuring Direct and Indirect Effects', *West European Politics* 29(2): 270–89.

Schmitt-Beck, R. (2017). 'The "Alternative für Deutschland in the Electorate": Between Single-Issue and Right-Wing Populist Party', *German Politics* 26(1): 124–48.

Schonfeld, W. (1986). 'Le RPR et l'UDF à l'épreuve de l'opposition', *Revue Française de Science Politique* 36(1): 14–29.

Schumacher, G. and van Kersbergen, K. (2016). 'Do Mainstream Parties Adapt to the Welfare Chauvinism of Populist Parties?', *Party Politics* 22(3): 300–12.

Schwander, H. and Manow, P. (2017). '"Modernize and Die"? German Social Democracy and the Electoral Consequences of the Agenda 2010', *Socio-Economic Review* 15(1): 117–34.

Seldon, A. and Snowdon, P. (2001). *A New Conservative Century?* London: Centre for Policy Studies.

  (2005). 'The Conservative Campaign', *Parliamentary Affairs* 58(4): 725–42.

Siaroff, A. (2003). 'Two-and-a-Half-Party Systems and the Comparative Role of the "Half"', *Party Politics* 9(3): 267–90.

Sides, J. and Citrin, J. (2007). 'European Opinion about Immigration: The Role of Identities, Interests and Information', *British Journal of Political Science* 37(3): 477–504.

Smith, G. (1988). 'Between Left and Right: The Ambivalence of European Liberalism', in E. Kirchner (ed.), *Liberal Parties in Western Europe*, Cambridge University Press, pp. 16–28.

Smith, M. (2019). 'Most Conservative Members Would See Party Destroyed to Achieve Brexit', YouGov, 18 June, available at: https://yougov.co.uk/topics/politics/articles-reports/2019/06/18/most-conservative-members-would-see-party-destroye, last accessed 25 July 2019.

Spierings, N., Lubbers, M. and Zaslove, A. (2017). '"Sexually Modern Nativist Voters": Do They Exist and Do They Vote for the Populist Radical Right?', *Gender and Education* 29(2): 216–37.

Spierings, N. and Zaslove, A. (2015). 'Gendering the Vote for Populist Radical-Right Parties', *Patterns of Prejudice* 49(1–2): 135–62.

Spies, D. (2013). 'Explaining Working-Class Support for Extreme Right Parties: A Party Competition Approach', *Acta Politica* 48(3): 296–325.

Spoon, J. J. and Klüver, H. (2020). 'Responding to Far Right Challengers: Does Accommodation Pay Off?' *Journal of European Public Policy* 27(2): 273–91.

Steenvoorden, E. and Harteveld, E. (2018). 'The Appeal of Nostalgia: The Influence of Societal Pessimism on Support for Populist Radical Right Parties', *West European Politics* 41(1): 28–52.

Stenberg, E. and Eriksson, K. (2016). 'De nya hårda moderaterna', *Dagens Nyheter*, 8 July, available at: www.dn.se/nyheter/politik/de-nya-harda-moderaterna, last accessed 20 June 2019.

Strøm, K. and Müller, W. (1999). *Policy, Office or Votes? How Political Parties in Western Europe Make Hard Decisions*, Cambridge University Press.

SVT (2018). Agenda, television broadcast, 29 April, Swedish public service television, Stockholm.

SVT NYHETER (2012). 'Skamligt att SVT gör sig till redskap för främlingsfientlighet', SVT NYHETER online, 12 October, available at: www.svt.se/opinion/skamligt-att-svt-gor-sig-till-redskap-for-fram lingsfientlighet, last accessed 20 June 2019.

——— (2014). 'Enkät: Var tredje M-kommunpolitiker säger ja till SD-samarbete', SVT NYHETER online, 11 December, available at: www.svt.se/nyh eter/inrikes/var-tredje-m-kommunpolitiker-sager-ja-till-sd-samarbete, last accessed 20 June 2019.

SVT VALU (2018). 'Väljarströmmar', SVT, available at: www.svt.se/special/valu2018-valjarstrommar, last accessed 20 June 2019.

Tarchi, M. (2016). 'Recalcitrant Allies: The Conflicting Foreign Policy Agenda of the Alleanza Nazionale and the Lega Nord', in C. Schori (ed.), *Europe for the Europeans: The Foreign and Security Politics of the Populist Radical Right*, London: Routledge, pp. 187–208.

——— (2018). 'Voters without a Party: The "Long Decade" of the Italian Centre-Right and Its Uncertain Future', *South European Society and Politics* 23(1): 147–62.

Taylor-Gooby, P. (2016). 'The Divisive Welfare State', *Social Policy and Administration* 50(6): 712–33.

Theborn, G. (1992). 'A Unique Chapter in History of Democracy: The Social Democrats in Sweden', in K. Misgeld, K. Molin and K. Åmark (eds), *Creating Social Democracy: A Century of the Social Democratic Labor Party in Sweden*, University Park, PA: Pennsylvania State University Press, pp. 1–34.

Thränhardt, D. (1995). 'The Political Uses of Xenophobia in England, France and Germany', *Party Politics* 1(3): 323–45.

Tonge, J. (2017). 'Supplying Confidence or Trouble? The Deal between the Democratic Unionist Party and the Conservative Party', *Political Quarterly* 88(3): 412–16.

Torcal, M. (1989). 'Dimensión materialista/postmaterialista en España: las variables del cambio cultural', *Revista Española de Investigaciones Sociológicas* 47: 227–54.

Tournier-Sol, K. (2015). 'Reworking the Eurosceptic and Conservative Traditions into a Populist Narrative: UKIP's Winning Formula?', *Journal of Common Market Studies* 53(1): 140–56.

Turnbull-Dugarte, S. (2019). 'Explaining the End of Spanish Exceptionalism and Electoral Support for Vox', *Research and Politics* 6(2): 1–8.

Twist, K. A. (2019). *Partnering with Extremists: Coalitions Between Mainstream and Far-right Parties in Western Europe*, Ann Arbor: University of Michigan Press.

Usherwood, S. (2008). 'The Dilemmas of a Single-Issue Party: The UK Independence Party', *Representation* 44(3): 255–64.

Valk, G. 2020. 'Stuurloos CDA snakt naar leider', *NRC Handelsblad*, 1 May, available at: www.nrc.nl/nieuws/2020/04/30/stuurloos-cda-snakt-naar-leider-a3998416, last accessed 29 September 2020.

van der Brug, W. and Fennema, M. (2009). 'The Support Base of Radical Right Parties in the Enlarged European Union', *Journal of European Integration* 31(5): 589–608.

van der Brug, W., Fennema, M., de Lange, S. L. and Baller, I. (2012). 'Radical Right Parties: Their Voters and Their Electoral Competitors', in J. Rydgren (ed.), *Class Politics and the Radical Right*, London: Routledge, pp. 52–74.

van der Brug, W. and van Spanje, J. (2009). 'Immigration, Europe and the "New" Cultural Dimension', *European Journal of Political Research* 48(3): 309–34.

van der Eijk, C. and Franklin, M. (2004). 'Potential for Contestation on European Matters at National Elections in Europe', in G. Marks and M Steenbergen (eds), *European Integration and Political Conflict: Themes in European Governance*, Cambridge University Press, pp. 33–50.

van der Meer, T. (2019). 'Zonder eigen kernwaarde zwabbert CDA', Stuk Rood Vlees blog, 14 February, available at: http://stukroodvlees.nl/zonder-eigen-kernwaarde-zwabbert-cda, last accessed 29 September 2020.

van der Meer, T., Lubbe, R., van Elsas, E., Elff, M. and van der Brug, W. (2012). 'Bounded Volatility in the Dutch Electoral Battlefield: A Panel Study on the Structure of Changing Vote Intentions in the Netherlands during 2006-2010', *Acta Politica* 47(4): 333–55.

van de Wardt, M., de Vries, C. and Hobolt, S. (2014). 'Exploiting the Cracks: Wedge Issues in Multiparty Competition', *Journal of Politics* 76(4): 986–99.

van Elsas, E. J., Miltenburg, E. M. and van der Meer, T. W. (2016). 'If I Recall Correctly: An Event History Analysis of Forgetting and Recollecting Past Voting Behavior', *Journal of Elections, Public Opinion and Parties* 26(3): 253–72.

van Hecke, S. (2004). 'Christian Democratic Parties and Europeanisation', in S. van Hecke and E. Gerard (eds), *Christian Democratic Parties in Europe since the End of the Cold War*, Leuven University Press, pp. 43–54.

van Heerden, S., de Lange, S., van der Brug, W. and Fennema, M. (2013). 'The Immigration and Integration Debate in the Netherlands: Discursive and Programmatic Reactions to the Rise of Anti-Immigration Parties', *Journal of Ethnic and Migration Studies* 40(1): 119–36.

van Kersbergen, K. (1995). *Social Capitalism: A Study of Christian Democracy and of the Welfare State*, London: Routledge.

van Kersbergen, K. and Krouwel, A. (2008). 'A Double-Edged Sword! The Dutch Centre-Right and the "Foreigners Issue"', *Journal of European Public Policy* 15(3): 398–414.

van Kessel, S. (2015). *Populist Parties in Europe: Agents of Discontent?* Basingstoke: Palgrave Macmillan.

(2016). 'Using Faith to Exclude: The Role of Religion in Dutch Populism', in N. Marzouki, D. McDonnell and O. Roy (eds), *Saving the People: How Populists Hijack Religion*, London: Hurst, pp. 61–77.

van Kessel, S., Chelotti, N., Drake, H., González, J. R. and Rodi, P. (2020). 'Eager to Leave? Populist Radical Right Parties' Responses to the UK's Brexit Vote', *British Journal of Politics and International Relations* 22(1): 65–84.

van Spanje, J. (2010). 'Contagious Parties: Anti-Immigration Parties and Their Impact on Other Parties' Immigration Stances in Contemporary Western Europe', *Party Politics* 16(5): 563–86.

van Spanje, J. and de Graaf, N. D. (2018). 'How Established Parties Reduce Other Parties' Electoral Support: The Strategy of Parroting the Pariah', *West European Politics* 41(1): 1–27.

van Spanje, J. and van der Brug, W. (2007). 'The Party as Pariah: The Exclusion of Anti-Immigration Parties and its Effect on Their Ideological Positions', *West European Politics* 30(5): 1022–40.

Vasilopoulou, S. and Halikiopoulou, D. (2015). *The Golden Dawn's 'Nationalist Solution': Explaining the Rise of the Far Right in Greece*, Houndmills: Palgrave Macmillan.

Verbeek, B. and Zaslove, A. (2015). 'Italy: A Case of Mutating Populism?', *Democratization* 23(2): 304–23.

Vidal, G. (2018). 'Challenging Business as Usual? The Rise of New Parties in Spain in Times of Crisis', *West European Politics* 41(2): 261–86.

Voigt, L. (2018). 'Let the Good Times Roll: Eine Bilanz der Sozialpolitik der dritten Großen Koalition 2013–2017', in R. Zohlnhöfer and T. Saalfeld (eds), *Zwischen Stillstand, Politikwandel und Krisen-management. Eine Bilanz der Regierung Merkel 2013–2017*, Wiesbaden: Springer, pp. 415–43.

Volkens, A., Krause, W., Lehmann, P., Matthieß, T., Merz, N., Regel, S. and Weßels, B. (2018). 'The Manifesto Data Collection', *Manifesto Project (MRG/CMP/MARPOR)*, Version 2018b, Berlin: Wissenschaftszentrum Berlin für Sozialforschung (WZB).

Vossen, K. (2017). *The Power of Populism: Geert Wilders and the Party for Freedom in the Netherlands*, Abingdon: Routledge.

VVD (2017a). 'Lees hier de brief van Mark', VVD, 22 January, available at: www.vvd.nl/nieuws/lees-hier-de-brief-van-mark, last accessed 29 September 2020.

VVD (2017b). 'Zeker Nederland. VVD Verkieizngsprogramma 2017–2021', VVD parliamentary election manifesto, Zeker, Amsterdam.

Wagner, M. (2014). *Wandel und Fortschritt in den Christdemokratien Europas: Christdemokratische Elegien Angesichts Fragiler Volksparteilicher Symmetrien*, Wiesbaden: VS Verlag.

Wagner, M. and Meyer, T. M. (2017). 'The Radical Right as Niche Parties? The Ideological Landscape of Party Systems in Western Europe, 1980–2014', *Political Studies* 65(1S): 84–107.

Webb, P. and Bale, T. (2014). 'Why Do Tories Defect to UKIP? Conservative Party Members and the Temptations of the Populist Radical Right', *Political Studies* 62(4): 961–70.

Widfeldt, A. (2008). 'Party Change as a Necessity: The Case of the Sweden Democrats', *Representation* 44(3): 265–76.

Wiliarty, S. E. (2010). *The CDU and the Politics of Gender in Germany: Bringing Women to the Party*, Cambridge University Press.

(2013). 'Gender as a Modernising Force in the German CDU', *German Politics* 22(1/2): 172–90.

Williams, M. H. (2009). 'Catch-all in the Twenty-First Century? Revisiting Kircheimer's Thesis 40 Years Later', *Party Politics* 15(5): 539–41.

Wilson, F. L. (1998). *The European Center-Right at the End of the Twentieth Century*, New York: St. Martin's Press.

Wodak, R. (2015). *The Politics of Fear: What Right-Wing Populist Discourses Mean*, London: Sage.

Wörlund, I. (1992). 'The Swedish Parliamentary Election of September 1991', *Scandinavian Political Studies* 15(2): 135–43.

Wottle, M. and Blomberg, E. (2011). 'Feminism och jämställdhet i en nyliberal kontext 1990–2010', *Tidskrift för genusvetenskap* 2/3: 97–116.

Wüst, A. M. (2016). 'Incorporation beyond Cleavages? Parties, Candidates, and Germany's Immigrant-Origin Electorate', *German Politics* 25(3): 414–32.

Ysmal, C. (1984). 'Le RPR et l'UDF face au FN: concurrence et convergence', Revue politique et parlementaire, 913: 6–20.

Zapata-Barrero, R. (2003). 'The "Discovery" of Immigration in Spain: The Politicization of Immigration in the Case of El Ejido', *Journal of International Migration and Integration* 4(4): 523–39.

Zaslove, A. (2004). 'The Dark Side of European Politics: Unmasking the Radical Right', *Journal of European Integration* 26(1): 61–81.

Zhirkov, K. (2014). 'Nativist but not Alienated: A Comparative Perspective on the Radical Right Vote in Western Europe', *Party Politics* 20(2): 286–96.

Ziblatt, D. (2017). *Conservative Parties and the Birth of Democracy*, Cambridge University Press.

Index

CPSIA information can be obtained
at www.ICGtesting.com
Printed in the USA
LVHW05084525251021
701445LV00008B/507